# Fuzzy Logic Handbook

# Fuzzy Logic Handbook

Edited by **Frank West**

New York

Published by NY Research Press,
23 West, 55th Street, Suite 816,
New York, NY 10019, USA
www.nyresearchpress.com

**Fuzzy Logic Handbook**
Edited by Frank West

© 2015 NY Research Press

International Standard Book Number: 978-1-63238-211-5 (Hardback)

Printed in the United States of America.

# Contents

# Preface

This book aims to highlight the current researches and provides a platform to further the scope of innovations in this area. This book is a product of the combined efforts of many researchers and scientists, after going through thorough studies and analysis from different parts of the world. The objective of this book is to provide the readers with the latest information of the field.

Fuzzy logic has developed into an important means of solving problems in all domains. It has a huge impact on the design of autonomous intelligent systems. This book discusses hybrid algorithms, techniques, and implementations of fuzzy logic. The main focus of the book is on the models and fundamentals of fuzzy logic and issues related to its technique and implementations. This book will prove beneficial to engineers, researchers, and graduate students who are working in the field of fuzzy logic.

I would like to express my sincere thanks to the authors for their dedicated efforts in the completion of this book. I acknowledge the efforts of the publisher for providing constant support. Lastly, I would like to thank my family for their support in all academic endeavors.

Editor

# Part 1

# Hybrid Fuzzy Logic Algorithms

# Ambiguity and Social Judgment: Fuzzy Set Model and Data Analysis

Kazuhisa Takemura
*Waseda University,*
*Japan*

## 1. Introduction

Comparative judgment is essential in human social lives. Comparative judgment is a type of human judgment procedure, in which the evaluator is asked which alternative is preferred (e.g., "Do you prefer Brand A to Brand B?" or "How do you estimate the probability of choosing Brand A over Brand B when you compare the two brands? "). This type of judgment is distinguished from absolute judgment, in which the evaluator is asked to assess the attractiveness of an object (e.g., "How much do you like this brand on a scale of 0 to 100?").

The ambiguity of social judgment has been conceptualized by the fuzzy set theory. The fuzzy set theory provides a formal framework for the presentation of the ambiguity. Fuzzy sets were defined by Zadeh(1965) who also outlined how they could be used to characterize complex systems and decision processes ( Zadeh, 1973). Zadeh argues that the capacity of humans to manipulate fuzzy concepts should be viewed as a major asset, not a liability. The complexities in the real world often defy precise measurement and fuzzy logic defines concepts and its techniques provide a mathematical method able to deal with thought processes which are often too imprecise and ambiguous to deal with by classical mathematical techniques.

This chapter introduces a model of ambiguous comparative judgment (Takemura,2007) and provides a method of data analysis for the model, and then shows some examples of the data analysis of social judgments. Comparative judgments in social situations often involve ambiguity with regard to confidence, and people may be unable to make judgments without some confidence intervals. To measure the ambiguity (or vagueness) of human judgment, the fuzzy rating method has been proposed and developed (Hesketh, Pryor, Gleitzman, & Hesketh, 1988). In fuzzy rating, respondents select a representative rating point on a scale and indicate higher or lower rating points, depending on the relative ambiguity of their judgment. For example, fuzzy rating would be useful for perceived temperature, with the evaluator indicating a representative value and lower and upper values. This rating scale allows for asymmetries and overcomes the problem, identified by Smithson (1987), of researchers arbitrarily deciding the most representative value from a range of scores. By making certain simplifying assumptions (which is not uncommon in fuzzy set theory), the rating can be viewed as an L-R fuzzy number, thereby making the use of fuzzy set theoretical operations possible (Hesketh et al., 1988; Takemura, 2000). Lastly, numerical illustrations of psychological experiments are provided to examine the ambiguous comparative judgment model (Takemura, 2007) using the proposed data analysis.

## 2. Model of ambiguous comparative judgment

### 2.1 Overview of ambiguous comparative judgment and the judgment model

Social psychological theory and research have demonstrated that comparative evaluation has a crucial role in the cognitive processes and structures that underlie people's judgments, decisions, and behaviors(e.g.,Mussweiler,2003). People comparison processes are almost ubiquitous in human social cognition. For example, people tend to compare their performance of others in situations that are ambiguous (Festinger,1954). It is also obvious that they are critical in forming personal evaluations, and making purchase decisions (Kühberger,,.Schulte-Mecklenbeck, & Ranyard, 2011; Takemura,2011).

The ambiguity or vagueness is inherent in people's comparative social judgment. Traditionally, psychological and philosophical theories implicitly had assumed the ambiguity of thought processes ( Smithson, 1987, 1989). For example, Wittgenstein (1953) pointed out that lay categories were better characterized by a " family resemblance" model which assumed vague boundaries of concepts rather than a classical set-theoretic model. Rosch (1975) and Rosch & Mervice(1975) also suggested vagueness of lay categories in her prototype model and reinterpret-ed the family resemblance model. Moreover, the social judgment theory (Sherif & Hovland,1961) and the information integration theory (Anderson,1988) for describing judgment and decision making assumed that people evaluate the objects using natural languages which were inherently ambiguous. However, psychological theories did not explicitly treat the ambiguity in social judgment with the exception of using random error of judgment.

Takemura (2007) proposed fuzzy set models that explain ambiguous comparative judgment in social situations. Because ambiguous comparative judgment may not always hold transitivity and comparability properties, the models assume parameters based on biased responses that may not hold transitivity and comparability properties. The models consist of two types of fuzzy set components for ambiguous comparative judgment. The first is a fuzzy theoretical extension of the additive difference model for preference, which is used to explain ambiguous preference strength and does not always assume judgment scale boundaries, such as a willing to pay (WTP) measure. The second type of model is a fuzzy logistic model of the additive difference preference, which is used to explain ambiguous preference in which preference strength is bounded, such as a probability measure (e.g., a certain interval within a bounded interval from 0 to 100%).

Because judgment of a bounded scale, such as a probability judgment, causes a methodological problem when fuzzy linear regression is used, a fuzzy logistic function to prevent this problem was proposed. In both models, multi-attribute weighting parameters and all attribute values are assumed to be asymmetric fuzzy L-R numbers. For each model, A method of parameter estimation using fuzzy regression analysis was proposed. That is, a fuzzy linear regression model using the least squares method (Takemura, 1999, 2005) was applied for the analysis of the former model, and a fuzzy logistic regression model (Takemura, 2004) was proposed for the analysis of the latter model.

## 2.2 Assumptions of the model

### 2.2.1 Definition 1: Set of multidimensional alternatives

Let $X = X_1 \times X_2 \times .... \times X_n$ be a set of multidimensional alternatives with elements of the form $X_1 = (X_{11}, X_{12},...,X_{1n})$, $X_2 = (X_{21}, X_{22},...,X_{2n})$,..., $X_m = (X_{m1}, X_{m2},...,X_{mn})$, where $X_{ij}$ ($i = 1.m$; $j = 1.,n$) is the value of alternative $X_i$ on dimension $j$. Note that the components of $X_i$ may be ambiguous linguistic variables rather than crisp numbers.

### 2.2.2 Definition 2: Classic preference relation

Let $\succ$ be a binary relation on X, that is, $\succ$ is a subset of $X \times X$.

The relational structure $< X, \succ >$ is a weak order if, and only if, for all $X_a$, $X_b$, $X_c$, the following two axioms are satisfied.

1.  Connectedness (Comparability): $X_a \succ X_b$ or $X_b \succ X_a$,

2.  Transitivity: If $X_a \succ X_b$ and $X_b \succ X_c$, then $X_a \succ X_c$.

However, the weak order relation is not always assumed in this paper. That is, transitivity or connectedness may be violated in the preference relations.

### 2.2.3 Definition 3: Fuzzy preference relation

As a classical preference relation $\succ$ is a subset of $X \times X$, $\succ$ is a classical set often viewed as a characteristic function $c$ from $X \times X$ to $\{0,1\}$ such that:

$$c(X_j \succ X_k) = \begin{cases} 1 & \text{iff} & X_a \succ X_b \\ 0 & \text{iff} & \text{not}(X_a \succ X_b) \end{cases}.$$

Note that "iff" is short for "if and only if" and $\{0,1\}$ is called the valuation set. If the valuation set is allowed to be the real interval [0,1], $\succ$ is called a fuzzy preference relation. That is, the membership function $\mu_a$ is defined as:

$$\mu_a: X \times X \rightarrow [0,1].$$

### 2.2.4 Definition 4: Ambiguous preference relation

Ambiguous preference relations are defined as a fuzzy set of $X \times X \times S$, where $S$ is a subset of one-dimensional real number space. $S$ is interpreted as a domain of preference strength. $S$ may be bounded, for example, $S = [0,1]$. The membership function $\mu_\beta$ is defined as:

$$\mu_\beta:: X \times X \times S \rightarrow [0,1].$$

Ambiguous preference relation is interpreted as a fuzzified version of a classical characteristic function $c(X_a \succ X_b)$.

Therefore, the ambiguous preference relation for $X_a \succ X_b$ is represented as the fuzzy set $v(X_a \succ X_b)$. For simplicity, $v(X_a \succ X_b)$ will be assumed to be an asymmetrical L-R fuzzy number (see Figure 1).

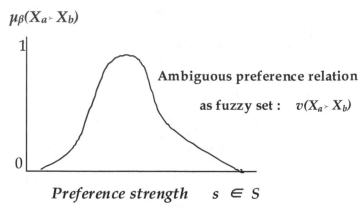

Fig. 1. Example of Ambiguous Preference Relation

### 2.2.5 Additive difference model of ambiguous comparative judgement

The ambiguous preference relation $v(X_a \succ X_b)$ for $X_a \succ X_b$ is represented as the following additive difference model using L-R fuzzy numbers:

$v(X_a \succ X_b) =$

$A_{ab0} \oplus A_{ab1} \otimes (X_{a1} \ominus X_{b1}) \oplus \cdots \oplus A_{abn} \otimes (X_{an} \ominus -X_{bn})$ (1)

where $\otimes$, $\oplus$, and $\ominus$ are the product, additive, and difference operation based on the extension principle for the fuzzy set, respectively.

The parameter $A_{jk0}$ involves a response bias owing to presentation order, context effects, and the scale parameter of the dependent variables. The parameter $A_{jk0}$ would be a fuzzy variable and larger than $A_{ab0}$ if $X_a$ were more salient than $X_b$. This model can be reduced to the Fuzzy Utility Difference Model (Nakamura, 1992) if multi-attribute weighting parameters are assumed to be crisp numbers, and reduced to the Additive Difference Model (Tversky, 1969) if multi-attribute weighting parameters and the values of multi-attributes are assumed to be crisp numbers.

### 2.2.6 Logistic model of ambiguous comparative judgement

Let an ambiguous preference relation that is bounded (e.g., fuzzy probability in [0,1]) be $p(X_a \succ X_b)$ for $X_a \succ X_b$. $p(X_a \succ X_b)$ and be represented as the following logistic model using L-R fuzzy numbers:

$l og \left( p(Xa \succ Xb) \oplus \left( 1 \ominus p(Xj \succ Xk) \right) \right) = 1 n Xb1)ype$ correction and drawing figures.mments and $Aab0 \oplus Aab1 \otimes (Xa1 \ominus Xb1) \oplus \cdots \oplus Aabn \otimes (Xan \ominus -Xbn)$ (2)

where $log$, $\oplus$, $\otimes$, $\oplus$, and $\ominus$ are logarithmic, division, product, additive, and difference operations based on the extension principle for the fuzzy set, respectively.

The second model of the equation (2) is the model for [0,1]. However, the model could apply to not only the interval [0,1] but also any finite interval [a,b](a<b). Therefore, the model of the equation (2)is considered to be a special case for the finite interval model.

### 2.2.7 Explaining non-comparability and intransitivity

Non-comparability and intransitivity properties are explained if a threshold of comparative judgment is assumed, if intransitivity is indicated by the necessity measure of fuzzy comparative relation resulting from the existence of the threshold, and if a necessity measure for fuzzy relation does not always lead to comparability. That is,

$$Xa \succ Xb \ iff \ Nes \left( v(Xa \succ Xb) > \theta \right) \quad (3)$$

or

$$X_a \succ X_b \ iff \ Nes( p(X_a \succ X_b) \oplus \left( 1 \ominus p(X_a \succ X_b) \right) > P_\theta) \quad (4)$$

where $Nes \left( \cdot \right)$ is a necessity measure, and $\theta$ and $P_\theta$ are threshold parameters for the additive difference model and the logistic regression model, respectively. Assuming the above relation of (3) or (4), it is clear that intransitivity and non-comparability hold in the comparative judgment.

## 3. Fuzzy data analysis for the ambiguous comparative judgment model

### 3.1 Fuzzy rating data and fuzzy set

Traditional approaches to the measurement of social judgment have involved methods such as the semantic differential, the Likert scale, or the Thurstone scale. Although insights into the ambiguous nature of social judgment were identified early in the development of measurement of social judgment, the subsequent methods used failed to capture this ambiguity, no doubt because traditional mathematics was not well developed for dealing with vagueness of judgment (Hesketh et al.,1988).

In order to measure the vagueness of human judgment, the fuzzy rating method has recently been proposed and developed (Hesketh et al.,1988; Takemura,1996). In the fuzzy rating method, respondents select a representative rating point on a scale and indicate lower or upper rating points if they wish depending upon the relative vagueness of their judgment (see Figure 2). For example, the fuzzy rating method would be useful for measuring perceived temperature indicating the representative value and the lower or upper values. This rating scale allows for asymmetries, and overcomes the problem, identified by Smithson (1987), of researchers arbitrarily deciding most representative value from a range of scores. By making certain simplifying assumptions ( not uncommon within fuzzy set theory), the rating can be viewed as a L-R fuzzy number, hence making possible the use of fuzzy set theoretic operations).

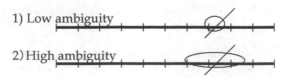

1) Low ambiguity

2) High ambiguity

Fig. 2. Example of Fuzzy Rating

A fuzzy set A is defined as follows. Let $X$ denote a universal set, such as $X=\{x_1,x_2,....,x_n\}$. Then, the membership function $\mu A \subseteq X$ by which a fuzzy set A is defined has the form

$$\mu A \,:\, X \rightarrow [\,0,1\,]\,,$$

where [0,1] denotes the interval of real numbers from 0 to 1, inclusive.

The concept of a fuzzy set is the foundation for analysis where fuzziness exists (Zadeh, 1965). a fuzzy set may be expressed as:

$$A = \mu A(x_1)/x_1 \oplus \mu A(x_2)/x_2 \oplus .\ \ .\ \ .\ \oplus \mu A(x_n)/x_n$$

$$= \sum_{i=1}^{n} \mu A(x_i)/x_i,$$

where $\mu A(x_i)$ represents the "grade of membership" of $X_i$ in $A$, or the degree to which $X_i$ satisfies the properties of the set $A$. It should be noted that here the symbol '"+ " does not refer to the ordinary addition.

$\mu A$ is called a membership function, or a possibility function. The $X_i$ values are drawn from a global set of all possible values, $X$. Grade of membership take values between 0 and 1. The membership function has a value of 0 when the properties of the fuzzy set are not at all satisfied, and 1 when the properties of fuzzy set are completely satisfied.

Hesketh et al.(1988) pointed out that fuzzy rating data can be represented as fuzzy sets by making certain implifying assumptions, which are not uncommon within fuzzy set theory. According to Hesketh et al.(1988), those assumptions are:

1.    The fuzzy set has a convex membership function.
2.    The global set $X$ is represented along the horizontal axis.
3.    The fuzzy membership function takes its maximum value, one, at the point on the fuzzy support represented by the representative point.
4.    The extent of the fuzzy support is represented by the horizontal lines to either side of evaluated point.
5.    The fuzzy membership function tapers uniformly from its value of one at the representative point to a value of zero beyond the fuzzy support or the left and right extensions. The membership value of the lower point and the upper point is 0.

Making those assumptions, fuzzy rating data in this study can be expressed as a fuzzy number which is a kind of fuzzy set. The concept of the fuzzy number can be defined from the concept of the fuzzy subset(Kaufman & Gupta,1985). The properties of fuzzy numbers are the convexity and the normality of a fuzzy subset.

Firstly, the convexity of the fuzzy subset is defined as follows: A fuzzy subset $A \subseteq R$ is convex if and only if every ordinary

$$A_\alpha = \{x \mid \mu A(x) \geq \alpha\}, \alpha \in [0,1],$$

subset is convex( That is, in the case of a closed interval of R).

Secondly, the normality of the fuzzy subset is defined as follows: A fuzzy subset $A \subseteq R$ is normal if and only if

$\forall x \in R$, $\max_x \mu A(x) = 1$.

One of the most well known fuzzy numbers is the L-R fuzzy number (Dubois & Prade,1980). The L-R fuzzy number is defined as follows:

$\forall x \in R$:

$$\begin{cases} \mu A(x) = L((x - m)/u), -\infty < x < m, \\ = 1, x = m, \\ = R((x - m)/v), m < x < \infty, \end{cases}$$

where $L((x - m)/u)$ is a increasing monotonic function, $R((x - m)/v)$ is a decreasing monotonic function, u>0, and v>0.

An example of the fuzzy rating scale and of the representation of the rating data using L-R fuzzy number are shown in Figure 3. Note in Figure 3 that representations of variables are abbreviated as follows: $x_{ij}{}^L$ for $x_{ij\,(0l}{}^L$, $x_{ij}{}^R$ for $x_{ij\,(0l}{}^R$, $x_{ij}{}^M$ for $x_{ij\,(1l}{}^L = x_{ij\,(1l}{}^R$.

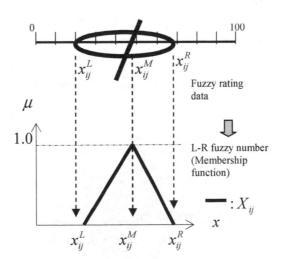

Fig. 3. Fuzzy Rating Data and Its Representation by L-R Fuzzy Numbers

## 3.2 Analysis of the additive difference type model

The set of fuzzy input-output data for the $k$-th observation is defined as:

$$\left(Y_{abk}; X_{a1k}, X_{a2k},...,X_{ank}; X_{b1k}, X_{b2k},...,X_{bnk;}\right) \qquad (5)$$

where $Y_{abk}$ indicates the $k$-th observation's ambiguous preference for the $a$-th alternative (a) over the $b$-th alternative (b), which represented by fuzzy L-R numbers, and $X_{ajk}$ and $X_{bjk}$ are the $j$-th attribute values of the alternatives (a and b) for observation $k$.

Let $X_{abjk}$ be $X_{ajk} - X_{bjk}$, where $-$ is a difference operator based on the fuzzy extension principle, and denote $X_{k.}$ as the abbreviation of $X_{abk}$ in the following section. Therefore, a set of fuzzy input-output data for the $i$-th observation is re-written as:

$$\left(Y_k; X_{1k}, X_{2k},...,X_{nk}\right), k=1,2,....,N \qquad (6)$$

where $Y_k$ is a fuzzy dependent variable, and $X_{jk}$ is a fuzzy independent variable represented by L-R fuzzy numbers. For simplicity, assume that $Y_k$ and $X_{jk}$ are positive for any membership value, $\alpha \in (0,1)$.

The fuzzy linear regression model (where both input and output data are fuzzy numbers) is represented as follows:

$$\overline{Y}_k = A_0 \oplus A_1 \otimes X_{1k} \oplus ... \oplus A_n \otimes X_{nk} \qquad (7)$$

where is a fuzzy estimated variable, $A_j(j = 1,...,n)$ is a fuzzy regression parameter represented by an L-R fuzzy number, $\otimes$ is an additive operator, and $\oplus$ is the product operator based on the extension principle.

It should be noted that although the explicit form of the membership function of $\overline{Y}_k$ cannot be directly obtained, the $\alpha$-level set of $\overline{Y}_k$ can be obtained from Nguyen's theorem (Nguyen, 1978).

Let $z^L_{k(\alpha)}$ be a lower value of $\overline{Y}_k$, and $z^R_{k(\alpha)}$ be an upper value of $\overline{Y}_k$.

Then,

$$Z_k = \left[z^L_{k(\alpha)}, z^R_{k(\alpha)}\right], \quad \alpha \in (0,1] \qquad (8)$$

Where

$$z^L_{k(\alpha)} = \sum_{j=0}^{n}\left\{\min\left(a^L_{j(\alpha)}x^L_{jk(\alpha)}, a^L_{j(\alpha)}x^R_{jk(\alpha)}\right)\right\} \qquad (9)$$

$$z^R_{k(\alpha)} = \sum_{j=0}^{n}\left\{\max\left(a^R_{j(\alpha)}x^L_{jk(\alpha)}, a^R_{j(\alpha)}x^R_{jk(\alpha)}\right)\right\} \qquad (10)$$

$$x^L_{0k(\alpha)} = x^R_{0k(\alpha)} = 1 \tag{11}$$

In the above Equation (9), $a^L_{j(\alpha)}x^L_{jk(\alpha)}$ is a product between the lower value of the $\alpha$-level fuzzy coefficient for the $j$-th attribute and the $\alpha$-level set of fuzzy input data $X_{jk}$, $a^L_{j(\alpha)}x^R_{jk(\alpha)}$, $a^R_{j(\alpha)}x^L_{jk(\alpha)}$, or $a^R_{j(\alpha)}x^R_{jk(\alpha)}$ is defined in the same manner, respectively. $x^L_{0k(\alpha)}$ and $x^R_{0k(\alpha)}$ are assumed to be 1 (a crisp number) for the purpose of estimation for the fuzzy bias parameter $A_0$.

To define the dissimilarity between the predicted and observed values of the dependent variable, the following indicator $D_{k(\alpha)}{}^2$ was adopted:

$$D_k{}_{(\alpha)}{}^2 = (y^L_{k(\alpha)} - z^L_{k(\alpha)})^2 + (y^R_{k(\alpha)} - z^R_{k(\alpha)})^2 \tag{12}$$

The definition in Equation (12) can be applied to interval data as well as to L-R fuzzy numbers. That is, Equation (12) represents the sum of squares for the distance between interval data.

To generalize, a dissimilarity indicator representing the square of the distance for L-R fuzzy numbers can be written as follows:

$$Dk^2 = \sum_{j=0}^{n} wj((y^L_{k(\alpha j)} - z^L_{k(\alpha j)})^2 + (y^R_{k(\alpha j)} - z^R_{k(\alpha j)})^2) \tag{13}$$

where $\alpha_j = jh/n$, $j = 0,...,n$, $h$ is an equal interval, and $w_j$ is a weight for the $j$-th level.

In the case of a triangular fuzzy number with $w_j = 1$, the above equation is approximately represented as:

$$Dk^2 = (y^L_{k(0)} - z^L_{k(0)})^2 + (y^L_{k(1)} - z^R_{k(1)})^2 + (y^R_{k(0)} - z^R_{k(0)})^2 \tag{14}$$

The proposed method is to estimate fuzzy coefficients using minimization of the sum of $D_k^2$ respecting $k$. That is,

$$\text{Objective function: Min} \sum_{k=1}^{N} D_k{}^2 \tag{15}$$

$$\text{Subject to:} \quad a^L_{j(h)} \geq 0, \ j \in J_1 \tag{16}$$

$$a^L_{j(h)} \leq 0, \ a^R_{j(h)} \geq 0, \ j \in J_2 \tag{17}$$

$$a^R_{j(h)} \leq 0, \ j \in J_3 \tag{18}$$

$$-a^L_{j(h)} + a^R_{j(h)} \geq 0 \tag{19}$$

Where $j \in \{0,....,n\} = J_1 \cup J_2 \cup J_3, \ J_1 \cap J_2 = \varphi, \ J_2 \cap J_3 = \varphi, \ J_3 \cap J_1 = \varphi,$

$$z_{k(\alpha)}^L = \sum_{j \in J_1} a_{j(\alpha)}^L x_{jk(\alpha)}^L + \sum_{j \in J_2 J_3} a_{j(\alpha)}^L x_{jk(\alpha)}^R \tag{20}$$

$$z_{k(\alpha)}^R = \sum_{j \in J_1, J_{12}} a_{j(\alpha)}^R x_{jk(\alpha)}^R + \sum_{j \in J_3} a_{j(\alpha)}^R x_{jk(\alpha)}^L \tag{21}$$

The estimated coefficients can be derived through quadratic programming. The proposed fuzzy least squares method is also shown in Figure 4.

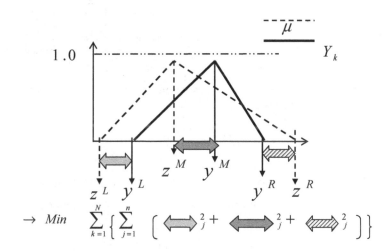

Fig. 4. Fuzzy Least Squares Regressions Analysis for Fuzzy Input and Output Data

### 3.3 Analysis of the logistic type model

Although the fuzzy linear regression analysis in the fuzzy additive difference model can give satisfactory results, these fuzzy regression analyses may fail to interpret psychological judgment data that have bounds on a psychological scale. For example, a perceived purchase probability has [0,1] interval and cannot be greater than 1 or less than 0. For such data, these fuzzy regression analyses may predict the values that are greater than 1 or less than 0. It may happen that the predicted values are greater than the highest bound or less than the lowest bound, and this causes a significant problem if the predicted values are used in a subsequent analysis. Therefore, the present study also attempted to solve this problem by setting predicted values to be greater than the lowest value (such as 0) or less than the highest value (such as 1). The present study develops the concept of logistic regression for the crisp numbers, and then proposes the fuzzy version of logistic regression analysis for fuzzy input and output data.

The set of fuzzy input-output data for the $k$-th observation is defined as:

$$(P_{abk}; X_{a1k}, X_{a2k}, \ldots, X_{ank}; X_{b1k}, X_{b2k}, \ldots, X_{bnk}) \tag{22}$$

where $P_{abk}$ indicates the $k$-th observation's ambiguous preference for the $a$-th alternative (a) over the $b$-th alternative (b), which is represented by fuzzy L-R numbers, and $X_{ajk}$ and $X_{bjk}$ are the $j$-th attribute values of the alternatives (a and b) for observation $k$.

Let $X_{abjk}$ be $X_{ajk} \ominus X_{bjk}$, where $\ominus$ is a difference operator based on the fuzzy extension principle, and denote $X_{k.}$ as the abbreviation of $X_{abk}$ in the following section. Therefore, a set of fuzzy input-output data for the $i$-th observation is re-written as:

$$(P_k; X_{1k}, X_{2k}, \ldots, X_{nk}) \,, k=1,2,\ldots,N \tag{23}$$

where $P_k$ is a fuzzy dependent variable, and $X_{jk}$ is a fuzzy independent variable represented by L-R fuzzy numbers. For simplicity, I assume that $P_k$ and $X_{jk}$ are positive for any membership value, $\alpha \in (0,1)$.

The fuzzy logic regression model (where both input and output data are fuzzy numbers) is represented as follows:

$$\overline{log(P_k \oslash (1 \ominus P_k))} = A_0 \otimes X_{i0} \oplus A_1 \otimes X_{i1} \oplus \ldots \oplus \Lambda_m \otimes X_{im} \tag{24}$$

where $\overline{log(P_k \oslash (1 \ominus P_k))}$ is the estimated fuzzy log odds, $\oslash$ is the division operator, $\ominus$ is the difference operator, $\otimes$ is the product operator, and $\oplus$ is the additive operator based on the extension principle for the fuzzy set, respectively.

It should be noted that although the explicit form of the membership function of $\overline{log(P_k \oslash (1 \ominus P_k))}$ cannot be directly obtained, the $\alpha$-level set of $\overline{log(P_k \oslash (1 \ominus P_k))}$ can be obtained using Nguyen's theorem (Nguyen, 1978).

Let $P_{k(\alpha)}^L$ be the lower bound of the dependent fuzzy variable and $P_{k(\alpha)}^R$ be the upper bound. Then, the $\alpha$ level set of the fuzzy dependent variable $P_k$ can be represented as $P_{k\alpha} = \left[ P_{k(\alpha)}^L, P_{k(\alpha)}^R \right] \,, \alpha \in (0,1]$ .

Therefore, the $\alpha$ level set of the left term in Equation (24) is as follows:

$$[log(P_k \oslash (1 \ominus P_k))]_{\alpha=}$$

$$[\min(\overline{\log(P_{k(\alpha)}^L / (1 - P_{k(\alpha)}^L))}, \overline{\log(P_{k(\alpha)}^R / (1 - P_{k(\alpha)}^R))})$$

$$\max(\overline{\log(P_{k(\alpha)}^L / (1 - P_{k(\alpha)}^L))}, \overline{\log(P_{k(\alpha)}^R / (1 - P_{k(\alpha)}^R))})] \tag{25}$$

Let $z^L_{k(\alpha)}$ be a lower value of $\overline{[log(P_k \oplus (1 \ominus P_k))]}_\alpha$, and $z^R_{k(\alpha)}$ be an upper value of $[log(P_k \oplus (1 \ominus P_k))]_\alpha$

where

$$z^L_{k(\alpha)} = \sum_{j=0}^{n} \left\{ \min\left(a^L_{j(\alpha)} x^L_{jk(\alpha)}, a^L_{j(\alpha)} x^R_{jk(\alpha)}\right) \right\} \tag{26}$$

$$z^R_{k(\alpha)} = \sum_{j=0}^{n} \left\{ \max\left(a^R_{j(\alpha)} x^L_{jk(\alpha)}, a^R_{j(\alpha)} x^R_{jk(\alpha)}\right) \right\} \tag{27}$$

$$x^L_{0k(\alpha)} = x^R_{0k(\alpha)} = 1 \tag{28}$$

In the above Equation (26), is a product between the lower value of the □-level fuzzy coefficient for the $j$-th attribute and the $\alpha$-level set of fuzzy input data $X_{jk}$, , or is defined in the same manner, respectively. and are assumed to be 1 (a crisp number) for the purpose of estimation for the fuzzy bias parameter $A_0$. The parameter estimation method is basically the same as the fuzzy logistic regression method and a more concrete procedure is described in Takemura (2004).

## 4. Numerical example of the data analysis method

To demonstrate the appropriateness of the proposed data analysis methods, the detail numerical examples are shown for the individual level analysis (Takemura,2007) and group level analysis (Takemura, Matsumoto, Matsuyama, & Kobayashi, 2011) of ambiguous comparative judgments.

### 4.1. Individual level analysis of ambiguous comparative model

### 4.1.1 Example of additive difference model

#### 4.1.1.1 Participant and procedure

The participant was a 43-year-old faculty member of Waseda University. The participant rated differences in WTP for two different computers (DELL brand) with three types of attribute information (hard disk: 100 or 60 GB; memory: 2.80 or 2.40 GHz; new or used product). The participant compared a certain alternative with seven different alternatives. The participant provided representative values and lower and upper WTP values using a fuzzy rating method. (see Figure 5)

The participant was asked the amount of money he would be willing to pay to upgrade the inferior from inferior alternative to superior alternative using fuzzy rating method. That is, the participant answered the lower value, the representative value, and upper value for the amount of money he would be willing to pay.

| Lower Value | Representative Value | Upper Value |
|---|---|---|
| (    ) Yen | (    ) Yen | (    ) Yen |

Fig. 5. Example of a Fuzzy Rating in WTP Task.

The participant also rated the desirability of the attribute information for each computer using a fuzzy rating method. The fuzzy rating scale of desirability ranged from 0 point to 100 points. (see Figure 6). That is, the participant answered the lower value, the representative value , and upper value for each attribute value.

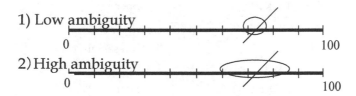

Fig. 6. Example of a Fuzzy Desirability Rating.

### 4.1.1.2 Analysis and results

The fuzzy coefficients were obtained by fuzzy linear regression analysis using the least squares under constraints, as shown in Tables 1 and 2. The dependent variable of Table 1 was the same as that in Table 2. However, the independent variables in Table 1 are objective values measured by crisp numbers, whereas in Table 2 the independent variables are fuzzy rating values measured by an L-R fuzzy number. The parameter of $A_{jk0}$ involves a response bias owing to presentation order, context effects, and the scale parameter of the dependent variables. The parameter $A_{jk0}$ would be a fuzzy variable and larger than $A_{ab0}$ if $X_a$ were more salient than $X_b$. This model can be reduced to the Fuzzy Utility Difference Model (Nakamura, 1992) if multi-attribute weighting parameters are assumed to be crisp numbers, and reduced to the Additive Difference Model (Tversky, 1969) if multi-attribute weighting parameters and the values of multi-attributes are assumed to be crisp numbers as explained before. According to Tables 1 and 2, the preference strength concerning comparative judgment was influenced most by whether the target computer was new or used. The impact of the hard disks' attributes was smaller than that of the new-used dimension.

### 4.1.2 Example of the logistic model

### 4.1.2.1 Participant and procedure

The participant was a 43-year-old adult. The participant rated the ambiguous probability of preferring a certain computer (DELL brand) out of seven different computers. Three types of attribute information (hard disk: 100 or 60 GB; memory: 2.80 or 2.40 GHz; new or used product) were manipulated in the same manner as in the previous judgment task.. That is, the participant answered the lower value, the representative value , and upper value for the probability that superior alternative is preferred to inferior alternative. The participant used the fuzzy rating method to provide representative, lower, and upper values of probabilities (see Figure 7 ).

|            | Attribute | Value | |
|------------|-----------|-------|-------|
|            | Hard Disk(L) | Lower | 78.5 |
|            | Hard Disk (M) | Representative | 85.7 |
|            | Hard Disk (R) | Upper | 986.8 |
| Fuzzy      | Memory(L) | Lower | 0.0 |
| Coefficient | Memory(M) | Representative | 0.0 |
|            | Memory(R) | Upper | 0.0 |
|            | New or Used (R) | Lower | 22 332.5 |
|            | New or Used (M) | Representative | 22 332.5 |
|            | New or Used (L) | Upper | 22 332.5 |
|            | $A_{jk0}$ (L) | Lower | 25 450.8 |
|            | $A_{jk0}$ (M) | Representative | 29 420.1 |
|            | $A_{jk0}$ (R) | Upper | 33 111.2 |

Note: The independent variables are crisp numbers.

Table 1. Coefficients of Fuzzy Regression Analysis

|            | Attribute | Value | |
|------------|-----------|-------|-------|
|            | Hard Disk(L) | Lower | 33.9 |
|            | Hard Disk (M) | Representative | 33.9 |
|            | Hard Disk (R) | Upper | 33.9 |
| Fuzzy      | Memory(L) | Lower | 0.0 |
| Coefficient | Memory(M) | Representative | 0.0 |
|            | Memory(R) | Upper | 0.0 |
|            | New or Used (R) | Lower | 446.1 |
|            | New or Used (M) | Representative | 446.1 |
|            | New or Used (L) | Upper | 446.1 |
|            | $A_{jk0}$ (L) | Lower | 36 082.1 |
|            | $A_{jk0}$ (M) | Representative | 36 082.1 |
|            | $A_{jk0}$ (R) | Upper | 48 004.0 |

Note: The independent variables are fuzzy L-R numbers.

Table 2. Coefficients of Fuzzy Regression Analysis

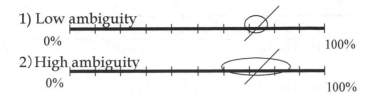

Fig. 7. Example of Fuzzy Probability Rating.

### 4.1.2.2 Analysis and results

The fuzzy coefficients were obtained by fuzzy linear regression analysis using least squares under constraints, as shown in Tables 3 and 4. However, in Table 3 the independent variables are objective values measured by crisp numbers, whereas in Table 4 the independent variables are fuzzy rating values measured by an L-R fuzzy number. The parameter $A_{jk0}$ involves a response bias owing to presentation order, context effects, and the scale parameter of the dependent variables. According to Tables 3 and 4, the bounded preference strength was influenced most by whether the target computer was new or used. Interestingly, the impact of the attribute for memory was slightly greater than was the case in Tables 1 and 2.

|  | Attribute | Value |  |
| --- | --- | --- | --- |
|  | Hard Disk (L) | Lower | 0.000 |
|  | Hard Disk(M) | Representative | 0.000 |
|  | Hard Disk (R) | Upper | 0.009 |
| Fuzzy | Memory(L) | Lower | 1.781 |
| Coefficient | Memory(M) | Representative | 1.781 |
|  | Memory(R) | Upper | 1.881 |
|  | New or Used (R) | Lower | 1.791 |
|  | New or Used (M) | Representative | 2.097 |
|  | New or Used (L) | Upper | 2.777 |
|  | $A_{jk0}$ (L) | Lower | 0.847 |
|  | $A_{jk0}$ (M) | Representative | 1.201 |
|  | $A_{jk0}$ (R) | Upper | 1.443 |

Note: The independent variables are crisp numbers.

Table 3. Coefficients of Fuzzy Logistic Regression Analysis

|                    | Attribute          | Value          |       |
|--------------------|--------------------|----------------|-------|
|                    | Hard Disk(L)       | Lower          | 0.000 |
|                    | Hard Disk (M)      | Representative  | 0.000 |
|                    | Hard Disk (R)      | Upper          | 0.000 |
| Fuzzy              | Memory(L)          | Lower          | 0.008 |
| Coefficient        | Memory(M)          | Representative  | 0.008 |
|                    | Memory(R)          | Upper          | 0.008 |
|                    | New or Used (R)    | Lower          | 0.043 |
|                    | New or Used (M)    | Representative  | 0.043 |
|                    | New or Used (L)    | Upper          | 0.043 |
|                    | $A_{jk0}$ (L)      | Lower          | 1.806 |
|                    | $A_{jk0}$ (M)      | Representative  | 1.806 |
|                    | $A_{jk0}$ (R)      | Upper          | 1.806 |

Note: The independent variables are fuzzy L-R numbers.

Table 4. Coefficients of Fuzzy Logistic Regression Analysis

## 4.2 Group level analysis of ambiguous comparative model

### 4.2.1 Example of additive difference model

#### 4.2.1.1 Participants and procedure

The participant s were 100 undergraduate university students (68 female and 32 male students) enrolled in an economic

psychology class at Waseda University. They were recruited for an experiment investigating "consumer preference ".

Their average age was 21.3 years old. The participants rated differences in WTP for two different digital cameras with three types of attribute information (weight: 130 gram or1 60 gram; memory: 25 or 50 MB; display size:2.5 or 5.0 inches). The participants compared a certain alternative with seven different alternatives. The participants also rated differences in WTP for two different mobile phones with three types of attribute information (weight: 123 gram or132 gram; pixel number:3,200,000 or 5,070,000 pixels; display size:2.8 or 3.0 inches). The participants compared a certain alternative with seven different mobile phones. The participant provided representative values and lower and upper WTP values using a fuzzy rating method. The participants were asked the amount of money he would be willing to pay to upgrade the inferior from  inferior  alternative to superior alternative using fuzzy rating method. That is, the participants answered the lower value, the representative value , and upper value for the amount of money he would be willing to pay. An example of fuzzy WTP rating is illustrated in the Figure 8.

**Question:**

Which alternative do you prefer ? Please circle the superior alternative.

Then, please estimate the amount of money you would be willing to pay to upgrade the inferior alternative from inferior alternative to superior alternative using fuzzy rating method. That is, the participants answered the lower value, the representative value, and upper value for the amount of money you would be willing to pay.

<table>
<tr><td>**Brand A**</td><td>**Brand B**</td></tr>
<tr><td>Weight: 130g</td><td>Weight: 160g</td></tr>
<tr><td>Memory: 25MB</td><td>Memory: 50MB</td></tr>
<tr><td>Display: 50 inches</td><td>Display: 25 inches</td></tr>
</table>

**Difference**

Minimum: <u>2,000 yen</u> ----- Maximum: <u>10, 000 yen</u>
Representative Value: <u>5,000 yen</u>

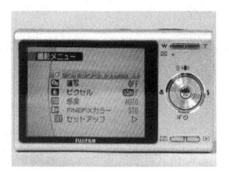

Fig. 8. Example of Fuzzy WTP Rating

### 4.2.1.2 Analysis and results

The fuzzy coefficients were obtained by fuzzy linear regression analysis using the least squares under constraints, as shown in Tables 5 for the digital camera data and Table 6 for mobile phone data. The independent variables in Table5 and Table 6 are objective values measured by crisp numbers. The parameter of $A_{jk0}$ involves a response bias owing to presentation order, context effects, and the scale parameter of the dependent variables.According to Tables 5, the preference strength concerning comparative judgment was influenced most by whether the target digital camera was 2.5 or 5.0 inches. The impact of the memory's attribute was smaller than those of display size and weight dimensions. According to Tables 6, the preference strength concerning comparative judgment was influenced most by whether the target mobile phone was 2.8 or 3.0 inches. The impact of the pixel number's attribute was smaller than those of display size and weight dimensions. The participants also rated the desirability of the attribute information for each computer using a fuzzy rating method. The fuzzy rating scale of desirability ranged from 0 point to 100 points. (see Figure 6). That is, the participant answered the lower value, the representative value , and upper value for each attribute value.

|  | Attribute | Value | |
|---|---|---|---|
|  | Weight(L) | Lower | 48.57 |
|  | Weight (M) | Representative | 48.57 |
|  | Weight (R) | Upper | 68.33 |
| Fuzzy | Memory(L) | Lower | 8.29 |
| Coefficient | Memory(M) | Representative | 8.29 |
|  | Memory(R) | Upper | 14.62 |
|  | Display Size (R) | Lower | 223.10 |
|  | Display Size (M) | Representative | 4791.98 |
|  | Display Size (L) | Upper | 4791.98 |
|  | $A_{jk0}$  (L) | Lower | 11361.25 |
|  | $A_{jk0}$  (M) | Representative | 11361.25 |
|  | $A_{jk0}$  (R) | Upper | 15447.54 |

Note: The independent variables are crisp numbers.

Table 5. Coefficients of Fuzzy Regression Analysis for Digital Camera Data

|  | Attribute | Value | |
|---|---|---|---|
|  | Weight(L) | Lower | 28.84 |
|  | Weight (M) | Representative | 28.84 |
|  | Weight (R) | Upper | 53.44 |
| Fuzzy | Pixel Number(L) | Lower | -12.12 |
| Coefficient | Pixel Number(M) | Representative | 28.55 |
|  | Pixel Number(R) | Upper | 28.55 |
|  | Display Size (R) | Lower | -233.73 |
|  | Display Size (M) | Representative | 190.29 |
|  | Display Size (L) | Upper | 190.29 |
|  | $A_{jk0}$  (L) | Lower | 7758.98 |
|  | $A_{jk0}$  (M) | Representative | 8234.94 |
|  | $A_{jk0}$  (R) | Upper | 12569.35 |

Note: The independent variables are crisp numbers.

Table 6. Coefficients of Fuzzy Regression Analysis for Mobile Phone Data

## 4.2.2 Example of the logistic model

### 4.2.2.1 Participants and procedure

The participant s were 100 undergraduate university students (68 female and 32 male students). Their average age was 21.3 years old. The participants rated the ambiguous probability of preferring a certain digital camera out of seven different digital cameras. The three types of attribute information (weight: 130 gram or1 60 gram; memory: 25 or 50 MB; display size:2.5 or 5.0 inches) were manipulated in the same manner as in the previous individual judgment task. They also rated the ambiguous probability of preferring a certain mobile phone out of seven different mobile phones. The three types of attribute information (weight: 123 gram or132 gram; pixel number:3,200,000 or 5,070,000 pixels; display size:2.8 or 3.0 inches) were manipulated in the same manner in the previous judgment task. The participant provided representative values and lower and upper values of probabilities. That is, the participants answered the lower value, the representative value , and upper value for the probability that superior alternative is preferred to inferior alternative. The participants used the fuzzy rating method to provide representative, lower, and upper values of probabilities (see Figure 7 ).

### 4.2.2.2 Analysis and results

The fuzzy coefficients were obtained by fuzzy logistic regression analysis using the least squares under constraints, as shown in Tables 7 for the digital camera data and Table 8 for mobile phone data. The independent variables in Table 7 and Table 8 are objective values measured by crisp numbers. The parameter of $A_{jk0}$ involves a response bias owing to presentation order, context effects, and the scale parameter of the dependent variables. According to Tables 7, the bounded preference strength was influenced most by whether the target digital camera was 2.5 or 5.0 inches. The impact of the memory's attribute was smaller than those of display size and weight dimensions. According to Tables 8, the bounded preference strength t was influenced most by whether the target mobile phone was 2.8 or 3.0 inches. The impact of the weight's attribute was smaller than those of display size and pixel number dimensions.

|  | Attribute | Value |  |
|---|---|---|---|
|  | Weight(L) | Lower | 0.035 |
|  | Weight (M) | Representative | 0.038 |
|  | Weight (R) | Upper | 0.054 |
| Fuzzy | Memory(L) | Lower | 0.003 |
| Coefficient | Memory(M) | Representative | 0.003 |
|  | Memory(R) | Upper | 0.003 |
|  | Display Size(R) | Lower | 2.625 |
|  | Display Size (M) | Representative | 2.625 |
|  | Display Size(L) | Upper | 2.625 |
|  | $A_{jk0}$ (L) | Lower | -0.122 |
|  | $A_{jk0}$ (M) | Representative | 0.459 |
|  | $A_{jk0}$ (R) | Upper | 1.072 |

Note: The independent variables are crisp numbers.

Table 7. Coefficients of Fuzzy Logistic Regression Analysis for Digital Camera Data

| | Attribute | Value | |
| --- | --- | --- | --- |
| | Weight(L) | Lower | 0.002 |
| | Weight (M) | Representative | 0.002 |
| | Weight (R) | Upper | 0.009 |
| Fuzzy | Pixel Number(L) | Lower | 0.012 |
| Coefficient | Pixel Number(M) | Representative | 0.017 |
| | Pixel Number(R) | Upper | 0.024 |
| | Display Size(R) | Lower | 0.161 |
| | Display Size(M) | Representative | 0.165 |
| | Display Size(L) | Upper | 0.232 |
| | $A_{jk0}$ (L) | Lower | -0.871 |
| | $A_{jk0}$ (M) | Representative | 0.030 |
| | $A_{jk0}$ (R) | Upper | 0.887 |

Note: The independent variables are crisp numbers.

Table 8. Coefficients of Fuzzy Logistic Regression Analysis for Mobile Phone Data

## 5. Conclusion

This chapter introduce fuzzy set models for ambiguous comparative judgments, which do not always hold transitivity and comparability properties. The first type of model was a fuzzy theoretical extension of the additive difference model for preference that is used to explain ambiguous preference strength. This model can be reduced to the Fuzzy Utility Difference Model (Nakamura, 1992) if multi-attribute weighting parameters are assumed to be crisp numbers, and can be reduced to the Additive Difference Model (Tversky, 1969) if multi-attribute weighting parameters and the values of multi-attributes are assumed to be crisp numbers. The second type of model was a fuzzy logistic model for explaining ambiguous preference in which preference strength is bounded, such as a probability measure.

In both models, multi-attribute weighting parameters and all attribute values were assumed to be asymmetric fuzzy L-R numbers. For each model, parameter estimation method using fuzzy regression analysis was introduced. Numerical examples for comparison were also demonstrated. As the objective of the numerical examples was to demonstrate that the proposed estimation might be viable, further empiric studies will be needed. Moreover, because the two models require different evaluation methods, comparisons of the psychological effects of the two methods must be studied further.

In this chapter, the least squares method was used for data analyses of the two models. However, the possibilistic linear regression analysis (Sakawa & Yano, 1992) and the possibilistic logistic regression analysis (Takemura, 2004) could also be used in the data analysis of the additive difference type model and the logistic type model, respectively. The proposed models and the analyses for ambiguous comparative judgments will be applied to marketing research, risk perception research, and human judgment and decision-making research. Empirical research using possibilistic analysis and least squares analysis will be needed to examine the validity of these models.

Results of these applications to psychological study indicated that the parameter estimated in the proposed analysis was meaningful for social judgment study. This study has a methodological restriction on statistical inferences for fuzzy parameters. Therefore, we plan further work on the fuzzy theoretic analysis of social judgment directed toward the statistical study of fuzzy regression analysis and fuzzy logistic regression analysis such as statistical tests of parameters, outlier detection, and step-wise variable selection.

# 6. Acknowledgment

This work was supported in part by Grants in Aids for Grant-in-Aid for Scientific Research on Priority Area, The Ministry of Education, Culture, Sports, Science and Technology(MEXT). I thank Matsumoto,T., Matsuyama,S.,and Kobayashi,M.. for their assistance, and the editor and the reviewers for their valuable comments.

# 7. References

Anderson,N.H.(1988). A functional approach to person cognition. In T.K.Srull & R.S. Wyer (Eds.), *Advances in social cognition.* vol.1. Hiisdale, New Jersey: Lawrence Erlbaum Associates, pp.37-51.

Dubois D. & Prade,H. (1980). Fuzzy sets and systems: Theory and applications, New York: Academic Press.

Festinger, L. (1954). A theory of social comparison processes. *Human Relations, 7,* 114–140.

Hesketh, B., Pryor, R., Gleitzman, M., & Hesketh, T. (1988). Practical applications and psychometric evaluation of a computerised fuzzy graphic rating scale. In T. Zetenyi (Ed.), *Fuzzy sets in psychology* (pp. 425–454). New York: North Holland.

Kühberger,A.,.Schulte-Mecklenbeck,M. & Ranyard,R. (2011). Introduction: Windows for understanding the mind, In M.Schulte-Mecklenbeck, A.Kühberger, & R. Ranyard(Eds.), A handbook of process tracing methods for decision research,New Yorrk: Psychologgy Press, pp.3-17.

Mussweiler, T. (2003). Comparison processes in social judgment: Mechanisms and consequences. *Psychological Review, 110,* 472–489.

Nakamura, K. (1992). On the nature of intransitivity in human referential judgments. In V. Novak (Ed.), *Fuzzy approach to reasoning and decision making, academia* (pp. 147–162). Prague: Kluwer Academic Publishers.

Nguyen, H. T. (1978). A note on the extension principle for fuzzy sets. *Journal of Mathematical Analysis and Application,* 64, 369–380.

Rosch,E. (1975). Cognitive representation of semantic categories. Journal of Experimental Psychology: General, 104, 192-233.

Rosch,E., & Mervis,C.B. (1975). Family resemblances: Studies in the internal structure of categories. *Cognitive Psychology, 7,* 573-603.

Sakawa, M., & Yano, H. (1992). Multiobjective fuzzy linear regression analysis for fuzzy input-output data. *Fuzzy Sets and Systems, 47,* 173-181.

Sherif,M.,& Hovland,C,I. (1961). *Social judgment: Assimilation and contrast effects in communication and attitude change.* New Haven: Yale University Press.

Smithson, M. (1987). *Fuzzy set analysis for the behavioral and social sciences.* New York: Springer-Verlag.

Smithson,M.(1989) Ignorance and uncertainty. New York: Springer-Verlag-

Takemura, K. (1999). A fuzzy linear regression analysis for fuzzy input-output data using the least squares method under linear constraints and its application to fuzzy rating data. *Journal of Advanced Computational Intelligence,* 3, 36–40.

Takemura, K. (2000). Vagueness in human judgment and decision making. In Z. Q. Liu & S. Miyamoto (Eds), *Soft Computing for Human Centered Machines* (pp. 249–281). Tokyo: Springer Verlag.

Takemura, K. (2004). Fuzzy logistic regression analysis for fuzzy input and output data. Proceedings of the joint 2nd International Conference on Soft Computing and Intelligent Systems and the 5th International Symposium on Advanced Intelligent Systems 2004 (WE8-5), Yokohama, Japan.

Takemura, K. (2005). Fuzzy least squares regression analysis for social judgment study. *Journal of Advanced Computational Intelligence,* 9, 461–466.

Takemura, K. (2007). Ambiguous comparative judgment: Fuzzy set model and data analysis. *Japanese Psychology Research,* 49, 148–156.

Takemura, K. ,Matsumoto,T.,Matsuyama,S.,& Kobayashi,M., (2011). Analysis of consumer's ambiguous comparative judgment. *Discussion Paper, Department of Psychology, Waseda University.*

Takemura,K. (1996). *Psychology of decision making.* Tokyo:Fukumura Syuppan. (in Japanese).

Takemura,K. (2011) Model of multi-attribute decision making and good decision. Operations Research，56(10),583－590 (In Japanese)

Tversky, A. (1969). Intransitivity of preferences. *Psychological Review,* 76, 31–48.

Wittgenstein,L. (1953). *Philosophical investigations.* New York:MacMillan.

Zadeh,A. (1965). Fuzzy sets, *Information and Control,* 8, 338-353.

Zadeh,A. (1973). Outline of a new approach to the analysis of complex systems and decision processes, *IEEE Transactions on Systems, Man and Cybernetics,* SMC 3(1), 28-44.

# 2

# Resolution Principle and Fuzzy Logic

Hashim Habiballa
*University of Ostrava*
*Czech Republic*

## 1. Introduction

Fuzzy Predicate Logic with Evaluated Syntax (FPL) (Novák, V.) is a well-studied and wide-used logic capable of expressing vagueness. It has a lot of applications based on robust theoretical background. It also requires an efficient formal proof theory. However the most widely applied resolution principle (Dukić, N.) brings syntactically several obstacles mainly arising from normal form transformation. FPL is associating with even harder problems when trying to use the resolution principle. Solutions to these obstacles based on the non-clausal resolution (Bachmair, L.) were already proposed in (Habiballa, H.).

In this article it would be presented a natural integration of these two formal logical systems into fully functioning inference system with effective proof search strategies. It leads to the refutational resolution theorem prover for FPL ($RRTP_{FPL}$). Another issue addressed in the paper concerns to the efficiency of presented inference strategies developed originally for the proving system. It is showed their perspectives in combination with standard proof-search strategies. The main problem for the fuzzy logic theorem proving lies in the large amount of possible proofs with different degrees and there is presented an algorithm (Detection of Consequent Formulas - DCF) solving this problem. The algorithm is based on detection of such redundant formulas (proofs) with different degrees.

The article presents the method which is the main point of the work on any automated prover. There is a lot of strategies which makes proofs more efficient when we use refutational proving. We consider well-known strategies - orderings, filtration strategy, set of support etc. One of the most effective strategies is the elimination of consequent formulas. It means the check if a resolvent is not a logical consequence of a formula in set of axioms or a previous resolvent. If such a condition holds it is reasonable to not include the resolvent into the set of resolvents, because if the refutation can be deduced from it, then so it can be deduced from the original resolvent, which it implies of.

## 2. First-order logic

For the purposes of ($RRTP_{FPL}$) it will be used generalized principle of resolution, which is defined in the research report (Bachmair, L.). There is a propositional form of the rule defined at first and further it is lifted into first-order logic. It is introduced the propositional form of the general resolution.

**General resolution - propositional version**

$$\frac{F[G] \quad F'[G]}{F[G/\bot] \vee F'[G/\top]} \tag{1}$$

where the propositional logic formulas $F$ and $F'$ are the premises of inference and $G$ is an occurrence of a subformula of both $F$ and $F'$. The expression $F[G/\bot] \vee F'[G/\top]$ is the resolvent of the premises on $G$. Every occurrence of G is replaced by false in the first formula and by true in the second one. It is also called F the positive, F' the negative premise, and G the resolved subformula.

The proof of the soundness of the rule is similar to clausal resolution rule proof. Suppose the Interpretation I in which both premises are valid. In I, G is either true or false. If G ($\neg G$) is true in I, so is $F'[G/\top]$ ($F[G/\bot]$).

Revised version of the paper which forms the core of the handbook (Bachmair, L.) is closely related with notion of selection functions and ordering constraints. By a selection functions it is meant a mapping $S$ that assigns to each clause $C$ a (possibly empty) multiset $S(C)$ of negative literals in C. In other words, the function S selects (a possibly empty) negative subclause of C. We say that an atom $A$, or a literal $\neg A$, is selected by $S$ if $\neg A$ occurs in $S(C)$. There are no selected atoms or literals if $S(C)$ is empty. Lexicographic path ordering can be used as an usual ordering over a total precedence. But in this case the ordering is admissible if predicate symbols have higher precedence than logical symbols and the constants $\top$ and $\bot$ are smaller than the other logical symbols. It means the ordering is following $A \succ \equiv \succ \supset \succ \neg \succ \vee \succ \wedge \succ \top \succ \bot$. The handbook also addresses another key issues for automated theorem proving - the efficiency of the proof search. This efficiency is closely related with the notion of *redundancy*.

If we want to generalize the notion of resolution and lift it into first-order case we have to define first the notion of selection function for general clauses. General clauses are multisets of arbitrary quantifier-free formulas, denoting the disjunction of their elements. Note that we can also work with a special case of such general clause with one element, which yields to a standard quantifier-free formula of first-order logic. A (general selection) function is a mapping $S$ that assigns to each general clause $C$ a (possibly empty) set $C$ of non-empty sequences of (distinct) atoms in C such that either $S(C)$ is empty or else, for all interpretations $I$ in which C is false, there exists a sequence $A_1, ..., A_k$ in $S(C)$, all atoms of which are true in I. A sequence $A_1, ..., A_k$ in $S(C)$ is said to be *selected* (by S).

We have to define the notion of polarity for these reasons according to the handbook (Bachmair, L.). It is based on the following assumption that a subformula $F'$ in $E[F']$ is *positive* (resp. *negative*), if $E[F'/\top]$ (resp. $E[F'/\bot]$) is a tautology. Thus, if $F'$ is *positive* (resp. *negative*) in E, F' (resp. $\neg F'$) logically implies E. Even it should seem that determining of the polarity of any subformula is NP-complete (hard) problem, we can use syntactic criteria for this computation. In this case the complexity of the algorithm is linear (note that we base our theory on similar syntactic criteria below - structural notions definition).

**Proposition 1.** *Polarity criteria*

1. *F is a positive subformula of F.*

2. *If $\neg G$ is a positive (resp. negative) subformula of F, then G is a negative (resp. positive) subformula of F.*

3. *If $G \vee H$ is a positive subformula of F, then G and H are both positive subformulas of F.*

4. *If $G \wedge H$ is a negative subformula of F, then G and H are both negative subformulas of F.*

5. *If $G \to H$ is a positive subformula of F, then G is a negative subformula and H is a positive subformula of F.*

6. *If $G \to \bot$ is a negative subformula of F, then G is a positive subformula of F.*

7. *F is positive in a clause C if it is an element of C.*

Note that this proposition applies both to formulas and clauses and allows us to determine polarity of any subformula in a formula. It is safe to *select any sequence of negative atoms* in a general clause, since a negative atom cannot be false in an interpretation the clause is false. With the notion of the polarity as a selection function there is possible to state another notion of General resolution based on orderings applied to clauses.

**General ordered resolution with selection $O_S^\succ$**

$$\frac{C_1(A_1)...C_n(A_n) \quad D(A_1,...,A_n)}{C_1(\bot)...C_n(\bot) \quad D(\top,...,\top)} \tag{2}$$

where (i) either $A_1, ..., A_n$ is selected by $S$ in $D$, or else $S(D)$ is empty, $n = 1$, $A_1$ is maximal in $D$, (ii) each atom $A_i$ is maximal in $C_i$, and (iii) no clause $C_i$ contains a selected atom.

According to the (Bachmair, L.) an inference system based on this rule is refutationally complete. When trying to extend this into the first-order case we to use lifting lemma.

**Lemma 1.** *Lifting lemma*
Let $M$ be a set of clauses and $K = G(M)$ *(set of ground instances). If*

$$\frac{C_1...C_n \quad C_0}{C}$$

*is an inference in* $O_{S_M}^\succ(K)$ *then there exist clauses* $C_i'$ *in* $M$, *a clause* $C'$, *and a ground substitution* $\sigma$ *such that*

$$\frac{C_1'...C_n' \quad C_0'}{C'}$$

*is an inference in* $O_S^\succ(M)$, $C_i = C_i'\sigma$, *and* $C = C'\sigma$.

**Example 1.** *General resolution - polarity based selection*
1. $\neg a \vee \neg b \vee c$ *(axiom),*
2. $a$ *(axiom),* 3. $b$ *(axiom)*
4. $\bot \quad \vee \quad \neg\top \vee \neg b \vee c$ *(a is a negative atom in (1) - selected in (1) as negative premise, and (2) as positive premise respectively)* $\Rightarrow \neg b \vee c$
5. $\bot \quad \vee \quad \neg\top \vee c$ *(b is a negative atom in (4) - selected in (4) as negative premise, and (3) as positive premise respectively)* $\Rightarrow c$

In the example we used the notion of polarity as a selection function. For example in the line 4 we select the atom a upon negative polarity (according the proposition criteria 1, 3 and 2 - level ordered) in formula 1 (it means 1. is a negative premise).

Further we can observe the behavior of the rule within the frame of clausal form resolution. Consider following table showing various cases of resolution on clauses.

**Example 2.** *General resolution with equivalence*
1. $a \wedge c \leftrightarrow b \wedge d$ *(axiom),* 2. $a \wedge c$ *(axiom),* 3.$\neg[b \wedge d]$ *(axiom) - negated goal*
4. $[a \wedge \bot] \vee [a \wedge \top]$ *(resolvent from (2), (2) on c)* $\Rightarrow a$
5. $[a \wedge \bot] \vee [a \wedge \top \leftrightarrow b \wedge d]$ *((2), (1) on c)* $\Rightarrow a \leftrightarrow b \wedge d$
6. $\bot \vee [\top \leftrightarrow b \wedge d]$ *((4), (5) on a)* $\Rightarrow b \wedge d$
7. $\bot \wedge d \vee \top \wedge d$ *((6), (6) on b)* $\Rightarrow d$
8. $b \wedge \bot \vee b \wedge \top$ *((6), (6) on d)* $\Rightarrow b$

| Premise1 | Premise2 | Resolvent | Simplified | Comments |
|----------|----------|-----------|------------|----------|
| $a \vee b$ | $b \vee c$ | $(a \vee \bot) \vee (\top \vee c)$ | $\top$ | no compl. pair |
| $a \vee \neg b$ | $b \vee c$ | $(a \vee \top) \vee (\top \vee c)$ | $\top$ | redundant inference |
| $a \vee b$ | $\neg b \vee c$ | $(a \vee \bot) \vee (\bot \vee c)$ | $a \vee c$ | clausal resolution |
| $a \vee \neg b$ | $\neg b \vee c$ | $(a \vee \top) \vee (\bot \vee c)$ | $\top$ | no compl. pair |

Table 1. Clausal resolution in the context of the non-clausal resolution

9. $\bot \vee \neg [\top \wedge d]$ ((8), (3) on b) $\Rightarrow \neg d$
10. $\bot \vee \neg \top$ ((7), (9) on d) $\Rightarrow \bot$ (refutation)

When trying to refine the general resolution rule for fuzzy predicate logic, it is important to devise a sound and complete unification algorithm. Standard unification algorithms require variables to be treated only as universally quantified ones. We will present a more general unification algorithm, which can deal with existentially quantified variables without the need for those variables be eliminated by skolemization. It should be stated that the following unification process does not allow an occurrence of the equivalence connective. It is needed to remove equivalence by rewrite rule: $A \leftrightarrow B \Leftrightarrow [A \rightarrow B] \wedge [B \rightarrow A]$.

We assume that the language and semantics of FOL is standard. We use terms - individuals $(a, b, c, ...)$, functions (with n arguments) $(f, g, h, ...)$, variables $(X, Y, Z, ...)$, predicates(with n arguments) $(p, q, r, ...)$, logical connectives $(\wedge, \vee, \rightarrow, \neg)$, quantifiers $(\exists, \forall)$ and logical constants $(\bot, \top)$. We also work with standard notions of logical and special axioms (sets LAx, SAx), logical consequence, consistency etc. as they are used in mathematical logic.

**Definition 1.** *Structural notions of a FOL formula*
*Let F be a formula of FOL then the structural mappings Sub (subformula), Sup (superformula), Pol (polarity) and Lev (level) are defined as follows:*

| $F = G \wedge H$ or $F = G \vee H$ | $Sub(F) = \{G, H\}, Sup(G) = F, Sup(H) = F$ $Pol(G) = Pol(F), Pol(H) = Pol(F)$ |
|---|---|
| $F = G \rightarrow H$ | $Sub(F) = \{G, H\}, Sup(G) = F, Sup(H) = F$ $Pol(G) = -Pol(F), Pol(H) = Pol(F)$ |
| $F = \neg G$ | $Sub(F) = \{G\}, Sup(G) = F$ $Pol(G) = -Pol(F)$ |
| $F = \exists \alpha G$ or $F = \forall \alpha G$ ($\alpha$ is a variable) | $Sub(F) = \{G\}, Sup(G) = F$ $Pol(G) = Pol(F)$ |

$Sup(F) = \emptyset \Rightarrow Lev(F) = 0, Pol(F) = 1,$
$Sup(F) \neq \emptyset \Rightarrow Lev(F) = Lev(Sup(F)) + 1$
*For mappings Sub and Sup reflexive and transitive closures Sub\* and Sup\* are defined recursively as follows:*
1. $Sub^*(F) \supseteq \{F\}, Sup^*(F) \supseteq \{F\}$
2. $Sub^*(F) \supseteq \{H | G \in Sub^*(F) \wedge H \in Sub(G)\}, Sup^*(F) \supseteq \{H | G \in Sup^*(F) \wedge H \in Sup(G)\}$

Example: $A \rightarrow B$ - $Pol(A) = -1, Pol(B) = 1, Lev(A) = 1$

These structural mappings provide framework for assignment of quantifiers to variable occurrences. It is needed for the correct simulation of skolemization (the information about a variable quantification in the prenex form). Subformula and superformula mappings and its closures encapsulate essential hierarchical information of a formula structure. Level gives the ordering with respect to the scope of variables (which is also essential for skolemization simulation - unification is restricted for existential variables). Polarity enables to decide the global meaning of a variable (e.g. globally an existential variable is universal if its quantification subformula has negative polarity). Sound unification requires further definitions on variable quantification. We will introduce notions of the corresponding quantifier for a variable occurrence, substitution mapping and significance mapping (we have to distinguish between original variables occurring in special axioms and newly introduced ones in the proof sequence).

**Definition 2.** *Variable assignment, substitution and significance*
*Let F be a formula of FOL, $G = p(t_1, ..., t_n) \in Sub^*(F)$ atom in F and $\alpha$ a variable occurring in $t_i$.*
*Variable mappings Qnt(quantifier assignment), Sbt (variable substitution) and Sig(significance) are defined as follows:*

$Qnt(\alpha) = Q\alpha H, where Q = \exists \lor Q = \forall, H, I \in Sub^*(F), Q\alpha H \in Sup^*(G),$
$\forall Q\alpha I \in Sup^*(G) \Rightarrow Lev(Q\alpha I) < Lev(Q\alpha H).$
$F[\alpha / t']$ *is a substitution of term $t'$ into $\alpha$ in $F \Rightarrow Sbt(\alpha) = t'$.*
*A variable $\alpha$ occurring in $F \in LAx \cup SAx$ is significant w.r.t. existential substitution, $Sig(\alpha) = 1$ iff variable is significant, $Sig(\alpha) = 0$ otherwise.*

Example: $\forall x(\forall x A(x) \rightarrow B(x))$ - $Qnt(x) = \forall x A(x)$, for $x$ in $A(x)$ and $Qnt(x) = \forall x(\forall x A(x) \rightarrow B(x))$, for $x$ in $B(x)$.

Note that with Qnt mapping (assignment of first name matching quantifier variable in a formula hierarchy from bottom) we are able to distinguish between variables of the same name and there is no need to rename any variable. Sbt mapping holds substituted terms in a quantifier and there is no need to rewrite all occurrences of a variable when working with this mapping within unification. It is also clear that if $Qnt(\alpha) = \emptyset$ then $\alpha$ is a free variable. These variables could be simply avoided by introducing new universal quantifiers to F. Significance mapping is important for differentiating between original formula universal variables and newly introduced ones during proof search (an existential variable can't be bounded with it).

Before we can introduce the standard unification algorithm, we should formulate the notion of global universal and global existential variable (it simulates conversion into prenex normal form).

**Definition 3.** *Global quantification*
*Let F be a formula without free variables and $\alpha$ be a variable occurrence in a term of F.*

1. *$\alpha$ is a global universal variable ($\alpha \in Var_\forall(F)$) iff $(Qnt(\alpha) = \forall \alpha H$*
   *$\land Pol(Qnt(\alpha)) = 1)$ or $(Qnt(\alpha) = \exists \alpha H \land Pol(Qnt(\alpha)) = -1)$*
2. *$\alpha$ is a global existential variable ($\alpha \in Var_\exists(F)$) iff $(Qnt(\alpha) = \exists \alpha H$*
   *$\land Pol(Qnt(\alpha)) = 1)$ or $(Qnt(\alpha) = \forall \alpha H \land Pol(Qnt(\alpha)) = -1)$*

*$Var_\forall(F)$ and $Var_\exists(F)$ are sets of global universal and existential variables.*

Example: $F = \forall y(\forall x A(x) \rightarrow B(y))$ - $x$ is a global existential variable, $y$ is a global universal variable.

It is clear w.r.t. skolemization technique that an existential variable can be substituted into an universal one only if all global universal variables over the scope of the existential one have been already substituted by a term. Skolem functors function in the same way. Now we can define the most general unification algorithm based on recursive conditions (extended unification in contrast to standard MGU).

**Definition 4.** *Most general unifier algorithm*

*Let $G = p(t_1, ..., t_n)$ and $G' = r(u_1, ..., u_n)$ be atoms. Most general unifier (substitution mapping) MGU(G, G') = $\sigma$ is obtained by following atom and term unification steps or the algorithm returns fail-state for unification. For the purposes of the algorithm we define the Variable Unification Restriction (VUR).*

## Variable Unification Restriction

*Let $F_1$ be a formula and $\alpha$ be a variable occurring in $F_1$, $F_2$ be a formula, $t$ be a term occurring in $F_2$ and $\beta$ be a variable occurring in $F_2$. Variable Unification Restriction (VUR) for $(\alpha, t)$ holds if one of the conditions 1. and 2. holds:*

1. *$\alpha$ is a global universal variable and $t \neq \beta$, where $\beta$ is a global existential variable and $\alpha$ not occurring in $t$ (non-existential substitution)*

2. *$\alpha$ is a global universal variable and $t = \beta$, where $\beta$ is a global existential variable and $\forall F \in Sup^*(Qnt(\beta))$, $F = Q\gamma G$, $Q \in \{\forall, \exists\}$, $\gamma$ is a global universal variable, $Sig(\gamma) = 1 \Rightarrow (Sbt(\gamma) = r') \in \sigma$, $r'$ is a term (existential substitution).*

## Atom unification

1. *if $n = 0$ and $p = r$ then $\sigma = \emptyset$ and the unifier exists (success-state).*

2. *if $n > 0$ and $p = r$ then perform term unification for pairs $(t_1, u_1), \ldots, (t_n, u_n)$; If for every pair unifier exists then MGU(G, G') = $\sigma$ obtained during term unification (success state).*

3. *In any other case unifier does not exist (fail-state).*

## Term unification $(t', u')$

1. *if $u' = \alpha$, $t' = \beta$ are variables and $Qnt(\alpha) = Qnt(\beta)$ then unifier exists for $(t', u')$ (success-state) (occurrence of the same variable).*

2. *if $t' = \alpha$ is a variable and $(Sbt(\alpha) = v') \in \sigma$ then perform term unification for $(v', u')$; The unifier for $(t', u')$ exists iff it exists for $(v', u')$ (success-state for an already substituted variable).*

3. *if $u' = \alpha$ is a variable and $(Sbt(\alpha) = v') \in \sigma$ then perform term unification for $(t', v')$; The unifier for $(t', u')$ exists iff it exists for $(t', v')$ (success-state for an already substituted variable).*

4. *if $t' = a$, $u' = b$ are individual constants and $a = b$ then for $(t', u')$ unifier exists (success-state).*

5. *if $t' = f(t'_1, ..., t'_m)$, $u' = g(u'_1, ..., u'_n)$ are function symbols with arguments and $f = g$ then unifier for $(t', u')$ exists iff unifier exists for every pair $(t'_1, u'_1), ..., (t'_n, u'_n)$ (success-state).*

6. *if $t' = \alpha$ is a variable and VUR for $(t', u')$ holds then unifier exists for $(t', u')$ holds and $\sigma = \sigma \cup (Sbt(\alpha) = u')$ (success-state).*

7. *if $u' = \alpha$ is a variable and VUR for $(u', t')$ holds then unifier exists for $(t', u')$ holds and $\sigma = \sigma \cup (Sbt(\alpha) = t')$ (success-state).*

8. *In any other case unifier does not exist (fail-state).*

*MGU(A) = $\sigma$ for a set of atoms $A = \{G_1, \ldots, G_k\}$ is computed by the atom unification for $(G_1, G_i), \sigma_i = MGU(G_1, G_i), \forall i, \sigma_0 = \emptyset$, where before every atom unification $(G_1, G_i)$, $\sigma$ is set to $\sigma_{i-1}$.*

With above defined notions it is simple to state the general resolution rule for FOL (without the equivalence connective). It conforms to the definition from (Bachmair, L.).

**Definition 5.** *General resolution for first-order logic* $(GR_{FOL})$

$$\frac{F[G_1,,...,G_k] \quad F'[G'_1,...,G'_n]}{F\sigma[G/\perp] \vee F'\sigma[G/\top]} \tag{3}$$

*where* $\sigma = MGU(A)$ *is the most general unifier (MGU) of the set of the atoms* $A = \{G_1,...,G_k,G'_1,...,G'_n\}$ , $G = G_1\sigma$. *For every variable* $\alpha$ *in F or F'*, $(Sbt(\gamma) = \alpha) \cap \sigma = \emptyset$ $\Rightarrow Sig(\alpha) = 1$ *in F or F' iff* $Sig(\alpha) = 1$ *in* $F\sigma[G/\perp] \vee F'\sigma[G/\top]$. *F is called positive and F' is called negative premise, G represents an occurrence of an atom. The expression* $F\sigma[G/\perp] \vee F'\sigma[G/\top]$ *is the resolvent of the premises on G.*

Note that with Qnt mapping we are able to distinguish variables not only by its name (which may not be unique) but also with this mapping (it is unique). Sig property enables to separate variables, which were not originally in the scope of an existential variable. When utilizing the rule it should be set the Sig mapping for every variable in axioms and negated goal to one. We present a very simple example of existential variable unification before we introduce the refutational theorem prover for FOL.

**Example 3.** *Variable Unification Restriction*
*We would try to prove if* $\forall X \exists Y p(X,Y) \vdash \exists Y \forall X p(X,Y)$? *We will use refutational proving and therefore we will construct a special axiom from the first formula and negation of the second formula:* $F_0 : \forall X \exists Y p(X,Y)$. $F_1(\neg query) : \neg \exists Y \forall X p(X,Y)$.
*There are 2 trivial and 2 non-trivial combinations how to resolve* $F_0$ *and* $F_1$ *(combinations with the same formula as the positive and the negative premise could not lead to refutation since they are consistent):*
*Trivial cases:* $R[F_1 \& F_1] : \perp \vee \top$ *and* $R[F_0 \& F_0] : \perp \vee \top$. *Both of them lead to* $\top$ *and the atoms are simply unifiable since the variables are the same.*
*Non-trivial cases:* $[F_1 \& F_0]$ : *no resolution is possible.*
$Y \in Var_\forall(F_1)$ *and* $Y \in Var_\exists(F_0)$ *can't unify since VUR for* $(Y,Y)$ *does not hold - there is a variable* $X \in Sup^*(Qnt(Y))$ *(over the scope),* $X \in Var_\forall(F_0), Sbt(X) = \emptyset$); *the case with variable X is identical.*
$[F_0 \& F_1]$ : *no resolution is possible (the same reason as above).*
*No refutation could be derived from* $F_0$ *and* $F_1$ *due to VUR.*

*Further we would like to prove* $\exists Y \forall X p(X,Y) \vdash \forall X \exists Y p(X,Y)$.
$F0 : \exists Y \forall X p(X,Y)$. $F1$ *(¬query)* : $\neg \forall X \exists Y p(X,Y)$
*In this case we can simply derive a refutation:*
$R[F_1 \& F_0] : \perp \vee \neg \top (refutation)$
$X \in Var_\forall(F_0)$ *and* $X \in Var_\exists(F_1)$ *can unify since VUR for* $(X,X)$ *holds - there is no global universal variable over the scope of X in* $F_1$; $Sbt(X) = X$ *and* $Sbt(Y) = Y$.

## 3. Fuzzy predicate logic and refutational proof

The fuzzy predicate logic with evaluated syntax is a flexible and fully complete formalism, which will be used for the below presented extension (Novák, V.). In order to use an efficient form of the resolution principle we have to extend the standard notion of a proof (provability value and degree) with the notion of refutational proof (refutation degree). Propositonal version of the fuzzy resolution principle has been already presented in (Habiballa, H.). We suppose that set of truth values is Łukasiewicz algebra. Therefore we assume standard notions of conjunction, disjunction etc. to be bound with Łukasiewicz operators.

We will assume Łukasewicz algebra to be

$$\mathcal{L}_{\text{Ł}} = \langle [0,1], \wedge, \vee, \otimes, \rightarrow, 0, 1 \rangle$$

where [0, 1] is the interval of reals between 0 and 1, which are the smallest and greatest elements respectively. Basic and additional operations are defined as follows:

$$a \otimes b = 0 \vee (a + b - 1) \quad a \rightarrow b = 1 \wedge (1 - a + b) \quad a \oplus b = 1 \wedge (a + b) \quad \neg a = 1 - a$$

The biresiduation operation $\leftrightarrow$ could be defined $a \leftrightarrow b =_{df} (a \rightarrow b) \wedge (b \rightarrow a)$, where $\wedge$ is infimum operation. The following properties of $\mathcal{L}_{\text{Ł}}$ will be used in the sequel:
$a \otimes 1 = a, a \otimes 0 = 0, a \oplus 1 = 1, a \oplus 0 = a, a \rightarrow 1 = 1, a \rightarrow 0 = \neg a, 1 \rightarrow a = a, 0 \rightarrow a = 1$
The syntax and semantics of fuzzy predicate logic is following:

- terms $t_1, ..., t_n$ are defined as in FOL
- predicates with $p_1, ..., p_m$ are syntactically equivalent to FOL ones. Instead of 0 we write $\bot$ and instead of 1 we write $\top$, connectives - & (Łukasiewicz conjunction), $\nabla$ (Łukasiewicz disjunction), $\Rightarrow$ (implication), $\neg$ (negation), $\forall X$ (universal quantifier), $\exists X$ (existential quantifier) and furthermore by $F_J$ we denote set of all formulas of fuzzy logic in language $J$
- FPL formulas have the following semantic interpretations (D is the universe): Interpretation of terms is equivalent to FOL, $\mathcal{D}(p_i(t_{i_1}, ..., t_{i_n})) = P_i(\mathcal{D}(t_{i_1}), ..., \mathcal{D}(t_{i_n}))$ where $P_i$ is a fuzzy relation assigned to $p_i$, $\mathcal{D}(a) = a$ for $a \in [0, 1]$, $\mathcal{D}(A \& B) = \mathcal{D}(A) \otimes \mathcal{D}(B)$, $\mathcal{D}(A \nabla B) = \mathcal{D}(A) \oplus \mathcal{D}(B)$, $\mathcal{D}(A \Rightarrow B) = \mathcal{D}(A) \rightarrow \mathcal{D}(B)$, $\mathcal{D}(\neg A) = \neg \mathcal{D}(A)$, $\mathcal{D}(\forall X(A)) = \wedge \mathcal{D}(A[x/d] | d \in D)$, $\mathcal{D}(\exists X(A)) = \vee \mathcal{D}(A[x/d] | d \in D)$
- for every subformula defined above $Sub, Sup, Pol, Lev, Qnt, Sbt, Sig$ and other derived properties defined for classical logic hold (where the classical FOL connective is presented the Łukasiewicz one has the same mapping value).

Graded fuzzy predicate calculus assigns grade to every axiom, in which the formula is valid. It will be written as $a/A$ where A is a formula and $a$ is a syntactic evaluation. We use several standard notions defined in (Novák, V.) namely: inference rule, formal fuzzy theory with set of logical and special axioms, evaluated formal proof.

**Definition 6.** *Inference rule*
*An n-ary inference rule r in the graded logical system is a scheme*

$$r : \frac{a_1/A_1, ..., \ a_n/A_n}{r^{evl}(a_1, ..., a_n)/r^{syn}(A_1, ..., A_n)} \tag{4}$$

*using which the evaluated formulas $a_1/A_1, ..., \ a_n/A_n$ are assigned the evaluated formula*
$r^{evl}(a_1, ..., a_n)/r^{syn}(A_1, ..., A_n)$. *The syntactic operation $r^{syn}$ is a partial n-ary operation on $F_J$ and the evaluation operation $r^{evl}$ is an n-ary lower semicontinous operation on L (i.e. it preserves arbitrary suprema in all variables).*

**Definition 7.** *Formal fuzzy theory*
*A formal fuzzy theory T in the language J is a triple*

$$T = \langle \text{LAx}, \text{SAx}, R \rangle$$

*where* $\text{LAx} \subseteq_{\sim} F_J$ *is a fuzzy set of logical axioms,* $\text{SAx} \subseteq_{\sim} F_J$ *is a fuzzy set of special axioms, and R is a set of sound inference rules.*

**Definition 8.** *Evaluated proof, refutational proof and refutation degree*
An *evaluated formal proof of a formula A from the fuzzy set* $X \subseteq F_J$ *is a finite sequence of evaluated formulas* $w := a_0/A_0, a_1/A_1, ..., a_n/A_n$ *such that* $A_n := A$ *and for each* $i \leq n$, *either there exists an m-ary inference rule r such that*

$a_i/A_i := r^{evl}(a_{i_1}, ..., a_{i_m})/r^{syn}(A_{i_1}, ..., A_{i_m}), \quad i_1, ..., i_m < n$ *or* $a_i/A_i := X(A_i)/A_i$.
*We will denote the value of the evaluated proof by* $Val(w) = a_n$.
*An evaluated refutational formal proof of a formula A from X is w, where additionally* $a_0/A_0 := 1/\neg A$ *and* $A_n := \perp$. $Val(w) = a_n$ *is called refutation degree of A.*

**Definition 9.** *Provability and truth*
Let *T be a fuzzy theory and* $A \in F_J$ *a formula. We write* $T \vdash_a A$ *and say that the formula A is a theorem in the degree a, or provable in the degree a in the fuzzy theory T.*

$$T \vdash_a A \text{ iff } a = \bigvee \{Val(w) | \text{ w is a proof of A from } LAx \cup SAx\} \tag{5}$$

*We write* $T \models_a A$ *and say that the formula A is true in the degree a in the fuzzy theory T.*

$$\mathcal{D} \models T \text{ if } \forall A \in LAx : LAx(A) \leq \mathcal{D}(A), A \in SAx : SAx(A) \leq \mathcal{D}(A) \tag{6}$$

$$T \models_a A \text{ iff } a = \bigwedge \{\mathcal{D}(A) | \mathcal{D} \models T\} \tag{7}$$

The fuzzy modus ponens rule could be formulated:

**Definition 10.** *Fuzzy modus ponens*

$$r_{MP} : \frac{a/A, b/A \Rightarrow B}{a \otimes b/B} \tag{8}$$

*where from premise A holding in the degree a and premise* $A \Rightarrow B$ *holding in the degree b we infer B holding in the degree* $a \otimes b$.

In classical logic $r_{MP}$ could be viewed as a special case of the resolution. The fuzzy resolution rule presented below is also able to simulate fuzzy $r_{MP}$. From this fact the completeness of a system based on resolution can be deduced. It will only remain to prove the soundness. It is possible to introduce following notion of resolution w.r.t. the modus ponens.

**Definition 11.** *General resolution for fuzzy predicate logic* $(GR_{FPL})$

$$r_{GR} : \frac{a/F[G_1, ..., G_k], b/F'[G'_1, ..., G'_n]}{a \otimes b/F\sigma[G/\perp]\nabla F'\sigma[G/\top]} \tag{9}$$

*where* $\sigma = MGU(A)$ *is the most general unifier (MGU) of the set of the atoms*
$A = \{G_1, ..., G_k, G'_1, ..., G'_n\}$, $G = G_1\sigma$. *For every variable* $\alpha$ *in F or F',* $(Sbt(\gamma) = \alpha) \cap \sigma = \emptyset$
$\Rightarrow Sig(\alpha) = 1$ *in*

*F or F' iff* $Sig(\alpha) = 1$ *in* $F\sigma[G/\perp] \vee F'\sigma[G/\top]$. *F is called positive and F' is called negative premise, G represents an occurrence of an atom. The expression* $F\sigma[G/\perp] \vee F'\sigma[G/\top]$ *is the resolvent of the premises on G.*

**Lemma 2.** *Soundness of $r_{GR}$*
*The inference rule $r_{GR}$ for FPL based on $\mathcal{L}_{\L}$ is sound i.e. for every truth valuation $\mathcal{D}$,*

$$\mathcal{D}(r^{syn}(A_1, ..., A_n)) \geq r^{evl}(\mathcal{D}(A_1), ..., \mathcal{D}(A_n)) \tag{10}$$

*holds true.*

*Proof.* Before we solve the core of $GR_{FPL}$ we should prove that the unification algorithm preserves soundness. But it could be simply proved since in the classical FPL with the rule of Modus-Ponens (Novák, V.) from the axiom $\vdash (\forall x)A \Rightarrow A[x/t]$ and $\vdash (\forall x)A$ we can prove $A[x/t]$. For $r_{GR}$ we may rewrite the values of the left and right parts of equation (10):

$$\mathcal{D}(r^{syn}(A_1, ..., A_n)) = \mathcal{D}[\mathcal{D}(F_1[G/\bot]) \nabla \mathcal{D}(F_2[G/\top])]$$

$$r^{evl}(\mathcal{D}(A_1), ..., \mathcal{D}(A_n)) = \mathcal{D}(F_1[G]) \otimes \mathcal{D}(F_2[G])$$

It is sufficient to prove the equality for $\Rightarrow$ since all other connectives could be defined by it. By induction on the complexity of formula $|A|$, defined as the number of occurrences of connectives, we can prove:

Let premises $F_1$ and $F_2$ be atomic formulas. Since they must contain the same subformula then $F_1 = F_2 = G$ and it holds

$$\mathcal{D}[\mathcal{D}(F_1[G/\bot]) \nabla \mathcal{D}(F_2[G/\top])] = D(\bot \nabla \top) = 0 \oplus 1 = 1 \geq \mathcal{D}(F_1[G]) \otimes \mathcal{D}(F_2[G])$$

Induction step: Let premises $F_1$ and $F_2$ be complex formulas and let $A$ and $B$ are subformulas of $F_1$, $C$ and $D$ are subformulas of $F_2$ and $G$ is an atom where generally $F_1 = (A \Rightarrow B)$ and $F_2 = (C \Rightarrow D)$. The complexity of $|F_1| = |A| + 1$ or $|F_1| = |B| + 1$ and $|F_2| = |C| + 1$ or $|F_2| = |D| + 1$. Since they must contain the same subformula and for $A, B, C, D$ the induction presupposition hold it remain to analyze the following cases:

1. $F_1 = A \Rightarrow G$  $F_2 = G \Rightarrow D$ : $\mathcal{D}[\mathcal{D}(F_1[G/\bot]) \nabla \mathcal{D}(F_2[G/\top])] = \mathcal{D}([A \Rightarrow \bot] \nabla [\top \Rightarrow D]) = \mathcal{D}(\neg A \nabla D) = 1 \wedge (1 - a + d)$
   We have rewritten the expression into Łukasiewicz interpretation. Now we will try to rewrite the right side of the inequality, which has to be proven.
   $\mathcal{D}(F_1[G]) \otimes \mathcal{D}(F_2[G]) = \mathcal{D}(A \Rightarrow G) \otimes \mathcal{D}(G \Rightarrow D) = 0 \vee ((1 \wedge (1 - a + g)) + (1 \wedge (1 - g + d)) - 1) = 1 \wedge (1 - a + d)$ The left and right side of the equation (10) are equal and therefore

   $$\mathcal{D}[\mathcal{D}(F_1[G/\bot]) \nabla \mathcal{D}(F_2[G/\top])] \geq \mathcal{D}(F_1[G]) \otimes \mathcal{D}(F_2[G])$$

   for this case holds.

2. $F_1 = A \Rightarrow G$  $F_2 = C \Rightarrow G$ : $\mathcal{D}[\mathcal{D}(F_1[G/\bot]) \nabla \mathcal{D}(F_2[G/\top])] = \mathcal{D}([A \Rightarrow \bot] \nabla [C \Rightarrow \top]) = 1 \geq \mathcal{D}(F_1[G]) \otimes \mathcal{D}(F_2[G])$

3. $F_1 = G \Rightarrow B$  $F_2 = G \Rightarrow D$ : $\mathcal{D}[\mathcal{D}(F_1[G/\bot]) \nabla \mathcal{D}(F_2[G/\top])] = \mathcal{D}([\bot \Rightarrow B] \nabla [\top \Rightarrow D]) = 1 \geq \mathcal{D}(F_1[G]) \otimes \mathcal{D}(F_2[G])$

4. $F_1 = G \Rightarrow B$  $F_2 = C \Rightarrow G$ : $\mathcal{D}[\mathcal{D}(F_1[G/\bot]) \nabla \mathcal{D}(F_2[G/\top])] = \mathcal{D}([\bot \Rightarrow B] \nabla [C \Rightarrow \top]) = 1 \geq \mathcal{D}(F_1[G]) \otimes \mathcal{D}(F_2[G])$

By induction we have proven that the inequality holds and the $r_R$ is sound. The induction of the case where only one of the premises has greater complexity is included in the above solved induction step. □

**Definition 12.** *Refutational resolution theorem prover for FPL*
*Refutational non-clausal resolution theorem prover for FPL* ($RRTP_{FPL}$) *is the inference system with the inference rule* $GR_{FPL}$ *and sound simplification rules for* $\bot$, $\top$ *(standard equivalencies for logical constants). A refutational proof by definition 8 represents a proof of a formula G (goal) from the set of special axioms N. It is assumed that* $Sig(\alpha) = 1$ *for* $\forall \alpha$ *in* $F \in N \cup \neg G$ *formula, every formula in a proof has no free variable and has no quantifier for a variable not occurring in the formula.*

**Definition 13.** *Simplification rules for* $\nabla, \Rightarrow$

$$r_{s\nabla} : \frac{a/\bot\nabla A}{a/A} \quad and \quad r_{s\Rightarrow} : \frac{a/\top\Rightarrow A}{a/A}$$

**Lemma 3.** *Provability and refutation degree for* $GR_{FPL}$
$T \vdash_a A$ iff $a = \bigvee\{Val(w)|$ w is a refutational proof of A from LAx $\cup$ SAx$\}$

*Proof.* If $T \vdash_a A$ then $a = \bigvee\{Val(w)|$ w is a proof of A from LAx $\cup$ SAx$\}$ and for every such a proof of we can construct refutational proof as follows $(Val(w) \leq a)$:
$w := a/A$ {proof A}, $1/\neg A$ {member of refutational proof}, $a \otimes 1/\bot$ $\{r_{GR}\}$
If $a = \bigvee\{Val(w)|$ w is refutational proof of A from LAx $\cup$ SAx$\}(Val(w) \leq a)$:
$w := a_0/A_0, ..., a_i/A_i, 1/\neg A, ..., a/\bot$, where $A_0, ..., A_i$ are axioms.
There is a proof:
$w' := a_0/A_0, ..., a_i/A_i, 1/\neg A\nabla A, a_{i+2}/A_{i+2}\nabla A, ..., a/\bot\nabla A$.
All the schemes of the type $A_j\nabla A$, $j > i$ could be simplified by sound simplification rules and the formula $\neg A\nabla A$ may be removed.
The proof $w'' := a_0/A_0, ..., a_i/A_i, a_{i+2}/A_{i+2}\nabla A, ..., a/A$ is a correct proof of A in the degree a since the formulas are either axioms or results of application of resolution.                    $\square$

**Theorem 1.** *Completeness for fuzzy logic with* $r_{GR}, r_{s\nabla}, r_{s\Rightarrow}$ *instead of* $r_{MP}$
*Formal fuzzy theory, where* $r_{MP}$ *is replaced with* $r_{GR}, r_{s\nabla}, r_{s\Rightarrow}$, *is complete i.e. for every A from the set of formulas* $T \vdash_a A$ iff $T \models_a A$.

*Proof.* The left to right implication (soundness of such formal theory) could be easily done from the soundness of the resolution rule. Conversely it is sufficient to prove that the rule $r_{MP}$ can be replaced by $r_{GR}, r_{s\nabla}, r_{s\Rightarrow}$. Indeed, let $w$ be a proof:
$w := a/A$ {proof $w_a$}, $b/A \Rightarrow B$ {proof $w_{A\Rightarrow B}$}, $a \otimes b/B$ $\{r_{MP}\}$. Then we can replace it by the proof:
$w := a/A\{proof w_a\}, b/A \Rightarrow B\{proof w_{A\Rightarrow B}\}, a \otimes b/\bot\nabla[\top\Rightarrow B]\{r_{GR}\},$
$a \otimes b/\top\Rightarrow B\{r_{s\nabla}, a \otimes b/B\{r_{s\Rightarrow}\}$

Using the last sequence we can easily make a proof with $r_{MP}$ also with the proposed $r_R$ and simplification rules. Since usual formal theory with $r_{MP}$ is complete as it is proved in (Novák, V.), every fuzzy formal theory with these rules is also complete. Note that the non-ground case (requiring unification) could be simulated in the same way like in the proof of soundness.    $\square$

## 4. Implementation and efficiency

The author also currently implements the non-clausal theorem prover into fuzzy logic as an extension of previous prover for FOL (GEneralized Resolution Deductive System - GERDS) (Habiballa, H.). Experiments concerning prospective inference strategies can be performed with this extension.   The prover called Fuzzy Predicate Logic GEneralized Resolution

Deductive System (Fig. 1) - FPLGERDS provides standard interface for input (knowledge base and goals) and output (proof sequence and results of fuzzy inference, statistics).

Fig. 1. Fuzzy Predicate Logic GEneralized Resolution Deductive System

There are already several efficient strategies proposed by author (mainly Detection of Consequent Formulas (DCF) adopted for the usage also in FPL). With these strategies the proving engine can be implemented in real-life applications since the complexity of theorem proving in FPL is dimensionally harder than in FOL (the need to search for all possible proofs - we try to find the best refutation degree). The DCF idea is to forbid the addition of a resolvent which is a logical consequence of any previously added resolvent. For refutational theorem proving it is a sound and complete strategy and it is emiprically very effective. Completeness of such a strategy is also straight-forward in FOL:

$$(R_{old} \vdash R_{new}) \wedge (U, R_{new} \vdash \perp) \Rightarrow (U, R_{old} \vdash \perp)$$

Example: $R_{new} = p(a)$, $R_{old} = \forall x(p(x))$, $R_{old} \vdash R_{new}$.

DCF could be implemented by the same procedures like General Resolution (we may utilize self-resolution). Self-resolution has the same positive and negative premise and needs to resolve all possible combinations of an atom. It uses the following scheme:

$$R_{old} \vdash R_{new} \Leftrightarrow \neg(R_{old} \to R_{new}) \vdash \bot$$

Even the usage of this teachnique is a semidecidable problem, we can use time or step limitation of the algorithm and it will not affect the completeness of the $RRTP_{FOL}$.

Example: $R_{new} = p(a)$, $R_{old} = \forall x(p(x))$, $\neg(\forall x(p(x)) \to p(a))$

MGU: $Sbt(x) = a$, $Res = \neg(\bot \to \bot) \vee \neg(\top \to \top) \Rightarrow \bot$

We have proved that $R_{new}$ is a logical consequence of $R_{old}$.

In FPL we have to enrich the DCF procedure by the limitation on the provability degree. if $U \vdash_a R_{old} \wedge U \vdash_b R_{new} \wedge b \leq a$ then we can apply DCF. DCF Trivial check performs a symbolic comparison of $R_{old}$ and $R_{new}$ we use the same provability degree condition. In other cases we have to add $R_{new}$ into the set of resolvents and we can apply DCF Kill procedure. DCF Kill searches for every $R_{old}$ being a logical consequence of $R_{new}$ and if $U \vdash_a R_{old} \wedge U \vdash_b R_{new} \wedge b \geq a$ then Kill $R_{old}$ (resolvent is removed).

We will now show some efficiency results concerning many-valued logic both for Fuzzy Predicate Logic. We have used the above mentioned application FPLGERDS and originally developed DCF strategy for FPL. It is clear that inference in $RRTP_{FPL}$ and $RRTP_{FDL}$ on general knowledge bases is a problem solved in exponential time. Nevertheless as we would like to demonstrate the need to search for every possible proof (in contrast to the two-valued logic) will not necessarily in particular cases lead to the inefficient theory. We have devised knowledge bases (KB) on the following typical problems related to the use of fuzzy logic.

We have performed experimental measurements concerning efficiency of the presented non-clausal resolution principle and also DCF technique. These measurements were done using the FPLGERDS application (Habiballa, H.). Special testing knowledge bases were prepared and several types of inference were tested on a PC with standard Intel Pentium 4 processor as described below.

**Fuzzy predicate Logic redundancy-based inefficient knowledge bases**

As it was shown above in the theorem proving example the problem of proof search is quite different in FPL and FDL in comparison with the two-valued logic. We have to search for the best refutation degree using refutational theorem proving in order to make sensible conclusions from the inference process. It means we cannot accept the **first successful** proof, but we have to check **"all possible proofs"** or we have to be sure that every omitted proof is **worse** that some another one. The presented DCF and DCF Kill technique belong to the third sort of proof search strategies, i.e. they omit proofs that are really worse than some another (see the explication above). Proofs and formulas causing this could be called redundant proofs and redundant formulas. Fuzzy logic makes this redundancy dimensionally harder since we could produce not only equivalent formulas but also equivalent formulas of different evaluation degree.

**Example 4.** *Redundant knowledge base*
*Consider the following knowledge base (fragment):*

....,
$0.51/a \wedge b_1 \Rightarrow z$,
$0.61/a \wedge b_1 \wedge b_1 \Rightarrow z$,
$0.71/a \wedge b_1 \wedge b_1 \wedge b_1 \Rightarrow z$,
$0.81/a \wedge b_1 \wedge b_1 \wedge b_1 \wedge b_1 \Rightarrow z$,

| Search method | | Description |
|---|---|---|
| Breadth | B | Level order generation, start - special axioms + goal |
| Linear | L | Resolvent $\Rightarrow$ premise, start - goal |
| Modified-Linear | M | Resolvent $\Rightarrow$ premise, start - goal + special axioms |

Table 2. Proof search algorithms

| DCF Method | | Description |
|---|---|---|
| Trivial | T | Exact symbolic comparison |
| DCF | DC | Potential resolvent is consequent (no addition) |
| DCF Kill | DK | DCF + remove all consequent resolvents |

Table 3. DCF heuristics

$0.91/a \wedge b_1 \wedge b_1 \wedge b_1 \wedge b_1 \wedge b_1 \Rightarrow z, 1/b_1,$

...,

$0.52/a \wedge b_2 \Rightarrow z,$

$0.62/a \wedge b_2 \wedge b_2 \Rightarrow z,$

$0.72/a \wedge b_2 \wedge b_2 \wedge b_2 \Rightarrow z,$

$0.82/a \wedge b_2 \wedge b_2 \wedge b_2 \wedge b_2 \Rightarrow z,$

$0.92/a \wedge b_2 \wedge b_2 \wedge b_2 \wedge b_2 \wedge b_2 \Rightarrow z, 1/b_2,$

...,

Goal: $? - a \Rightarrow z$

*Searching for the best proof of a goal will produce a lot of logically equivalent formulas with different degrees. These resolvents make the inference process inefficient and one of the essential demands to the presented refutational theorem prover is a reasonable inference strategy with acceptable time complexity.*

We have compared efficiency of the standard **breadth-first search**, **linear search** and **modified linear search** (starting from every formula in knowledge base) and also combinations with DCF and DCF-kill technique (Habiballa, H.). We have prepared knowledge bases of the size 120, 240, 360, 480 and 600 formulas. It has been compared the time and space efficiency on the criterion of 2 redundancy levels. This level represents the number of redundant formulas to which the formula is equivalent (including the original formula). For example the level 5 means the knowledge base contain 5 equivalent redundant formulas for every formula (including the formula itself). The basic possible state space search techniques and DCF heuristics and their combinations are presented in the following tables.

We use standard state space search algorithms in the FPLGERDS application - Breadth-first and Linear search. Breadth-first method searches for every possible resolvent from the formulas of the level 0 (goal and special axioms). These resolvents form formulas of the level 1 and we try to combine them with all formulas of the same and lower level and continue by the same procedure until no other non-redundant resolvent could be found. Linear search performs depth-first search procedure, where every produced resolvent is used as one of the premises in succeeding step of inference. The first produced resolvents arises from the goal formula. Modified linear search method posses the same procedure as linear one, but it starts from goal and also from all the special axioms.

DCF methods for reduction of resolvent space are basically three. The simplest is trivial DCF method, which detects redundant resolvent only by its exact symbolic comparison, i.e. formulas are equivalent only if the are syntactically the same. Even it is a very rough method,

| Search | DCF | Code | Description |
|---|---|---|---|
| Breadth | Trivial | BT | Complete |
| Breadth | DCF | BDC | Complete |
| Breadth | DCF Kill | BDK | Complete |
| Mod. Linear | Trivial | MT | Incomplete (+) |
| Mod. Linear | DCF | MDC | Incomplete (+) |
| Mod. Linear | DCF Kill | MDK | Incomplete (+) |
| Linear | Trivial | LT | Incomplete |
| Linear | DCF | LDC | Incomplete |
| Linear | DCF Kill | LDK | Incomplete |

Table 4. Inference strategies

it is computationally very simple and forms necessary essential restriction for possibly infinite inference process. The next method of DCF technique enables do detect the equivalency of a formula (potential new resolvent) by the means described above. DCF Kill technique additionally tries to remove every redundant resolvent from the set of resolvents. The important aspect of the theorem DCF lies in its simple implementation into an automated theorem prover based on general resolution. The prover handles formulas in the form of syntactical tree. It is programmed a procedure performing general resolution with two formulas on an atom. This procedure is also used for the implementation of the theorem. A "virtual tree" is created from candidate and former resolvent (axiom) connected by negated implication. Then it remains to perform self-resolution on such formula until a logical value is obtained. Let us compare the efficiency of standard strategies and the above-defined one. We have built-up 9 combinations of inference strategies from the mentioned proof search and DCF heuristics. They have different computational strength, i.e. their completeness is different for various classes of formulas. Fully complete (as described above) for general formulas of FPL and FDL are only breadth-first search combinations. Linear search strategies are not complete even for two-valued logic and horn clauses. Modified linear search has generally bad completeness results when an infinite loop is present in proofs, but for guarded knowledge bases it can assure completeness preserving better space efficiency than breadth-first search. We tested presented inference strategies on sample knowledge bases with redundancy level 5 with 20, 40, 60, 80 and 100 groups of mutually redundant formulas (total number of formulas in knowledge base is 120, 240, 360, 480 and 600). At first we have tested their time efficiency for inference process. As it could be observed from figure 2, the best results have **LDK and LDC** strategies. For simple guarded knowledge bases (not leading to an infinite loop in proof search and where the goal itself assures the best refutation degree) these two methods are **very efficient**. DCF strategies significantly reduces the proof search even in comparison with LT strategy (standard), therefore the usage of any non-trivial DCF heuristics is significant. Next important result concludes from the comparison of BDK and MDK, MDC strategies. We can conclude that MDK and MDC strategies are relatively comparable to BDK and moreover BDK preserves completeness for general knowledge bases.

Space complexity is even more significantly affected by the DCF heuristics. There is an interesting comparison of trivial and non-trivial DCF heuristics in figure 3. Even BDK strategy brings significant reduction of resolvents amount, while LDK, LDC, MDK, MDC strategies have minimal necessary amount of kept resolvents during inference process. The second examined redundancy level 10 shows also important comparison for increasing redundancy in knowledge bases. Tested knowledge bases contained 10, 20, 30, 40 and 50 groups of 10 equivalent formulas (the total number of formulas was 110, 220, 330, 440 and 550 formulas).

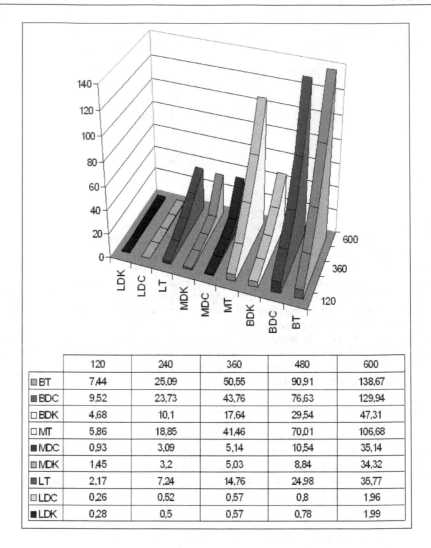

| | 120 | 240 | 360 | 480 | 600 |
|---|---|---|---|---|---|
| ▣ BT | 7,44 | 25,09 | 50,55 | 90,91 | 138,67 |
| ■ BDC | 9,52 | 23,73 | 43,76 | 76,63 | 129,94 |
| □ BDK | 4,68 | 10,1 | 17,64 | 29,54 | 47,31 |
| □ MT | 5,86 | 18,85 | 41,46 | 70,01 | 106,68 |
| ■ MDC | 0,93 | 3,09 | 5,14 | 10,54 | 35,14 |
| ▣ MDK | 1,45 | 3,2 | 5,03 | 8,84 | 34,32 |
| ■ LT | 2,17 | 7,24 | 14,76 | 24,98 | 35,77 |
| □ LDC | 0,26 | 0,52 | 0,57 | 0,8 | 1,96 |
| ■ LDK | 0,28 | 0,5 | 0,57 | 0,78 | 1,99 |

Fig. 2. Time complexity for redundancy level 5 (seconds)

Time efficiency results shows that higher redundancy level causes expected increase in the necessary time for the best proof search (figure 4). The approximate increase is double, while the proportion shows good results for MDK, MDC and LDK, LDC (linear search based) strategies. This property also holds for space complexity as shown in figure 5. Performed experiments shows the significance of originally developed DCF strategies in combination with standard breadth-first search (important for general knowledge bases - **BDK**). We also outlined high efficiency for linear search based strategies (mainly **LDK**). Even this strategy is not fully complete and could be used only for guarded fragment of FDL, this problem is already known in classical (two-valued) logic programming and automated theorem proving. We also use these highly efficient linear search strategies, even they are not complete.

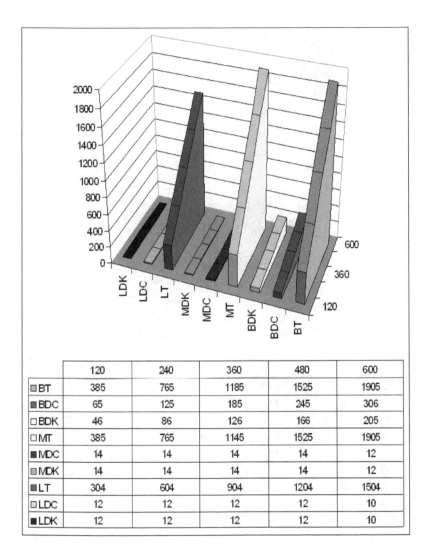

|       | 120 | 240 | 360 | 480 | 600 |
|-------|-----|-----|-----|-----|-----|
| ▨ BT  | 385 | 765 | 1185 | 1525 | 1905 |
| ▪ BDC | 65  | 125 | 185 | 245 | 306 |
| ☐ BDK | 46  | 86  | 126 | 166 | 205 |
| ☐ MT  | 385 | 765 | 1145 | 1525 | 1905 |
| ▪ MDC | 14  | 14  | 14  | 14  | 12  |
| ▨ MDK | 14  | 14  | 14  | 14  | 12  |
| ▪ LT  | 304 | 604 | 904 | 1204 | 1504 |
| ☐ LDC | 12  | 12  | 12  | 12  | 10  |
| ▪ LDK | 12  | 12  | 12  | 12  | 10  |

Fig. 3. Space complexity for redundancy level 5 (resolvents)

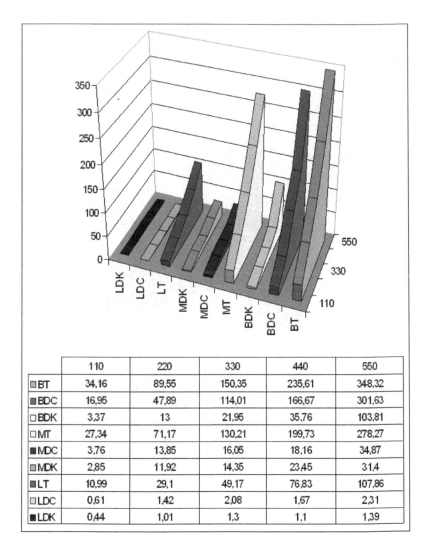

|      | 110   | 220   | 330    | 440    | 550    |
|------|-------|-------|--------|--------|--------|
| ▣BT  | 34,16 | 89,55 | 150,35 | 235,61 | 348,32 |
| ▪BDC | 16,95 | 47,89 | 114,01 | 166,67 | 301,63 |
| ▢BDK | 3,37  | 13    | 21,95  | 35,76  | 103,81 |
| ▢MT  | 27,34 | 71,17 | 130,21 | 199,73 | 278,27 |
| ▪MDC | 3,76  | 13,85 | 16,05  | 18,16  | 34,87  |
| ▣MDK | 2,85  | 11,92 | 14,35  | 23,45  | 31,4   |
| ▪LT  | 10,99 | 29,1  | 49,17  | 76,83  | 107,86 |
| ▢LDC | 0,61  | 1,42  | 2,08   | 1,67   | 2,31   |
| ▪LDK | 0,44  | 1,01  | 1,3    | 1,1    | 1,39   |

Fig. 4. Time complexity for redundancy level 10 (seconds)

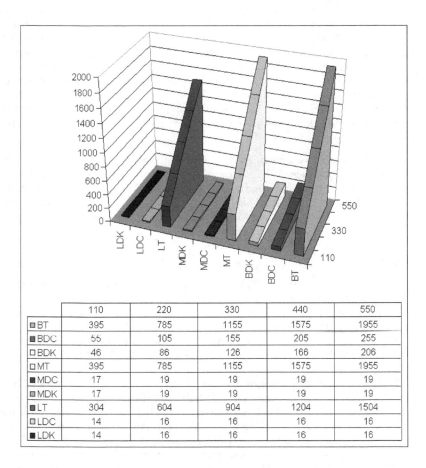

| | 110 | 220 | 330 | 440 | 550 |
|---|---|---|---|---|---|
| ⊡ BT | 395 | 785 | 1155 | 1575 | 1955 |
| ■ BDC | 55 | 105 | 155 | 205 | 255 |
| ☐ BDK | 46 | 86 | 126 | 166 | 206 |
| ☐ MT | 395 | 785 | 1155 | 1575 | 1955 |
| ■ MDC | 17 | 19 | 19 | 19 | 19 |
| ☐ MDK | 17 | 19 | 19 | 19 | 19 |
| ■ LT | 304 | 604 | 904 | 1204 | 1504 |
| ☐ LDC | 14 | 16 | 16 | 16 | 16 |
| ■ LDK | 14 | 16 | 16 | 16 | 16 |

Fig. 5. Space complexity for redundancy level 10 (resolvents)

## 5. Conclusions and further research

The *Non-clausal Refutational Resolution Theorem Prover* forms a powerful inference system for automated theorem proving in fuzzy predicate logic. The main advantage in contrast with other inference systems lies in the possibility to utilize various inference strategies for effective reasoning. Therefore it is essential for practically successful theorem proving.

The Detection of Consequent Formulas algorithms family brings significant improvements in time and space efficiency for the best proof search. It has been shown results indicating specific behavior of some combinations of the DCF and standard proof search (breadth-first and linear search). DCF strategies (BDC, BDK) have interesting results even for fully general fuzzy predicate logic with evaluated syntax, where the strategy makes the inference process practically manageable (in contrast to unrestricted blind proof-search). However it seems to be more promising for practical applications to utilize incomplete strategies with high time efficiency like LDK (even for large knowledge bases it has very short solving times). It conforms to another successful practical applications in two-valued logic like logic programming or deductive databases where there are also used efficient incomplete strategies for fragments of fully general logics.

It has been briefly presented some efficiency results for the presented automated theorem prover and inference strategies. They show the significant reduction of time and space complexity for the DCF technique. Experimental application FPLGERDS can be obtained from URL:// *http://www1.osu.cz/home/habibal/files/gerds.zip*. The package contains current version of the application, source codes, examples and documentation. This work was supported by project DAR (1M0572).

## 6. References

Bachmair, L., Ganzinger, H. (1997). A theory of resolution. Technical report: Max-Planck-Institut, 1997.

Bachmair, L., Ganzinger, H. (2001). Resolution theorem proving. In Handbook of Automated Reasoning, MIT Press, 2001.

Dukić, N., Avdagić, Z. (2005). Fuzzy Functional Dependency and the Resolution Principle. In Informatica, Vilnius: Lith. Acad. Sci. (IOSPRESS), 2005, Vol.16, No. 1, pp. 45 - 60, 2005.

Habiballa, H. (2000). Non-clausal resolution - theory and practice. Research report: University of Ostrava, 2000, http://www.volny.cz/habiballa/files/gerds.pdf

Habiballa, H., Novák, V. (2002). Fuzzy General Resolution. In Proc. of Intl. Conf. Aplimat 2002. Bratislava, Slovak Technical University, 2002. pp. 199-206, also available as research rep. at http://ac030.osu.cz/irafm/ps/rep47.ps

Habiballa, H. (2006). Resolution Based Reasoning in Description Logic. In Proc. of Intl. Conf. ZNALOSTI 2006, Univ. of Hradec Kralove, 2006, also available as research rep. at http://ac030.osu.cz/irafm/ps/rep66.ps.gz.

Habiballa, H.(2006a). Fuzzy Predicate Logic Generalized Resolution Deductive System. Technical Report, Institute for Research and Application of Fuzzy Modeling, University of Ostrava, 2006.

Hájek, P. (2000). Metamathematics of fuzzy logic. Kluwer Academic Publishers - Dordrecht, 2000.

Hájek, P. (2005). Making fuzzy description logic more general. Fuzzy Sets and Systems 154(2005),pp. 1-15.

Novák, V., Perfilieva, I., Močkoř, J. (1999). Mathematical principles of fuzzy logic. Kluwer, 1999.

# 3

# Standard Fuzzy Sets and some Many-Valued Logics

Jorma K. Mattila
*Lappeenranta University of Technology*
*Finland*

## 1. Introduction

The aim of this chapter is to consider the relationship between standard fuzzy set theory and some many-valued logics. Prof. Lotfi A. Zadeh introduced his theory of fuzzy sets in sixties, and his first paper that circulated widely around the world is "Fuzzy Sets" (Zadeh, 1965). In the long run, this theory was began to call by the name *theory of standard fuzzy sets*.

After Zadeh has introduced his theory, many-valued logic began to have a new interest. Especially, Łukasiewicz logic was enclosed quite closely in fuzzy sets. There is a strong opinion that Łukasiewicz infinite-valued logic has the role as the logic of fuzzy sets, similarly as classical logic has the role as the logic of crisp sets. But actually, it seems that Kleene's 3-valued logic was the closest logic connecting to fuzzy sets, when Zadeh created his theory. We will discuss this thing later. In the books Rescher (Rescher, 1969) and Bergmann (Bergmann, 2008) descriptions about Kleene's logic are given.

In Section 2 we consider the main concepts of fuzzy set theory. We will not do it completely, because our purpose is not to present the whole theory of standard fuzzy sets. We restrict our consideration on those things we need when we are "building a bridge" between fuzzy sets and some closely related logics. The section is based on Zadeh (Zadeh, 1965).

In Section 3 we consider De Morgan algebras in general in order to have a formal base to our consideration. There are many sources for this topic. One remarkable one is Rasiowa's book (Rasiowa, 1974).

In Section 4 we introduce an algebraic approach for standard fuzzy set theory by applying De Morgan algebras. We choose an algebra from the infinite large collection of De Morgan algebras that fits completely to standard fuzzy set theory. We call this De Morgan algebra by the name *Zadeh algebra*. The concept "Zadeh algebra" was introduced by the author in an international symposium "Fuzziness in Finland" in 2004. Also Prof. Zadeh attended this event. In the same year, a more comprehensive article about Zahed algebra (*cf.* (Mattila, 2004)) was published by the author. This algebra gives a tool for studying connections between standard fuzzy sets and certain many-valued logics. Two of these logics are Kleene's logic and Łukasiewicz logic. Some analysis about Łukasiewicz and Kleene's logic is given for example in Mattila (Mattila, 2009). Especially, connections to modal logic are considered in that paper.

In Section 5 we make some analysis about the essence of fuzziness from the formal point of view. We try to find the original point where fuzziness appears and how it "moves" from its hiding-place making some concepts fuzzy.

In Section 6 we give the definition of *propositional language* by introducing its alphabet and how the expressions, i.e., *wellformed formulas* (or *formulas*, for short) can be formed from the alphabet. This formal language can be used as classical propositional logic and as many-valued propositional logic, too. We do not consider any other logical properties here, because they are not necessary for our purpose. In addition to the formal language, only the concept *valuation* and *truth-function* are needed. About the truth value evaluation, we consider the common things for several logics. The counterparts are obtainable also from Zadeh algebra. We also construct a *propositional algebra* that appears to be a Zadeh algebra.

In Section 7 an important logic for fuzzy sets is Kleene's 3-valued logic, as we already noticed above. Hence, the consideration of this logic deserves its own section. We tell about Kleene's motivation for constructing his 3-valued logic and give the truth value evaluation rules for the basic connectives. These rules fit completely well to the fuzzy set operations Zadeh introduced. We also explain the connections between standard fuzzy sets and this logic from Zadeh's point of view. In the end of this section, we give a short description about *Kleene-Dienes many-valued logic* that is an extension of Kleene's 3-valued logic into infinite-valued logic.

In Section 8 we consider the main features of Łukasiewicz ifinite-valued logic. Our main problem is included in this section. Łukasiewicz chose the connectives negation and implication as primitive connectives and derived the connectives conjunction, disjunction, and equivalence from these primitives. This starting point does not fit together with the operations of Zadeh algebra. Only the counterpart of negation (the complementarity operation) is included in Zadeh algebra but implication does not appear in it. in Łukasiewicz logic the two other connectives, disjunction and conjunction, belongs to the derived connectives. But they have such a form that their truth value evaluation rules are exactly the same as the corresponding operations in Zadeh algebra. So, using the set negation, disjunction, and conjunction of Łukasiewicz logic's connectives, we have to derive the connective Łukasiewicz implication. Actually, for this task we need only negation and disjunction, as is seen in Proposition 8.2 and its proof. Our final result is presented in Proposition 8.3. Some considerations on this topic can be found in Mattila (Mattila, 2005).

In Section 9 we consider briefly MV-algebras and give some hints how the connection between standard fuzzy sets and Łukasiewicz logic can be found. MV-algebras and their applications to fuzzy set theory and soft computing are widely studied, and the study of this topic actually forms a mainstream in this research area. Three books are mentioned in References representing this topic, namely M. Bergmann (Bergmann, 2008), R. L. O. Cignoli et al. (Cignoli et al., 2000), and P. Hájek (Hájek, 1998). These books belongs to a quite central literature of the topic.

MV-algebras are more general than De Morgan algebras, but formally it can be proved that De Morgan algebras belong to MV-algebras as a special case. But according to our problem, the used ways to apply general MV-algebras seems to give a circuitous route rather than a straightforward bridge between standard fuzzy set theory and Łukasiewicz logic.

In Section 10 we point out the main results and other concluding remarks.

## 2. Zadeh's theory of standard fuzzy sets

For considering the standard system of fuzzy sets, the range of fuzzy sets (i.e., that of membership functions) is the unit interval $\mathbb{I} = [0,1]$. We give the definition of the concept *fuzzy set* using Zadeh's original definition. However, some symbols have been changed. Usually, the symbol of a fuzzy set, in general, is denoted by $\mu$. A membership function of a fuzzy set $A$ in a reference set $X$ can be written as $\mu_A(x)$ or $A(x)$ where $x \in X$.

**Definition 2.1** (Standard fuzzy set). A *fuzzy subset* $A$ of a set $X$ is characterized by a *membership function* $A(x)$ which associates with each point $x$ in $X$ a real number in the interval $[0,1]$, with the value of $A(x)$ at $x$ representing the "grade of membership" of $x$ in $A$. Thus, the nearer the value of $A(x)$ to unity, the higher the grade of membership of $x$ in $A$.

This definition means that a fuzzy subset $A$ of a universe of discourse $X$ is represented by a function

$$A : X \longrightarrow \mathbb{I}.$$

The *power set* of all fuzzy subsets of the set $X$ is

$$\mathbb{I}^X = \{ A \mid A : X \longrightarrow \mathbb{I} \} \tag{2.1}$$

An important subset of the set of all membership functions (2.1) is the set of functions taking only values 1 or 0, i.e., the set of all characteristic functions of the crisp subsets of $X$

$$2^X = \{ f \mid f : X \longrightarrow \{0,1\} \}$$

as a special case.

It is also a well-known fact that $\mathbb{I}$ and $\mathbb{I}^X$ are partially ordered sets. (Actually, $\mathbb{I}$ is a totally ordered set, but hence it is also prtially ordered.) In fact, they are also distributive complete lattices. Generally, some main properties of $\mathbb{I}$ can be embedded to $\mathbb{I}^X$ (*cf.* e.g. Lowen (Lowen, 1996)).

We consider operations, properties, and some concepts involved in fuzzy sets given by Zadeh (Zadeh, 1965).

**Definition 2.2** (Basic operations). Let $A, B \in \mathbb{I}^X$ and $x \in X$. In $\mathbb{I}^X$ there are defined the following operations:

$$(A \vee B)(x) = \max\{A(x), B(x)\} \qquad \textit{union}$$
$$(A \wedge B)(x) = \min\{A(x), B(x)\} \qquad \textit{intersection}$$
$$\overline{A}(x) = 1 - A(x) \qquad \textit{complementarity}$$

Two fuzzy sets $A, B \in \mathbb{I}^X$ are *equal*, denoted by $A = B$, if

$$\forall x \in X, \quad A(x) = B(x).$$

A fuzzy set $A$ is *contained* in a fuzzy set $B$, i.e., $A$ is a *subset* of $B$, denoted by $A \subseteq B$, if their membership functions satisfy the condition

$$\forall x \in X, \quad A(x) \leq B(x)$$

Zadeh also shows that the operations max and min are associative, distributive to each other, and De Morgan's laws hold, and they have the form

$$1 - \min\{\mathcal{A}(x), \mathcal{B}(x)\} = \max\{1 - \mathcal{A}(x), 1 - \mathcal{B}(x)\} \tag{2.2}$$

$$1 - \max\{\mathcal{A}(x), \mathcal{B}(x)\} = \min\{1 - \mathcal{A}(x), 1 - \mathcal{B}(x)\} \tag{2.3}$$

Actually, Zadeh gives the building materials for an algebra in his paper (Zadeh, 1965). However, he did not think any algebras when he created his paper "Fuzzy Sets". He thought the problem from another point of view. We return to this matter in the end of Section 4.

Finally, we present the following theorem due to C. V. Negoiță and D. A. Ralescu (Negoiță & Ralescu, 1975).

**Theorem 2.1.** *The set* $\mathbb{I}^X$ *is a complete distributive lattice.*

*Proof.* The reference set $X$ has the membership function

$$\mu_X(x) = 1, \quad x \in X$$

and the empty set $\emptyset$ the membership function

$$\mu_\emptyset(x) = 0, \quad x \in X.$$

This corresponds to the fact that $\mathbf{1}, \mathbf{0} \in \mathbb{I}^X$ where $\mathbf{1}(x) = 1$ and $\mathbf{0}(x) = 0$ for any $x \in X$. Hence, the result follows by the definition of complete lattice and the order properties of the unit interval.                                                                                                    □

## 3. On De Morgan algebras

To get an algebra of standard fuzzy sets we start by considering the concept of De Morgan algebras. The main source is Helena Rasiowa's book (Rasiowa, 1974).

**Definition 3.1** (De Morgan algebra). An abstract algebra $\mathcal{A} = \langle A, \vee, \wedge, \neg, \mathbf{1} \rangle$ is called *De Morgan algebra*, if $(A, \vee, \wedge)$ is a distributive lattice with unit element $\mathbf{1}$ (the neutral element of $\wedge$ operation), and $\neg$ is a unary operation on $A$ satisfying the following conditions:

(DM1)    for all $a \in A$,    $\neg\neg a = a$,
(DM2)    for all $a, b \in A$,    $\neg(a \vee b) = \neg a \wedge \neg b$.

It is easy to prove that in any De Morgan algebra $\langle A, \vee, \wedge, \neg, \mathbf{1} \rangle$ the following properties hold:

(DM3)    there is a zero element $\mathbf{0}$ (the neutral element of $\vee$ operation),
(DM4)    $\neg\mathbf{0} = \mathbf{1}$    and    $\neg\mathbf{1} = \mathbf{0}$,
(DM5)    $\neg(a \wedge b) = \neg a \vee \neg b$.

The unit element is the greatest element and the zero element the least element of $A$. By (DM3), we sometimes add the zero element of a De Morgan algebra into the component list of the entities belonging to the algebra: $\mathcal{A} = \langle A, \vee, \wedge, \neg, \mathbf{0}, \mathbf{1} \rangle$.

Consider the unit interval lattice $\mathbb{I} = ([0,1], \leq)$. Sometimes we write $\mathbb{I} = [0,1]$, for short. As is well known, the order relation $\leq$ and the operations $\vee$ and $\wedge$ have the connection

$$\forall x, y \in X, \ x \leq y \iff \begin{cases} x \vee y = y \\ x \wedge y = x \end{cases} \tag{3.1}$$

Hence, we can write the lattice $\mathbb{I}$ into the form $\mathbb{I} = ([0,1], \vee, \wedge)$. We will prove it is a distributive lattice. We consider it in the proof of Theorem 3.1 when we prove that $\mathbb{I}$ forms a De Morgan algebra. Especially, the order relation $\leq$ is a total order on $[0,1]$ because it is an order and any two elements from the interval $[0,1]$ are comparable with each other under it, i.e., for any $x, y \in \mathbb{I}$, we can state whether the order $x \leq y$ either holds or not.

The interval $[0,1]$ is a metric space with the natural metric *distance* between two points of $[0,1]$ given by the condition

$$d(x,y) = |x - y|, \quad x, y \in [0,1] \tag{3.2}$$

We will see that this equality measure can be used in Łukasiewicz infinite-valued logic as the evaluation rule for the connective *equivalency*.

**Theorem 3.1.** *The system* $L_{\mathbb{I}} = \langle \mathbb{I}, \vee, \wedge, \neg, 0, 1 \rangle$ *is De Morgan algebra, where for all* $x \in [0,1]$, $\neg x = 1 - x$.

*Proof.* First, we show that $\mathbb{I}$ is a distributive lattice. It is clear that $\mathbb{I}$ is a lattice. For showing distributivity, we choose arbitrarily elements $a, b, c \in [0,1]$. Without loss of generality, we can suppose that $a \leq b \leq c$. Then, by (3.1) we have

$$\begin{cases} a \vee (b \wedge c) = a \vee b = b \\ (a \vee b) \wedge (a \vee c) = b \wedge c = b \end{cases} \implies a \vee (b \wedge c) = (a \vee b) \wedge (a \vee c)$$

Similarly, we have $a \wedge (b \vee c) = (a \wedge b) \vee (a \wedge c)$. Hence, $\mathbb{I} = ([0,1], \vee, \wedge)$ is a distributive lattice.

(DM1) holds because for all $a \in [0,1]$,

$$\neg \neg a = 1 - (1 - a) = a$$

(DM2) holds because for all $a, b \in [0,1]$,

$$\begin{cases} \neg(a \vee b) = 1 - (a \vee b) = 1 - b & \text{if } a \leq b \\ \neg a \wedge \neg b = (1 - a) \wedge (1 - b) = 1 - b & \text{if } a \leq b \end{cases} \implies \neg(a \vee b) = \neg a \wedge \neg b$$

Hence, by Def. 3.1, $L_{\mathbb{I}}$ is a De Morgan algebra. $\qquad \square$

From the ordering property (3.1) it follows that for all $x, y \in \mathbb{I}$

$$x \vee y = \max\{x, y\} \tag{3.3}$$
$$x \wedge y = \min\{x, y\} \tag{3.4}$$

Hence, we can express the algebra of Theorem 3.1 in the form

$$L_{\mathbb{I}} = \langle \mathbb{I}, \max, \min, \neg, 0, 1 \rangle \tag{3.5}$$

Let $X$ be a nonempty set. Consider a set of functions $\mu : X \longrightarrow \mathbb{I}$, i.e., the function set

$$\mathbb{I}^X = \{\mu \mid \mu : X \longrightarrow \mathbb{I}\} \tag{3.6}$$

We extend the algebra of Theorem 3.1 into an *algebra of functions* (3.6)

$$L_{\mathbb{I}^X} = \langle \mathbb{I}^X, \vee, \wedge, \neg, \mathbf{0}, \mathbf{1} \rangle \tag{3.7}$$

by pointwise calculation. Here $\mathbf{0}$ and $\mathbf{1}$ are constant functions, such that

$$\forall x \in X, \quad \mathbf{0} : x \mapsto 0, \quad \mathbf{1} : x \mapsto 1 \tag{3.8}$$

The algebra (3.7) is a De Morgan algebra by its construction. This means that we calculate expressions $\mu(x) \vee \nu(x), \mu(x) \wedge \nu(x), \neg\mu(x)$ etc. pointwise for any $x \in X$. Hence, the formulas (3.3) and (3.4) are applicable also in the function algebra (3.7).

As a special case, the algebra (3.7) has a subalgebra

$$L_{\{0,1\}^X} = \langle \{0,1\}^X, \max, \min, \neg, \mathbf{0}, \mathbf{1} \rangle \tag{3.9}$$

being an algebra of characteristic functions of classical sets, $f : X \longrightarrow \{0,1\}$. Sometimes we write $\mathbf{2}$ instead of $\{0,1\}$, so, especially,

$$\mathbf{2}^X = \{f_A \mid f_A : X \longrightarrow \{0,1\}, A \subset X\}$$

is the classical power set of a set $X$ expressed by characteristic functions. The characteristic function of a given set $A \subset X$, $f_A$, is the function

$$f_A(x) = \begin{cases} 1 & \text{if} \quad x \in A, \\ 0 & \text{if} \quad x \notin A \end{cases}$$

This function indicates by the value $f_A(x) = 1$ that the element $x \in X$ is an element of $A$ and all the elements of $X$ having the value $f_A(x) = 0$ are elements of the complement of $A$. As a subalgebra of the algebra (3.7), the algebra (3.9) is a special De Morgan algebra, namely a *Boolean algebra*.

## 4. Algebra of standard fuzzy sets

Consider the algebra (3.7). We may give a new label to it and use operation symbols max and min instead of $\vee$ and $\wedge$, respectively, by the formulas (3.3) and (3.4). Hence, we have

$$\mathcal{Z}_{\aleph_1} = \langle \mathbb{I}^X, \max, \min, \neg, \mathbf{0}, \mathbf{1} \rangle \tag{4.1}$$

The subscript $\aleph_1$ means the cardinality of continuum, so, $\mathbb{I}^X$ is a continuum because $\mathbb{I}$ is continuum, too. For short, we may refer to $\mathcal{Z}_{\aleph_1}$ by $\mathcal{Z}$, without the subscript, if there is no possibility for confusion. The complementarity operation $\neg$ is a mapping

$$\neg : \mathbb{I}^X \longrightarrow \mathbb{I}^X, \ \mu \mapsto \mathbf{1} - \mu \tag{4.2}$$

Hence, the complement function of a function $\mu$ is $\mathbf{1} - \mu$, such that for all $x \in X$, $(\mathbf{1} - \mu)(x) = \mathbf{1}(x) - \mu(x) = 1 - \mu(x)$. (The proof, that $\neg$ defined in this way is really a membership function, is given in the proof of Theorem 4.1.) This thing is analogous to the classical set complement expressed by subtraction a set $A$ to be complemented from the universe of discourse $X$, i.e., $A^c = X \setminus A$ where $A \subset X$ and $A^c$ is the complement of $A$.

The operations max and min are clearly commutative. Based on the fact that the algebra (3.7) is De Morgan algebra, the algebra (4.1) is De Morgan algebra, too. We call this algebra *Zadeh algebra* because it is an algebraic description of standard fuzzy set theory, similarly as in classical set theory, a certain Boolean algebra (set algebra or algebra of characteristic functions) is the algebraic description of the system of classical sets. Now, we have the following

**Theorem 4.1.** *Zadeh algebra* $\mathcal{Z} = \langle \mathbb{I}^X, \max, \min, \neg, 0, 1 \rangle$ *is an algebraic approach to standard fuzzy set theory.*

*Proof.*

(i) The operations max and min are exactly the same as in Zadeh's theory by Def. 2.2.

(ii) The operations max and min are commutative and associative on $\mathbb{I}^X$, i.e.,

$$\max\{\mu, \nu\} = \max\{\nu, \mu\} \quad \text{and} \quad \max\{\mu, \max\{\nu, \tau\}\} = \max\{\max\{\mu, \nu\}, \tau\}$$

for all $\mu, \nu, \tau \in \mathbb{I}^X$ because these laws clearly hold for the elements of $\mathbb{I}$, and these laws can be embedded to $\mathbb{I}^X$ by pointwise calculation of values of the functions $\mu \in \mathbb{I}^X$ (cf. Lowen (Lowen, 1996)). The same properties hold for min, too.

(iii) From Theorem 2.1, distributive laws follows for max and min on $\mathbb{I}^X$ because $(\mathbb{I}^X, \max, \min)$ is a distributive lattice and Zaheh-algebra (4.1) is De Morgan algebra. Zadeh (Zadeh, 1965) has also proved these laws.

(iv) For all $\mu \in \mathbb{I}^X$, $\max\{\mu, 0\} = \mu$ and $\min\{\mu, 1\} = \mu$, because for any $x \in X$,

$$(\max\{\mu, 0\})(x) = \max\{\mu(x), 0(x)\} = \max\{\mu(x), 0\} = \mu(x)$$

Similarly, for any $x \in X$,
$$(\min\{\mu, 0\})(x) = \mu(x)$$

(v) For any membership function $\mu \in \mathbb{I}^X$, there exists $\neg\mu \in \mathbb{I}^X$, such that for any $x \in X$,

$$(\neg\mu)(x) = (1 - \mu)(x) = 1(x) - \mu(x) = 1 - \mu(x)$$

taking values from the unit interval $[0, 1]$. Hence, $\neg\mu \in \mathbb{I}^X$, and $\neg$ is the complementarity operation of Zadeh's theory.

(vi) Clearly, Zadeh algebra $\mathcal{Z}$ satisfies the condition $0 \neq 1$, by (iv). Hence, $2^X \subset \mathbb{I}^X$. The constant functions $0$ and $1$ are the zero element and unit element of the algebra.

This competes the proof.                                                                 □

In classical set theory, an element either is or is not an element of a given set. In fuzzy set theory, we have three possibilities: a membership grade of an element in a given fuzzy set equals either to zero or one, or is between them.

For practical use, we may postulate Zadeh algebra by collecting the nevessary properties together. This means that we build Theor. 4.1 again using the main laws and properties like postulates. The result is as follows.

**Proposition 4.1.** *Let* $\mathbb{I}^X = \{\mu \mid \mu : X \longrightarrow \mathbb{I}\}$ *be the set of all functions from $X$ to $\mathbb{I}$, where the operations* max *and* min *are pointwise defined between membership functions, and* $\neg\mu \overset{\text{def}}{=} 1 - \mu$. *Then* $\mathcal{Z} = \langle \mathbb{I}^X, \text{max}, \text{min}, \neg, \mathbf{0}, \mathbf{1}\rangle$ *is Zadeh algebra if it satisfies the conditions*

($\mathcal{Z}$1) *The operations* max *and* min *are commutative on* $\mathbb{I}^X$;

($\mathcal{Z}$2) *The operations* max *and* min *are associative on* $\mathbb{I}^X$;

($\mathcal{Z}$3) *The operations* max *and* min *are distributive to each other;*

($\mathcal{Z}$4) *The neutral elements of the operations* max *and* min *are* $\mathbf{0}$ *and* $\mathbf{1}$, *respectively, i.e., for all* $\mu \in \mathbb{I}^X$, $\text{max}\{\mu, \mathbf{0}\} = \mu$ *and* $\text{min}\{\mu, \mathbf{1}\} = \mu$;

($\mathcal{Z}$5) *For any membership function* $\mu \in \mathbb{I}^X$, *there exists* $\neg\mu \in \mathbb{I}^X$, *such that* $(\neg\mu) = 1 - \mu$;

($\mathcal{Z}$6) $\mathbf{0} \neq \mathbf{1}$.

**Definition 4.1** (Kleene algebra). De Morgan algebra is *Kleene algebra* if it satisfies the additional condition

(K)     $x \wedge \neg x \leq y \vee \neg y$.

**Theorem 4.2.** *Zadeh algebra (4.1) is a Kleene algebra.*

*Proof.* Zadeh algebra is De Morgan algebra. The condition (K) in Zadeh algebra has the form

$$\text{min}\{\mu, \neg\mu\} \leq \text{max}\{\nu, \neg\nu\}$$

for all $\mu, \nu \in \mathbb{I}^X$.

To prove this, we can easily show that always $\text{min}\{\mu, \neg\mu\} \leq \frac{1}{2}$ and $\frac{1}{2} \leq \text{max}\{\nu, \neg\nu\}$ for arbitrary $\mu, \nu \in \mathbb{I}^X$, where the result follows immediately.

An alternative way is an easy task to check the four cases: $(1°)$ $\mu \leq \frac{1}{2}, \nu \leq \frac{1}{2}$, $(2°)$ $\mu \leq \frac{1}{2}, \nu > \frac{1}{2}$, $(3°)$ $\mu > \frac{1}{2}, \nu \leq \frac{1}{2}$, and $(4°)$ $\mu > \frac{1}{2}, \nu > \frac{1}{2}$, and find out that each of these cases satisfies the condition (K).                                                                            $\square$

Zadeh algebra $\mathcal{Z}_{\aleph_1}$ has subalgebras which are Zadeh algebras, too. A range of membership functions can be a suitable subset of the unit interval $[0,1]$, such that the postulates of Prop. 4.1 are satisfied. Here the suitability means that the set is closed under the operations of the algebra.

**Example 4.1.** Consider a set $A = \{0,1\}$ which is a subset of $[0,1]$ consisting of the extreme cases of the unit interval. The algebra $\langle A^X, \text{max}, \text{min}, \neg, \mathbf{0}, \mathbf{1}\rangle$ satisfies the conditions of Zadeh algebra. This algebra is really an extreme case, because it is the Boolean algebra of characteristic functions of strict (i.e., usual) sets. It is a subalgebra of $\mathcal{Z}_{\aleph_1}$.

**Example 4.2.** Consider a set $A = \{0, \frac{1}{2}, 1\}$ being a subset of $[0,1]$. The set $A$ is the range of functions $\mu : X \longrightarrow A$ where $X \neq \varnothing$ is a set. These functions belong to the set $\mathbb{I}^X$, by means of which $A$ is a subset of $\mathbb{I}^X$. The conditions of Prop. 4.1 are clearly satisfied. Hence, $\mathcal{Z}_3 = \langle A^X, \text{max}, \text{min}, \neg, \mathbf{0}, \mathbf{1}\rangle$ is a 3-valued Zadeh algebra, and hence, a subalgebra of $\mathcal{Z}_{\aleph_1}$.

**Example 4.3.** Consider a set $A$ consisting of all the rationals from the unit interval $[0,1]$. The number of the elements of $A$ is countable, but infinite. Hence, the cardinality of $A$ is $\aleph_0$. Making similar considerations as in the previous example, we verify that $\mathcal{Z}_{\aleph_0} = \langle A^X, \text{max}, \text{min}, \neg, \mathbf{0}, \mathbf{1}\rangle$ is a subalgebra of $\mathcal{Z}_{\aleph_1}$.

Zadeh-algebra as a special case of De Morgan algebras give rise to closer analysis. Here we have done some part of it. The author thinks that Prof. Zadeh did not necessarily think about De Morgan algebras, when he created his crucial paper "Fuzzy Sets" (Zadeh, 1965). He thought the problem from another point of view, as can be seen in the construction of the paper. His leading idea was to model things in the eventful real world. In any way, it was a happy event that Prof. Zadeh's ideas met such a mathematical frame we have considered here. No others have been so successful to find such a *right interpretation* to some formal tools for modeling real world incidences. In the same time the *problem of interpretation* of many-valued logic got a solution. Many-valued logic began to give meaningful tools for analyzing and modeling things in real world. The role of many-valued logics were very nominal before Prof. Zadeh invented fuzzy set theory. After this, the study of many-valued logic met a new rise. Fuzzy set theory and fuzzy logic has helped the researchers to find new aspects from already existing mathematical theories. This kind of work is now going on very strongly.

## 5. Where is the hiding-place of fuzziness?

For example, imagine a set of beautiful women. Let us denote this set by $A$. There are women who do not belong to $A$ with the highest grade 1. So, such a woman *does not* have some features which would make her beautiful. But she may have some of those features anyway. An intuitive hint about a possible answer to the question: "Where is the hiding-place of fuzziness?" can be found just on the second line above: "... *does not* ..." It seems that a partial complementarity is somehow involved in this problem.

Let us compare Zadeh algebra with a general Boolean algebra with a supposition that the binary operations are associative because associativity holds in Zadeh algebra. The definition of this kind of Boolean algebra can be postulated as follows.

**Definition 5.1.** Let $\wedge$ (*meet*) and $\vee$ (*join*) be binary operations, and $'$ (*complement*) a unary operation on a set $B(\neq \varnothing)$, and let $0$ and $1$ be the elements of $B$, such that the following axioms hold:

(BA1) $\wedge$ and $\vee$ are commutative in $B$, i.e., $\forall x, y \in B, x \vee y = y \vee x$ ja $x \wedge y = y \wedge x$;

(BA2) The operations $\wedge$ and $\vee$ are associative in $B$;

(BA3) The operations $\wedge$ and $\vee$ are distributive, i.e.,

$$\forall x, y, z \in B, \quad x \wedge (y \vee z) = (x \wedge y) \vee (x \wedge z),$$
$$x \vee (y \wedge z) = (x \vee y) \wedge (x \vee z).$$

(BA4) $\forall x \in B, x \vee 0 = x$ and $x \wedge 1 = x$, i.e., $0$ and $1$ are the neutral elements (or identity elements) of the operations $\vee$ and $\wedge$.

(BA5) For every element $x \in B$ there exists an element $x' \in B$, such that $x \vee x' = 1$ and $x \wedge x' = 0$.

(BA6) For the elements $0$ and $1$ of $B$ the condition $0 \neq 1$ holds.

Hence, the set $B$ together with these operations forms a *Boolean algebra* $\mathcal{B} = (B, \vee, \wedge, ', 0, 1)$.

The only *structural difference* between these algebras is that between the axioms Z5 and BA 5. BA 5 is characteristic for complement operation, but Z5 does not satisfy the conditions of complement. So, fuzziness lies in the axiom Z5. The influence of this axiom is that also other values can be considered as membership degrees than only 0 and 1. In Boolean algebras with the universe of discourse $\{0, 1\}$ the postulate BA5 do not cause conflicts, like the intermediate values may do if these values are added to the universe.

Because complement operation satisfies the conditions of strong negation, a Boolean algebra $\mathcal{B} = (\{0, 1\}, \vee, \wedge, ', \mathbf{0}, \mathbf{1})$ is a special case of $\mathcal{Z}$, i.e., the classical case is included in $\mathcal{Z}$. Trivially, $\{0, 1\} \subset [0, 1]$. This means that crisp sets are special cases of fuzzy sets, as they should be also according to Zadeh's own theory. See also the proof of Theorem 2.1.

We may conclude that formally the core hiding-place of fuzziness is the statement Z5 in Proposition 4.1. In a concept being fuzzy there is always something that *does not* hold, i.e., some missing particle the concept does not have. Hence, the complementarity is somehow involved in a fuzzy concept.

## 6. Common features of many-valued logics based on Zadeh algebra

We consider here some preliminary things being common for several many-valued logics. The main purpose is to find a connection between Zaheh algebra and the structures of some many-valued logics. We consider only some propositional logics, because the main concepts we consider here are basic to higher order many-valued logics, too. We restrict our considerations only to structural properties.

First, we need a formal language for our considerations. This language is that of propositional logic.

**Definition 6.1.** A propositional lanuage $\mathcal{L}$ consists of

1. a set of propositional letters $p_0, p_1, \ldots, p_k, \ldots$ and
2. the truth-functional connectives $'\wedge'$, $'\vee'$, and $'\neg'$.

These symbols are the *aplhabets* of the propositional language.

Usually only the so-called *primitive connectives* belong to the alphabet, but it is possible to choose some other connectives to the alphabet, too. Hence, we could drop either conjunction or disjunction from the alphabet if we like. Primitive connectives are connectives from which we can derive the other connectives.

In a standard nonclassical propositional language, the meanings of the connectives $'\wedge'$ (*conjunction*), $'\vee'$ (*disjunction*), and $'\neg'$ (*negation*) can be given as follows: negation $\neg$ is a stong negation (i.e., it is a negation with involution property $\neg\neg p \equiv p$), conjunction $\wedge$ is *glb* (greatest lower bound), and disjunction $\vee$ is *lub* (least upper bound). The symbol $'\equiv'$ and $\Longleftrightarrow$ are used as a *meta-symbols* of equivalency, i.e., this symbol does not belong to the alphabet of the *object language* which is the language of a formal logic under consideration.

**Definition 6.2.** Well-formed formulas of $\mathcal{L}$ are given as follows:

$$\alpha ::= p_k \mid \neg\varphi \mid \varphi \wedge \psi \mid \varphi \vee \psi. \tag{6.1}$$

In this recursive production system of well formed formulas (wff's, for short) the symbol $p_k$ represents any propositional letter and lower case Greek letters are labels of any atomic or connected wff's. Hence, $\alpha$ is a label for any wff, and similarly $\varphi$ and $\psi$ represent any propositional wff's. Starting with propositional letters, we can combine them by connectives in the way shown by the production system (6.1). And finally, we can combine any formulas according to the production system.

We can refer to the propositional letters also by lower case letters in general, and to combined formulas by lower case Greek letters or by usual capital letters. These letters belong to the metalanguage we use when we discuss and describe object language. Here we use English equipped by some formal symbols (so-called meta-symbols) as a metalanguage.

The definitions 6.1 and 6.2 above defines the language of propositional logic. Second, we consider some central semantical concepts being necessary for our consideration. This means that we will not present the whole machinery of formal semantics of standard many-valued logics.

We have two important functions, *valuation* and *truth-function* we need in our consideration. They are defined as follows.

**Definition 6.3.** *Valuation* $v$ is a function

$$v : \textbf{Prop} \longrightarrow \mathbb{I} \tag{6.2}$$

that associates truth values to propositional letters. **Prop** is a set of propositional variables.

*Truth-function* is a function

$$V_n : \mathbb{I}^n \longrightarrow \mathbb{I}, \quad n = 1, 2, 3, \ldots, \tag{6.3}$$

where $n$ is the number of propositional variables $p$, $q$, ... in the formula defining a truth function.

In general, truth-functions are functions of several variables defined on the $n$-tuple of the set of truth values, $[0,1]^n$ where the independent variables are proposition letters. The subindices $n = 1, 2, 3, \ldots$ are usually dropped. Actually, a propositional formula $\varphi$ itself is a truth-function. Suppose that a formula $\varphi$ consists of the propositional letters $p$, $q$, and $r$. Then we may write $\varphi = V(p, q, r)$. The equality sign is used only between truth-functions and truth values.

In connected formulas, valuations of propositional variables give the values for the variables of the corresponding truth-function presented by the connected formula. Hence, a "valuation" of a connected formula is the value of the corresponding truth-function. Hence, to evaluate a truth value of the whole connected formula corresponding a given valuation for propositional variables, we calculate the value of the truth-function where the given valuation $v$ first determines the values of the arguments of the truth-function. We may denote the truth value of a connected formula $\varphi$ by $V(\varphi)$, being like a valuation depending on a given valuation $v$ for propositional letters.

**Example 6.1.** Evaluate the truth value of a formula $p \wedge (\neg q \vee r)$ with regard to a given valuation $v$ for $p$, $q$, and $r$. Actually the formula is a truth-function $f(p, q, r) = p \wedge (\neg q \vee r)$ where $p$, $q$, and $r$ obtain their values from $[0, 1]$. These values are $v(p)$, $v(q)$, and $v(r)$. Now, the truth value of the formula, given by this valuation $v$, is

$$V(p \wedge (\neg q \vee r)) = v(p) \wedge (\neg v(q) \vee v(r)$$

Suppose that $v$ is a valuation where $v(p) = 0.5, v(q) = 0.3$, and $v(r) = 1$. Hence,

$$V(p \wedge (\neg q \vee r)) = 0.5 \wedge ((1 - 0.3) \vee 1) = 0.5 \wedge (0.7 \vee 1) = 0.5 \wedge 1 = 0.5$$

If we have two wff's representing the same state of affairs we use meta-equivalence sign $'\equiv'$ or $'\Longleftrightarrow'$ between them because the formulas are equivalent to each other, not identical. For example, the wff $\varphi$ is the formula $p \wedge (\neg q \vee r)$. So, we can write $\varphi \equiv p \wedge (\neg q \vee r)$, or $\varphi \Longleftrightarrow p \wedge (\neg q \vee r)$ to denote that we use an abbreviation $\varphi$ for the formula $p \wedge (\neg q \vee r)$. Another case is that we have two formulas being equivalent to each other, for example, $\neg p \vee \neg q \equiv \neg(p \wedge q)$. This equivalency describes one of De Morgan's laws. However, the expression

$$\forall x, y \in [0, 1], \quad \neg x \vee \neg y = \neg(x \wedge y)$$

emphasizes that two truth-functions $\neg x \vee \neg y$ and $\neg(x \wedge y)$ are identical.

Instead of propositional letters, we prefer to use "usual" variable symbols as variables of a truth-function, because of possible confusions.

We are interested in the logics where the *evaluation rules* for these connectives are

$$V(p \vee q) = \max\{v(p), v(q)\} \tag{6.4}$$
$$V(p \wedge q) = \min\{v(p), v(q)\} \tag{6.5}$$
$$V(\neg p) = 1 - v(p) \tag{6.6}$$

where $v(p), v(q) \in [0, 1]$, or $v(p), v(q) \in A$ where $A$ is a suitable subset of $[0, 1]$.

Evaluation rules are rules for evaluating truth values to connected logical formulas in a given logic.

We must remember that all the logics are not truth-functional. For example, modal logics are non-truth-functional.

In practice, we need some other connectives, too. Two of them are the connectives *implication* and *equivalency*.

The way to choose implication separates the logics based on Zadeh algebra or any De Morgan algebra. Hence, implication must be presented by means of disjunction and negation, or by means of conjunction and negation. There are several ways to define different implications from other connectives, depending on the logic in question. We consider these things in the case of each logic to be considered below.

The formulas (6.4), (6.5), and (6.6) somehow emphasize the relationship to algebraic construction. We have two binary operations and one unary operation defined on a nonempty set just as in usual algebraic system. Additionally, the binary operations are combined together, for example, being distributive. The formulas (6.4), (6.5), and (6.6) are the same as Zadeh's operations defined on the set of fuzzy sets. The bridge between standard fuzzy sets and some many-valued logics seems to be obvious. Having got this kind of motivation, we continue our construction of the bridge between standard fuzzy sets and some many-valued logics.

Consider Zadeh algebra $\mathcal{Z}_{\aleph_1} = \langle \mathbb{I}^X, \max, \min, \neg, \mathbf{0}, \mathbf{1} \rangle$ (*cf.* formula (4.1)). Now the question is wether there is a counterpart to this algebra in the scope of many-valued logic. According to the evaluation rules (6.4), (6.5), and (6.6), the operations max, min, and $\neg$ exist at least in the logics having these evaluation rules. Let us compare the power set of fuzzy sets of the set $X$, i.e., the set $\mathbb{I}^X$, to the set of all valuations $v :$ **Prop** $\longrightarrow \mathbb{I}$. Hence, the set of all valuations is $\mathbb{I}^{\textbf{Prop}}$. Especially, **1** and **0** are constant valuations, such that **1** gives the truth value 1 to every propositional letters, and similarly, **0** gives the truth value 0. Hence, we also have the neutral elements corresponding those in Zadeh algebra. It seems that if we replace the set $\mathbb{I}^X$ by $\mathbb{I}^{\textbf{Prop}}$ then we have a special Zadeh algebra, namely, say, *propositional algebra*

$$\mathcal{L}_{\aleph_1} = \langle \mathbb{I}^{\textbf{Prop}}, \max, \min, \neg, 0, 1 \rangle. \tag{6.7}$$

The values of valuations are truth values and those of membership functions are membership grades. Can these two interpretations for the elements $[0,1]$ be considered to be anyhow similar? According to formal consideration, we say *yes*. The both values are obtainable from the same set, namely from the unit interval $[0,1]$, and the construction of the both algebras are exactly the same. On the other hand, membership grades are in principle subjective opinions about the membership of an element in a given set. About truth values, a *degree of truth* of a given propositional letter in a given situation depends on the state of affairs associated to this situation. But there is a valuation for every state of affairs in any situation representing a suitable degree of truth expressed by a number obtained from $[0,1]$. Hence, these degrees of truth correspond to suitable membership grades even so that for any valuation there exists a membership function that is identical with the valuation. Hence, these two apparently different interpretations can be considered to be the same. This means that we can interpret the values of the functions of the algebra (6.7) as truth values, or more accurately, degrees of truth.

## 7. Description of Kleene's logic

For historical reasons, we consider a piece of Kleene's 3-valued logic. S. C. Kleene was Zadeh's logic teacher, and it is natural that Zadeh compared his concept of fuzzy set with Kleene's 3-valued logic. Zadeh ((Zadeh, 1965) p. 341-342) gives the following comment:

"Note that the notion of belonging", which plays a fundamental role in the case of ordinary sets, does not have the same role in the case of fuzzy sets. Thus, it is not meaningful to speak of a point $x$ "belonging" to a fuzzy set $A$ except in the trivial sense of $f_A(x)$ being positive. Less trivially, one can introduce two levels $\alpha$ and $\beta$ $(0 < \alpha < 1, 0 < \beta < 1, \alpha > \beta)$ and agree to say that (1) "$x$ belongs to $A$" if $f_A(x) \geq \alpha$; (2) "$x$ does not belong to $A$" if $f_A(x) \leq \beta$; and (3) "$x$ has an intermediate status relative to $A$" if $\beta < f_A(x) < \alpha$. This leads to a three-valued logic (Kleene, 1952) with three truth values $T$ $(f_A(x) \geq \alpha)$, $F$ $(f_A(x) \leq \beta)$, and $U$ $(\beta < f_A(x) < \alpha)$.

The symbols of the truth values of Kleene's 3-valued logic are $T$ (*true*), $U$ (*unknown*), and $F$ (*false*). In the literature, there are also some alternative symbols for the intermediate truth value. For example, Rescher (Rescher, 1969) uses the symbol $I$.

Kleene introduced his 3-vaued logic in 1938. We denote it by $\mathbf{K}_3$. In order to describe Kleene's logic, we refer to Rescher (Rescher, 1969), p. 34 - 36. He writes:

"In Kleene's system, a proposition is to bear the third truth-value $I$ not for fact-related, ontological reasons but for knowledge-related, epistemological ones: it is not to be excluded that the proposition may *in fact* be true or false, but it is merely *unknown* or undeterminable what its specific truth status may be.

In $K_3$, we have the following truth value evaluation rules for the connectives negation $\neg$, conjunction $\wedge$, and disjunction $\vee$:

$$V(\neg p) = T - v(p), \tag{7.1}$$

$$V(p \wedge q) = \min\{v(p), v(q)\}, \tag{7.2}$$

$$V(p \vee q) = \max\{v(p), v(q)\}. \tag{7.3}$$

Two of these connectives can form a set of *primitive connectives*. One of the primitives must be negation. Hence, for example, the connectives negation and disjunction can be chosen as primitives, and all the other connectives can be defined by means of these primitive connectives. The alternative case for primitives are negation and conjunction. Hence, we can define the nonprimitive one by negation and the fact that disjunction and conjunction are dual (i.e., by using a suitable De Morgan's law). The implication defined by means of negation and disjunction is given by the formula (7.4).

We see immediately that there is a strong analogy between the basic operations of fuzzy sets (*cf.* Def. 2.2) and these three connectives of Kleene's 3-valued logic. In addition to this, an analogy can be found between Kleene's valuations and Zadeh's membership functions, too, although they have different ranges. Zadeh's comment above connects these two concepts "membership" ($\mu : X \longrightarrow \mathbb{I}$) and "valuation" ($v : \textbf{Prop} \longrightarrow \{F, U, T\}$) together. We can compare the set $\{F, U, T\}$ with the set $\{0, \frac{1}{2}, 1\}$ where $F = 0$, $U = \frac{1}{2}$, and $T = 1$. Hence, by analogy of the sets, we can understand some arithmetic operations in some evaluation rules.

Kleene defined the implication of his 3-valued logic, denoted by $\ni$, analogously to material implication:

$$p \ni q \stackrel{\text{def}}{\Longleftrightarrow} \neg p \vee q, \tag{7.4}$$

hence, the evaluation rule of $p \ni q$ is

$$p \ni q = \max\{T - v(p), v(q)\}. \tag{7.5}$$

We may construct the truth tables according to the evaluation rules. Rescher tells that Kleene motivated the construction of his truth tables in terms of a mathematical application. He has in mind the case of a mathematical predicate $P$ (i.e., a propositional function) of a variable $x$ ranging over a domain $D$ where "$P(x)$" is defined for only a part of this domain. For example, we might have the condition

$$P(x) \quad \text{iff} \quad 1 \le \frac{1}{x} \le 2.$$

Here $P(x)$ will be:

(1) *true* if $x$ lies within the range from $\frac{1}{2}$ to $1$,
(2) *undefined* (or undetermined) if $x = 0$,
(3) *false* in all other cases.

Kleene presented his truth tables to formulate the rules of combination by logical connectives for such propositional functions. He writes:

"From this standpoint, the meaning of $Q \vee R$ is brought out clearly by the statement in words: $Q \vee R$ is true, if $Q$ is true (here nothing is said about $R$) or if $R$ is true (similarly); false, if $Q$ and $R$ are both false; defined only in these cases (and hence undefined, otherwise)."[1]

---

[1] Kleene, *Introduction to Metamathematics* (1952).

Clearly, the algebraic approach to $K_3$ is Kleene algebra, i.e., a 3-valued Zadeh algebra with the property (K).

*Kleene-Dienes many-valued logic:*

*Kleene-Dienes many-valued logic* is an extension of $K_3$ into $K_{\aleph_1}$ having the set of truth values $[0,1]$. The evaluation rules for conjunction, disjunction, and negation are the same as in the formulas (6.4), (6.5), and (6.6) above.

Implication of Kleene-Dienes many-valued logic is defined by

$$p \to q \overset{\text{def}}{\Longleftrightarrow} \neg p \vee q \tag{7.6}$$

being in accordance with the implication of $K_3$. This means that the evaluation rule for implication is as follows. For any $x,y \in [0,1]$,

$$x \to y = \max \{1 - x, y\} \tag{7.7}$$

Now, the connective *equivalence* is defined in the usual way:

$$p \leftrightarrow q \overset{\text{def}}{\Longleftrightarrow} (p \to q) \wedge (q \to p) \tag{7.8}$$

Hence, the evaluation rule for equivalence is

$$\forall x,y \in [0,1], \quad x \leftrightarrow y = \min\{x \to y, y \to x\} \tag{7.9}$$

The equations (6.4), (6.5), (6.6), (7.7), and (7.9) are the truth value evaluation rules for disjunction, conjunction, negation, implication, and equivalence, respectively, of Kleene-Dienes many-valued logic with the set of truth values $[0,1]$.

The implication operation of Kleene-Dienes many-valued logic is a typical example about a so-called *S-implication*. Another example is the implication operation of classical logic. The general principle for S-implication is just the formula (7.6).

# 8. On Łukasiewicz' many-valued logic

We begin with Łukasiewicz' many-valued logic $Ł_{\aleph_1}$ having the closed unit interval $[0,1]$ as the set of truth values.[2]

As we know, Łukasiewicz chose the connectives of *negation* and *implication* as primitives. This is a remarkable difference, for example, between Kleene's logic and Łukasiewicz logic. Hence, the connection between standard fuzzy set theory and $Ł_{\aleph_1}$ cannot be seen immediately.

Let $v$ be any valuation of $Ł_{\aleph}$, then the truth value evaluation rules for negation and implication are

$$v(\neg p) = 1 - v(p) \tag{Neg.}$$
$$v(p \to q) = \min\{1, 1 - v(p) + v(q)\} \tag{Impl.}$$

---

[2] *Cf.* Rescher (Rescher, 1969), p.36, and 337.

By means of these connectives, Łukasiewicz defined the other connectives by the rules

$$p \vee q \stackrel{\text{def}}{\Longleftrightarrow} (p \to q) \to q \tag{Disj.}$$

$$p \wedge q \stackrel{\text{def}}{\Longleftrightarrow} \neg(\neg p \vee \neg q) \tag{Conj.}$$

$$p \leftrightarrow q \stackrel{\text{def}}{\Longleftrightarrow} (p \to q) \wedge (q \to p) \tag{Eq.}$$

The truth value evaluation rules for these derived connectives are

$$\max\{v(p), v(q)\} \qquad \text{for } p \vee q, \tag{8.1}$$

$$\min\{v(p), v(q)\} \qquad \text{for } p \wedge q, \tag{8.2}$$

$$1 - |v(p) - v(q)| \qquad \text{for } p \leftrightarrow q \tag{8.3}$$

for any valuation $v$ of $Ł_{\aleph_1}$.

In Zadeh algebra we have the operations representing disjunction, conjunction, and negation as given. Negation in Zadeh algebra has the same construction as that in Łukasiewicz' logic $Ł_{\aleph_1}$, so, we need not to do anything with it. Now our task is to derive algebraically the *implication* of $Ł_{\aleph_1}$ by means of these three other connectives. For this we use the operations of Zadeh algebra. Actually, we need only complementarity and max operations in our solution. After succeeding to solve this problem we know that standard fuzzy sets and $Ł_{\aleph_1}$ fits together completely, i.e., we can derive all the connectives of $Ł_{\aleph_1}$ in terms of Zadeh algebra. The final result is given in Proposition 8.3. This is the main task in this section.

Consider again the special case of Zadeh algebra (6.7)

$$\mathcal{L}_{\aleph_1} = \langle \mathbb{I}^{\text{Prop}}, \max, \min, \neg, \mathbf{0}, \mathbf{1} \rangle.$$

From the considertations above, we know that

- $\mathcal{L}_{\aleph_1}$ is a special Zadeh algebra, namely propositional algebra.
- The binary operations max and min are commutative and associative.
- The operations max and min are distributive to each others.
- The unary operation $\neg$ is a complementarity operation with the property of involution.

We observed in Section 3 that $[0, 1]$ is a metric space with the natural metric distance (3.2)

$$d(x, y) = |x - y|, \quad x, y \in [0, 1].$$

This formula satisfies the general definition of the concept *metric*. We need it in the following consideration where we manipulate expressions involving maxima and minima.

In manipulating maxima and minima, the consideration can sometimes be done easier by using the following expressions for max and min operations:

$$\max\{x, y\} = \frac{x + y + |x - y|}{2}, \qquad \min\{x, y\} = \frac{x + y - |x - y|}{2} \tag{8.4}$$

These formulas hold on the set of real numbers $\mathbb{R}$, and especially on the unit interval $[0, 1]$.

First, consider the case where the operations min and max are used in the form of the formulas (8.4), and $\neg$ is defined in the usual way: $\neg x = 1 - x$.

**Proposition 8.1.** *Suppose $x, y \in [0,1]$. Then De Morgan's laws hold for $\min\{x,y\}$ and $\max\{x,y\}$.*

*Proof.* Consider the operation $\min(x,y)$ and $\max(x,y)$, where $x$ and $y$ are variables taking their values from the interval $[0,1]$. Using the arithmetical formula for min operation (i.e., the expression for min in (8.4)), we have

$$\min\{x,y\} = \frac{x+y-|x-y|}{2}$$

$$= \frac{2-1-1+x+y-|1-1+x-y|}{2}$$

$$= 1 - \frac{1+1-x-y+|1-1+x-y|}{2}$$

$$= 1 - \frac{(1-x)+(1-y)+|(1-y)-(1-x)|}{2}$$

$$= 1 - \max\{(1-x),(1-y)\}. \tag{8.5}$$

From the formula (8.5), by replacing $x$ by $1-x$ and $y$ by $1-y$, and then solving $\max(x,y)$, the following formula follows:

$$\max\{x,y\} = 1 - \min\{1-x, 1-y\}. \tag{8.6}$$

The formulas (8.5) and (8.6) show that DeMorgan laws hold for max and min, and they are dual of each other.

This completes the proof. □

Łukasiewicz knew that the operations max and min are dual of each other. Actually, this property is easily found in the classical special case, i.e. using characteristic functions in presenting crisp sets. But the general proof for this is easily done by using the expressions (8.4) for max and min in such cases where a distance metric is defined in the universe of discourse. This always holds at least for real numbers.

Second, consider the connection between max and Łukasiewicz implication using Zadeh algebra (similar considerations are done in Mattila (Mattila, 2005), but the following proposition 8.2 is not completely proved).

**Proposition 8.2.** *For all $x, y \in [0,1]$,*

$$\max(x,y) = (x \underset{\text{Ł}}{\rightarrow} y) \underset{\text{Ł}}{\rightarrow} y, \tag{8.7}$$

*where $x \underset{\text{Ł}}{\rightarrow} y$ is Łukasiewicz implication.*

*Proof.* Consider disjunction operation $x \vee y = \max(x,y)$. Because $0 \leq x, y \leq 1$, using the arithmetical formula (8.4) for max, we have

$$\max(x,y) = \min\{1, \max(x,y)\} = \min\{1, \frac{x+y+|x-y|}{2}\}$$

$$= \min\left\{1, \frac{2-1-1+x+2y-y+|1-1+x-y|}{2}\right\}$$

$$= \min\left\{1, 1 - \frac{1+(1-x+y)-|1-(1-x+y)|}{2} + y\right\}$$

$$= \min\{1, 1 - \min(1, 1-x+y) + y\} \tag{8.8}$$

On the other hand, in $Ł_{\aleph_1}$ disjunction is defined by(Disj.), i.e., by the formula

$$x \vee y = (x \underset{Ł}{\to} y) \underset{Ł}{\to} y \tag{8.9}$$

When we apply the evaluation rule of implication (Impl.) to the right side of the equation (8.9) we get the equation

$$x \vee y = (x \underset{Ł}{\to} y) \underset{Ł}{\to} y = \min\{1, 1 - \min(1, 1-x+y) + y\} = \max(x,y) \tag{8.10}$$

by (8.8). Hence, the assertion (8.7) follows, and the proof is complete. $\square$

Of course, Łukasiewicz must have known the connection between maximum operation and his truth evaluation formula (Impl.) of the implication because without any knowledge about this, he would have not been sure that everything fits well together in his logic. But how he has inferred this is not known. Maybe, he has shown this in some special cases by truth tables with $n$ truth values where $n$ is finite.

The result of the proof of the formula (8.7) shows that from the join operation max of our algebra we deduce a formula that expresses the rule of Łukasiewicz' implication, and this formula is the truth value evaluation rule in $Ł_{\aleph_1}$. Hence, we have shown that from our algebra (6.7) it is possible to derive similar rules as the truth value evaluation rules in $Ł_{\aleph_1}$.

Hence, we may conclude our main result in a formal way:

**Proposition 8.3.** *If the cases*

1. $\neg x = 1 - x$;
2. $x \vee y = \max(x,y)$;

*hold, then the other cases*

3. $x \wedge y = \min(x,y)$;
4. $x \to y = \min(1, 1-x+y)$;
5. $x \leftrightarrow y = (x \to y) \wedge (y \to x) = 1 - |x-y|$,

*can be derived based on Zadeh algebra (6.7).*

*Proof.* The case 3 follows from the case 2 by duality. (Actually, this operation already belongs to Zadeh algebra, and hence to $Ł_{\aleph_1}$.)

The case 4 follows from the case 2 by Prop. 8.2 as follows. When we consider the equation (8.10) in the proof of Prop. 8.2, we find two min-stuctures corresponding to the evaluation rule of implication, so that one of them is an inside part of the whole formula. If we denote the inner min-structure $\min(1, 1 - x + y)$ by $z$ then the outer min-structure is $\min(1, 1 - z + y)$, i.e., the min-structures are formally the same. The implication operations in (8.9) are situated in the same way. Hence, $\min(1, 1 - x + y)$ must be the evaluation rule of $x \underset{\text{Ł}}{\to} y$, by (Impl.).

The case 5 is deduced as follows:

$$
\begin{aligned}
x \leftrightarrow y &= \min\{(x \to y), (y \to x)\} \\
&= \frac{(x \to y) + (y \to x) - |(x \to y) - (y \to x)|}{2} \\
&= \frac{\min(1, 1 - x + y) + \min(1, 1 - y + x)}{2} \\
&\quad - \frac{\min(1, 1 - x + y) - \min(1, 1 - y + x)}{2} \\
&= \frac{4 - 2|x - y| - |-2x + 2y - |x - y| + |x - y||}{4} \\
&= \frac{4 - 4|x - y|}{4} = 1 - |x - y|.
\end{aligned}
$$

Hence, the connectives of $Ł_{\aleph_1}$ can be created by Zadeh algebra. □

These cases are similar to the truth value evaluation rules for connected formulas in $Ł_{\aleph_1}$. Hence, if we want to use algebraic approach for $Ł_{\aleph_1}$ we need not necessarily to follow the mainstream described in Section 9 using the operations of MV-algebras for studying the connections between the connectives in $Ł_{\aleph_1}$.

However, in the next section, we give also a very brief description about the alternative approach starting from the definition of general MV-algebra. It is the mainstream in this research topic, but a circuitous route in the case of Łukasiewicz logic.

## 9. The relationship between Łukasiewicz logic and MV-algebras

We open another way a little for creating an algebra for Łukasiewicz logic. We adopt the definition and some properties of MV-algebras from Cignoli et. al. (Cignoli et al., 2000). Other sources are Bergmann (Bergmann, 2008) and Hájek (Hájek, 1998).

**Definition 9.1.** An *MV-algebra* is an algebra $\langle A, \oplus, \neg, 0 \rangle$ with a binary operation $\oplus$, a unary operation $\neg$ and a constant 0 satisfying the following equations:

(MV1)    $x \oplus (y \oplus z) = (x \oplus y) \oplus z$
(MV2)    $x \oplus y = y \oplus x$
(MV3)    $x \oplus 0 = x$
(MV4)    $\neg\neg x = x$
(MV5)    $x \oplus \neg 0 = \neg 0$
(MV6)    $\neg(\neg x \oplus y) \oplus y = \neg(\neg y \oplus x) \oplus x$

A non-empty set $A$ is the universe of the MV-algebra $\langle A, \oplus, \neg, 0 \rangle$.

In particular, axioms (MV1) - (MV3) state that $\langle A, \oplus, 0 \rangle$ is an *abelian monoid*.

Given an MV-algebra $A$ and a set $X$, the set $A^X$ of all functions $f : X \longrightarrow A$ becomes an MV-algebra if the operations $\oplus$ and $\neg$ and the element 0 are defined pointwise. It is obvious that the unit interval $[0, 1]$ is an MV-algebra. The continuous functions from $[0, 1]$ into $[0, 1]$ form a subalgebra of the MV-algebra $[0, 1]^{[0,1]}$.

On each MV-algebra $A$ we define the constant 1 and the operations $\odot$ and $\ominus$ as follows:

$$1 \stackrel{\text{def}}{=} \neg 0, \tag{9.1}$$

$$x \odot y \stackrel{\text{def}}{=} \neg(\neg x \oplus \neg y), \tag{9.2}$$

$$x \ominus y \stackrel{\text{def}}{=} x \odot \neg y. \tag{9.3}$$

An MV-algebra is nontrivial is and only if $0 \neq 1$. The following identities are immediate consequences of (MV4):

(MV7)    $\neg 1 = 0$,

(MV8)    $x \oplus y = \neg(\neg x \odot \neg y)$.

Axioms (MV5) and (MV6) can now be written as:

(MV5')    $x \oplus 1 = 1$,

(MV6')    $(x \ominus y) \oplus y = (y \ominus x) \oplus x$.

Setting $y = \neg 0$ in (MV6) we obtain

(MV9)    $x \oplus \neg x = 1$,

In the MV-algebra $\langle [0, 1], \oplus, \neg, 0 \rangle$ we have

$$x \odot y = \max(0, x + y - 1) \tag{9.4}$$
$$x \ominus y = \max(0, x - y) \tag{9.5}$$

*Notation*: Following common usage, we consider the $\neg$ operation more binding than any other operation, and the $\odot$ operation more binding than $\oplus$ and $\ominus$.

Consider the question about the connection between Łukasiewicz implication and operations in MV-algebra.

Given an MV-algebra $\langle A, \oplus, \neg, 0 \rangle$ and a set $X$, the set

$$A^X = \{ f \mid f : X \longrightarrow A \}$$

becomes an MV-algebra if the operations $\oplus$ and $\neg$ and the element 0 are defined pointwice (Cignoli et al. (Cignoli et al., 2000), p. 8). To define 0 pointwice means here that the result is a constant function $\mathbf{0} : x \mapsto 0$ for any $x$ in the universe of that algebra.

Further, Łukasiewicz implication

$$x \to y \stackrel{\text{def}}{=} \min\{1, 1 - x + y\}$$

can be expressed in MV-algebra in the form (*cf.* Cignoli et al. (Cignoli et al., 2000), p. 78)

$$x \rightarrow y = \neg x \oplus y \qquad (9.6)$$

whence,

$$x \oplus y = \neg x \rightarrow y. \qquad (9.7)$$

The equation (9.6) shows that between Łukasiewicz implication ant the operation $\oplus$ there is a similar connection as in S-implications which are defined by means of disjunction. But $\oplus$ is not disjunction in Łukasiewicz logic. In many cases $\oplus$ is interpreted as disjunction, but defined on the unit interval it gives different values as Łukasiewicz disjunction operation max. However, it is possible to define the operations max and min by means of the operations of MV-algebra, but then the result usually is a logic with additional operations having no reasonable interpretations (*cf.* for example, the logic Fuzzy$_L$ in Bergmann's book (Bergmann, 2008). Some comments on Fuzzy$_L$ is given in (Mattila, 2010)).

Wajsberg created an algebra, called by *Wajsberg algebra* (*W-algebra*, for short) which is know to serve an algebraic approach to Łukasiewicz infinite-valued logic. The following lemma (*cf.* Cignoli et al. (Cignoli et al., 2000), p. 83) gives the connection between Wajsberg algebras and MV-algebras.

**Lemma 9.1.** *Let $A$ be an MV-algebra, and put $x \rightarrow y \overset{\text{def}}{=} \neg x \oplus y$ and $1 \overset{\text{def}}{=} \neg 0$. Then $\langle A, \rightarrow, 1 \rangle$ is a W-algebra.*

The binary operation of W-algebra is implication operation. In this algebra a unary operation is $\neg$ because it is needed to create the unit element 1. The zero element 0 belongs to this algebra because it implies the unit element by means of negation. Hence, the algebra is in a suitable form according to Łukasiewicz logic. Now, we have counterparts of the primitive connectives of Łukasiewicz logic as the operations of W-algebra. The other connectives can be created in the similar way in W-algebra as Łukasiewicz has introduced them.

One consequence from this consideration is that in MV-algebras the operations max and min can be created by the operations of W-algebra, i.e., by the primitive connectives of Łukasiewicz logic by means of the evaluation rule of (9.6).

## 10. Conclusion

The main problem we considered here is to find connections between standard fuzzy sets and Łukasiewicz logic $Ł_{\aleph_1}$ and to find a suitable algebra for it, especially, because the primitive connectives are negation and implication. In De Morgan algebras the counterparts for the logical connectives disjunction, conjunction, and negation appear as the algebraic operations. It cannot immediately be seen how Łukasiewicz implication, that belongs to the primitive connectives, are derived from the disjunction (max) and negation ($\neg x = 1 - x, x \in \mathbb{I}$). We have done it here using a special De Morgan algebra, namely, Zadeh algebra. Hence, the connection between standard fuzzy sets and Łukasiewicz logic $Ł_{\aleph_1}$ becomes clear. The key result, where Łukasiewicz implication is derived algebraically from disjunction and negation, is given in Proposition 8.3.

Kleene's logic is considered because of its close connection to standard fuzzy sets, already motivated by Zadeh. The sections 2, 3, 4, 6, and 8 gives the method we have used for creating our results.

The section 9 tells very briefly how the others consider this topic. That way is different and alternative to ours. MV-algebra is quite general, and many algebras, like Boolean algebras and also De Morgan algebras belong to its scope. The reader may become familiar with this topic, for example, by reading the Bergmann's, Cignoli's et. al, and Hájek's books mentioned in References. A lot of other material is available, too.

Our alternative way we have considered the topic here, is not totally new, because these things are considered in (Mattila, 2004), (Mattila, 2005), and (Mattila, 2010), but our key result, Proposition 8.3 is. Proposition 8.2 is the core of this result. It makes the connection of max operation and Łukasiewicz inmplication clear by means of Zadeh algebra. Using the expressions (8.4) for the operations max and min is usually not used in general, but it makes the consideration easy. As we can see from the used references, De Morgan algebras have already been well known relatively long time having, in the long run, different alternative names, like "quasi Boolean algebras", and "soft algebras".

H. Rasiowa has considered *implicative algebras* and *implication algebras* in her book ((Rasiowa, 1974)). Hence, the future research policy may be based on these algebras. Also, the connections between implicative/implication algebras and De Morgan algebras or MV-algebras restricted to many-valued or modal logics are included to the future research.

## 11. References

Bergmann, M. (2008). *An Introduction to Many-Valued and Fuzzy Logic*, Cambridge University Press, New York, Melbourne, Madrid,Cape Town, Singapore, São Paulo, Delhi.

Cignoli, L. & D'Ottaviano, M. & Mundici, D. (2000). *Algebraic Foundations of Many-valued Reasoning*, Kluwer Academic Publishers, Dordrecht, Boston, London.

Hájek, P. (1998). *Metamathematics of Fuzzy Logic*, Kluwer Academic Publishers, Dordrecht, Boston, London.

Lowen, R. (1996). *Fuzzy Set Theory. Basic Concepts, Techniques and Bibliography*, Kluwer Academic Publishers, Dordrecht, Boston, London.

Mattila, J. K. (2004). Zadeh algebras as a syntactical approach to fuzzy sets, *Current Issues in Data and Knowledge Engineering*, Springer-Verlag, Warszawa, Poland, pp. 343–349.

Mattila, J. K. (year 2005). On łukasiewicz modifier logic, *Journal of Advanced Computational Intelligence and Intelligent Informatics* Vol. 9(No. 5): 506–510.
     URL: *www.fujipress.jp*

Mattila, J. K. (2009). Many-valuation, modality, and fuzziness, *in* Seising R. (ed.), *Views on Fuzzy Sets and Systems from Different Perspectives. Philosophy and Logic, Criticisms and Applications*, Springer-Verlag, Berlin, Heidelberg, pp. 271–300.

Mattila, J. K. (2010). On Łukasiewicz' infinite-Valued logic and Fuzzy$_L$, *in*, *KES 2010 Knowledge-Based Intelligent Information and Engineering Systems*, Part IV, LNAI 6279, Springer-Verlag, Berlin, Heidelberg, pp. 108–115.

Negoiță, C. V. & Ralescu, D. A., (1975). *Applications of Fuzzy Sets to Systems Analysis*, Birkhäuser, Basel, Stuttgart.

Rasiowa, H. (1974). *An Algebraic Approach to non-classical Logics*, North-Holland.

Rescher, N. (1969). *Many-Valued Logic*, McGraw-Hill, New York, St. Louis, San Francisco, London, Sydney, Toronto, Mexiko, Panama.

Zadeh, L. A. (1965). Fuzzy Sets, *Information and Controll* 8.

# 4

# Parametric Type-2 Fuzzy Logic Systems

Arturo Tellez, Heron Molina, Luis Villa,
Elsa Rubio and Ildar Batyrshin
*IPN, CIC, Mexico City,*
*Mexico*

## 1. Introduction

The use of Fuzzy Logic Systems (FLS) for control applications has increased since they became popular from 80's. After Mendel in 90's showed how uncertainty can be computed in order to achieve more robust systems, Type-2 Fuzzy Logic Systems (T2FLS) are in the focus of researchers and recently they became a new research topic.

At same time, Batyrshin et al demonstrated that parametric conjunctions can be useful for tuning a FLS in order to achieve better performance beyond the set parameter tuning. In signal processing and system identification, this fact let the designer to add freedom degrees to adjust a general FLS.

This chapter presents the parametric T2FLS and shows that this new FLS is a very useful option for sharper approximations in control. In order to verify the advantages of the parametric T2FLS, it is used the Ball and Plate System as a testbench. This study case helps us to understand how a parametric conjunction affects the controller behavior in measures like response time or overshoot. Also, this application let us observe how the controller works in noise presence.

## 2. Parametric T2FLS

A Parametric Type-2 Fuzzy Logic Systems (PT2FLS) is a general FLS which can be fully adjusted through a single or multiple parameters in order to achieve a benefit in its general performance. It means that a PT2FLS has several options to adjust set parameters (i.e. membership function parameters), rule parameters and output set parameters. Fig. 1 shows the structure of a PT2FLS which it is almost equal to a general T2FLS.

In this figure the Defuzzification stage comprises the Output Processing Block and the Defuzzifier as Mendel stated in (Karnik, Mendel et al. 1999). For Interval Type-2 Fuzzy Logic Systems (IT2FLS) this block represents only the centroid calculation for example considering the WM Algorithm (Wu and Mendel 2002). As it can be seen, a dashed arrow crosses every stage; this means that every stage is tunable for optimization purposes.

A general Fuzzy System is a function where all input variables are mapped to the output variables according to the knowledge base defined by rules. Rule Set represents the configuration of the T2FLS.

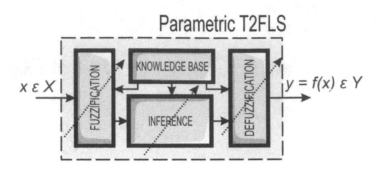

Fig. 1. Parametric Type-2 Fuzzy Logic Systems

Every input variable (where $X$ is the input vector) for a T2FLS has associated a single or multiple Fuzzy Sets (FS), in this case a Type-2 Fuzzy Set (T2FS). Those T2FS express the uncertainty associated with ideas or linguistic expressions of the people. A T2FS is characterized by a complex Membership Function (MF) (defined by their outer MFs, which has several parameters that define it) called Footprint of Uncertainty (FOU). In FLS, those equivalent parameters help the expert to improve the entire system performance when performing adaptation. In case of T2FS, additional parameters are needed.

In the other hand, every output variable (where $Y$ is the output vector) has associated also a FOU. This FOU has its own parameters which can be also tuned. Adaptation for output T2FS or FS when defuzzifying implies in adjusting their output centroids. This stage is not very used for adaptation, but it can be realized.

Adaptation in inference stage is not used, because of the complexity of the parametric operation. Adding more complexity in a system which is by its own very complex is not suitable. For this reason, it is introduced an operation which is simpler, the *Parametric Conjunction* (Batyrshin and Kaynak 1999; Batyrshin, Rudas et al. 2009; Prometeo Cortes, Ildar Z. Batyrshin et al. 2010).

## 2.1 Overview

In a T2FLS the inference step combines every rule and maps input sets to output sets (premises to consequents). Each premise that is related with another premise (implied sets) is related by a rule using a Conjunction Operation. This conjunction operation normally is performed with a t-norm operation. Suppose a rule $l$ in the rule set with $M$ rules of a given MISO T2FLS with $m$ inputs $(x_1 \in X_1, x_2 \in X_2, \ldots, x_p \in X_m)$ and $n = 1$ output $(y_1 \in Y_1)$, so that $R^l$: IF $x_1$ is $\tilde{A}_1^j \wedge x_2$ is $\tilde{A}_2^j \ldots x_p$ is $\tilde{A}_m^j \rightarrow y$ is $\tilde{B}^j$, where $\tilde{A}_i^j$ denotes a specific set that belongs to a specific input variable. Symbol "$\wedge$" represents a conjunction operation performed with a basic t-norm, typically a minimum, which can be replaced for a parametric operation.

This rule represents the relation between the input space of every variable $X_1 \times X_2 \times \ldots \times X_m$ (where $i = 1, 2, \ldots m$) and the output space $Y$ and the relation of those variables are expressed as $\mu_{\tilde{A}_1 \times \tilde{A}_2 \times \ldots \times \tilde{A}_m \to \tilde{B}}$ $(x, y)$. Suppose any input variable with a T2FS defined as $\tilde{F}_i^j\left(x_i; \mathbb{p}_{s_i}^j\right) = FOU\left(x_i; \mathbb{p}_{s_i}^j\right)$, where $1 \leq j \leq m$, $1 \leq j \leq k$ and function $FOU(\cdot)$ is the characterization of the T2FS defined between its Upper Membership Function (UMF) and its Lower Membership Function (LMF), i.e. the FOU; $\mathbb{p}_s$ represents the set of parameter of the T2FS which defines its basic FOU shape (triangular, trapezoidal, Gaussian, etc.). Such parameters let the expert or an extern intelligent system to modify its behavior.

A parametric fuzzy conjunction operation represents the variable intersection of two premises related by a parameter, i.e. that two premises are implied in a measured way in order to take a specific decision. Those premises are T2FS $(\tilde{A}_i^j)$.

For a specific rule $R^l$, a firing strength $F^l$ for the implication of two or more premises is expressed as

$$F^l = \left[\overline{F}^l; \underline{F}^l\right] = \left[\overline{\mu}_{\tilde{A}_i^j}(x_i); \underline{\mu}_{\tilde{A}_i^j}(x_i)\right]$$

$$\overline{F}^l = \overline{\mu}_{\tilde{A}_1^j}(x_1) \wedge \overline{\mu}_{\tilde{A}_2^j}(x_2) \wedge \ldots \wedge \overline{\mu}_{\tilde{A}_m^j}(x_m)$$

$$\underline{F}^l = \underline{\mu}_{\tilde{A}_1^j}(x_1) \wedge \underline{\mu}_{\tilde{A}_2^j}(x_2) \wedge \ldots \wedge \underline{\mu}_{\tilde{A}_m^j}(x_m)$$

Until here, upper and lower firing strengths are defined using non-parametric conjunctions for operator "$\wedge$". Once it is considered a parametric conjunction operation for performing implication of the premises, every firing strength can be controlled by a parameter, arising to a parametric inference process, as it is used for FLS in (Batyrshin, Rudas et al. 2009). So a parametric firing strength is expressed as

$$\overline{F}^l = \mathbf{T}\left(\overline{\mu}_{\tilde{A}_1^j}(x_1), \overline{\mu}_{\tilde{A}_2^j}(x_2), \ldots, \overline{\mu}_{\tilde{A}_m^j}(x_m); \mathbb{p}_r\right) = \mathbf{T}\left(\overline{\mu}_{\tilde{A}_i^j}(x_i); \mathbb{p}_r^l\right) \tag{1}$$

$$\underline{F}^l = \mathbf{T}\left(\underline{\mu}_{\tilde{A}_1^j}(x_1), \underline{\mu}_{\tilde{A}_2^j}(x_2), \ldots, \underline{\mu}_{\tilde{A}_m^j}(x_m); \mathbb{p}_r\right) = \mathbf{T}\left(\underline{\mu}_{\tilde{A}_i^j}(x_i); \mathbb{p}_r^l\right) \tag{2}$$

where $\mathbf{T}$ is a parametric conjunction and $\mathbb{p}_r^l$ is the set of parameters used to manipulate the implication of the premises related in $l$th rule.

Finally, every firing strength must be aggregated by a disjunction operator or t-conorn operator in order to complete the composition.

$$\overline{\mu}_{\tilde{B}_1^j}(y) = \sqcup_{x \in X}\left(\mathbf{T}\left(\overline{\mu}_{\tilde{A}_i^j}(x_i); \mathbb{p}_r\right)\right) \tag{3}$$

$$\underline{\mu}_{\tilde{B}_1^j}(y) = \sqcup_{x \in X}\left(\mathbf{T}\left(\underline{\mu}_{\tilde{A}_i^j}(x_i); \mathbb{p}_r\right)\right) \tag{4}$$

For the defuzzification stage in a T2FLS, the corresponding centroids of an output T2FS can be parametric also. However, if an expert tries to calculate them all using the KM algorithm, it can be a complex task. Instead of calculation of output centroids it is suggested the use heuristically techniques. Next section, explains two suitable parametric conjunctions used in FLS and T2FLS.

## 2.2 Parametric conjunctions

A fuzzy conjunction is the operation between two values of membership degrees that relate two fuzzy sets considered as premises in an inference scheme. Those premises let the system to decide for a specific decision in a given moment. This process is called Implication. Every rule describes an implication as shown in Fig. 2.

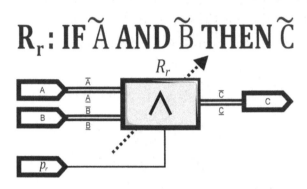

Fig. 2. Implication of premises of a single rule using (p)-Monotone Sum of Conjunctions

Most popular conjunction and disjunction operations are t-norm $T$ and t-conorm $S$ (also called s-norm), respectively. They are defined as functions $T, S: [0,1] \times [0,1] \rightarrow [0,1]$ satisfying the following axioms of commutativity, associativity, monotonicity and boundary conditions (E. P. Klement, R. Mesiar et al. 2000):

$$
\begin{array}{lll}
T(a,b) = T(b,a) & S(a,b) = S(b,a) & \text{commutativity} \\
T(T(a,b),c) = T(a,T(b,c)) & S(S(a,b),c) = S(a,S(b,c)) & \text{associativity} \\
T(a,b) \le T(c,d) & S(a,b) \le S(c,d) \qquad a \le c, b \le d & \text{monotonicity} \\
T(a,1) = a & S(a,0) = a & \text{boundary conditions}
\end{array}
$$

A parametric fuzzy conjunction uses some parameters to control the way the inference will be done. In order to simplify the complexity of a traditional parametric conjunction, it was proposed in (Batyrshin and Kaynak 1999) to use non-associative conjunction operations, due to the lack of use of this property and the usage of only two operands in applied fuzzy systems. For this reason in definition of conjunctions T further we use only axioms of commutativity, monotonicity and boundary conditions.

A single parametric conjunction may behave in different ways depending of a parameter value. There are some works today about the parametric conjunctions (Batyrshin and Kaynak 1999; Batyrshin, Rudas et al. 2009; Rudas, Batyrshin et al. 2009; Prometeo Cortes, Ildar Z. Batyrshin et al. 2010). Next subsections describe briefly some parametric conjunctions suitable for software and hardware implementations, which share the usage of basic t-norms and other simple functions.

## 2.3 Monotone sum of conjunctions

This parametric conjunction is characterized depending of a parameter value and also fulfill with properties of monotonicity, boundary conditions and commutativity (Batyrshin, Rudas et al. 2009). Other suitable parametric conjunctions can be found in (Batyrshin and Kaynak 1999).

Suppose $G = \{1,2, \dots, n\}; n \geq 2$ be an index set and H is a *partition* of $[0,1]$ on pairwise disjoint intervals $\{H_1, H_2, \dots, H_n\}$ such that if $i < j$ then $a < b$ for all $a \in H_i$ and $b \in H_j$. Denote a *section* as $D_{ij} = H_i \times H_j$ and suppose $G = \{1,2, \dots, n\}; n \geq 2$ be an index set and H is a partition of $[0,1]$ on pairwise disjoint intervals $\{H_1, H_2, \dots, H_n\}$ such that if $i < j$ then $a < b$ for all $a \in H_i$ and $b \in H_j$. Suppose Q is some index set and $(T_q, \leq)_{q \in Q}$ is a partially ordered set of fuzzy conjunctions, e.g. a set of all basic t-norms. Then assign to each section $D_{ij} = H_i \times H_j$ in $[0,1] \times [0,1]$ some $T_{ij} = T_q$ from this set such that $T_{ij}(a,b) \leq T_{st}(u,v)$ if $i \leq s, j \leq t$ and $a \leq u, b \leq v$ where $(a,b) \in D_{ij}$ and $(u,v) \in D_{st}$. Define a function T on $[0,1] \times [0,1]$ by

$$T(a,b) = T_{ij}(a,b) \ if \ (a,b) \in D_{ij}; i,j \in G \tag{5}$$

Then T is a conjunction called a monotone sum (Batyrshin, Rudas et al. 2009) of $(D_{ij}, T_{ij})_{i,j \in G}$ or monotone sum of fuzzy conjunctions $T_{ij}$; $i,j \in G$. If it is desirable to construct commutative conjunctions then it should be considered:

$$T_{i,j} = T_{j,i} \tag{6}$$

Next subsections describe two types of monotone sums using a single parameter.

## 2.3.1 (p) – Monotone sum

Suppose a partition on two intervals is defined by some parameter $0 \leq p \leq 1$ as $H_1 = [0,p]$ and $H_2 = (p,1]$. Assign to each $D_{ij}$, $i = [1,2]$, fuzzy conjunctions $T_{11}, T_{21}, T_{12}$ and $T_{22}$ ordered as follows: $T_{11} \leq T_{12} \leq T_{22}, T_{11} \leq T_{21} \leq T_{22}$. Then define the $(p)$ −monotone sum of fuzzy conjunctions from (5) as follows:

$$T(a,b,p) = \begin{cases} T_{11}(a,b), & (a \leq p) \wedge (b \leq p) \\ T_{21}(a,b), & (a > p) \wedge (b \leq p) \\ T_{12}(a,b), & (a \leq p) \wedge (b > p) \\ T_{22}(a,b), & (a > p) \wedge (b > p) \end{cases} \tag{7}$$

As it can be seen all four sections are defined by parameter $p$, then a monotone sum of conjunctions is able to behave in different ways depending of this parameter. For example, if $p = 0$ then its behavior will be $T_{22}$ as stated in (6).

## 2.3.2 (p, 1 − p) – Monotone sum

Suppose three partitions defined by some parameter $p$ as $H_1 = [1,p]$, $H_2 = (p, 1-p]$ and $H_3 = (1-p, 1]$. Assign to each section $D_{i,j}, i = [1,2,3]$ fuzzy conjunctions $T_{11}, T_{12}, T_{13}, T_{21}, T_{22}, T_{23}, T_{31}, T_{32}$ and $T_{33}$ ordered as follows: $T_{11} \leq T_{12} \leq T_{13} \leq T_{23} \leq T_{33}, T_{11} \leq T_{21} \leq T_{31} \leq T_{32} \leq T_{33}, T_{12} \leq T_{22} \leq T_{32}, T_{21} \leq T_{22} \leq T_{23}$. Then define the $(p, 1-p) −$ monotone sum of fuzzy conjunctions from (5) as follows:

$$T(a,b,p) = \begin{cases} T_{11}(a,b), & (a \leq p) \wedge (b \leq p) \\ T_{21}(a,b), & (a > p) \wedge (a \leq 1-p) \wedge (b \leq p) \\ T_{31}(a,b), & (a > 1-p) \wedge (b \leq p) \\ T_{12}(a,b), & (a \leq p) \wedge (b > p) \wedge (b \leq 1-p) \\ T_{22}(a,b), & (a > p) \wedge (a \leq 1-p) \wedge (b > p) \wedge (b \leq 1-p) \\ T_{32}(a,b), & (a > 1-p) \wedge (b > p) \wedge (b \leq 1-p) \\ T_{13}(a,b), & (a \leq p) \wedge (b > p) \\ T_{23}(a,b), & (a > p) \wedge (a \leq 1-p) \wedge (b > p) \\ T_{33}(a,b), & (a > p) \wedge (b > p) \end{cases} \tag{8}$$

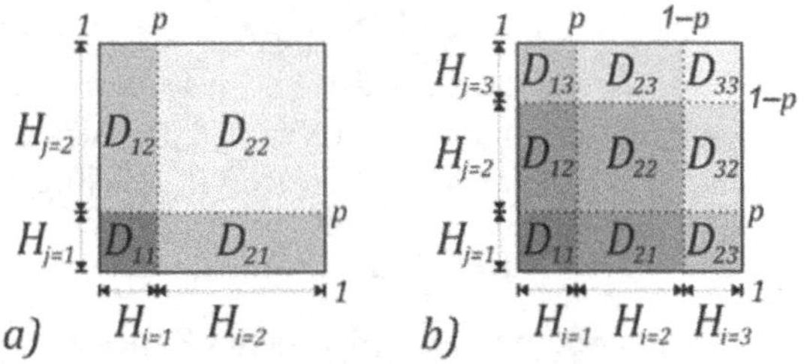

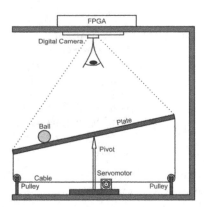

Fig. 3. Monotone sum of conjunctions a) (p) and b) (p,1-p)

Fig. 3 shows both monotone sums described here and its construction is very similar between them. Next section describes a case of study for PT2FLS application: the Ball and Plate System.

fig. 4. Mechanical Model of B&P System

Fig. 4. The tilt of plate let the ball to move from one point to another over its surface. The position of ball is captured from a digital camera that is mounted over the plate on a specific and convenient distance in order to scan the plate surface completely.

## 3. A case of study: The ball and plate system

As reported in (Moreno-Armendariz, Rubio-Espino et al. 2010), it was built a prototype of B&P mechanism that can be used as a testbench for control implementations. This model consists of a plate mounted over a pivot that let the plate to tilt along any of its axes using two servomotors. Fig. 4 shows this description only for a single axis.

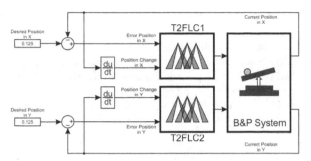

Fig. 5. PT2FLC for B&P System

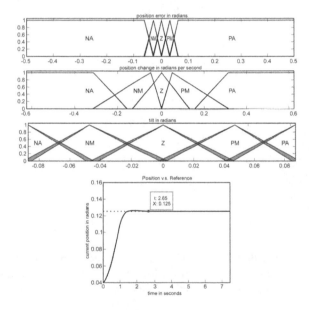

Fig. 6. Initial set distribution for input and output variables for every PT2FLC

The computer vision is implemented in a Field Programmable Gate Array (FPGA) using a development kit, manufactured by Terasic (DE2 Development Kit). This kit has several interfaces to test a digital system and let the usage of an embedded vision system in the same chip. The vision system calculates with (10) the centroid of the ball and determines its position (coordinates). It was implemented the T1FLC that controls the B&P system also, embedding it in the same chip using just the 15% of the Cyclone II EP2C35F672C6N.

In this work, B&P System is controlled using PT2FLC. This system is shown in Fig. 5 and describes a control system that establishes a desired position in axis X and a desired position in axis Y. Servomotors perform the adequate tilt over both axes. Every tilt value is calculated by its corresponding PT2FLC using the error position and the position change. Position change is the differential of the feedback of the plant, i.e. the current position.

It is noteworthy that PT2FLC hardware has not been implemented and tested for this application. Only simulations are performed in order to show all advantages of the use of PT2FLC in control applications. Mechanical model proposed in (Moreno-Armendariz, Rubio-Espino et al. 2010) has the characteristic of designing and testing new and improved controllers, which it is a suitable future work, because of the flexibility of FPGA.

$$A = \begin{bmatrix} 0 & 1 & 0 & 0 & 0 & 0 & 0 & 0 \\ 0 & 0 & -9.81 & 0 & 0 & 0 & 0 & 0 \\ 0 & 0 & 0 & 1 & 0 & 0 & 0 & 0 \\ -6.1313 \times 10^4 & 0 & 0 & 0 & 0 & 0 & 0 & 0 \\ 0 & 0 & 0 & 0 & 0 & 1 & 0 & 0 \\ 0 & 0 & 0 & 0 & 0 & 0 & -9.81 & 0 \\ 0 & 0 & 0 & 0 & 0 & 0 & 0 & 1 \\ 0 & 0 & 0 & 0 & -6.1313 \times 10^4 & 0 & 0 & 0 \end{bmatrix}$$

$$B = \begin{bmatrix} 0 & 0 \\ 0 & 0 \\ 0 & 0 \\ 5.6818 \times 10^4 & 0 \\ 0 & 0 \\ 0 & 0 \\ 0 & 0 \\ 0 & 5.6818 \times 10^4 \end{bmatrix} \tag{9}$$

$$C = \begin{bmatrix} 1 & 0 & 0 & 0 & 0 & 0 & 0 & 0 \\ 0 & 0 & 0 & 0 & 1 & 0 & 0 & 0 \end{bmatrix}$$

$$D = [0]$$

$$x' = Ax + Bu$$

$$y = Cx$$

The characteristics of this B&P System (9) is a linearized state-space model, the same as described in (Moreno-Armendariz, Rubio-Espino et al. 2010). With (10), it can be calculated the current velocity, acceleration and position in axis x.

$$v(k) = \frac{(x(k) - x(k-1))}{T}$$
$$a(k) = v(k) - v(k-1)$$
$$x_e(k+1) = x(k) + \frac{v(k)}{T} + \frac{a(k)T^2}{2} \tag{10}$$
$$e(k+1) = x_d - x_e(k+1)$$

The vision system described in (Moreno-Armendariz, Rubio-Espino et al. 2010) uses a sampling time $T$ (50ms), which captures and processes a single image in that period. After the vision system process the image, FPGA calculates the current position of the ball in axis X, $x(k)$, where $k$ is the current sample. Once it is known the position, it is possible to find the current velocity component $v(k)$ and the current acceleration component $a(k)$ of the ball, over the axis X. If it is assumed that the velocity and the acceleration of the ball are constant at shorter values of $T$, it is possible to estimate the next position of ball with $x_e(k + 1)$ and finally the desired position $x_d$ and the estimated error $e(k + 1)$.

| Tilt | | Change | | | | |
|------|------|----|----|----|----|----|
| | | NA | NM | Z | PM | PA |
| Error | NA | NM | Z | PM | PA | PA |
| | NM | NM | NM | PA | PA | PA |
| | Z | NA | NA | Z | PA | PA |
| | PM | NA | NA | NA | PM | PM |
| | PA | NA | NA | NM | Z | PM |

Table 1. Optimal Rule Set of B&P System with T1FLC described in (Moreno-Armendariz, Rubio-Espino et al. 2010) used for the PT2FLC purposes.

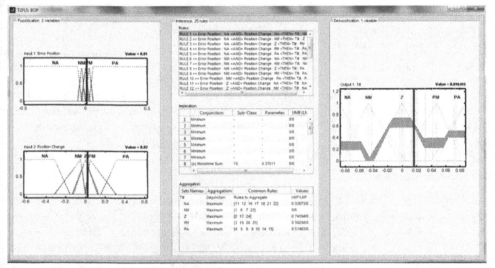

Fig. 7. IT2FLS Simulator for B&P System

It is proved that B&P System is a decoupled system over its two axes (Moreno-Armendariz, Rubio-Espino et al. 2010). So, (10) are similar for the axis Y. Fig 5 shows that B&P system block has two inputs and two outputs for our control purposes; so, every in-out pair corresponds to every axis.

T1FLC proposed by (Moreno-Armendariz, Rubio-Espino et al. 2010) has two inputs and one output. Every variable has 5 FS (Fig. 6) associated to linguistic variables "high positive" (PA), "medium positive" (PM), "zero or null" (Z), "medium negative" (NM), and "high negative" (NA). Rule set is described in Table 1.

The T1FLC controls the tilt of plate using the information that the FPGA takes form the camera and calculates the current position using (10) under perfect environment conditions. But what happens when some external forces (e.g. weather) complicate the system stability? Some equivalent phenomena may be introduced to the plate. For example, the illuminating variation due to light incidence over the plate, an unbalanced motor tied to the plate, a low quality image sensor or some interference noise added to the processed image, may be introduced as external disturbances.

| Experiment | Overshoot | SSE | Ripple |
|---|---|---|---|
| When all sets in every variable are T1, except the variable which set FOUs are increasing from zero. | Yes | No | No |
| When all sets in input variable error are T2 and their FOU are decreasing until they become T1. All other variable sets are wide as much as it can be possible. | No | No | Yes |
| When all sets in input variable change are T2 and their FOU are decreasing until they become T1. All other variable sets are wide as much as it can be possible. | Yes | No | No |
| When all sets in output variable tilt are T2 and their FOU are decreasing until they become T1. All other variable sets are wide as much as it can be possible. | No | Yes | No |

Table 2. Phenomena associated with the FOU of every set in system

In initial experiments, noise-free optimization is performed and similar results are achieved in order to compare it with T1FLC. For noise tests it is only considered an unbalanced motor tied to the plate that makes it tremble while a sine trajectory is performed, analyzing a single axis. This experiment helps us to verify the noise-proof ability of the T2FLC.

## 4. Experimental results

FS distribution, i.e., FS shape parameters may arise several characteristic phenomena that expert must take into account when designing applied-to-control fuzzy systems, so-called Fuzzy Logic Controller (FLC). As described in (Moreno-Armendariz, Rubio-Espino et al. 2010), authors found an optimal FS distribution where FLC shows a great performance in 3.8 seconds. However, when it is used this same configuration some phenomena arises when it is introduced T2FS.

Starting from the initial optimal set distribution and without considering any possible noise influence, it was tested several configurations modifying every set FOU, starting from a T1FS (without FOU) and increasing it as much as possible; or starting from a very wide FOU and collapsing it until it becomes a T1FS. Some phenomena are related to them as described in Table 2, but in general, when it is introduced a T2FS a certain level of overshoot is found, no matter which variable was modified; so, if every variable has a T2FS, then the expert has to deal with the influence of nonlinear aggregation of overshoot, steady-state error or offset (SSE) and ripple, when tuning a PT2FLC, which might be a complicated task.

For every experiment it was used an implemented simulator for IT2FLS. With some instructions it can be constructed any parametric IT2FLS and expert may choose from set shape, several parametric conjunctions and defuzzification options (Fig. 7).

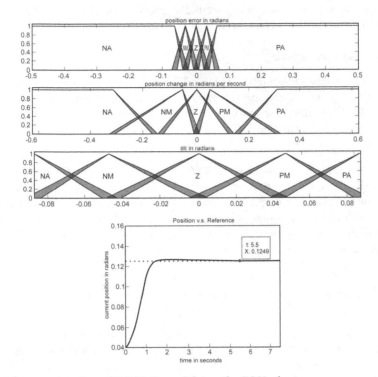

Fig. 8. Second approximation of PT2FLC modifying the FOU of sets

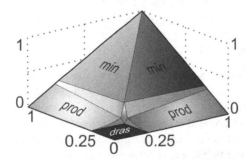

Fig. 9. Parametric Fuzzy Conjunction using (p) −Monotone Sum with parameter p = 0.25

In first experiments, (Fig. 6) it was re-adjusted the FOU of every set, leaving the set distribution intact, so it was found that only for a very thin FOU in every input set it is gotten a good convergence without overshoot and other phenomena. But, what is the sense of having a very short FOU like T1FS if they will not capture the associated uncertainties of the system? So, there should be a way of tuning the PT2FLC without changing this initial optimal set distribution.

In second experiments, it was moved the FOU of every set in every variable and found a very close approximation of time response as described in Fig. 8. This configuration has wider FOU in every input and output variable as much as necessary (with uniform spread) for supporting variations in error until 0.0075 radians, in change until 0.01 radians per second and in tilt until 0.004 radians, all around the mean of every point of its corresponding set and variable.

As it can be seen, every set exhibits a wider FOU and its time response has increased over 5 seconds. Also, some overshoot and ripple are present, but reference is reached, so SSE is eliminated. This is the first best approximation using the same optimal distribution of sets, although it does not mean that there could not be any other set distribution for this application.

As it is sated in (Batyrshin, Rudas et al. 2009), a parametric operator may help to tune a T1FLC through the inference step, so every rule of the knowledge base related with the implication of the premises might be a parametric conjunction. In third experiments, it is used commutative $(p)$ —monotone sum of conjunctions (11), where it is assigned to every section the following conjunctions: $D_{11} = T_d$ is the drastic intersection, $D_{12} = D_{21} = T_p$ is the product and $D_{22} = T_m$ is the minimum, using (7) as follows:

$$T(x,y,p) = \begin{cases} T_d(x,y), & (x \leq p) \wedge (y \leq p) \\ T_p(x,y), & [(x > p) \wedge (y \leq p)] \vee [(x \leq p) \wedge (y > p)] \\ T_m(x,y), & (x > p) \wedge (y > p) \end{cases} \tag{11}$$

In (10), it is possible to assure that when parameter $p = 0$ then the conjunction in (11) will have a minimum t-norm behavior, but when parameter $p = 1$, it will be a drastic product t-norm behavior as it can be seen in Fig. 9. If $p$ has any other value between the interval $(0,1)$, then it will have a drastic, product o minimum t-norm behavior depending on the membership values of operands. Resulting behavior of this monotone sum might help to diminish the fuzzy implication between two membership degrees of premises and therefore to reduce the resulting overshoot of system and then reach the reference faster. Now another task is to choose the values of every parameter of conjunctions.

Moreover the optimal FS distribution, it is used the same rule set of (Moreno-Armendariz, Rubio-Espino et al. 2010) as shown in Table 1 in order to show that any T1FLC can be extended to a PT2FLC. So, $M = 25$ rules define the T1FLC configuration, it means that there are 25 parametric conjunctions and therefore 25 parameters. When searching for an optimal value of every $p$, it is recommended to use an optimization algorithm in order to obtain optimal values and the resulting waste of time when calculating them manually.

According to (11), the initial values of $\mathbb{p}_r$, make the conjunctions to behave like min, i.e.

$$\mathbb{p}_r = [0,0,0,0,0,0,0,0,0,0,0,0,0,0,0,0,0,0,0,0,0,0,0,0,0]$$

It is proposed some values when optimization was performed with heuristics to get optimal rule parameters, i.e.

$$\mathbb{p}_r = [0,0.25,0.25,0,0,0,0,0.2,0,0,1,0,1,0,1,0,0,0.2,0,0,0,0,0.25,0.25,0] \tag{12}$$

| Rule Parameter | Description | Over shoot | SSE | Ripple |
|---|---|---|---|---|
| 1, 2, 5, 6, 10, 16, 17, 20, 21, 22, 25 | These rules have no influence with the final response, so their parameter values might be any. These rules may be quantified using non-parametric conjunctions. | No | No | No |
| 3, 4, 9, 11, 12, 15 | These rules have a very slight influence with the final response. Some of them reduce the ripple, but they are negligible. These rules may be quantified using non-parametric conjunctions also. | No | No | Yes |
| 13b, 14c, 18a, 23b, 24b | These rules have a very positive influence with the final response, especially the parameter value of rule 18. | Yes | No | No |
| 7b, 19c | These rules increase or decrease the offset of the final response, but could add some overshoot. | No | Yes | No |
| 8b | This rule help to stretch the ripple slightly but also might be useful to reduce small ripple. | No | No | Yes |

Table 3. Phenomena associated with the rule operator of every implication in inference

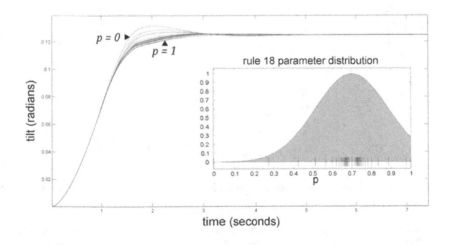

Fig. 10. Rule 18 parameter distribution for 43 experiments

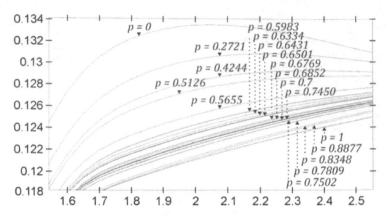

Fig. 11. Transient response for several values of parameter of rule 18

| Transient Values | Min | Max | μ | σ² |
|---|---|---|---|---|
| Overshoot (rads) | 0.0038 | 0.0529 | 0.0086 | 6.5267e-05 |
| Delay Time (s) | 0.95 | 0.95 | 0.95 | 0 |
| Rise Time (s) | 1.05 | 1.2 | 1.1465 | 8.5992e-04 |
| Peak Time (s) | 2.05 | 3.95 | 3.2162 | 0.1249 |
| Settling Time (s) | 2.35 | 3.95 | 3.2465 | 0.0774 |

Table 4. Transient characteristics for parameter variation of rule 18

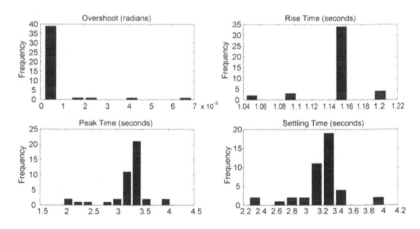

Fig. 12. Histograms for transient measures (overshoot, rise time, peak time and settling time) for rule parameter 18

Also, it was found that every rule parameter has a full, medium or null influence with final response. Table 3 shows the analysis made with every implication. For example, with rule 18 it can be diminished the overshoot when PT2FLC is just trying to control the system to reach a specific tilt of plate.

Suppose a PT2FLC where it is only modified the parameter value of rule 18 and a set of parameters that can be spread randomly around the mean of its value $p_r(18) = 0.7$. For this experiment, it was performed 43 iterations in order to show how the variation of $p_r(18)$ affects the overshoot attenuation and also other phenomena (Fig. 10-11).

Table 4 shows some results about the transient when trying to reach a tilt = 0.125 rads. Other phenomena can be analyzed for all 43 iterations. Also, in Fig.12 it can be seen that overshoot is attenuated drastically when $p_r(18) \to 1$, if it is only modified this rule. Time response (rise time, peak time and settling time) is also compromised due to parametric conjunctions. It can be seen also that drastic attenuation of overshoot occurs for $p_r(18) \lesssim 0.7$. Greater values do not affect it meaningfully. As it can be seen in (12), rule parameter proposed as the optimal for rule 18 is near to 1, which might be different with other configurations. This is because of the influence of the rest of rule parameters. However, this optimal configuration does not compromise the response time but it does eliminate the overshoot completely.

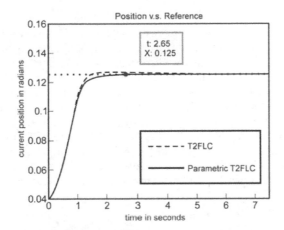

Fig. 13. Final approximation of T2FLC modifying rule parameters

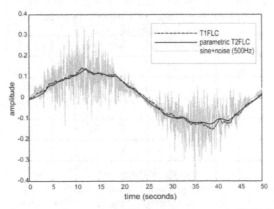

Fig. 14. Comparison of response between T1FLC and parametric T2FLC when reference is a noisy sine signal

Once it has been chosen the right parameter values of every rule it is possible to see that the influence of premises over a consequent may be regulated using a parametric conjunction. Then, overshoot and ripple have been completely removed and time response has been improved also as it can be seen in Fig. 13.

Finally Fig. 14 depicts this response of T1FLC and PT2FLC using the optimal set and rule parameters when reference cannot be determined in presence of noise. In this last experiment, signal to follow is a noisy sine signal with noise frequency equal to 500 Hz (applied to a single axis of plate). PT2FLC follows this shape very similar to T1FLC. It can be seen that PT2FLC filters all drastic changes of this noisy signal unlike T1FLC.

## 5. Discussion

Some of encountered problems and solutions are listed below.

### 5.1 Overshoot

The best results were obtained when it was reduced the FOU of every set, but reducing their FOU to zero converts the T2FLC into a T1FLC, so, this system could not deal with the uncertainties that could exist in feedback of control system (e.g. noise in sensor or noise due to illumination of room). The use of parametric conjunction operators instead the common t-norm operators, e.g. min, is the best solution to reduce the reminding overshoot after considering to modify the FOU of the sets. Due to overshoot is present when the ball is nearby the reference, inertia pulls the ball over the reference and no suitable control action could be applied. In order to smooth this action it is possible to decrease its effect diminishing the influence of premises using a parametric conjunction. A suitable value of parameter $p$ of certain rule let drop that excessive control action, and therefore decrease the overshoot. Parameters of rules 8 and 18 have the major influence on overshoot.

### 5.2 Steady-State Error

There is not a precise solution to decrease the SSE. But expert can play with FOU widths of variables. For example, reducing the SSE having a big FOU in sets of variable error and decreasing all FOUs of variable change is a good option to reduce all SSE. Also it is possible to reduce it modifying the centroids of output variable tilt. Unfortunately those actions could generate additional nonlinearities so an expert must evaluate this situation.

### 5.3 Ripple

Ripple can be controlled considering the FOU width of the variable error. Having a big FOU in sets of variable change can help to reduce the ripple.

### 5.4 Response time

A simpler approximation is possible considering the values of parameters of rules 8 and 18. If $p_8 = 1$ then all reminding ripple is cleared and if $p_{18} = 1$ then almost all overshoot is eliminated, but time response is increased. Hence, if the expert has not any timing constraints then the usage of those rule parameters might help to reduce the undesired phenomenon considering this compromise.

# 6. Conclusion

It is introduced a PT2FLC suitable for control system implementation using a new set of parametric conjunction called (p) —monotone sum of conjunctions.

Some phenomena are present when trying to tune a fuzzy system. Original B&P T1FLC was tuned to obtain the best results as in (Moreno-Armendariz, Rubio-Espino et al. 2010). When it was implemented a B&P PT2FLC with same set distribution in input and output with same rule set, as its counterpart, it was found that some phenomenon appears again. Final system response is related with all their variables, like set distribution, FOU width or conjunction parameters and they all have an implicit phenomenon which might be controlled, depending on the characteristics of the plant and the proposed rule set for a particular solution.

A parametric conjunction to perform the implication can be applied to any fuzzy system, no matter if it is type1 or type 2. The usage of parametric conjunctions in inference help to weight the influence of premises and therefore it can be forced to obtain a certain crisp value desired. Finally it was obtained an optimal result when trying to control the B&P system, reaching the reference without overshoot, SSE nor ripple in 2.65 seconds.

When the PT2FLC is subjected to external perturbations, i.e. an extra level of uncertainty is aggregated to the system; the PT2FLC exhibits a better response over its T1 counterpart. Therefore, uncertain variations in inputs of a general FLC require sets with an appropriated FOU that can capture and support them.

Therefore, the usage of PT2FLS for control purposes gives additional options for improving control precision and the usage of Monotone Sum of Conjunctions gives an opportunity to implement PT2FLC in hardware for real time applications.

Future research needs to examine the use of other parametric classes of conjunctions using simple functions. Moreover, this work can be extended using optimization techniques for calculating both better rule parameter selection and other parameters like set distribution and rule set. A hardware implementation is convenient in order to validate its behavior in real time applications.

# 7. Acknowledgements

This work was supported by the Instituto de Ciencia y Tecnologia del Distrito Federal (ICyTDF) under project number PICCT08-22. We also thank the support of the Secretaria de Investigacion y Posgrado of Instituto Politecnico Nacional (SIP-IPN) under project number SIP-20113813 and project number SIP-20113709, COFFA-IPN and PIFI-IPN. Any opinions, findings, conclusions or recommendations expressed in this publication are those of the authors and do not necessarily reflect the views of the sponsoring agency.

# 8. References

Batyrshin, I. Z. and O. Kaynak (1999). "Parametric Classes of Generalized Conjunction and Disjunction Operations for Fuzzy Modeling." IEEE Transactions on Fuzzy Systems 7(5): 586-596.

Batyrshin, I. Z., I. J. Rudas, et al. (2009). "On Generation of Digital Fuzzy Parametric Conjunctions." Studies in Computational Intelligence **243**: 79-89.

E. P. Klement, R. Mesiar, et al. (2000). Triangular norms. Dordrecht, Kluwer.

Karnik, N. N., J. M. Mendel, et al. (1999). "Type-2 Fuzzy Logic Systems." IEEE Transactions on Fuzzy Systems 7(6): 643-658

Moreno-Armendariz, M. A., E. Rubio-Espino, et al. (2010). Design and Implementation of a Visual Fuzzy Control in FPGA for the Ball and Plate System. IEEE International Conference on Reconfigurable Computing and FPGAs, Cancun, Mexico.

Prometeo Cortes, Ildar Z. Batyrshin, et al. (2010). FPGA Implementation of (p)-Monotone Sum of Basic t-norms. International Conference on Fuzzy Systems.

Rudas, I. J., I. Z. Batyrshin, et al. (2009). Digital Fuzzy Parametric Conjunctions for Hardware Implementation of Fuzzy Systems. IEEE International Conference on Computational Cybernetics, Budapest, Hungary.

Wu, H. and J. M. Mendel (2002). "Uncertainty Bounds and their Use in the Design of Interval Type-2 Fuzzy Logic Systems." IEEE Transactions on Fuzzy Systems **10**(5): 622-639.

# 5

# From Fuzzy Datalog to Multivalued Knowledge-Base

Agnes Achs

*University of Pecs Faculty of Engineering,*
*Hungary*

## 1. Introduction

Despite the fact that people have very different and ambiguous concepts and knowledge, they are able to talk to one another. How does human mind work? How can people give answers to questions? Modelling human conversation and knowledge demands to deal with uncertainty and deductions.

Human knowledge consists of static and dynamic knowledge chunks. The static ones include the so called lexical knowledge or the ability to sense similarities between facts and between predicates. Through dynamic attainments one can make deductions or one can give answers to a question. There are several and very different approaches to make a model of human knowledge, but one of the most common and widespread fields of research is based on fuzzy logic.

Fuzzy sets theory, proposed by Zadeh (1965), is a realistic and practical means to describe the world that we live in. The method has successfully been applied in various fields, among others in decision making, logic programming, and approximate reasoning. In the last decade, a number of papers have dealt with that subject, e.g. (Formato et al 2000, Sessa 2002, Medina et al 2004, Straccia et al 2009). They deal with different aspects of modelling and handling uncertainty. (Straccia 2008) gives a detailed overview of this topic with widespread references. Our investigations have begun independently of these works, and have run parallel to them. Of course there are some similar features, but our model differs from the others detailed in literature.

As a generalization of fuzzy sets, intuitionistic fuzzy sets were presented by Atanassov (Atanassov 1983), and have allowed people to deal with uncertainty and information in a much broader perspective. Another well-known generalization of an ordinary fuzzy set is the interval-valued fuzzy set, which was first introduced by Zadeh (Zadeh 1975). These generalizations make descriptions and models of the world more realistic, and practical.

In the beginning, our knowledge-base model was based on the concept of fuzzy logic, later on it was extended to intuitionistic and interval-valued logic. In this model, the static part is a background knowledge module, while the dynamic part consists of a Datalog based deduction mechanism. To develop this mechanism, it was necessary to generalize the Datalog language and to extend it into fuzzy and intuitionistic direction. (Achs 1995, 2007, 2010).

In many frameworks, in order to answer a query, we have to compute the whole intended model by a bottom-up fixed-point computation and then answer with the evaluation of the query in this model. This always requires computing a whole model, even if not all the facts and rules are required to determine answer. Therefore a possible top-down like evaluation algorithm has been developed for our model. This algorithm is not a pure top-down one but the combination of top down and bottom up evaluations. Our aim is to improve this algorithm and perhaps to develop a pure top down evaluation based on fuzzy or multivalued unification algorithm. There are fuzzy unification algorithms described for example in (Alsinet et al 1998, Formato et al 2000, Virtanen 1994), but they are inappropriate for evaluating our knowledge-base.

However, the concept of (Julian-Iranzo et al 2009, 2010) is similar but not identical with one of our former ideas about evaluating of special fuzzy Datalog programs (Achs 2006). Reading these papers has led to the assumption that this former idea may be the base of a top-down-like evaluation strategy in special multivalued cases as well. Based on this idea, a multivalued unification algorithm was developed and used for to determine the conclusion of a multivalued knowledge-base.

In this chapter this possible model for handling uncertain information will be provided. This model is based on the multivalued extensions of Datalog. Starting from fuzzy Datalog, the concept of intuitionistic Datalog and bipolar Datalog will be described. This will be the first pillar of the knowledge-base. The second one deals with the similarities of facts and concepts. These similarities are handled with proximity relations. The third component connects the first two with each other. In the final part of the paper, an evaluating algorithm is presented. It is discussed in general, but in special cases it is based on fuzzy, or multivalued unification, which is also mentioned.

## 2. Extensions of datalog

When one builds a knowledge-base, it is very important to deal with a database management system. It is based on the relational data model developed by Codd in 1970. This model is a very useful one, but it can not handle every problem. For example, the standard query language for relational databases (SQL) is not Turing-complete, in particular it lacks recursion and therefore concepts like transitive closure of a relation can not be expressed in SQL. Along with other problems this is why different extensions of the relational data model or the development of other kinds of models are necessary. A more complete one is the world of deductive databases. A deductive database consists of facts and rules, and a query is answered by building chains of deductions. Therefore the term of deductive database highlights the ability to use a logic programming style for expressing deductions concerning the contents of a database. One of the best known deductive database query languages is Datalog.

As any deductive database, a Datalog program consists of facts and rules, which can be regarded as first order logic formulas. Using these rules, new facts can be inferred from the program's facts so that the consequence of a program will be logically correct. This means that evaluating the program, the result is a model of the formulas belonging to the rules. On the other hand, it is also important that this model will contain only those true facts, which are the consequences of the program; that is, the minimality of this model is expected, i.e. in this model it is impossible to make any true fact false and still have a model consistent with the database.

An interpretation assigns truth or falsehood to every possible instance of the program's predicates. An interpretation is a model, if it makes the rules true, no matter what assignment of values from the domain is made for the variables in each rule. Although there are infinite many implications, it is proved that it is enough to consider only the Herbrand interpretation defined on the Herbrand universe and the Herbrand base.

The Herbrand universe of a program $P$ (denoted by $H_P$) is the set of all possible ground terms constructed by using constants and function symbols occurring in $P$. The Herbrand base of $P$ ($B_P$) is the set of all possible ground atoms whose predicate symbols occur in $P$ and whose arguments are elements of $H_P$.

In general, a term is a variable, a constant or a complex term of the form $f(t_1, \ldots, t_n)$, where $f$ is a function symbol and $t_1, \ldots, t_n$ are terms. An atom is a formula of the form $p(\underline{t})$, where $p$ is a predicate symbol of a finite arity (say $n$) and $\underline{t}$ is a sequence of terms of length $n$ (arguments). A literal is either an atom (positive literal) or its negation (negative literal). A term, atom or literal is ground if it is free of variables. As in fuzzy extension, we did not deal with function symbols, so in our case the ground terms are the constants of the program.

In the case of Datalog programs there are several equivalent approaches to define the semantics of the program. In fuzzy extension we mainly rely on the fixed-point base aspect. The above concepts are detailed in classical works such as (Ceri et al 1990, Loyd 1990, Ullman 1988).

## 2.1 Fuzzy Datalog

In fuzzy Datalog (fDATALOG) the facts can be completed with an uncertainty level, the rules with an uncertainty level and an implication operator. With the use of this operator and these levels deductions can be made. As in classical cases, logical correctness is extremely important as well, i.e., the consequence must be a model of the program. This means that for each rule of the program, the truth-value of the fuzzy implication following the rule has to be at least as large as the given uncertainty level.

### 2.1.1 Syntax and semantics of fuzzy datalog

More precisely, the notion of fuzzy rule is the following:

**Definition 1.** An fDATALOG rule is a triplet $r; \beta; I$, where r is a formula of the form

$$A \leftarrow A_1,\ldots,A_n \qquad (n \geq 0),$$

where $A$ is an atom (the head of the rule), $A_1,\ldots,A_n$ are literals (the body of the rule); $I$ is an implication operator and $\beta \in (0,1]$ (the level of the rule).

For getting a finite result, all the rules in the program must be safe. An fDATALOG rule is safe if all variables occurring in the head also occur in the body, and all variables occurring in a negative literal also occur in a positive one. An fDATALOG program is a finite set of safe fDATALOG rules.

There is a special type of rule, called fact. A fact has the form $A \leftarrow; \beta; I$. From now on, the facts are referred as $(A, \beta)$, because according to implication $I$, the level of $A$ easily can be computed and in the case of the implication operators detailed in this chapter it is $\beta$.

For defining the meaning of a program, we need again the concepts of Herbrand universe and Herbrand base, but this time they are based on fuzzy logic. Now a ground instance of a rule $r$; $\beta$; $I$ in $P$ is a rule obtained from $r$ by replacing every variable in $r$ with a constant of $H_P$. The set of all ground instances of $r$; $\beta$; $I$ is denoted by $ground(r)$; $\beta$; $I$. The ground instance of $P$ is $ground(P) = \cup_{(r;\, I;\, \beta) \in P} (ground(r); I; \beta)$.

An interpretation of a program $P$ is a fuzzy set of the program's Herbrand base, $B_P$, i.e. it is: $\cup_{A \in BP} (A;\, \alpha_A)$. An interpretation is a model of $P$ if for each $(A \leftarrow A_1,...,A_n;\, \beta;\, I) \in ground(P)$

$$I(\alpha_{A1 \wedge ... \wedge An},\, \alpha_A) \geq \beta.$$

A model $M$ is least if for any model $N$, $M \leq N$. A model $M$ is minimal if there is not any model $N$, where $N \leq M$.

To be short $\alpha_{A1 \wedge ... \wedge An}$ will be denoted as $\alpha_{body}$ and $\alpha_A$ as $\alpha_{head}$.

In the extensions of Datalog several implication operators are used, but all cases are restricted to min-max conjunction and disjunction, and to the complement to 1 as negation. So: $\alpha_{A \wedge B} = min(\alpha_A,\, \alpha_B)$, $\alpha_{A \vee B} = max(\alpha_A,\, \alpha_B)$ and $\alpha_{\neg A} = 1 - \alpha_A$.

The semantics of fDATALOG is defined as the fixed points of consequence transformations. Depending on evaluating sequences two semantics can be defined: a deterministic and a nondeterministic one. Further on only the nondeterministic semantics will be discussed, the deterministic one is detailed in (Achs 2010). It was proved that the two semantics are equivalent in the case of negation- and function-free fDatalog programs, but they differ if the program has any negation. In this case merely the nondeterministic semantics is applicable. The nondeterministic transformation is as follows:

**Definition 2.** Let $B_P$ be the Herbrand base of the program $P$, and let $F(B_P)$ denote the set of all fuzzy sets over $B_P$. The consequence transformation $NT_P : F(B_P) \rightarrow F(B_P)$ is defined as

$$NT_P(X) = \{(A,\, \alpha_A)\} \cup X, \tag{1}$$

where

$$(A \leftarrow A_1,...,A_n;\, \beta;\, I) \in ground(P),\, (|A_i|,\, \alpha_{Ai}) \in X,\, (1 \leq i \leq n);$$

$$\alpha_A = max(0,\, min\{\gamma \mid I(\alpha_{body},\, \gamma) \geq \beta\}).$$

$|A_i|$ denotes the kernel of the literal $A_i$, (i.e., it is the ground atom $A_i$, if $A_i$ is a positive literal, and $\neg A_i$, if $A_i$ is negative) and $\alpha_{body} = min(\alpha_{A1},...,\alpha_{An})$.

It can be proved that this transformation has a fixed point. To prove it, let us define the powers of a transformation:

For any $T : F(B_P) \rightarrow F(B_P)$ transformation let

$$T_0 = \{ \cup\{(A, \alpha_A)\} \mid (A \leftarrow;\, I;\, \beta) \in ground(P),\, \alpha_A = max(0,\, min\{\gamma \mid I(1,\, \gamma) \geq \beta\}) \} \cup$$
$$\{(A,\, 0) \mid \exists (B \leftarrow ... \neg A...;\, I;\, \beta) \in ground(P)\}$$

and let

$$T_1 = T(T_0)$$

$$T_n = T(T_{n-1})$$

...

$T_\omega$ = least upper bound of $\{ T_n \mid n < \omega \}$ if $\omega$ is a limit ordinal.

An ordering relation can be defined over $F(B_P)$. For $G; H : B_P \rightarrow [0; 1]$; $G \leq H$ iff $(\forall d \in B_P)$ $G(d) \leq H(d)$. It easily can be seen that $L = (F(B_P), \leq)$ is a complete lattice.

It is clear that $NT_P$ is inflationary transformation over $L$, and if $P$ is negation-free, then $NT_P$ is monotone as well. (A transformation $T$ is inflationary if $X \leq T(X)$ for every $X \in L$ and it is monotone if $T(X) \leq T(Y)$ if $X \leq Y$).

In (Ceri et al 1990) it is shown that an inflationary transformation over a complete lattice has a fixed point and if it is monotone then it has a least fixed point (Loyd 1990). Therefore $NT_P$ has a fixed point, i.e. there exists an $X \in F(B_P)$ for which $NT_P(X) = X$. If $P$ is positive, then $X$ is the least fixed point. (That is for any $Z=T(Z) : X \leq Z$.)

The fixed point of the transformation will be denoted by $lfp(NT_P)$. It can be shown (Achs 1995) that this fixed point is a model of $P$.

**Theorem 1.** $lfp(NT_P)$ is a model of $P$.

**Proof** In $ground(P)$ there are rules in the next forms:

a/ $(A \leftarrow; \beta; I)$.
b/ $(A \leftarrow A_1, ..., A_n; \beta; I)$; $(A, \alpha_A) \in lfp(NT_P)$ and $(|A_i|, \alpha_{A_i}) \in lfp(NT_P)$, $1 \leq i \leq n$.
c/ $(A \leftarrow A_1, ..., A_n; \beta; I)$; $\exists i : (|A_i|, \alpha_{A_i}) \notin lfp(NT_P)$.

In the case of a, b because of the construction of $\alpha_A$ the condition $I(\alpha_{body}, \alpha_A) \geq \beta$ is realized. In the case of c because of the construction of $T_0$ $A_i$ is not negative, that is $A_i$ is not among the facts, so $\alpha_{A_i} = 0$, therefore $\alpha_{body} = 0$, so $I(\alpha_{body}, \alpha_A) = 1 \geq \beta$, namely $lfp(NT_P)$ is a model.

Moreover, the next proposition is true as well.

**Proposition 1.** For negation-free fDATALOG program $P$ $lfp(NT_P)$ is the least model.

**Proof** In the case of a positive Datalog program, the least fixed point is the least model (Ceri et al 1990, Ullman 1988). In the case of fuzzy Datalog, according to the definition of the consequence transformation, the level of the rule's head is the least value satisfying the criterion of modelness. The application of the transformations may arise only one problem. A lower level would be ordered to the same rule's head, but according to the definitions we should accept the higher value. But such a case can arise only in the case of programs containing any negation. Therefore the proposition is true.

According to the above statements, the meaning of the programs can be defined by this fixed point:

**Definition 3.** $lfp(NT_P)$ is the nondeterministic semantics of fDATALOG $P$ program.

To compute the level of rule-heads, we need the concept of uncertainty level function.

**Definition 4.** The uncertainty-level function is:

$$f(I, \alpha, \beta) = min (\{ \gamma \mid I (\alpha, \gamma) \geq \beta \}).$$

According to this function the level of a rule-head is: $\alpha_{head} = f(I, \alpha_{body}, \beta)$.

It is an extremely important question whether the fixed-point algorithm terminates or not. It depends on the feature of uncertainty level function:

**Proposition 2.** If $f(I, \alpha, \beta) \leq \alpha$ for $\forall \alpha \in [0; 1]$ then the fixed point algorithm terminates.

**Proof** As $P$ is finite, therefore in the fixed point there are only finite many ground atoms. The only problem may occur with the level of recursive predicates, but according to the above property of the uncertainty-level function, the level of the rule's head cannot be greater than any former one, so this algorithm must terminate.

In former papers (Achs 1995, Achs 2006) several implications were detailed (the operators are detailed in (Dubois et al, 1991)), for now three are chosen from these. The values of their uncertainty-level functions can be easily computed. They are the following:

Gödel $\qquad I_G(\alpha,\gamma) = \begin{cases} 1 & \alpha \leq \gamma \\ \gamma & otherwise \end{cases}$ $\qquad f(I_G, \alpha, \beta) = min(\alpha, \beta)$

Lukasiewicz $\qquad I_L(\alpha,\gamma) = \begin{cases} 1 & \alpha \leq \gamma \\ 1-\alpha+\gamma & otherwise \end{cases}$ $\qquad f(I_L, \alpha, \beta) = max(0, \alpha + \beta - 1)$

Kleene-Dienes $\qquad I_K(\alpha,\gamma) = max(1-\alpha, \gamma)$ $\qquad f(I_K, \alpha, \beta) = \begin{cases} 0 & \alpha + \beta \leq 1 \\ \beta & \alpha + \beta > 1 \end{cases}$

It is obvious that $I_G$ and $I_L$ satisfy the condition of Proposition 2, and it is easy to see that in the case of $I_K$ the fixed point algorithm terminates as well. (Among the operators of (Dubois et al, 1991) there is one for which the algorithm does not terminate and one for which the uncertainty-level function does not exists.)

**Example 1.** Let us consider the next program:

$$(p(a), 0.8).$$
$$(r(b), 0.6).$$
$$q(x, y) \leftarrow p(x), r(y); 0.7; I_G.$$
$$q(x, y) \leftarrow q(y, x); 0.9; I_L.$$
$$s(x) \leftarrow q(x, y); 0.7; I_K.$$

Then $T_0 = \{(p(a), 0.8), (r(b), 0.6) \}$ and the computed atoms are:

$$(q(a, b), min(min(0.8, 0.6), 0.7) = 0.6);$$
$$(q(b, a), max(0, 0.6 + 0.9 - 1) = 0.5);$$
$$(s(a), \begin{cases} 0 & 0.6 + 0.7 \leq 1 \\ 0.7 & 0.6 + 0.7 > 1 \end{cases} = 0.7);$$
$$(s(b), \begin{cases} 0 & 0.5 + 0.7 \leq 1 \\ 0.7 & 0.5 + 0.7 > 1 \end{cases} = 0.7);$$

So $lfp(NT_P) = \{(p(a), 0.8), (r(b), 0.6), (q(a, b), 0.6), (q(b, a), 0.5), (s(a), 0.7), (s(b), 0.7) \}$.

As the next examples show, there some problems would arise if the program had any negation.

**Example 2.** Look at the next one-rule program:

$$p(a) \leftarrow \neg q(b); I_G; 0.7.$$

This program has no least model, only two minimal ones:

$$M_1 = \{(p(a), 0.7) \} \text{ and } M_2 = \{(q(b), 1) \}.$$

(The result of the above fixed point algorithm is $M_1$.)

**Example 3.** This example shows that there is a difference between the fixed points.

1. $(r(a), 0.8)$.
2. $p(x) \leftarrow r(x), \neg q(x); 0.6; I_G$.
3. $q(x) \leftarrow r(x); 0.5; I_G$.
4. $p(x) \leftarrow q(x); 0.8; I_G$.

The result depends on the evaluation order. If it is 1., 2., 3., 4., then

$$lfp(NT_P) = \{(r(a), 0.8), (p(a), 0.6), (q(a), 0.5)\},$$

while in the order 1., 3., 2., 4.

$$lfp(NT_P) = \{(r(a), 0.8), (p(a), 0.5), (q(a), 0.5)\}.$$

According to the above examples, in the case of programs containing negation there are problems with the model's minimality. However, the nondeterministic semantics – $lfp(NT_P)$ – is minimal under certain conditions. These conditions are referred to as stratification. Stratification gives an evaluating sequence in which the literals are evaluated before negating them.

## 2.1.2 Stratified fuzzy datalog

To stratify a program, it is necessary to define the concept of dependency graph. This is a directed graph, whose nodes are the predicates of $P$. There is an arc from predicate $p$ to predicate $q$ if there is a rule whose body contains $p$ or $\neg p$ and whose head predicate is $q$. A program is recursive, if its dependency graph has one or more cycles. A program is stratified if whenever there is a rule with head predicate $p$ and a negated body literal $\neg q$, there is no path in the dependency graph from $p$ to $q$.

The stratification of a program $P$ is a partition of the predicate symbols of $P$ into subsets $P_1,..., P_n$ such that the following conditions are satisfied:

a/ if $p \in P_i$ and $q \in P_j$ and there is an edge from $q$ to $p$ then $i \geq j$;

b/ if $p \in P_i$ and $q \in P_j$ and there is a rule with the head $p$ whose body contains $\neg q$, then $i > j$.

Stratification specifies an order of evaluation. The rules whose head-predicates are in $P_1$ are evaluated first, then those whose head-predicates are in $P_2$ and so on. The sets $P_1,..., P_n$ are called the strata of the stratification. A program $P$ is called stratified if and only if it admits stratification. There is a very simple method for finding stratification for a stratified program in (Ceri et al 1990, Ullman 1988). Because this algorithm groups the predicates of the program, this is suitable for the fDATALOG programs as well.

The first of the following Datalog programs is not stratified, the other one has more distinct stratifications.

**Example 4.** Consider the one-rule program:

$$p(x) \leftarrow \neg p(x).$$

This is not stratified.

The next program has more stratification (Abiteboul et al 1995):

1.  $s(x) \leftarrow r_1(x), \neg r(x).$
2.  $t(x) \leftarrow r_2(x), \neg r(x).$
3.  $u(x) \leftarrow r_3(x), \neg t(x).$
4.  $v(x) \leftarrow r_4(x), \neg s(x), \neg u(x).$

The program has five distinct stratifications, namely:

$$\{1.\}, \{2.\}, \{3.\}, \{4.\}$$
$$\{2.\}, \{1.\}, \{3.\}, \{4.\}$$
$$\{2.\}, \{3.\}, \{1.\}, \{4.\}$$
$$\{1., 2.\}, \{3.\}, \{4.\}$$
$$\{2.\}, \{1., 3.\}, \{4.\}$$

These lead to five different ways of reading the program. As will be seen later, each of them yields the same semantics.

Let $P$ be a stratified fDATALOG program with stratification $P_1, ..., P_n$. Let $P_i^*$ denote the set of all rules of $P$ corresponding to stratum $P_i$, that is the set of all rules whose head-predicate is in $P_i$. Let

$$L_1 = lfp(NT_{P_1^*}),$$

where the starting point of the computation is $T_0$ defined earlier.

$$L_2 = lfp\,(NT_{P_2^*}),$$

where the starting point of the computing is $L_1$.

$$L_n = lfp\,(NT_{P_n^*}),$$

where the starting point is $L_{n-1}$.

In other words: the least fixed point - $L_1$ - corresponding to the first stratum of $P$ is computed at first. Once this fixed point has been computed, we can take a step to the next strata.

By induction it will be shown that $L_n$ is a minimal model of $P$. For this purpose, we need the next definition and lemma.

**Definition 5.** An fDATALOG program $P$ is semi-positive if its negated predicates are solely facts.

**Lemma 1.** A semi-positive program $P$ has a minimal model: $L = lfp(NT_P)$.

**Proof.** A semi-positive program is almost the same as a positive one, because if $p$ is a negated predicate of a rule-body, then it can be replaced by the fact q = $\neg$p. As p is a fact predicate, therefore the uncertainty level of q may be easily calculated. So the negation can be eliminated from the program and this program has a least fixed point which is the least model.

According to the lemma, $L_1$ is the least fixed point for $P_1^*$. Generally $L_{i-1} \cup P_i^*$ is semi-positive, because according to the stratification each negative literal of the i-th strata belongs to a predicate of a lower level strata. So $L_i$ is the least fixed point for $P_i^*$, which is minimal model for the given stratification. Therefore the next theorem is true:

**Theorem 2.** If $P$ is a stratified fDATALOG program then $L_n$ is a minimal model of $P$.

This means that evaluating the rules in the order of stratification, the least fixed point of the program's nondeterministic transformation is the minimal model of the program as well. So:

**Proposition 3.** For stratified fDATALOG program $P$, there is an evaluation sequence, in which $lfp(NT_P)$ is a minimal model of $P$.

As shown in Example 4, a program can have more then one stratification. Will the different stratifications yield the same semantics? Fortunately, the answer is yes. (Ceri et al 1990) declares, (Abiteboul et al 1995) proves the theorem, according to which for stratified Datalog programs the resulting minimal model is independent of the actual stratification. That is, two stratifications of a Datalog program yield the same semantics on all inputs. As the order of stratification depends only on the predicates of the program and it is not influenced by the uncertainty levels, therefore this theorem is true in the case of fDATALOG programs as well.

**Theorem 3.** Let $P$ be a stratifiable fDATALOG program. The least fixed point according to an arbitrary order of stratification is a unique minimal model of the program.

**Example 5.** In Example 3. the right stratified order is 1., 3., 2., 4.; so the least fixed point of the program is: $lfp(NT_P) = \{(r(a), 0.8), (p(a), 0.5), (q(a), 0.5)\}$.

## 2.2 Multivalued datalog

In fuzzy theory, uncertainty is measured by a single value between zero and one, and negation can be calculated as its complement to 1. However, human beings sometimes hesitate expressing these values, that is, there may be some hesitation degree. This illuminates a well-known psychological fact that linguistic negation does not always correspond to the logical one. Based on this observation, as a generalization of fuzzy sets, the concept of intuitionistic fuzzy sets was introduced and developed by Atanassov in 1983 and later (Atanassov 1983, 1999, Atanassov & Gargov 1989). In the next paragraphs some possible multivalued extensions of Datalog will be discussed.

### 2.2.1 Intuitionistic- and interval-valued extensions of datalog

In intuitionistic fuzzy systems (IFS) and interval-valued systems (IVS) the uncertainty is represented by two values, $\underline{\mu} = (\mu_1, \mu_2)$ instead of a single one. In the intuitionistic case the two elements must satisfy the condition $\mu_1 + \mu_2 \leq 1$, while in the interval-valued case the condition is $\mu_1 \leq \mu_2$. If $\underline{\mu} = (\mu_1, \mu_2)$ belonging to a predicate $p$ is an IFS level, then $p$ is definitely true on level $\mu_1$ and definitely false on level $\mu_2$, while in IVS the truth value is between $\mu_1$ and $\mu_2$. It is obvious that the relation $\mu'_1 = \mu_1$, $\mu'_2 = 1 - \mu_2$ creates a mutual connection between the two systems. (The equivalence of IVS and IFS was stated first in (Atanassov & Gargov 1989).)

The fixed point theory of programming is based on the theory of lattices. So does the theory of fuzzy Datalog as well, which is based on the lattice of fuzzy sets. The extension of the programs into an intuitionistic and interval-valued direction needs the extension of lattices as well.

**Definition 6.** $L_F$ and $L_V$ are lattices of IFS and IVS respectively, where

$$L_F = \{(x_1, x_2) \in [0,1]^2 \mid x_1 + x_2 \leq 1\},\ (x_1, x_2) \leq_F (y_1, y_2) \Leftrightarrow x_1 \leq y_1 \text{ and } x_2 \geq y_2,$$

$$L_V = \{(x_1, x_2) \in [0,1]^2 \mid x_1 \leq x_2\},\ (x_1, x_2) \leq_V (y_1, y_2) \Leftrightarrow x_1 \leq y_1 \text{ and } x_2 \leq y_2$$

It can be proved that both $L_F$ and $L_V$ are complete lattices (Cornelis et al 2004), so it can be the base of intuitionistic Datalog (ifDATALOG) and interval-valued Datalog (ivDATALOG) as well. (If the distinction is not important, both of them will be denoted by iDATALOG.)

The so called i-extended DATALOG is defined on these lattices, and the necessary concepts are generalizations of the ones presented in Definition 1 and Definition 2. Let us continue to denote by $B_P$ the Herbrand base of the program $P$, and let $FV(B_P)$ the set of all IFS or IVS sets over $B_P$.

**Definition 7.** The i-extended Datalog program (iDATALOG) is a finite set of safe iDATALOG rules $r$; $\underline{\beta}$; $\underline{I}_{FV}$;

- the i-extended consequence transformation $iNT_P : FV(B_P) \to FV(B_P)$ is formally the same as $NT_P$ in (1) except:

$$\underline{\alpha}_A = max_{FV} (\underline{0}_{FV}, min_{FV}\{\gamma \mid \underline{I}_{FV}(\underline{\alpha}_{body}, \underline{\gamma}) \geq_{FV} \underline{\beta}\});$$

- the i-extended uncertainty-level function is

$$f(\underline{I}_{FV}, \underline{\alpha}, \underline{\beta}) = min_{FV}(\{\gamma \mid \underline{I}_{FV}(\underline{\alpha}, \gamma) \geq_{FV} \underline{\beta}\}),$$

where $\underline{\alpha}$, $\underline{\beta}$, $\gamma$ are elements of $L_F$, $L_V$ respectively, $\underline{I}_{FV} = \underline{I}_F$ or $\underline{I}_V$ is an implication of $L_F$ or $L_V$; $max_{FV} = max_F$ or $max_V$; $min_{FV} = min_F$ or $min_V$ are the max or min operator of $L_F$ or $L_V$; $\underline{0}_{FV}$ is $\underline{0}_F = (0,1)$ or $\underline{0}_V = (0,0)$ and $\geq_{FV}$ is $\geq_F$ or $\geq_V$.

As $iNT_P$ is inflationary transformation over the complete lattices $L_F$ or $L_V$, thus according to (Ceri et al 1990) it has an inflationary fixed point denoted by $lfp(iNT_P)$. If $P$ is positive (without negation), $iNT_P$ is a monotone transformation, so $lfp(iNT_P)$ is the least fixed point.

The next question is whether this fixed point is a model of $P$. The fixed point is an interpretation of $P$, which is a model, if for each

$$A \leftarrow A_1,\ldots, A_n; \underline{\beta}; \underline{I}_{FV} \in ground(P), \underline{I}_{FV}(\underline{\alpha}, \underline{\gamma}) \geq_{FV} \underline{\beta}.$$

Similarly to the proof of Theorem 1, it can easily be proved that this fixed point is a model of the program. For negation-free iDATALOG this is the least model of the program. (Achs 2010).

In fDATALOG a fact can be negated by completing its membership degree to 1. In iDATALOG the uncertainty level of a negated fact can be computed according to negators. A negator on $L_F$ or $L_V$ is a decreasing mapping ordering $\underline{0}_{FV}$ and $\underline{1}_{FV}$ together (Cornelis et al 2004). The applied negators are relevant for the computational meaning of a program, but they have no influence on the stratification. So for a stratified iDATALOG program $P$ there is an evaluation sequence in which $lfp(iNT_P)$ is a unique minimal model of $P$. Therefore $lfp(iNT_P)$ can be regarded as the semantics of iDATALOG.

After defining the syntax and semantics of extended fuzzy Datalog, it is necessary to examine the properties of possible implication operators and the extended uncertainty-level functions. A number of intuitionistic implications are discussed in (Cornelis et al 2004, Atanassov 2005, 2006) and other papers, four of them are the extensions of the above three fuzzy implication operators. Now these operators will be presented and completed by the suitable interval-value operators and the uncertainty-level functions. The computations will not be shown here, only the starting points and results are presented.

The coordinates of intuitionistic and interval-valued implication operators can be determined by each other. The uncertainty-level functions can be computed according to the applied implication. The connection between $\underline{I}_F$ and $\underline{I}_V$ and the extended versions of uncertainty-level functions are given below: For

$$\underline{I}_V(\underline{\alpha}, \underline{\gamma}) = (I_{V1}, I_{V2});$$

$$I_{V1}=I_{F1}(\underline{\alpha}',\underline{\gamma}'); \qquad \underline{\alpha}'=(\alpha_1, 1-\alpha_2);$$

$$I_{V2}=1-I_{F2}(\underline{\alpha}',\underline{\gamma}'); \qquad \underline{\gamma}'=(\gamma_1, 1-\gamma_2).$$

$$\underline{f}(\underline{I}_F, \underline{\alpha}, \underline{\beta}) = (min(\{ \gamma_1 \mid I_{F1}(\underline{\alpha}, \underline{\gamma}) \geq \beta_1 \}), max(\{ \gamma_2 \mid I_{F2}(\underline{\alpha}, \underline{\gamma}) \leq \beta_2 \}))$$

$$\underline{f}(\underline{I}_V, \underline{\alpha}, \underline{\beta}) = (min(\{ \gamma_1 \mid I_{V1}(\underline{\alpha}, \underline{\gamma}) \geq \beta_1 \}), min(\{ \gamma_2 \mid I_{V2}(\underline{\alpha}, \underline{\gamma}) \geq \beta_2 \}))$$

The studied operators and the related uncertainty-level functions are the following:

### 2.2.1.1 Extension of Kleene-dienes implication

One possible extension of Kleene-Dienes implication for IFS is:

$$\underline{I}_{FK}(\underline{\alpha}, \underline{\gamma}) = (max(\alpha_2, \gamma_1), min(\alpha_1, \gamma_2))$$

The appropriate computed elements are the following:

$$\underline{I}_{VK}(\underline{\alpha}, \underline{\gamma}) = (max(1-\alpha_2, \gamma_1), max(1-\alpha_1, \gamma_2))$$

$$f_1(\underline{I}_{FK}, \underline{\alpha}, \underline{\beta}) = \begin{cases} 0 & \alpha_2 \geq \beta_1 \\ \beta_1 & \text{otherwise} \end{cases} \qquad f_2(\underline{I}_{FK}, \underline{\alpha}, \underline{\beta}) = \begin{cases} 1 & \alpha_1 \leq \beta_2 \\ \beta_2 & \text{otherwise} \end{cases}$$

$$f_1(\underline{I}_{VK}, \underline{\alpha}, \underline{\beta}) = \begin{cases} 0 & 1 - \alpha_2 \geq \beta_1 \\ \beta_1 & \text{otherwise} \end{cases} \qquad f_2(\underline{I}_{VK}, \underline{\alpha}, \underline{\beta}) = \begin{cases} 0 & 1 - \alpha_1 \geq \beta_2 \\ \beta_2 & \text{otherwise} \end{cases}$$

### 2.2.1.2 Extension of Lukasiewicz implication

One possible extension of Lukasiewicz implication for IFS is:

$$\underline{I}_{FL}(\underline{\alpha}, \underline{\gamma}) = (min(\alpha_2, \gamma_1), min(\alpha_1, \gamma_2))$$

The appropriate computed elements are as follows:

$$\underline{I}_{VL}(\underline{\alpha}, \underline{\gamma}) = (max(1, \alpha_2 + \gamma_1), max(0, \alpha_1 + \gamma_2 - 1))$$

$$f_1(\underline{I}_{FL}, \underline{\alpha}, \underline{\beta}) = min(1 - \alpha_2, max(0, \beta_1 - \alpha_2))$$

$$f_2(\underline{I}_{FL}, \underline{\alpha}, \underline{\beta}) = max(1 - \alpha_1, min(1, 1 - \alpha_1 + \beta_2))$$

$$f_1(\underline{I}_{VL}, \underline{\alpha}, \underline{\beta}) = max(0, \alpha_2 + \beta_1 - 1)$$

$$f_2(\underline{I}_{VL}, \underline{\alpha}, \underline{\beta}) = max(0, \alpha_1 + \beta_2 - 1)$$

### 2.2.1.3 Extensions of Gödel implication

There are several alternative extensions of Gödel implication, two of them are presented here:

$$\underline{I}_{FG1}(\underline{\alpha}, \underline{\gamma}) = \begin{cases} (1,0) & \alpha_1 \leq \gamma_1 \\ (\gamma_1, 0) & \alpha_1 > \gamma_1, \alpha_2 \geq \gamma_2 \\ (\gamma_1, \gamma_2) & \alpha_1 > \gamma_1, \alpha_2 < \gamma_2 \end{cases} \qquad \underline{I}_{FG2}(\underline{\alpha}, \underline{\gamma}) = \begin{cases} (1,0) & \alpha_1 \leq \gamma_1, \alpha_2 \geq \gamma_2 \\ (\gamma_1, \gamma_2) & \text{otherwise} \end{cases}$$

The appropriate computed elements are:

$$\underline{I}_{VG1}(\underline{\alpha}, \underline{\gamma}) = \begin{cases} (1,1) & \alpha_1 \leq \gamma_1 \\ (\gamma_1, 1) & \alpha_1 > \gamma_1, \alpha_2 \geq \gamma_2 \\ (\gamma_1, \gamma_2) & \alpha_1 > \gamma_1, \alpha_2 < \gamma_2 \end{cases} \qquad \underline{I}_{VG2}(\underline{\alpha}, \underline{\gamma}) = \begin{cases} (1,1) & \alpha_1 \leq \gamma_1, \alpha_2 \leq \gamma_2 \\ (\gamma_1, \gamma_2) & \text{otherwise} \end{cases}$$

$$f_1(\underline{I}_{FG1}, \underline{\alpha}, \underline{\beta}) = min(\alpha_1, \beta_1)$$

$$f_2(\underline{I}_{FG1}, \underline{\alpha}, \underline{\beta}) = \begin{cases} 1 & \alpha_1 \leq \beta_2 \\ max(\alpha_2, \beta_2) & \text{otherwise} \end{cases}$$

$$f_1(\underline{I}_{VG1}, \underline{\alpha}, \underline{\beta}) = min(\alpha_1, \beta_1)$$

$$f_2(\underline{I}_{VG1}, \underline{\alpha}, \underline{\beta}) = \begin{cases} 0 & \alpha_1 \leq \beta_2 \\ min(\alpha_2, \beta_2) & \text{otherwise} \end{cases}$$

$$f_1(\underline{I}_{FG2}, \underline{\alpha}, \underline{\beta}) = min(\alpha_1, \beta_1)$$

$$f_2(\underline{I}_{FG2}, \underline{\alpha}, \underline{\beta}) = max(\alpha_2, \beta_2)$$

$$f_1(\underline{I}_{VG2}, \underline{\alpha}, \underline{\beta}) = min(\alpha_1, \beta_1)$$

$$f_2(\underline{I}_{VG2}, \underline{\alpha}, \underline{\beta}) = min(\alpha_2, \beta_2)$$

An important question is whether the resulting degrees satisfy the conditions referring to IFS and IVS respectively. Unfortunately, for implications other than $G_2$, the answer is "no", or rather "not in all cases". For example, in the case of the Kleene-Dienes and the Lukasiewicz intuitionistic operators the levels of a rule-head satisfy the condition of intuitionism only if the sum of the levels of the rule-body is at least as large as the sum of the levels of the rule. That is, the solution is inside the scope of IFS, if the level of the rule-body is less "intuitionistic" than the level of the rule. In the case of the first Gödel operator, the solution is inside the scope of IFS only if the level of the rule-body is more certain than the level of the rule (Achs 2010). However, for the second Gödel operator the next proposition can easily be proven:

**Proposition 4.** For $\underline{\alpha} = (\alpha_1, \alpha_2)$, $\underline{\beta} = (\beta_1, \beta_2)$

$$if\ \alpha_1 + \alpha_2 \leq 1,\ \beta_1 + \beta_2 \leq 1\ then\ f_1(\underline{I}_{FG2},\ \underline{\alpha},\ \underline{\beta}) + f_2(\underline{I}_{FG2},\ \underline{\alpha},\ \underline{\beta}) \leq 1$$

$$if\ \alpha_1 \leq \alpha_2,\ \beta_1 \leq \beta_2\ then\ f_1(\underline{I}_{VG2},\ \underline{\alpha},\ \underline{\beta}) \leq f_2(\underline{I}_{VG2},\ \underline{\alpha},\ \underline{\beta})$$

Similarly to Proposition 2, it can be seen that the fixed-point algorithm terminates if $\underline{f}(\underline{I}_{FV},\ \underline{\alpha},\ \underline{\beta}) \leq_{FV} \underline{\alpha}$ for each $\underline{\alpha} \in L_{FV}$ (Achs 2010). G2 satisfies this condition, so:

**Proposition 5.** In the case of G2 operator the fixed-point algorithm terminates.

### 2.2.2 Bipolar extension of datalog

The intuitive background of intuitionistic levels is some psychological perception. Experiments have shown that when making decisions people deal with positive and negative facts in different ways (Dubois et al 2000, 2005). Continuing this idea, it can be stated that there would be differences not only in the scaling of truth values, but in the way of concluding as well. This means that in a way similar to the facts, positive and negative inferences can be separated. The idea of bipolar Datalog is based on the above observation: two kinds of ordinary fuzzy implications are used for positive and negative deduction, namely, a pair of consequence transformations is defined instead of a single one. Since in the original transformations lower bounds are used with degrees of uncertainty, therefore starting from IFS or IVS facts, the resulting degrees will be lower bounds of membership and non-membership respectively, instead of the upper bound for non-membership. However, if each non-membership value $\mu$ is transformed into membership value $\mu' = 1 - \mu$, then both members of head-level can be deduced similarly. So the appropriate concepts are as follows.

**Definition 8.** The bipolar Datalog program (bDATALOG) defined on $L_F$ or $L_V$ is a finite set of safe bDATALOG rules $r$; $(\beta_1, \beta_2)$; $(I_1, I_2)$.

The elements of the bipolar nondeterministic consequence transformation $bNT_P = (NT_{P1}, NT_{P2})$ are similar to $NT_P$ in (1) except in $NT_{P2}$ the level of rule's head is:

$$\alpha'_2 = max_{FV2}\ (0,\ min_{FV2}\ \{\gamma'_2\ |\ I_2(\alpha'_{body2},\ \gamma'_2) \geq \beta'_2\});$$

where $\alpha'_{body2} = min_{FV2}\ (\alpha'_{A_12}, \ldots, \alpha'_{A_n2})$.

The uncertainty-level function is: $\underline{f} = (f_1, f_2)$ where

$$f_1 = min_{FV2}\ (\{\gamma_1\ |\ I_1(\alpha_1,\ \gamma_1) \geq \beta_1\});$$

$$f_2 = 1 - min_{FV2} (\{1 - \gamma_2 \mid I_2(1 - \alpha_2, 1 - \gamma_2) \geq 1 - \beta_2\}).$$

It is evident that applying the transformation $\mu'_1 = \mu_1$, $\mu'_2 = 1 - \mu_2$, for all IFS levels of the program, the above definition can be applied to IVS degrees as well. As a simple computation can show, contrary to the results of iDATALOG, the resulting degrees for most variants of bipolar Datalog satisfy the conditions referring to IFS:

**Proposition 5.** For $\underline{\alpha} = (\alpha_1, \alpha_2)$, $\underline{\beta} = (\beta_1, \beta_2)$ and for implication-pairs $\underline{I} = (I_G, I_G)$; $\underline{I} = (I_L, I_L)$; $\underline{I} = (I_L, I_G)$; $\underline{I} = (I_K, I_K)$; $\underline{I} = (I_L, I_K)$;

$$\text{if } \alpha_1 + \alpha_2 \leq 1, \beta_1 + \beta_2 \leq 1 \text{ then } f_1(I_1, \underline{\alpha}, \underline{\beta}) + f_2(I_2, \underline{\alpha}, \underline{\beta}) \leq 1$$

From the construction of bipolar consequence transformations follows:

**Proposition 6.** The nondeterministic bipolar consequence transformation has a least fixed point, which is a model of program $P$ in the following sense: for each $A \leftarrow A_1,...,A_n$; $\underline{\beta}$; $\underline{I} \in ground(P)$

$$I(\alpha_{body1}, \alpha_1) \geq \beta_1; I(\alpha'_{body2}, \alpha'_2) \geq \beta'_2$$

As the termination of the consequence transformations based on these three implication operators was proven in the case of fDATALOG (Achs 2006) and since this property does not change in bipolar case, the bipolar consequence transformations terminate as well.

The bipolar extension of Datalog has no influence on the stratification, so the propositions detailed in the case of stratified fDATALOG programs are true in the case of bipolar fuzzy Datalog programs as well, that is, for a stratified bDATALOG program $P$, there is an evaluation sequence, in which $lfp(bNT_P)$ is a unique minimal model of $P$.

**Example 6.** Consider the next IFS program:

$$(p(a), (0.7, 0.2)).$$
$$(q(b), (0.65, 0.3)).$$
$$(r(a, b), (0.7, 0.2)).$$
$$r(x, y) \leftarrow p(x), q(y); (0.75, 0.2); \underline{I}.$$

Let $\underline{I} = \underline{I}_{FG2}$, then according to the rule r(a,b) is inferred and uncertainty can be computed as follows: $\alpha_{body} = min_F((0.7, 0.2), (0.65, 0.3)) = (0.65, 0.3)$, $f_1(\underline{I}_{FG2}, \underline{\alpha}, \underline{\beta}) = min(\alpha_1, \beta_1) = min(0.65, 0.75) = 0.65$, $f_2(\underline{I}_{FG2}, \underline{\alpha}, \underline{\beta}) = max(\alpha_2, \beta_2) = 0.3$, that is, the level of the rule's head is (0.65, 0.3). There is a fact for r(a,b) as well, so the resulting level is the union of the level of the rule's head and the level of the fact: $max_F ((0.65, 0.3), (0.7, 0.2)) = (0.7, 0.2)$. So the fixed point of the program is:

$$\{(p(a), (0.7, 0.2)), (q(b), (0.65, 0.3)), (r(a, b), (0.7, 0.2)) \}.$$

Let us see the bipolar evaluation of the program. Let $\underline{I} = (I_L, I_G)$. That is let the first element of the uncertainty level be computed according to the Lukasiewicz operator and the second one according to the Gödel operator. The Lukasiewicz operator defines the uncertainty level function $f (I_L, \alpha, \beta) = max(0, \alpha + \beta - 1)$. Then $\alpha_{body1} = min(0.7, 0.65) = 0.65$, $\alpha'_{body2} = min(1 - 0.3, 1 - 0.2) = 0.7$; $f_1(I_L, \alpha_1, \beta_1) = max(0, \alpha_1 + \beta_1 - 1) = 0.65 + 0.75 - 1 = 0.4$, $f_2(I_G, \alpha'_2, \beta'_2) = 1 - $

$min(\alpha'_2, 1-\beta_2) = 1 - min(0.7, 0.8) = 0.3$. So the uncertainty level of rule's head is $(0.4, 0.3)$. Considering the other level of $r(a,b)$, its resulting level is $(max(0.4, 0.7), 1-max(1-0.3, 1-0.2)) = (0.7, 0.2)$, so the fixed point is:

$$\{(p(a), (0.7, 0.2)), (q(b), (0.65, 0.3)), (r(a,b), (0.7, 0.2)) \}.$$

**Example 7.** Consider the next (recursive) IVS program:

$$p(a, b), (0.7, 0.8)).$$
$$p(a, c), (0.8, 0.9)).$$
$$p(b, d), (0.75, 0.8)).$$
$$p(d, e), (0.9, 0.95)).$$
$$q(x, y) \leftarrow p(x, y); (0.85, 0.95); I_1.$$
$$q(x, y) \leftarrow p(x, z), q(z, y); (0.8, 0.9); I_2.$$

Let $I_1 = I_{VG2}$, $I_2 = I_{VL}$, that is the appropriate uncertainty level functions are:

$$f_1(I_{VG2}, \alpha, \beta) = min(\alpha_1, \beta_1) \qquad\qquad f_2(I_{VG2}, \alpha, \beta) = min(\alpha_2, \beta_2)$$

$$f_1(I_{VL}, \alpha, \beta) = max(0, \alpha_2+ \beta_1 -1) \qquad f_2(I_{VL}, \alpha, \beta) = max(0, \alpha_1+ \beta_2 -1)$$

Before showing the fixed point algorithm, two computations are set out. According to the first rule for $q(x, y)$ the uncertainty level of $q(a, b)$ is: $f(I_{VG2}, \alpha, \beta) = (min(\alpha_1, \beta_1), min(\alpha_2, \beta_2)) = (min(0.7, 0.85), min(0.8, 0.95)) = (0.7, 0.8)$.

According to the second rule, the uncertainty of $q(a, d)$ can be computed in this way:

The body of the rule is: $p(a, b)$, $q(b, d)$, so $\alpha_{body} = min((0.7, 0.8),(0.75, 0.8)) =(0.7, 0.8)$; $f(I_{VL}, \alpha, \beta) =( max(0, \alpha_2+ \beta_1 -1), max(0, \alpha_1+ \beta_2 -1) = (max(0, 0.8 + 0.8-1), max(0, 0.7 + 0.9 - 1)) = (0.6, 0.6)$.

The steps of fixed point algorithm are:

$$X_0 = \{(p(a, b), (0.7, 0.8)), (p(a, c), (0.8, 0.9)), (p(b, d), (0.75, 0.8)), (p(d, e), (0.9, 0.95))\}$$
$$X_1 = X_0 \cup \{ (q(a, b), (0.7, 0.8)), (q(a, c), (0.8, 0.9)), (q(b, d), (0.75, 0.8)), (q(d, e), (0.85, 0.95)),$$
$$(q(a, d), (0.6, 0.6), (q(b, e), (0.6, 0.65)) \}$$
$$X_2 = X_1 \cup \{ (q(a, e), (0.45, 0.5)) \}$$

$X_2$ is fixed point, so it is the result of the program.

As fuzzy Datalog is a special kind of its multivalued extensions, so further on both fDATALOG and any of above extensions will be called multivalued Datalog (mDATALOG).

## 3. Multivalued knowledge-base

The facts of an mDATALOG program can be regarded as any kind of lexical knowledge including uncertainty as well, and from this knowledge other facts can be deduced according to the rules. Therefore a multivalued Datalog program is suitable to be the deduction mechanism of a knowledge base. Sometimes, however, it is not enough for getting answer to a question. For example, if there are rules describing the options of loving a good composer, and there is a fact declaring that Vivaldi is a good composer, what is the possible answer to the question inquiring about liking Bach? Getting an answer needs the use of synonyms and similarities. For handling this kind of information, our model includes a background knowledge module.

## 3.1 Background knowledge

Some "synonyms" and "similarities" will be defined between the potential predicates and between the potential constants of a given problem, so it can be examined in a larger context. More precisely, proximity relations will be defined on the sets of the program's predicates and terms. These relations will serve as the basis for the background knowledge.

**Definition 9.** A multivalued proximity on a domain $D$ is an IFS or IVS valued relation $\underline{R}_{FV_D}$ : $D \times D \rightarrow [\underline{0}_{FV}, \underline{1}_{FV}]$ which satisfies the following properties:

$$\underline{R}_{F_D}(x, y) = \underline{\lambda}_F(x, y) = (\lambda_1, \lambda_2), \quad \lambda_1 + \lambda_2 \leq 1$$
$$\underline{R}_{V_D}(x, y) = \underline{\lambda}_V(x, y) = (\lambda_1, \lambda_2), \quad 0 \leq \lambda_1 \leq \lambda_2 \leq 1$$
$$\underline{R}_{FV_D}(x, y) = \underline{1}_{FV} \quad \forall x \in D \quad \text{(reflexivity)}$$
$$\underline{R}_{FV_D}(x, y) = R_{FV_D}(y, x) \quad \forall x \in D \quad \text{(symmetry)}.$$

A proximity is similarity if it is transitive, that is

$$\underline{R}_{FV_D}(x, z) \geq_{FV} min_{FV} (\underline{R}_{FV_D}(x, y), \underline{R}_{FV_D}(y, x)) \quad \forall x, y, z \in D.$$

In the case of similarity, equivalence classifications can be defined over $D$. The effect of this classification is perhaps a simpler or more effective algorithm, but in many cases the requirement of similarity is a too strict constraint. Therefore this chapter deals only with the more general proximity.

Background knowledge consists of the "synonyms" of each terms and each predicates of the program. The "synonyms" of any element form the proximity set of the element, and all of the proximity sets compose the background knowledge. More precisely:

**Definition 10.** Let $d \in D$ any element of domain $D$. The proximity set of $d$ is an IFS or IVS subset over $D$:

$$\mathcal{R}_{FV_d} = \{(d_1, \underline{\lambda}_{FV_1}), (d_2, \underline{\lambda}_{FV_2}), \dots (d_n, \underline{\lambda}_{FV_n})\},$$

where $d_i \in D$ and $\underline{\lambda}_{FV_i} = \underline{R}_{FV_D}(d, d_i)$ for $i = 1, \dots, n$.

**Definition 11.** Let $G$ be any set of ground terms and $S$ any set of predicate symbols. Let $\underline{RG}_{FV_G}$ and $\underline{RS}_{FV_S}$ be any proximity over $G$ and $S$ respectively. The background knowledge is the set of proximity sets:

$$Bk = \{\mathcal{RG}_{FV_g} \mid g \in G\} \cup \{\mathcal{RS}_{FV_s} \mid s \in S\}$$

## 3.2 Computing uncertainties

Up to now, the deduction mechanism and the background knowledge of a multivalued knowledge-base have been defined. Now, the question remains: how can the two parts be connected to each other? How can we find the "synonyms"? For example, if it is known that

Ann loves the music of Bach very much $((love(Ann, Bach), (0.9, 0.95)))$ and the concept of love is similar to the concept of like $(\underline{RS}_{VS} ("love", "like") = (0.8, 0.9))$ and the music of Bach is more or less similar to the music of Vivaldi $(\underline{RG}_{VG} (Bach, Vivaldi) = (0.7, 0.75))$ then how strongly can be stated that Ann likes Vivaldi, that is, what is the uncertainty of the predicate *like(Ann, Vivaldi)*?

To solve this problem, the concept of proximity-based uncertainty function will be introduced. According to this function, the uncertainty levels of "synonyms" can be computed from the levels of original fact and from the proximity values of actual predicates and its arguments. It is expectable that in the case of identity, the level must be unchanged, but in other cases it is should be equal or less than the original level or than the proximity values. Furthermore, this function is required to increase monotonically. This function will be ordered to each atom of a program.

Let $p$ be a predicate symbol with $n$ arguments, then $p/n$ is called the functor of the atom, characterized by this predicate symbol.

**Definition 12.** A proximity-based uncertainty function of $p/n$ is:

$$\varnothing_p(\alpha, \lambda, \lambda_1, ..., \lambda_n) : (\underline{0}_{FV}, \underline{1}_{FV}]^{n+2} \rightarrow [\underline{0}_{FV}, \underline{1}_{FV}]$$

where

$$\varnothing_p(\alpha, \lambda, \lambda_1, ..., \lambda_n) \leq min_{FV} (\alpha, \lambda, \lambda_1, ..., \lambda_n)$$

$$\varnothing_p(\alpha, \underline{1}_{FV}, \underline{1}_{FV}, ..., \underline{1}_{FV}) = \alpha$$

and $\varnothing_p(\alpha, \lambda, \lambda_1, ..., \lambda_n)$ is monotonically increasing in each argument.

Any triangular norm obeys the above constraints so they are appropriate proximity-based uncertainty functions.

**Example 8.** Let $(p(a), (0.7, 0.2))$ be an *IFS* fact and $\underline{RS}_{FS}(p, q) = (0.8, 0.1)$, $\underline{RG}_{FG}(a, b) = (0.7, 0.3)$ and $\varnothing_p(\alpha, \lambda, \lambda_1) = min_F(\alpha, \lambda \cdot \lambda_1)$.

(In IFS the product is defined as: $\mu \cdot \lambda = (\mu_1 \lambda_1, 1-(1-\mu_2) \cdot (1-\lambda_2))$.)

The uncertainty levels of $p(b)$, $q(a)$ and $q(b)$ are:

$(p(b), (min((0.7, 0.2), ((1, 0) \cdot (0.7, 0.3))) = (min(0.7, 0.7), max(0.2, 0.3)) = (0.7, 0.3));$

$(q(a), (min((0.7, 0.2), ((0.8, 0.1) \cdot (1, 0))) = (min(0.7, 0.8), max(0.2, 0.1)) = (0.7, 0.2));$

$(q(b), (min((0.7, 0.2), ((0.8, 0.1) \cdot (0.7, 0.3))) = (min(0.7, 0.56), max(0.2, 0.37)) = (0.56, 0.37));$

**Example 9.** Let $(love(Ann, Bach), (0.9, 0.95))$ be an *IVS* fact and $\underline{RS}_{VS}("love", "like") = (0.8, 0.9)$, $\underline{RG}_{VG} (Bach, Vivaldi) = (0.7, 0.75))$ and $\varnothing_{love}(\alpha, \lambda, \lambda_1, \lambda_2) = min_V(\alpha, \lambda, \lambda_1 \cdot \lambda_2)$. Then

$(love(Ann, Vivaldi), (min(0.9, 1, 1 \cdot 0.7), min(0.95, 1, 1 \cdot 0.75) = (0.7, 0.75));$

$(like(Ann, Bach), (min(0.9, 0.8, 1 \cdot 1), min(0.95, 0.9, 1 \cdot 1) = (0.8, 0.9));$

$(like(Ann, Vivaldi), (min(0.9, 0.8, 1 \cdot 0.7), min(0.95, 0.9, 1 \cdot 0.75) = (0.7, 0.75));$

As the above examples show, the levels of "synonyms" can be computed according to proximity-based uncertainty functions. To determine all direct or indirect conclusions of the facts and rules of a program, a proximity based uncertainty function has to be ordered to each predicate of the program. The set of these functions will be the decoding-set of the program.

**Definition 13.** Let $P$ be a multivalued Datalog program, and $F_P$ be the set of the program's functors. The decoding-set of $P$ is: $\Phi_P = \{ \underline{\varphi_p}(\alpha, \lambda, \underline{\lambda_1}, ..., \underline{\lambda_n}) \mid \forall p/n \in F_P \}$.

## 3.3 Deduction with background knowledge

The original deducing mechanism makes conclusions according to the rules of the program, but from now on the background knowledge must be considered as well. So the original mechanism has to be modified. This modified deduction consists of two alternating parts: starting from the facts, their "synonyms" are determined, then applying the suitable rules, other facts are derived, followed by their "synonyms" determined, and again the rules are applied, etc. To define it in a precise manner the concept of modified consecution transformation will be introduced.

The consequence transformation of a mDATALOG $P$ program is defined over the set of all multivalued sets of $P$'s Herbrand base, that is, over $FV(B_P)$. To define the modified transformation's domain, let us extend $P$'s Herbrand universe with all possible ground terms of the background knowledge, obtaining the so called modified Herbrand universe, $modH_P$. The modified Herbrand base, $modB_P$ is the set of all ground atoms, whose predicate symbols occur in $P \cup Bk$ and whose arguments are elements of $modH_P$.

However, it is possible, that there are some special predicates in $P$, which have no alternatives, even if their arguments have "synonyms". These predicates are named as bound predicates. For such predicates, the modified Herbrand base only includes atoms that are present in the original Herbrand base.

**Definition 14.** The modified consequence transformation $modNT_P : FV(modB_P) \rightarrow FV(modB_P)$ is defined as

$$modNT_P (X) = \{(q(s_1,...,s_n), \ \underline{\varphi_p}(\alpha_p, \lambda_q, \underline{\lambda_{s_1}}, ..., \underline{\lambda_{s_n}}) ) \mid$$

$$(q, \underline{\lambda_q}) \in \underline{RS}_{FV_p}; (s_i, \underline{\lambda_{s_i}}) \in \underline{RG}_{FVt_i}, \ 1 \le i \le n\} \cup X,$$

where

$$(p(t_1,...,t_n) \leftarrow A_1,...,A_k; \underline{\beta}, \underline{l} ) \in ground(P),$$

$$( |A_i|, \underline{\alpha_{A_i}}) \in X, 1 \le i \le k \quad ( |A_i| \ is \ the \ kernel \ of \ A_i)$$

and $\underline{\alpha_p}$ is computed according to the actual extension of (1).

This transformation is inflationary over $FV(modB_P)$ and it is monotone if $P$ is positive. So, according to (Ceri et al 1990) it has a least fixed point. If $P$ is positive, this is the least fixed point. This fixed point is a model of $P$, but because $lfp(NT_P) \subseteq lfp(mod \ NT_P)$, it is not a minimal one (Achs 2010).

The modifying algorithm is irrelevant to the evaluation sequence, so stratification can be applied with the same condition. That is, the modified consequence transformation has a least fixed point in the case of stratified programs as well. This transformation makes connections between an mDATALOG program, the background knowledge and the decoding-set of the program. So these four components can form a knowledge-base. However, there should be other transformations connecting the three other parts with each other, therefore the universal concept of a multivalued knowledge-base can be defined with an arbitrary deduction algorithm:

**Definition 15.** A multivalued knowledge-base ($mKB$) is a quadruple

$$mKB = (P, Bk, \Phi_P, dA(P, Bk, \Phi_P)),$$

where $P$ is a multivalued Datalog program, $Bk$ is a background knowledge, $\Phi_P$ is a decoding-set of $P$ and $dA$ is any deduction algorithm connecting the three other part with each other. The least fixed point of the deduction algorithm is called the consequence of the knowledge-base, denoted by

$$C(Bk, P, \Phi_P, dA) = lfp(dA(P, Bk, \Phi_P)).$$

Because the actual deduction algorithm is the modified consequence transformation, now the consequence is

$$C(Bk, P, \Phi_P, dA) = lfp(modNT_P).$$

Note: If it is important to underline that there are bound predicates in P, then $mKB$ can be denoted by $mKB = (P, Bp, Bk, \Phi_P, dA(P, Bp, Bk, \Phi_P))$, where $Bp$ is the set of bound predicates.

**Example 10.** Let us suppose that an internet agent's job is to send a message to its clients if the cinema ($C$) presents a film, which its clients like. The agent knows that people generally go ($go$) to the cinema if they can pay ($cp$) for the ticket and are interested in ($in$) the film presented ($pr$) in the cinema. It also knows that people usually want to see ($ws$) a film if they like ($li$) its actor ($ac$). Moreover it knows that Paul (P) has enough money ($hm$) and he enjoys ($en$) Chaplin ($Ch$) very much. In the cinema, a film of Stan and Pan ($SP$) is presented. Should the agent inform Paul about this film? How much will he want to go to the cinema?

This situation can be modelled, for example, by the following multivalued knowledge-base.

Let the IVS valued mDATALOG program and the background knowledge be as follows

$$go(x, C) \leftarrow pr(C, f), in(x, f), cp(x); (0.85, 0.95); I_{VL}. \qquad (R1)$$

$$ws(f, x) \leftarrow ac(f, y), li(x, y); (0.8, 0.85); I_{VG_2}. \qquad (R2)$$

$(hm(P), (0.75, 0.8))$.
$(en(P, Ch), (0.9, 0.95))$.

$(pr(C, Film), (1,1))$.
$(ac(Film, SP), (1,1))$.

According to their roll, $pr(C, Film)$ and $ac(Film, SP)$ have no alternatives.

Let the proximities be:

$$\underline{R}_V \ (in, \ ws) = (0.7, 0.8). \qquad \underline{R}_V \ (Ch, \ SP) = (0.8, 0.9).$$

$$\underline{R}_V \ (li, \ en) \ = (0.8, 0.9).$$

$$\underline{R}_V \ (cp, \ hm) = (0.9, 0.95).$$

According to the connecting algorithm, it is enough to consider only the proximity-based uncertainty functions of head-predicates. Let these functions be the minimum function:

$$\mathcal{Q}_{go}(\alpha, \lambda, \lambda_1, \lambda_2) = \mathcal{Q}_{ws}(\alpha, \lambda, \lambda_1, \lambda_2) = \mathcal{Q}_{en}(\alpha, \lambda, \lambda_1, \lambda_2) = \mathcal{Q}_{pr}(\alpha, \lambda, \lambda_1, \lambda_2) = \mathcal{Q}_{ac}(\alpha, \lambda, \lambda_1, \lambda_2) := min_V (\alpha, \lambda, \lambda_1, \lambda_2),$$

$$\mathcal{Q}_{hm}(\alpha, \lambda, \lambda_1) := min_V (\alpha, \lambda, \lambda_1),$$

The modified consequence transformation has the next steps:

$X_0 = \{(hm(P), (0.75, 0.8)), (en(P, Ch), (0.9, 0.95)), (pr(C, Film), (1,1)), (ac(Film, SP), (1,1))\}$

⇓           (according to the proximity)

$X_1 = modNT_P(X_0) = X_0 \cup$
  $\{(cp(P), \mathcal{Q}_{hm}((0.75, 0.8), (0.9, 0.95), (1,1)) = (min(0.75, 0.9, 1), min(0.8, 0.95, 1)) = (0.75, 0.8)),$
  $(en(P, SP), \mathcal{Q}_{en}((0.9, 0.95), (1,1), (1,1), (0.85, 0.9)) = (0.85, 0.9)),$
  $(li(P, Ch), \mathcal{Q}_{en}((0.9, 0.95), (0.8, 0.9), (1,1), (1,1)) = (0.8, 0.9)),$
  $(li(P, SP), \mathcal{Q}_{en}((0.9, 0.95), (0.8, 0.9), (1,1), (0.85, 0.9)) = (0.8, 0.9))\}$

⇓           (applying the rules – only (R2) can be applied)

$X_2 = modNT_P (X_1) = X_1 \cup$
  $\{(ws(Film, P), \underline{f}(\underline{l}_{VG2}, \alpha, \beta) = \underline{f}(\underline{l}_{VG2}, min_V((1,1), (0.8, 0.9)), (0.8, 0.85)) = min_V((0.8, 0.9),(0.8, 0.85)) = (0.8, 0.85)) \}$

⇓           (according to the proximity)

$X_3 = modNT_P (X_2) = X_2 \cup$
  $\{(in(Film, P), \mathcal{Q}_{ws}( (0.8, 0.85), (0.7, 0.8), (1,1), (1,1)) = (0.7, 0.8))\}$

⇓           (applying the rules – (R1) can be applied)

$X_4 = modNT_P (X_3) = X_3 \cup$
  $\{(go(P, C), \underline{f}(\underline{l}_{VL}, \alpha, \beta) = \underline{f}(\underline{l}_{VL}, min_V((1,1), (0.7, 0.8), (0.75, 0.8)), (0.85, 0.95)) = (max(0, 0.8 + 0.85 - 1), max(0, 0.7 + 0.95 - 1)) = (0.65, 0.65))\}$

$X_4$ is a fixed point, so it is the consequence of the knowledgebase.

According to this result, the agent will know that the message can be sent, because Paul will probably enjoy Stan and Pan at a likelihood level of 85-90% (level (0.85, 0.9)), and there is a good chance (65%) that Paul will go to the cinema.

## 4. Evaluating algorithms

The fixed point-query is a bottom-up evaluation algorithm, which may involve many superfluous calculations. However, very often, only a particular question is of interest and the answer to this question needs to be searched. If a goal (query) is specified together with the multivalued knowledge-base, it is not necessary to evaluate all facts and rules, and it is enough to consider only a part of them. A goal is a pair $(q(t_1, t_2, ..., t_n); \underline{\alpha})$, where $q(t_1, t_2, ..., t_n)$ is an atom, $\underline{\alpha}$ is the fuzzy, the intuitionistic, the interval-valued or the bipolar level of the atom. $q$ may contain variables, and its levels may be known or unknown values. The evaluation algorithm gives answer to this query.

In standard Datalog, the most common approach in top-down direction is called query – sub-query framework. A goal, together with a program, determines a query. Literals in the body of any one of the rules defining the goal predicate are sub-goals of the given goal. Thus, a sub-goal together with the program yields a sub-query. In order to answer the query, each goal is expanded in a list of sub-goals, which are recursively expanded in their turn. That is, considering a goal, all rule-heads unifying with the goal are selected and the literals of the rule-body are the new sub-goals of given goal, which are evaluated one by one in an arbitrary order. This procedure continues until the facts have been obtained.

The situation is the same with a multivalued knowledge-base as well, but in this case the algorithm is completed with the computation of the unification levels. However, it is possible that such rules do not exist, but perhaps they do exist for the synonyms. For example, the goal is to know if Ann likes Bach, but there are rules only for describing the options of loving somebody and there are facts only about Vivaldi. In such cases, the synonyms are used. Therefore, the algorithm has to consider the proximities and has to compute the uncertainty levels. It is a bidirectional evaluation: firstly, the uncertainty-free rules and the proximities are evaluated in a top-down manner, obtaining the required starting facts, then the computing of uncertainties is executed in the opposite direction, that is, according to the fixed-point algorithm.

## 4.1 Evaluation of a general knowledge-base

The uncertainty levels are not required in the top-down part of the evaluation, so, this part of the algorithm can be based on the concept of classical substitution and unification (Ceri et al 1990, Ullman 1988, etc.) However other kinds of substitutions may be necessary as well: to substitute some predicate $p$ or term $t$ with their proximity sets $RS_{FV_p}$ and $RG_{FV_t}$, and to substitute some proximity sets with their members.

From now on, for the sake of a simpler terminology, the terms "goal", "rule" and "fact" will refer to these concepts without uncertainty levels. An AND/OR tree arises during the evaluation, this is the searching tree. Its root is the goal; its leaves are either YES or NO. The parent nodes of YES are the facts, and uncertainty can be computed moving towards the direction of the root. This tree is built up by a periodic change of three kinds of steps: a proximity-based unification, a rule-based unification and a splitting step.

Proximity-based unification unifies the predicate symbols of sub-goals and the members of their proximity sets. Rule-based unification unifies the sub-goals with the head of suitable rules, and continues the evaluating by the bodies of these rules. The splitting step splits the rule-body into sub-goals if the body contains more literals or splits a literal of proximity sets into literals of the suitable ground atoms.

During the construction process, the edges are labelled by necessary information for computing the uncertainties. The searching graph according to its depth is build up in the following way.

If the goal is on depth *0*, then every successor of any node on depth $3k+2$ *(k = 0, 1, ...)* is in AND connection, and the others are in OR connection. The step after depth $3k$ *(k = 0, 1, ...)* is a proximity-based unification, after depth $3k+1$ *(k=0, 1, ...)* is a rule-based unification and after depth $3k+2$ *(k=0,1,...)* is a splitting step. In detail:

If the atom $p(t_1, t_2, ..., t_n)$ is in depth $3k$ *(k = 0, 1, ...)*, then the successor nodes let be all possible $p'(t_1, t_2, ..., t_n)$, where $p' \in RS_{FV_p}$. The edges starting from these nodes are labelled by the proximity-based uncertainty functions $\wp_{p'}$.

If the atom *L* is in depth $3k+1$ *(k=0, 1, ...)*, then the successor nodes will be

- the bodies of suitable unified rules or
- the unified facts if L is unifiable with any fact of the program, or
- NO, if there is not any unifiable rule or fact.

That is, if the head of rule $M \leftarrow M_1,...,M_n$, *(n>0)* is unifiable with *L*, then the successor of *L* will be $M_1\theta,...,M_n\theta$, where $\theta$ is the most general unification of *L* and *M*. The edges starting from these nodes are labelled by the uncertainty functions belonging to the implication operator of the applied rules and by the uncertainty level of the rule.

If *n=0*, that is, in the program there is any fact with the predicate symbol of *L*, then the successors will be the unified facts. If $L = p(t_1, t_2, ..., t_n)$ and in the program there is any fact with predicate symbol *p*, then let the successor nodes be all possible $p(t'_1, t'_2,..., t'_n)$, where $t'_i = t_i$ if $t_i$ is a ground term or $t'_i = RG_{FV_{ti}\theta}$ if $t_i$ is a variable and $\theta$ is a suitable unification. The edges starting from these nodes are not labelled.

According to the previous paragraph, there are three kinds of nodes in depth $3k+2$ *(k=0,1,...)*: a unified body of a rule; a unified fact the arguments of with are ordinary ground terms or proximity sets; or the symbol NO.

In the first case, the successors are the members of the body. They are in AND connection. The connected edges will not be labelled, but because of the AND connection, during the computation, the minimum value of the successor's levels will be regarded.

In the second case, the successors are the so called facts-sets. This means, that if the node is $p(t_1, t_2,..., t_n)$, where $t_i$ is a ground term or a proximity set, then the facts-set is the set of all possible $p(t'_1, t'_2,..., t'_n)$, where $t'_i \in RG_{FV_{ti}}$. The edges starting from these nodes are labelled by the proximity-based uncertainty functions $\wp_p$.

The facts-set has a further successor, the symbol YES.

The NO-node has no successor.

A solution can be achieved in the graph along the path ending in the symbol YES. According to the unification algorithm, one of the literals that are located at the parent node of YES can also be found among the original facts of the program. Knowing its uncertainty and using the proximity-based uncertainty function of the label leading to this facts-set, the uncertainty of other members of the facts-set can be computed. However, it is not necessary to compute all of them, only those ones, which are appropriate for the pattern of the literal being in the parent node of facts-set. This means, that if the literal is $p(t_1, t_2,..., t_n)$, and $t_i$ is a ground term, then it is enough to consider only $p(t'_1, t'_2,..., t_i,..., t'_n)$ from the facts-set, but if $t_i$ is a proximity set, then it is necessary to deal with all $p(t'_1, t'_2,..., t'_i,..., t'_n)$, where $t'_i \in RG_{FV_{ti}}$.

In this way each starting fact can be appointed. Then a solution can be determined by connecting the suitable unifications and computing in succession the uncertainties according to the labels of edges in the path from the symbol YES to the root of the graph. The union of these solutions is the answer to the given query.

From the construction of searching graph follows:

**Proposition 7.** For a given goal and in the case of finite evaluation graph, the top-down evaluation terminates and gives the same answer as the fixed point query.

**Example 11.** Consider the IFS program of Example 6, and let it be completed by proximities and proximity-based uncertainty functions

$$(p(a), (0.7, 0.2)).$$

$$(q(b), (0.65, 0.3)).$$

$$(r(a, b), (0.7, 0.2)).$$

$$r(x, y) \leftarrow p(x), q(y); (0.75, 0.2); I_{FG_2}.$$

$$\underline{R}_F (p, p_1) = (0.7, 0.1). \qquad \varphi_p(\alpha, \lambda, \lambda_1) \quad := \alpha \cdot \lambda \cdot \lambda_1.$$

$$\underline{R}_F (q, q_1) = (0.8, 0.1). \qquad \varphi_j(\alpha, \lambda, \lambda_1) \quad := min_F (\alpha, \lambda \cdot \lambda_1).$$

$$\underline{R}_F (r, r_1) = (0.75, 0.2). \qquad \varphi_r(\alpha, \lambda, \lambda_1, \lambda_2) := min_F (\alpha, \lambda, \lambda_1, \lambda_2).$$

$$\underline{R}_F (a, a_1) = (0.8, 0.1).$$

$$\underline{R}_F (b, b_1) = (0.6, 0.3).$$

Let the goal be: $(r_1(a_1, x); \alpha)$, where $x$ is a variable. Then the evaluation graph is on the next page.

The three facts-sets can easily be seen in the graph. From the first one, the uncertainty of $r(a_1, b)$ and $r(a_1, b_1)$ can be computed.

As $(r(a, b), (0.7, 0.2))$ is a known member of the set, so knowing this uncertainty, the proximity-based function and the proximities of knowledge base, the uncertainties can be determined:

$$r (a_1, b), (min_F ((0.7, 0.2), (1, 0), (0.8, 0.1), (1,0))= (0.7, 0.2)).$$

$$r (a_1, b_1), (min_F ((0.7, 0.2), (1, 0), (0.8, 0.1), (0.6,0.3))= (0.6, 0.3)).$$

Applying the next label of the path the uncertainty of $r_1(a_1, b)$ and $r_1(a_1, b_1)$ can be found. They are as follows:

$$(r_1(a_1, b), (0.7, 0.2))$$

$$(r_1(a_1, b_1), (0.6, 0.3))$$

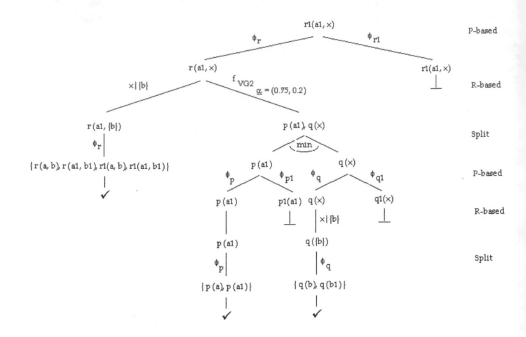

Fig. 1. The evaluation graph of Example 11.

In the second facts-set $(p(a), (0.7, 0.2))$ is the known fact, from this $(p(a_1), (0.56, 0.28))$.

Similarly $(q(b), (0.65, 0.3))$, $(q(b1), (0.6, 0.3))$. Applying the min, $f_{FG2}$ and $\varphi_r$ functions:

$$(r_1(a_1, b), (0.56, 0.3))$$

$$(r_1(a_1, b_1), (0.56, 0.3))$$

As the answer is the union of the different solutions, the final answer is:

$$(r_1(a_1, b), (0.7, 0.2))$$

$$(r_1(a_1, b_1), (0.6, 0.3))$$

## 4.2 Special evaluation based on multivalued unification

The necessity of bidirectional evaluation is derived from the generality of implications and proximity functions, because their values can be computed only from known arguments, namely in bottom-up manner. However, in special cases, computation can be realized parallel with the evaluation of rules and proximities, so the algorithm could be a more efficient pure top-down evaluation. This is the situation if all of the functions are the minimum function. That is, all implications that are used are the second Gödel implication (G2) and all proximity-based uncertainty functions are the minimum function.

As mentioned earlier, in the case of standard Datalog, the heart of the evaluation algorithm is the unification process. Our special evaluation of multivalued knowledge is based on unification as well, but on multivalued unification. The multivalued unification consists of two parts, one is the alternation of a rule-based-unification and the other is a proximity-based one. Both of them are the extensions of the classical unification algorithm. Now, the splitting step is inside these unifications: evaluating a fact, the last proximity-based unification unifies the fact with its facts-set, and a rule-based unification splits these sets into their members.

### 4.2.1 Rule-based unification

This unification algorithm is similar to the classical one, that is, the goal can be unified with the body of any one of the rules defining the goal predicate – if the body is not empty. The level of the unification is the level of the rule defining the goal predicate. In that case, a variable can be substituted with other variable or with a constant; a constant can be substituted with itself only. The next sub-goal of the evaluation process will be the first member of the body. It is possible that during the evaluation a variable of a later member is substituted by a proximity set. In such a case, in the course of later evaluation, this proximity set will be substituted with itself.

If the predicate symbol of the goal is the predicate symbol of a fact, its arguments can be substituted as follows:

- The variables of the goal can be substituted with the proximity set of the constants being the corresponding arguments of the fact. (E.g.: if $q(a,b)$ is a fact predicate and the goal is $q(x, y)$, then $x$ can be substituted with $R_{FV_a}$ and $y$ with $R_{FV_b}$.)
- The constants of the goal can be substituted
  - with themselves, if the goal contains any variable or
  - with their proximity set if the goal does not contain any variable.
- The proximity set argument of a goal can be substituted with itself.

The level of the unification is $1_{FV}$.

If there is no fact with the same predicate symbol, the unification process fails.

There is a special case of unification: the facts-set of a predicate is unified with its members in the following way:

According to the previous unifications, between the literals of these facts-set there is one from the facts of the program. Knowing its uncertainty and the level of proximities, the uncertainty of other members can be computed. Then these members can be unified respectively:

- with the empty clause, if there is no other literal to evaluate in the parent-node;
- with the remaining part of the body to be evaluated.

The level of this unification is the level of the fitting member, and the former proximity set-substitution of a variable is replaced by the suitable member of this set.

(E.g. : if there is a former $x \mid R_{FV_a}$ substitution for literal $p(x)$, and $R_{FV_a} = \{a, b\}$, then the facts-set of unification is $\{p(a), p(b)\}$, which is unified with empty clauses . The substitutions for $x$ are $x \mid a$ and $x \mid b$, and the levels are the computed levels of $p(a)$ and $p(b)$ respectively. )

## 4.2.2 Proximity-based unification

This unification serves for handling proximities. When these steps are implemented, the following substitutions can be realized:

- A constant or a variable can be substituted with itself only.
- A predicate symbol can be substituted with the elements of its proximity set. The level of the unification is the current proximity value.
- A proximity set can be substituted with itself except in the last step of the evaluation of a literal. In this case, that is if each argument of the literal is a proximity set, the literal can be unified with its facts-set. The level of the unification is $\underline{1}_{FV}$.

## 4.2.3 The unification algorithm

The evaluation algorithm combines the two kinds of unification. It starts with the proximity based unification and after it is finished, they alternate. The query is successful if the unification algorithm ends with an empty clause or a failure. In the first case the variables get the values defined during the substitutions. If all uncertainties are regarded as a minimum value, the actual level of unification can be computed as the minimum of former levels and when the algorithm reaches the empty clause, its level will be the level of the goal as well.

If the unification algorithm ends with a failure, there is no answer on this path.

If more answers arise during the evaluation, their union will be the resolution of the query.

According to the construction of unifications, the following proposition is true.

**Proposition 8.** For a given goal, and in the case of a finite evaluation graph, the above top-down evaluation gives the same answer as the fixed point query.

Notes:

- Although this algorithm was described for a knowledge-base based on a negation free program, it is similar in the case of stratified programs; the only difference is the calculation of the uncertainty of the negated sub-goal, but the computing of minimum remains the same.
- With a good depth limit this algorithm is suitable for evaluating recursive programs or infinite graphs as well.

**Example 12.** Let us consider a part of Example 10, and let it be completed with a new rule and new facts. That is now the internet agent knows that people usually want to see (*ws*) a film if they like (*li*) its actor (*ac*), or they like more or less the subject (*su*) of the film. Moreover, it knows that Paul (P) enjoys (*en*) Chaplin (*Ch*) very much and mostly enjoys the historical films (*H*). In the cinema, a film (*F1*) of Stan and Pan (*SP*) is presented. There are two other films (*F2*, *F3*). Both films' topics (*to*) are the war (*W*), but in different manner. The first one's central message is the war, the second one play in wartime, but it is only a background. From the former example it is known, that the agent wants to know the interest of Paul. Therefore let our goal be (*in(P,x)*; $\underline{\alpha}$).

Let the IVS valued mDATALOG program and the background knowledge be as follows

$$ws(f, x) \leftarrow ac(f, y), li(x, y); (0.8, 0.85); I_{VG_2}. \qquad (R1)$$

$$ws(f, x) \leftarrow su(f, y), li(x, y); (0.75, 0.85); I_{VG_2}. \qquad (R2)$$

(en(P, Ch), (0.9, 0.95)).
(en(P, H), (0.6, 0.7)).

(ac(F1, SP), (1, 1)).
(to(F2, W), (0.9, 0.95)).
(to(F3, W), (0.55, 0.6)).

According to its roll, *ac(F1, SP)* has no alternatives. Let the other proximities be:

$\underline{R}_V$ (in, ws) = (0.7, 0.8).      $\underline{R}_V$ (Ch, SP) = (0.8, 0.9).

$\underline{R}_V$ (li, en)  = (0.8, 0.9).      $\underline{R}_V$ (H, W) = (0.6, 0.8).

$\underline{R}_V$ (to, su ) = (0.9, 1).

Then the evaluation graph is Fig.2.

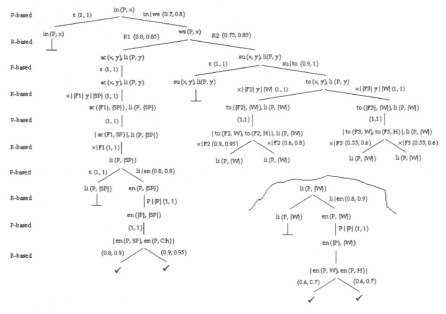

Fig. 2. The evaluation graph of Example 12.

Let each proximity-based uncertainty function be the minimum function.

According to the left path of the graph one can see, that *(in (P, F1), (0.7, 0.8))* because the applied substitution is *x | F1* and the minimum of levels is *(0.7, 0.8)*.

The other paths are only half-drawn, and they are continued in a partial graph, because this part of evaluation is similar in all cases. The only differences are in uncertainty levels.

So, according to these paths the other answers for the query are:

*(in (P, F2), (0.6, 0.7)), (in (P, F3), (0.55, 0.6))*

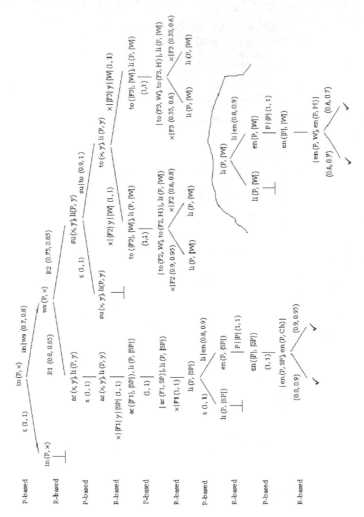

Fig. 3. The enlarged evaluation graph of Example 12.

## 5. Conclusion

In this chapter, a possible multivalued knowledge-base was presented as a quadruple of background knowledge, a deduction mechanism, a decoding set and an algorithm connecting the background knowledge to the deduction mechanism.

The background knowledge is based on proximity relations between terms and between predicates and it serves as a mechanism handling "synonyms".

The deduction mechanism can be any of the extensions of Datalog. These extensions are the fuzzy Datalog, based on fuzzy logic, the intuitionistic- or interval-value Datalog, based on the suitable logics and bipolar Datalog, which is some kind of coexistence of the former ones.

The semantics of Datalog is a fixed-point semantics, so the algorithm, which connects the two main pillars of the knowledge-base is the generalization of the consequence transformation determining this fixed-point. This transformation is defined on the extended Herbrand base of the knowledge-base, which is generated from the ground terms of knowledge base and its background knowledge.

Applying this transformation it is necessary to compute the uncertainty levels of "synonyms". The proximity-based uncertainty functions can do it, giving uncertainty values from the levels of the original fact and from the proximity values. The set of this kind of functions is the decoding set.

Two possible evaluation strategies were presented as well. One of them evaluates a general knowledgebase with arbitrary proximity-based uncertainty functions and arbitrary implication operators. The other one allows minimum functions only as proximity based uncertainty functions, and the special extension of Gödel operator, but in this case a multivalued unification algorithm can be determined. This strategy is based on the alternating rule-based- and proximity-based unification.

The improvement of this strategy and/or the deduction algorithm and/or the structure of background knowledge is a subject of further investigations.

A well structured multivalued knowledge-base and an efficient evaluating algorithm determining its consequence could be the basis of making decisions based on uncertain information, or it would be useful for handling argumentation or negotiation of agents. An implementation of this model would be an interesting future development as well.

# 6. References

Abiteboul, S.; Hull, R. and Vianu, V. (1995). *Foundations of Databases*. Addison-Wesley Publishing Company, Reading, Massachusetts.

Achs, A. & Kiss, A. (1995). Fuzzy extension of datalog, *Acta Cybernetica Szeged*, Vol.12, pp. 153-166.

Achs, A. (2006). Models for handling uncertainty, *PhD thesis*, University of Debrecen, 2006.

Achs, A. (2007). From Fuzzy- to Bipolar- Datalog, In: *Proceedings of 5th EUSFLAT Conference*, Ostrava, Czech Republic, pp. 221-227.

Achs, A. (2010). A multivalued knowledge-base model, *Acta Universitatis Sapientiae, Informatica*, Vol.2, No.1, pp. 51-79.

Alsinet, T. & Godo, L. (1998). Fuzzy Unification Degree, In: *Proceedings 2nd Int Workshop on Logic Programming and Soft Computing '98, in conjunction with JICSLP'98*, Manchester, UK, pp. 23-43.

Atanassov, K. (1983). Intuitionistic fuzzy sets, *VII ITKR's Session, Sofia* (deposed in Central Science-Technical Library of Bulgarian Academy of Science, 1697/84).

Atanassov, K. & Gargov, G. (1989). Interval-valued intuitionistic fuzzy sets, *Fuzzy Sets and Systems*, Vol.31, No.3, pp. 343-349.

Atanassov, K. (1994). Remark on intuitionistic fuzzy expert systems. *BUSEFAL*, Vol.59, pp. 71-76.

Atanassov, K. (2005). Intuitionistic fuzzy implications and modus ponens. *Notes on Intuitionistic Fuzzy Sets*, Vol. 11, pp. 1-5.

Atanassov, K. (2006). On some intuitionistic fuzzy implications. *Comptes Rendus de l'Academie Bulgare des Sciences, Tome*, Vol. 59, pp. 19-24.

Atanassov, K. (1999). *Intuitionistic Fuzzy Sets*, Springer-Verlag, Heidelberg

Ceri, S.; Gottlob, G. & Tanca, L. (1990). *Logic Programming and Databases*, Springer-Verlag, Berlin

Cornelis, C.; Deschrijver, G. & Kerre, E.E. (2004). Implication in intuitionistic fuzzy and interval-valued fuzzy set theory: construction, classification, application, *International Journal of Approximate Reasoning*, Vol.35, pp. 55-95.

Dubois, D. & Prade, H. (1991). Fuzzy sets in approximate reasoning, Part 1: Inference with possibility distributions, *Fuzzy Sets and Systems*, Vol.40, pp. 143-202.

Dubois, D.; Hajek, P. & Prade, H. (2000). Knowledge-Driven versus Data-Driven Logics, *Journal of Logic, Language, and Information*, Vol.9, pp. 65-89.

Dubois, D.; Gottwald, S.; Hajek, P.; Kacprzyk, J. & Prade, H. (2005). Terminological difficulties in fuzzy set theory – The case of Intuitionistic Fuzzy Sets, *Fuzzy Sets and Systems*, Vol.15, pp. 485-491.

Formato, F.; Gerla, G. & Sessa, M.I. (2000). Similarity-based Unification, *Fundamenta Informaticae*, Vol.41, pp. 393-414.

Julian-Iranzo, P. & Rubio-Manzano, C. (2009). A declarative semantics for Bousi~Prolog, *PPDP '09: Proceedings of the 11th ACM SIGPLAN conference on Principles and practice of declarative programming*.

Julian-Iranzo, P. & Rubio-Manzano, C. (2010). An Efficient Fuzzy Unification Method and its Implementation into the BousiProlog System, *WCCI2010 IEEE World Congress On Computational Intelligence, Barcelona*.

Lloyd, J.W. (1990). *Foundations of Logic Programming*, Springer-Verlag, Berlin

Medina, J.; Ojeda-Aciego, M. & Vojtas, P. (2004). Similarity-based unification: a multi-adjoint approach, *Fuzzy Sets and Systems*, Vol.146, No.1, pp. 43-62.

Sessa, M. I. (2002). Approximate reasoning by similarity-based SLD resolution, *Theoretical Computer Science*, Vol.275, No.1-2, pp. 389-426.

Straccia, U. (2008). Managing Uncertainty and Vagueness in Description Logics, Logic Programs and Description Logic Programs, In: Reasoning Web 2008, C. Baroglio et al. (Eds), pp. 54-103, Springer-Verlag, Berlin

Straccia, U.; Ojeda-Aciego, M. & Damasio, C.V. (2009). On Fixed-points of Multi-valued Functions on Complete Lattices and their Application to Generalized Logic Programs, *SIAM Journal on Computing*, Vol.8, pp. 1881-1911.

Ullman, J.D. (1988). *Principles of Database and Knowledge-base Systems*, Computer Science Press, Rockville

Virtanen, H.E. (1994) Fuzzy Unification, *Proc. of IPMU'94, Paris (France)*, pp. 1147–1152.

Zadeh, L. A. (1975) The concept of a linguistic variable and its application to approximate reasoning (I–II–III), *Information Sciences*, Vol.8, pp. 199-249; 301-357; Vol.9 pp. 43-80.

# 6

# Fuzzy Image Segmentation Algorithms in Wavelet Domain

Heydy Castillejos and Volodymyr Ponomaryov
*National Polytechnic Institute of Mexico*
*Mexico*

## 1. Introduction

The images are considered one of the most important means of information transmission; therefore the image processing has become an important tool in a variety of fields such as video coding, computer vision and medical imaging. Within the image processing, there is the segmentation process that involves partitioning an image into a set of homogeneous and meaningful regions, such that the pixels in each partitioned region possess an identical set of properties or attributes (Gonzalez & Woods, 1992). The sets of properties of the image may include gray levels, contrast, spectral values, or texture properties, etc. The result of segmentation is a number of homogeneous regions, each having a unique label. Image segmentation is often considered to be the most important task in computer vision. However, the segmentation in images is a challenging task due to several reasons: irregular and dispersive lesion borders, low contrast, artifacts in the image and variety of colors within the interest region. Therefore, numerous methods have been developed for image segmentation within applications in the computer vision. Image segmentation can be classified into three categories: A) *Supervised.*- These methods require the interactivity in which the pixels belonging to the same intensity range pointed out manually and segmented. B) *Automatic.*- This is also known as unsupervised methods, where the algorithms need some priori information, so these methods are more complex, and C) *Semi-automatic.*- That is the combination of manual and automatic segmentation. Some of practical applications of image segmentation are: the medical imaging tasks that consist of location of tumors and other pathologies, recognition of the objects in images of remote sensing obtained via satellite or aerial platforms, automated-recognition systems to inspect the electronic assemblies, biometrics, automatic traffic controlling systems, machine vision, separating and tracking the regions appearing in consequent frames of an sequence, and finally, the real time mobile robot applications employing vision systems. [1].

## 2. Related work

A lot of methods have been developed in the image segmentation. Let present brief description of the several promising frameworks.

---

[1] (Gonzalez & Woods, 1992)

## 2.1 *Adaptive thresholding (AT)*

In (Argenziano & Soyer, 1996), the automatic adaptive thresholding (AT) performs the image segmentation comparing the color of each a pixel with a threshold. The pixel is classified as a lesion if it is darker than the threshold, finally, presenting the output as a binary image. Morphological post-processing is then applied to fill the holes and to select the largest connected component in the binary image. For color images, an automatic selection of the color component based on the entropy of the color component $i$ is used:

$$S(i) = - \sum_{k=0}^{L-1} h_i(k) log[h_i(k)], \tag{1}$$

where $h_i(k)$ is the histogram of the color component $i$. It is assumed that the image $I_i(x, y)$ varies in the range $0, \ldots, 255$ and the histogram is computed using bins of length $L = 25$. The block diagram in Fig.1 explains in detail the operation for AT method.

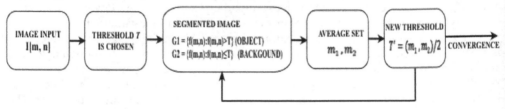

Fig. 1. Block diagram of Adaptive thresholding.

## 2.2 *Statistical region merging*

In (M. Celebi, 2008), the authors use a variant of region growing and merging technique, called as statistical region merging (SRM). The authors propose the following strategy:

- Regions are defied as the sets of pixels with homogeneous properties that then are iteratively growing by combining smaller regions.
- Region growing/merging techniques is used employing a statistical test to form the merging of regions.

The SRM framework uses the image generation homogeneity property and performs as follows in Fig. 2:

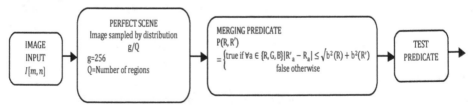

Fig. 2. Block diagram of Statistical region merging.

Ideally, the order in testing the region merging is when any test between two true regions occurs, which means that all tests inside each of the two true regions have previously occurred.

## Clustering based segmentation

The most promising in segmentation of the images in general is the approach based on clustering. Cluster oriented-segmentation uses the multidimensional data to partition of the image pixels into clusters. Such kind of technique may be more appropriate than histogram-oriented ones in segmenting images, where each pixel has several attributes and is represented by a vector. Cluster analysis has attracted much attention since the 1960's and has been applied in many fields such as OCR (*Optical Character Recognition*) system. Below, let present three most successful frameworks based on this technique that we apply in segmentation applications.

### 2.3 K-Means clustering algorithm

K-Means algorithm is an unsupervised clustering algorithm that classifies the input data point into multiple classes based on their inherent distance from each other. The algorithm assumes that the data features from a vector space and tries to find natural clustering in them (Hartigan & Wong, 1979). It works an iterative manner according to the following steps:

1. Choose initial centroids $m_1, \ldots, m_k$ of the clusters $C_1, \ldots, C_k$.
2. Calculate new cluster membership. A feature vector $x_j$ is assigned to the cluster $C_i$ if and only if:

$$i = argmin_{k=1,,K} \|x_j - m_k\|^2. \tag{2}$$

3. Recalculate the centroids for the clusters according to

$$m_i = \frac{1}{|C_i|} \sum_{x_j \in C_i} x_j, \tag{3}$$

where $x_j$ belong to data set $X = x_1,,x_i, x_N$.

4. If none of the cluster centroids has been changed, finish the algorithm. Otherwise, go to step 2.

In Fig.3, the segmentation process using the K-Means algorithm is exposed:

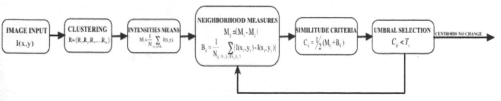

Fig. 3. Block diagram for K-Means algorithm.

## Image segmentation using fuzzy methods

### Preliminaries and background

The conventional set theory is based on a binary valued membership, which implies that a particular element either belongs to a particular set or it does not belong to it. A crisp set is defined as one whose elements fully belong to the set and they possess well-defined common attributes, which can be measured quantitatively. In a crisp set the common attributes are equally shared by all the elements of the set. On the other hand, in fuzzy sets, the degree of membership of an element to the set is indicated by a membership value, which signifies the extent to which the element belongs to the set. The membership value lies between 0 and 1, with membership "0" indicating no membership and "1" indicating full membership of the element to the set. In a crisp set, the membership values of its elements are either 0 or 1. The membership of an element $z$ in a fuzzy set is obtained using a membership function $\mu(x)$ that maps every element belonging to the fuzzy set $X_F$ to the interval $[0, 1]$. Formally, this mapping can be written as:

$$\mu(x) : X_F \to [0, 1] \tag{4}$$

The membership assignment is primarily subjective in the sense that the users specify the membership values.

*Selection of the Membership Function* The assignment of the membership function may be performed by several ways.

- *Membership based on visual model*: The membership function may be assigned in accordance with the human visual perceptual model. We may model the variation of the membership values of the pixels in a linear fashion as the pixel gray value changes from 0 to L - 1 (for an L level image).
- Statistical Distribution: The membership values of the pixels may be assigned on the basis of image statistics as a whole or on the basis of local information at a pixel calculated from the surrounding pixels. The probability density function of the Gaussian or gamma distribution may be used for assignment of membership values (Chaira & Ray, 2003).

### 2.4 Fuzzy C-Means algorithm

Details of fuzzy approach to supervised pattern classification and clustering may be found in (Bezdek, 1981) In fuzzy clustering, a pattern is assigned with a degree of belongings to each cluster in a partition. Here, let present the most popular and efficient fuzzy clustering algorithm: *Fuzzy C-Means Algorithm*. The algorithm should find the center of $'n'$ number of clusters iteratively adjusting their position via evaluation of an objective function. Additionally, it permits more flexibility by introducing the partial membership to the other clusters. The classical variant of this algorithm uses the following objective function:

$$E = \sum_{j=1}^{C} \sum_{i=1}^{N} \mu_{ij}^{k} \|x_i - c_j\|^2, \tag{5}$$

where $\mu_{ij}^{k}$ is the fuzzy membership of the pixel $x_i$; here, the cluster is identified by its center $c_j$, and $k \in [1, \infty]$ is an exponent weight factor. There is no fixed rule for choosing the exponent weight factor. However, in many applications $k = 2$ is a common choice. In case of crisp clustering, k may be chosen as 1. The membership value is proportional to the probability that a pixel belongs to some specific cluster where the probability is only dependent on the distance between the pixel and each independent cluster center. So, the criterion E has minimal value when for the pixels that are nearby the corresponding cluster center, higher membership values are assigned, while lower membership values are assigned to the pixels that are far from a center. This algorithm runs with the clusters' number and initial center positions that should be done at beginning, and then, the algorithm determines how many pixels belong to each cluster. The membership function and centers are determined as follows:

$$\mu_{ij} = \frac{1}{\sum_{m=1}^{C} \left( \frac{\|x_i - c_j\|}{\|x_i - c_m\|}^{\left(\frac{2}{(k-1)}\right)} \right)},$$
(6)

$$c_i = \frac{\sum_{j=1}^{N} u_{ij}^k x_j}{\sum_{j=1}^{N} u_{ij}^k}.$$
(7)

The FCM algorithm runs four simple steps:

1. The center is initialized with the first value 't' of the data to be equal to zero, and this value is used as a counter for number of iterations.
2. The fuzzy partition membership functions $\mu_{ij}$ are initialized according to (6).
3. The value $'t = t + 1'$ is changed and novel centers are computed using (7).
4. The steps 2 and 3 run until criterion E convergence.

Criterion E approaches to minimum value when its variations are decreased according to the restriction that a user should decide. The algorithm also can be interrupted if a user determines that only a certain number of iterations to be done Bezdek (1981).

## 2.5 Cluster pre-selection fuzzy C-Means

The FCM algorithm, which is one of the most commonly used procedures, has the following drawback: the number of clusters should be pre-determined by a user before it starts to work. Therefore, sometimes the correct number of clusters in the concrete application may not be the same that the number being chosen by a user. Therefore, a method that should add a process based on fuzzy logic to find the number of clusters to be used. To realize this, we take into consideration the difference between the max ($Vmax$) and the min ($Vmin$) values of intensity in an image $D = Vmax - Vmin$, these proportions determine the number of clusters. Following, obtained data are applied in the determination of the centers, reducing the operational time of the FCM algorithm. This value is the first data of our fuzzy system called 'Distance', that has six fuzzy sets, 'minimum', 'shorter', 'short', 'regular', 'large' and 'maximum' (see Tab. 1). For value of data of our fuzzy system called 'Size', that has five fuzzy sets, 'Min', 'Small', 'Medium', 'Big' and 'Max' (see Tab. 2). Finally, For value of data of our fuzzy system called 'Cluster', that has five fuzzy sets, 'Very few', 'Few', 'Some', 'Many' and 'Too Many' (see Tab. 3)

| Fuzzy set | Function | Center | Variance |
|-----------|----------|--------|----------|
| Minimum | Gauss | 15 | 16 |
| Shorter | Gauss | 53 | 24 |
| Short | Gauss | 105 | 30 |
| Regular | Gauss | 150 | 30 |
| Large | Gauss | 222 | 45 |
| Maximum | Gauss | 255 | 15 |

Table 1. Member functions of "Distance"

| Fuzzy set | Function | Center | Variance |
|-----------|----------|--------|----------|
| Min | Gauss | 9000 | 1.789e+005 |
| Small | Gauss | 3.015e+005 | 1.626e+005 |
| Medium | Gauss | 6.53e+005 | 1.968e+005 |
| Big | Gauss | 9.728e+005 | 2.236e+005 |
| Max | Gauss | 1.44e+006 | 2.862e+005 |

Table 2. Member functions of "Size"

| Fuzzy set | Function | Center | Variance |
|-----------|----------|--------|----------|
| Very few | Gauss | 2 | 3 |
| Few | Gauss | 7 | 3 |
| Some | Gauss | 16 | 5 |
| Many | Gauss | 23 | 5 |
| Too many | Gauss | 33 | 7 |

Table 3. Member functions of "Clusters"

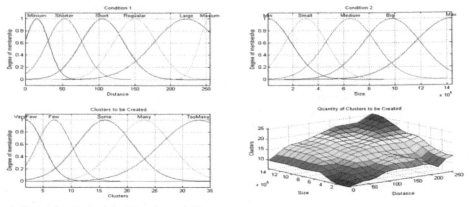

Fig. 4. Pre-selection of the Number of Clusters.

In the second phase, the number of clusters and its centers are already known, simply dividing the difference $D$ into the 'N' clusters and determining its center.

$$c_j = j\frac{D}{N}, \qquad\qquad j = 1, 2, 3, , N, \qquad\qquad (8)$$

where 'N' represents the number of clusters to be created and 'j' is a counter to define all the centers. This looks like a hard type of algorithm, but the centers are still a bit far from the final ones, therefore, there are still a certain number of iterations that should be applied to find them, but the number of iterations is a lot less than for original system, permitting to reduce the computation time. RGB image is discomposed into its three-color channels, and the Euclidean distance is employed (L.A. & Zadeh, 1965) to determine, which one is the difference between three distances.

$$d_1(x_{red}, x_{blue}) = \sqrt{\sum_{k=1}^{P}(x_{red}^k - x_{blue}^k)^2}, \tag{9}$$

$$d_2(x_{red}, x_{green}) = \sqrt{\sum_{k=1}^{P}(x_{red}^k - x_{green}^k)^2},$$

$$d_3(x_{green}, x_{blue}) = \sqrt{\sum_{k=1}^{P}(x_{green}^k - x_{blue}^k)^2}.$$

Two distances that are more alike should be combined into one gray scale image, and it is processed as a correct image, then the method proposed is used to determine the number of clusters to be created. The CPSFCM consists of the next steps:

1. Divide RGB image into three different images, use (9) to find two images that are more similar each to other and use them to create a new gray scale image.
2. Calculate the distance between intensity levels in the image $D$, and obtain the size of an image.
3. Feed with these data the fuzzy pre selective system and obtain the number of centers to be created.
4. Use (8) to obtain the approximate centers. The initial value 't' is equal to zero and it is used as a counter for the number of the iterations.
5. The fuzzy partition membership functions $\mu_{ij}$ are initialized according to (6).
6. Let the value be 't=t+1' and compute the new centers using (7).
7. The steps 5 and 6 should be done until criterion E converges.

## 3. Wavelet texture analysis

### 3.1 Continuous wavelet transform

The proposed frameworks in segmentation are based on wavelet analysis, so let present some brief introduction in this part. The continuous wavelet transform (CWT) (Grossman & Morlet, 1985) can be written as follows:

$$W(a,b) = \int_{-\infty}^{+\infty} x(t) \frac{1}{\sqrt{|a|}} \psi^*\left(\frac{t-b}{a}\right) dt, \tag{10}$$

where $b$ acts to translate the function across $x(t)$, and the variable $a$ acts to vary the time scale of the probing function, $\psi$. If value $a$ is greater than one, the wavelet function, $\psi$ is stretched along the time axis, and if it is less than one (but still positive) it contacts the function. Wavelets are functions generated from one single function (basis function) called the prototype or mother wavelet by dilations (scalings) and translations (shifts) in time (frequency) domain. If the mother wavelet is denoted by $\psi(t)$, the other wavelets $\psi_{a,b}(t)$ can be represented as:

$$\psi_{a,b}(t) = \frac{1}{\sqrt{|a|}} \psi^* \left( \frac{t-b}{a} \right). \tag{11}$$

The variables $a$ and $b$ represent the parameters for *dilations* and *translations*, respectively in the time axis. If the wavelet function $\psi(t)$ is appropriately chosen, then it is possible to reconstruct the original waveform from the wavelet coefficients just as in the Fourier transform. Since the CWT decomposes the waveform into coefficients of two variables, a and b, a double summation en discrete case (or integration in continuous case) is required to recover the original signal from the coefficients (Meyers, 1993):

$$x(t) = \frac{1}{C} \int_{a-\infty}^{+\infty} \int_{b=-\infty}^{+\infty} W(a,b)\psi_{a,b}(t)dadb, \tag{12}$$

where$C = \int_{-\infty}^{+\infty} \frac{|\Psi(\omega)|^2}{|\omega|} d\omega$ and $0 < C < -\infty$ (so called a*dmissibility* condition). In fact, reconstruction of the original waveform is rarely performed using the CWT coefficients because of its redundancy.

## 3.2 Discrete wavelet transforms

The CWT has one serious problem: it is highly redundant. The CWT provides an oversampling of the original waveform: many more coefficients are generated than are actually needed to uniquely specify the signal. The discrete wavelet transform (DWT) achieves this parsimony by restricting the variation in translation and scale, usually to powers of two that is the case of the dyadic wavelet transform. The basic analytical expressions for the DWT is usually implemented using filter banks (Mallat, 1989):

$$x(t) = \sum_{k=-\infty}^{\infty} \sum_{l=-\infty}^{\infty} d(k,l)2^{-k/2}\psi(2^{-k}t - l). \tag{13}$$

Here, $k$ is related to $a$ as: $a = 2k$ ; $b$ is related to $\lambda$ as $b = 2k$ ; and $d(k,\lambda)$ is a sampling of $W(a,b)$ at discrete points k and $\lambda$. In the DWT, it is introduced the scaling function, a function that facilitates computation of the DWT. To implement the DWT efficiently, the finest resolution is computed first. The computation then proceeds to coarser resolutions, but rather than start over on the original waveform, the computation uses a smoothed version of the fine resolution waveform. This smoothed version is obtained with the help of the scaling function. The definition of the scaling function uses a dilation or a two-scale difference equation:

$$\phi(t) = \sum_{n=-\infty}^{\infty} \sqrt{2}c(n)\phi(2t - n). \tag{14}$$

Here, $c(n)$ are the series of scalars that define the specific scaling function. This equation involves two time scales ($t$ and $2t$) and can be quite difficult to solve. In the DWT, the wavelet itself can be defined from the scaling function (Rao & Bopardikar, 1998):

$$\psi(t) = \sum_{n=-\infty}^{\infty} \sqrt{2}d(n)\phi(2t - n), \qquad (15)$$

where $d(n)$ are the series of scalars that are related to the waveform $x(t)$ and that define the discrete wavelet in terms of the scaling function. While the DWT can be implemented using the above equations, it is usually implemented using filter bank techniques. The use of a group of filters to divide up a signal into various spectral components is termed sub-band coding. The most used implementation of the DWT for 2-D signal applies only two filters for rows and columns, as in the filter bank, which is shown in 5.

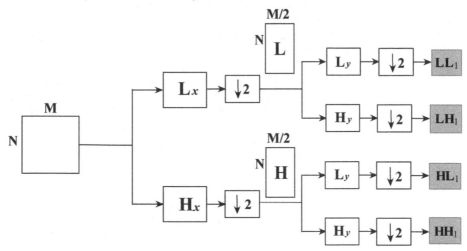

Fig. 5. Structure of the analysis filter bank for 2-D image.

## 4. Wavelet based texture analysis

A recent overview of methods applied to segmentation of skin lesions in dermoscopic images (M. Celebi & Stoecker, 2009) results that clustering is the most popular segmentation technique, probably due to their robustness. In the image analysis, texture is an important characteristic, including natural scenes and medical images. It has been noticed that the wavelet transform (WT)provides an ideal representation for texture analysis presenting spatial-frequency properties via a pyramid of tree structures, which is similar to sub-band decomposition. The hierarchical decomposition allows analyzing the high frequencies in the image, which features are importantin the segmentation task. Several works beneficially use the image features within a WT domain during the segmentation process.In paper (Bello, 1994), the image data firstly are decomposed into channels for a selected set of resolution levels using wavelet packets transform, then the Markov random field (MRF) segmentation is applied to the sub-bands coefficients for each scale, starting with the coarsest level, and propagating the segmentation process from current level to segmentation at the next level. Strickland et al. (Strickland & Hahn, 2009) apply the image features extracted in the WT domain for detection of microcalcifications in mammograms using a matching process and some a priori knowledge on the target objects.

Zhang et al. (Zhang & Desai, 2001) employ a Bayes classifier on wavelet coefficients to determine an appropriate scale and threshold that can separate segmentation targets from other features.

## 5. Proposed framework

The idea of our approach is consisted in employing the feature extraction in WT space before the segmentation process where the main difference with other algorithms presented in literature is in usage the information from three color channels in WT space gathering the color channels via a nearest neighbour interpolation (NNI). Developed approach uses the procedure that consists of the following stages: a digital color image I[n,m] is separated in R, G and Bchannels in the color space, where each a color channel is decomposed calculating their wavelets coefficients using Mallat's pyramid algorithm (Mallat, 1989). For chosen wavelet family is being used, the original image is decomposed into four sub-bands (Fig.5). These sub-bands labeled as LH, HL and HH represent the finest scale wavelet coefficient (detail images), while the sub-band LL corresponds to coarse level coefficients (approximation image), noted below as $D_h^{(2^i)}, D_v^{(2^i)}, D_d^{(2^i)}$ and $A^{(2^i)}$, respectively at given scale $2^j$, for $j = 1, 2, \ldots, J$, where J is the numbers of scales used in the DWT (Kravchenko, 2009). Finally, the DWT can be represented as follows:

$$W_i = |W_i| exp(j\Theta_i), \tag{16}$$

$$|W_i| = \left(\sqrt{|D_{h,i}|^2 + |D_{v,i}|^2 + |D_{d,i}|^2}\right)^2, \tag{17}$$

$$\Theta_i = \begin{cases} \alpha_i & \text{if } D_{h,i} > 0 \\ \pi - \Theta_i & \text{if } D_{h,i} < 0, \end{cases} \tag{18}$$

$$\Theta_i = \tan^{-1}\left(\frac{D_{v,i}}{D_{h,i}}\right).$$

Therefore, $W_i$ is considered as a new image for each color channel. The following process employed in the wavelet transform space is consisted of the stages: the classic segmentation method is applied to images; the image segmented corresponding to the red channel is interpolated with the image segmented corresponding to the green channel, the found image after applying *NNI* process is interpolated with the image segmented corresponding to the blue channel using *NNI* again, finally, this image is considerers the output of the segmentation procedure, Fig. 6 shows the block diagram of the above. The importance of considering the information of the three-color channels is an advantage in the segmentation process as it is judged to clusters formed in each of them.

The block diagram in Fig. 7 explains the operations for: a) image segmentation if K-Means algorithm is used where the WT is applied, named as WK-Means; b) image segmentation if FCM algorithm is used where the WT is applied, named as W-FCM; finally c) image segmentation if CPSFCM algorithm is used where the WT is applied, named as W-CPSFCM.

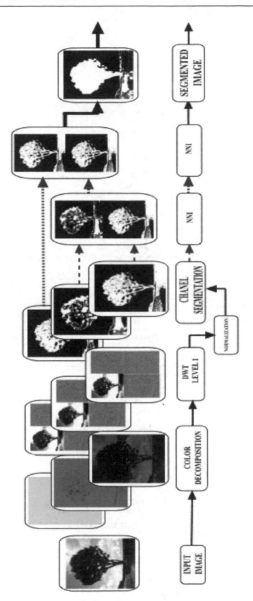

Fig. 6. Block diagram of proposed framework.

## 6. Evaluation criteria

In this section, let present the evaluation criteria focusing them in segmentation process in dermoscopic image. The same measures can be used for segmentation in other applications. Different objective measures are used in literature for the purpose of evaluation of the segmentation performance in dermoscopic images. For objective measures, there is needed

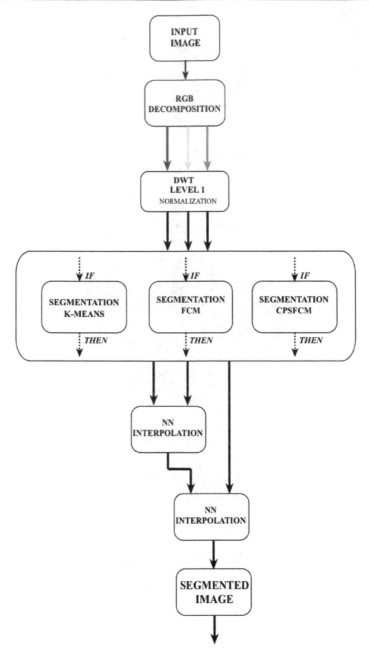

Fig. 7. Block diagram of the proposed algorithms: a) segmentation with WK-MEANS; b) segmentation with W-FCM; c) segmentation with W-CPSFCM.

the ground truth (GT) image, which is determined by dermatologist manually drawing the border around the lesion.

Employing GT image Hance *et al.* (Hance, 1996) calculated the operation exclusive disjunction (XOR) measure, other metrics used in segmentation performance are presented in(Garnavi, 2011): the *sensitivity* and *specificity, precision and recall, true positive rate, false positive rate, pixel misclassification probability,* the *weighted performance index,* among others. Below, let consider the *sensitivity* and *specificity* measure. Sensitivity and specificity are statistical measures of the performance of a binary classification test, commonly used in medical studies. In the context of segmentation of skin lesions, sensitivity measures the proportion of actual lesion pixels that are correctly identified as such. Specificity measures the proportion of background skin pixels that are correctly identified. Given the following definitions:

**TP**  true positive, object pixels that are correctly classified as interest object.

**FP**  false positive, background pixels that are incorrectly identified as interest object.

**TN**  true negative, background pixels that are correctly identified as background.

**FN**  false negative, object pixels that are incorrectly identified as background.

In each of the above categories, the sensitivity and specificity are given by:

$$sensitivity = \frac{TP}{TP + FN} \tag{19}$$

$$specificity = \frac{TN}{FP + TN} \tag{20}$$

We also apply the *Receiver Operating Characteristic* (ROC) analysis (Fig. 8) that permits to evaluate the image segmentation quality in terms of the ability of human observer or a computer algorithm using image data to classify patients as *"positive"* or *"negative"* with respect to any particular disease. This characteristic represents the second level of diagnostic efficacy in the hierarchical model described by Fryback and Thornbury (Fryback DG, 1991). Fig. 8 presents the points of the ROC curve that are obtained by sweeping the classification threshold from the most positive classification value to the most negative. These points are desirable to produce quantitative summary measure using the ROC curve, called as an area under the ROC curve (AUC).

## 7. Dermoscopic images

In the processing area of biomedical image processing, we applied the developed and existed segmentation techniques to dermoscopic images. Let present some definitions of commonly used terms in this application area. The term "skin cancer" refers to three different conditions that are from the least to the most dangerous can be presented as follows:

*   Basal cell carcinoma (or basal cell *carcinomaepithelioma*)
*   Squamous cell carcinoma (the first stage of which is called *actinic keratosis*)
*   *Melanoma*

The two most common forms of skin cancer are basal cell carcinoma and squamous cell carcinoma. Together, these two are also referred to as nonmelanoma skin cancer.

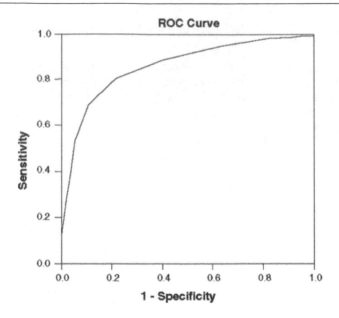

Fig. 8. ROC curve.

Melanoma is generally the most serious form of skin cancer because it tends to spread (metastasize) throughout the body quickly. For a diagnosis, doctors usually remove all or a part of the growth by performing a biopsy but is considered an invasive technique. Alternative, dermatoscopy reduces the need for a biopsy applying a dermatoscope device, which magnifies the sub surface structures with the use of oil and illumination, also called epiluminescence. Dermatoscopy is a particularly helpful standard method of diagnosing the malignancy of skin lesions (Argenziano & Soyer, 2001). A mayor advantage is the accuracy of dermatoscopy is increased to 20% in the case of sensitivity and up to 10% in the case of specificity, compared with naked-eye examination, permitting to reduce the frequency of unnecessary surgical excisions of benign lesions (Vestergaard, 2001). Several instruments designed for a computer aided diagnosis (CAD) (Fig. 9 of skin lesions have been proposed, which usually work in four steps: data acquisition of skin (dermoscopic images), segmentation, feature extraction and classification. The most relevant step is segmentation process because it provides fundamental information to the next stages. Image segmentation is the process of adequately grouping pixels into a few regions, which pixels share some similar characteristics. Automated analysis of edges, colors, and shape of the lesion relies upon an accurate segmentation and is an important first step in any CAD system but irregular shape, nonuniform color, and ambiguous structures make the problem difficult.

## 8. Simulation results

This section presents numerous experimental results in segmentation obtained by developed and existed techniques. The segmentation algorithms were evaluated on a set of 50 images of dermoscopic images obtained from http://www.dermoscopyatlas.com and http://www.wisdom.weizmann.ac.il. The GT images were found via human based

Fig. 9. Block diagram of CAD system.

segmentation. The dataset presents 24-bits color images in JPEG format with 600 x 600 pixel size. Below, we only expose five different images with different texture characteristics where the sensitivity and specificity are used as the evaluation criteria for segmentation accuracy. We also plotted the ROC curves to examine the classifier performance. Additionally, the diagnostic performance was quantified by AUC measure. Fig. 10 shows the images of different nature used in this study.

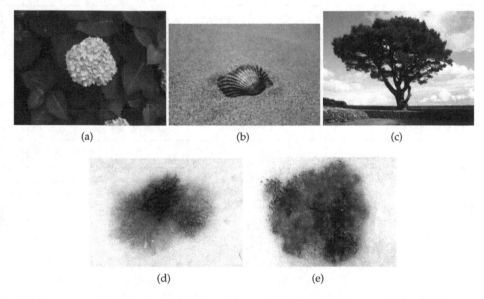

Fig. 10. Images used in this study:a) *Flower* b) *sea shell* c) *Tree* d)*Melanoma* (lesion1) e)) Melanoma (lesion2)

The simulation results in Table present the values of AUC for the proposed framework based on different wavelet families confirming their better performance in comparison with classical techniques. The maximum value of AUC is obtained when WF Daubechies 4 is used, followed by the WAF $\pi_6$. According to (Fryback DG, 1991) AUC measure should have values greater than 0.8 to consider a good test, but our study is focused in the best approximation of segmented image to GT, this means to get the value of AUC approximated to one.

Based on the objective quantity metrics and subjective visual results presented in Fig.4, one can see that the W-FCM presents borders that characterize the lesion (green color), in Fig.11

| | Lesion 1 | Lesion 2 | Flower | Sea shell | Tree | | Lesion 1 | Lesion 2 | Flower | Sea shell | Tree |
|---|---|---|---|---|---|---|---|---|---|---|---|
| **Without wavelet** | | | | | | **WAF Up$_2$** | | | | | |
| CPSFCM | 0.954 | 0.915 | 0.530 | 0.914 | 0.946 | W-CSPFCM | 0.798 | 0.787 | 0.886 | 0.906 | 0.921 |
| FCM | 0.967 | 0.936 | 0.955 | 0.954 | 0.960 | W-FCM | 0.826 | 0.929 | 0.901 | 0.935 | 0.913 |
| K-Means | 0.969 | 0.935 | 0.955 | 0.952 | 0.959 | WK-Means | 0.858 | 0.957 | 0.922 | 0.956 | 0.925 |
| **WF Coiflets 3** | | | | | | **WAF $\pi_6$** | | | | | |
| W-CSPFCM | 0.851 | 0.841 | 0.923 | 0.949 | 0.932 | W-CSPFCM | 0.832 | 0.956 | 0.887 | 0.929 | 0.943 |
| W-FCM | 0.966 | 0.948 | 0.956 | 0.961 | 0.963 | W-FCM | 0.874 | 0.953 | 0.926 | 0.953 | 0.931 |
| WK-Means | 0.871 | 0.959 | 0.928 | 0.953 | 0.928 | WK-Means | 0.898 | 0.961 | 0.941 | **0.965** | 0.934 |
| **WF Daubechies 4** | | | | | | **WAF fup$_2$** | | | | | |
| W-CSPFCM | 0.886 | 0.956 | **0.961** | 0.949 | 0.961 | W-CSPFCM | 0.811 | 0.758 | 0.868 | 0.914 | 0.936 |
| W-FCM | **0.971** | 0.945 | 0.957 | 0.959 | **0.970** | W-FCM | 0.846 | 0.940 | 0.911 | 0.943 | 0.920 |
| WK-Means | 0.874 | **0.964** | 0.937 | 0.960 | 0.939 | WK-Means | 0.878 | 0.960 | 0.931 | 0.957 | 0.931 |
| **WF biorthogonal 6.8** | | | | | | **WAF e$_2$** | | | | | |
| W-CSPFCM | 0.878 | 0.939 | 0.913 | 0.955 | 0.947 | W-CSPFCM | 0.811 | 0.763 | 0.870 | 0.911 | 0.935 |
| W-FCM | 0.966 | 0.949 | 0.956 | 0.962 | 0.964 | W-FCM | 0.844 | 0.939 | 0.910 | 0.942 | 0.919 |
| WK-Means | 0.869 | 0.958 | 0.927 | 0.953 | 0.928 | WK-Means | 0.875 | 0.960 | 0.929 | 0.959 | 0.932 |

Table 4. AUC simulation results using different segmentation algorithms

c-f, it is easy to note that the segmentation procedure has performed only around the lesion. On other hand, in Fig. 11 g-j, where WAF results are presented, one can see that together with segmentation of lesion boarder there are some areas into the lesion segmented.

Figure 12 presents ROC curves for lesion 1 comparing the classic and proposed algorithms. In particular, Fig.11c) exposes the ROC curves for WK-means and K-Means algorithms where one can see superiority of proposed WK-Means algorithm that uses WAFp6 (see ROC curve in light green color), Fig.12 d) presents ROC curves for W-FCM and FCM algorithms where it is easy to observe the better performance of WK-Means that employs the WF biorthogonal 6.8 (seeROC curve in red color), and finally, in Fig. 12 e), theROC curves for W-CPSFCM and CPSFCM algorithms have confirmed the better performance of the first one for WF biorthogonal 6.8usage (see ROC curve in red color).

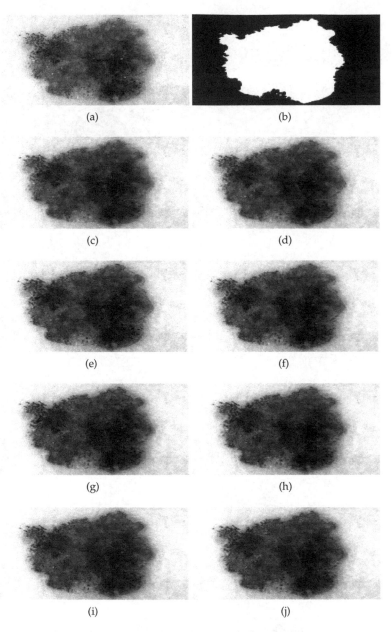

Fig. 11. Image segmentation results under different algorithms using: a) Melanoma, b) Ground Truth, c) FCM, d) W-FCM with WF Coiflets 3, e) W-FCM with Daubechies 4, f) W-FCM with WF biorthogonal 6.8, g) W-FCM with WAF $up_2$, h) W-FCM with WAF $\pi6_{\prime\prime}$, i) W-FCM with WAF $fup_2$, j) W-FCM with WAF $e_2$.

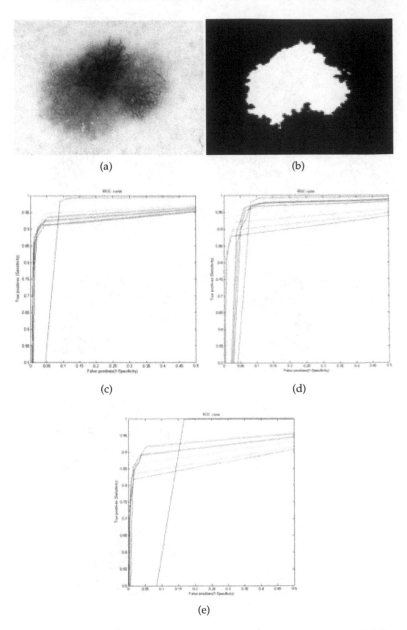

Fig. 12. a) Lesion 1 Melanoma b) Ground Truth image; ROC curves for c) WK-Means algorithm d) FCM algorithm e) W-CPSFCM: for WF Daubechies 4(dark blue), for WF biorthogonal 6.8 (red), for WF Coiflets 3 (purple), for WAF $up_2$ (dark green), for WAF fup2 (aqua), for WAF $\pi_6$ (light green); FCM (black).

# 9. Conclusion

The segmentation process involves the partition of an image into a set of homogeneous and meaningful regions allowing the detection of an object of interest in a specific task, and is an important stage in the different problems such as computer vision, remote sensing, medical images, etc. In this chapter, we present a review of existed promising methods of image segmentation; some of them are popular because they are used in various applications. Novel approach in segmentation exposed here has generated several frameworks that use traditional and fuzzy logic techniques (WK-Means, W-FCM, W-CPSFCM), all of them involve the wavelet transform space and approximation procedures for inter color channels processing, permitting better extraction of the image features. Numerous simulation results summarize the performance of all investigated algorithms for segmentation in images of different nature exposing quality in form of ROC curves (sensitivity-specificity parameters) and AUC values. It has been justified sufficiently better performance of the developed frameworks (WK-Means, W-FCM, and W-CPSFCM) that apply different classic wavelets families and WAF in comparison with traditional existed techniques.

# 10. Acknowledgement

The authors thank the National Polytechnic Institute of Mexico and CONACYT (grant 81599) for their support to realize this work.

# 11. References

Garnavi,R. (Aldeen, M. (Celebi, M. E. (2011). Weighted performance index for objective evaluation of border detection methods in dermoscopy images, Skin Research and Technology 17(1): 33–44.

Fryback, D. G. (Thornbury, J.R. (1991). The efficacy of diagnostic imaging, Med Decis Making 11(1): 88–94.

Hance, G. A (Umbaugh, S.E. ((Moss, R. H. (Stoecker, W. V. 1991). Unsupercised Color Image Segmentation with Application to Skin Tumor Borders, IEEE Engineering in Medicine and Biology Magazine 15(1): 104–111.

Argenziano, G. & Soyer, H. (1996). Adaptive thresholding of wavelet coefficients, Computational Statistics and amp. Data Analysis Vol.22(No.4): 351 – 361.

Argenziano, G. & Soyer, H. (2001). Dermoscopy of pigmented skin lesions-a valuable tool for early diagnosis of melanoma, The Lancet Oncology 2(7): 443Ǔ449.

Bello, M. (1994). A combined markov random field and wave-packet transform-based approach for image segmentation, IEEE Trans. Image Processing 3(6): 834–846.
URL: *www.intechweb.org*

Bezdek, J. (1981). *Pattern Recognition with Fuzzy Objective Function Algorithms, Plenum press,* New York.

Chaira & Ray, A. K. (2003). Fuzzy approach to color region extraction, *Pattern Recognition Letters* 12(24): 1943–1950.

Fryback DG, T. J. (1991). The efficacy of diagnostic imaging, Med Decis Making 11(1): 88Ǔ94.

Gonzalez, R. C. & Woods, R. E. (1992). *Digital Image Processing*, Addison Wesley, Place of publication.

Grossman, A. & Morlet, J. . (1985). *Mathematics and Physics: Lectures on Recent Results*, L. Streit, Place of publication.

Hartigan, A. & Wong, M. A. (1979). A k-means clustering algorithm, Applied Statistics 28(1): 100–108.

Kravchenko, V., M. H. P. V. . (2009). *Adaptive digital processing of multidimensional signals with applications.*, FizMatLit, Place of publication.

L.A. & Zadeh (1965). Fuzzy approach to color region extraction, *Information and Control* 8(3): 338 – 353.

M. Celebi, H. Iyatomi, G. S. & Stoecker, W. (2009). Lesion border detection in dermoscopy images, Computerized Medical Imaging and Graphics 33(2): 148Ű153.

M. Celebi, H. Kingravi, H. I. e. a. (2008). Border detection in dermoscopy images using statistical region merging, Skin Research and Technology Vol. 3(No. 14): 347–353.

Mallat, S. (1989). A theory for multiresolution signal decomposition: The wavelet representation, IEEE Trans. on Pattern Analysis and Machine Intelligence 11(7): 338 – 353.

Meyers, Y. (1993). *Wavelet: Algorithms and Applications*, SIAM, Place of publication.

Rao, R. M. & Bopardikar, A. S. (1998). *Wavelet Transforms: Introduction to Theory and Applications.*, Addison-Wesley, Place of publication.

Strickland, R. N. & Hahn, H. I. (2009). Wavelet transform matched filters for the detection and classification of microcalcifications in mammography, Proceedings of the International Conference on Image Processing, Washington 1(2): 422–425.

Vestergaard, ME; Macaskill, P. H. P. M. (2001). Dermoscopy compared with naked eye examination for the diagnosis of primary melanoma: a metaanalysis of studies performed in a clinical setting, British Journal of Dermatology 159(3): 669Ű76.

Zhang, X. & Desai, M. (2001). Segmentation of bright targets using wavelets and adaptive thresholding, IEEE Trans. Image Processing 10(7): 1020–1030.

# 7

# Application of Adaptive Neuro Fuzzy Inference System in Supply Chain Management Evaluation

Thoedtida Thipparat
*Faculty of Management Sciences,*
*Prince of Songkla Universit, Kohong Hatyai, Songkhla,*
*Thailand*

## 1. Introduction

Each construction project has unique features that differentiate it from even resembling projects. Construction techniques, design, contract types, liabilities, weather, soil conditions, politic-economic environment and many other aspects may be different for every new commitment. Uncertainty is a reality of construction business. Leung et al. (2007) developed a model to deal with uncertain demand by considering a multi-site production planning problem. The inventory control problem and quantify the value of advanced demand information were examined (Ozer and Wei, 2004). Mula et al. (2010) proposed mathematical programming models to address supply chain production and transport planning problems. A model for making multi-criteria decision was developed for both the manufacturers and the distributors Dong et al. (2005). A stochastic planning model was constructed for a two-echelon supply chain of a petroleum company Al-Othman et al. (2008). Weng and McClurg (2003) and Ray et al. (2005) focused supply uncertainty along with demand uncertainty in supply chains. Bollapragada et al. (2004) examined uncertain lead time for random demand and supply capacity in assembly Systems.

A number of methods were developed by researches to solve problems associated with uncertainties, including scenario programming (Wullink et al., 2004; Chang et al., 2007), stochastic programming (Popescu, 2007; Santoso et al., 2005), fuzzy approach (Petrovic et al., 1999; Schultmann et al., 2006; Liang, 2008), and computer simulation and intelligent algorithms (Kalyanmoy, 2001; Coello, 2005). However, each method is suitable for particular situations. The decision makers have to select the appropriate method for solving a problem.

For a uncertain construction project, the fuzzy atmosphere has been represented with the terms 'uncertainty' or 'risk' by construction managers and researchers, and they tried to control this systematically through risk management and analysis methods since the early 1990s (Edwards L., 2004). Some researchers like Flanagan et al. Flanagan R, Norman G. (1993) and Pilcher R. (1985) put differentiation between these two terms. They have mentioned that uncertainty represents the situations in which there is no historical data; and risk, in contrast, can be used for situations where success or failure is determined in probabilistic quantities by benefiting from the previous data available. Since such a separation is regarded as meaningless in the construction literature, risk turns out to be the most consistent term to be used for construction projects because some probability values can be attached intuitively and judgmentally to even the most uncertain events (Flanagan R, Norman G., 1993). The uncertainty represented quantitatively at some level is not the uncertainty any more; rather it is the risk henceforth and needs to be managed.

Construction companies are trying to make their supply chain more effective, and more efficient. Supply chain management has the potential to make construction projects less fragmented, improve project quality, reduce project duration, and hence reduce total project cost, while creating more satisfied customers. Construction companies need to respond of uncertain environment by using the concept of flexibility. Construction companies have recognized that flexibility is crucial for their survival and competitiveness. Several definitions of flexibility have been proposed since the construct is still in its initial stage of application to organizational phenomenon. Flexibility is defined as "the agility of a supply chain to respond to market changes in demand in order to gain or maintain its competitive advantage" (Bolstorff, P., Rosenbaum, R., 2007). The combination of Supply Chain Management (SCM) and flexibility is a significant source of competitiveness which has come to be named Agile Supply Chain (ASC). This paper argues that it is important to establish the flexibility of the construction supply chain. After embracing ASC an important question must be asked: How construction companies can evaluate flexibility in supply chains? This evaluation is essential for construction managers as it assists in achieving flexibility effectively by performing gap analysis between existent flexibility level and the desired one and also provides more informative and reliable information for decision making. Therefore, this study attempts to answer this question with a particular focus on measuring flexibility.

An approach based on Adaptive Neuro Fuzzy Inference System (ANFIS) for measurement of agility in Supply Chain was developed (Seyedhoseini, S.M., et al., 2010). The researchers used ANFIS to deal with complexity and vagueness of agility in global markets. ANFIS was applied order to inject different and complicated agility capabilities (that is, flexibility, competency, cost, responsiveness and quickness) to the model in an ambiguous environment. In addition, this study developed different potential attributes of ANFIS. Membership functions for each agility capabilities were constructed. The collected data was trained by using the functions through an adaptive procedure, using fuzzy concepts in order to model objective attributes. The proposed approach was useful for surveying real life problems. The proposed procedure had efficiently been applied to a large scale automobile manufacturing company in Iran. Statistical analysis illustrated that there were no meaningful difference between experts' opinion and our proposed procedure for supply chain agility measurement.

A procedure with aforementioned functionality must be develop to cope with uncertain environment of construction projects and lack of efficient measuring tool for flexibility of supply chain system. This study is to apply fuzzy concepts and aggregate this powerful tool with Artificial Neural Network concepts in favor of gaining ANFIS to handle the imprecise nature of attributes for associated concepts of flexibility. ANFIS is considered as an efficient tool for development and surveying of the novel procedure. Due to our best knowledge this combination has never been reported in literature before. This paper is organized as follows.

Section 2 reviews the literature on construction supply chain, supply chain performance evaluation and Agile Supply Chain (ASC); Section 3 represents the conceptual model using the capabilities of construction supply chain such as reliability, flexibility, responsiveness, cost, and asset, Section four contains an adaptive neuro fuzzy inference system (ANFIS) model which is proposed to evaluate flexibility in construction supply chains and the applicability of the proposed model has been tested by using construction companies in Thailand. Finally, in section 5 the main conclusion of this study is discussed.

## 2. Construction supply chain

Considering the construction industry, the client represents a unique customer with unique requirements. Stakeholders in the supply chain will provide these requirements. They must have the required primary competencies to make possible the fulfilment of these requirements.

### 2.1 Construction supply chain

In reality, organisations within a supply network delivering an office development will differ from those required to deliver a residential project. It may be useful to consider the chain as a network of organisations or a network organisations operating within the same market or industry to satisfy a variety of clients. Stakeholders involved in the construction supply-chain were classified into five categories related to the construction stages (H. Ismail & Sharif., 2005). The contract is the predominant approach for managing the relationship between organisations that operate in a construction project to deliver the client's required project. Although contracts are a sufficient basis for the delivery of a completed project, they are not sufficient to deliver a construction efficiently, at minimum cost, and right first time'.

### 2.2 Flexibility supply chain

The definition of flexibility is still fuzzy, mainly because it largely deals with things already being addressed by industry and which are covered by existing research projects and programs. Many researchers provide conceptual over views, different reference and mature models of flexibility. For instance, Siemieniuch and Sinclair (2000) presented that to become a truly agile supply chain key enablers are classified into four categories: Collaborative relationship as the supply chain strategy, Process integration as the foundation of supply chain, Information integration as the infrastructure of supply chain and Customer /marketing sensitivity as the mechanism of supply chain. The aggregation of current approaches can be criticized as they haven't considered the impact of enablers in assessing supply chain flexibility and also the scale used to aggregate the flexibility capabilities has the limitations.

Several papers present application of theories of measurement systems for managing performance of supply chain. However, there is no measurement system for managing performance of the entire supply chain. The adoption of metrics that cross of the borders of organization considering dimensions of performance related to inter and intra organization processes (Lapide, L., 2000). The metrics developed by the SCOR model (Supply-Chain Council (SCC), 2011) were proposed to analyze a supply chain form three perspectives: process, metrics and best practice. The connections between the inter-organizational processes in each company in a supply chain are created based on the SCOR framework. The common and standardized language among the company within a supply chain is developed in order to compare supply chain performance as a whole.

There are five performance attributes in top level SCOR metric, namely reliability, responsiveness, flexibility, cost and asset management efficiency (Bolstorff, P., Rosenbaum, R., 2007). Reliability is defined as the performance related to the delivery, i.e., whether the correct product (according to specifications) is delivered to the correct place, it the correct quantity, at the correct time, with the correct documentation and the right customer. The definition of responsiveness is the speed at which a supply chain provides the products to customers. Flexibility is the agility of a supply chain to respond to market changes in demand in order to gain or maintain its competitive advantage. All the costs related to the operation of supply chain are included in the cost attribute. The asset management efficiency is the efficiency of an organization in managing its resources to meet demand. The management of all the resources (i.e., fixed and working capital) is considered.

The first limitation of supply chain flexibility evaluation is that the techniques do not consider the ambiguity and multi possibility associated with mapping of individual judgment to a number. The second limitation is the subjective judgment, selection and preference of evaluators having a significant influence on these methods. Because of the fact that the qualitative and ambiguous attributes are linked to flexibility assessment, most measures are described subjectively using linguistic terms, and cannot be handled effectively using conventional assessment approaches. The fuzzy logic provides an effective means of handling problems involving imprecise and vague phenomena. Fuzzy concepts enable assessors to use linguistic terms to assess indicators in natural language expressions, and each linguistic term can be associated with a membership function. In addition, fuzzy logic has generally found significant applications in management decisions. This study applies a fuzzy inference system for mapping input space (tangible and intangible) to output space in order to assist construction companies in better achieving an flexibility supply chain. The proposed Fuzzy Inference System (FIS) has been based on the experiences of experts to evaluate flexibility of construction supply chains.

## 3. Methodology

To evaluate flexibility of the construction supply chain two main steps are performed. At the first step, measurement criteria are identified. A conceptual model is developed based on literature review. Capabilities of supply chain are employed to define supply chain performance in three basic segments: sourcing, construction and delivery. In this study the conceptual model involves four attributes: reliability, flexibility, responsiveness, cost, and asset. Twenty seven sub-attributes are the basis of the conceptual model as shown in Table 1. At the Second step, the design of an ANFIS architecture is performed by constructing an input-output mapping based on both human knowledge in the form of fuzzy if-then rules with appropriate membership functions and stipulated input-output data based- for deriving performance in supply chains.

| Reliability | Flexibility | Responsiveness | Cost | Asset |
|---|---|---|---|---|
| Perfect order fulfillment | Upside flexibility supply chain | Order fulfillment | Total cost supply chain management | Cash to cash |
| Orders in full | Upside source flexibility | Source cycle time | Finance and planning cost | Days sales outstanding |
| Delivery to commit day | Upside make flexibility | Make cycle time | Inventory carrying cost | Days payable outstanding |
| Delivery to commit day | Upside delivery flexibility | Delivery cycle time | IT cost for supply chain | Inventory days of supply |
| Perfect condition | | | Material acquisition cost | Return of asset |
| Accurate documentation | | | Order management cost | Asset turns Net profit |

Table 1. Input/Output indicators

## 4. Neurofuzzy model

The neuro-fuzzy system attempts to model the uncertainty in the factor assessments, accounting for their qualitative nature. A combination of classic stochastic simulations and fuzzy logic operations on the ANN inputs as a supplement to artificial neural network is employed. Artificial Neural Networks (ANN) has the capability of self-learning, while fuzzy logic inference system (FLIS) is capable of dealing with fuzzy language information and simulating judgment and decision making of the human brain. It is currently the research focus to combine ANN with FLIS to produce fuzzy network system. ANFIS is an example of such a readily available system, which uses ANN to accomplish fuzzification, fuzzy inference and defuzzification of a fuzzy system. ANFIS utilizes ANN's learning mechanisms to draw rules from input and output data pairs. The system possesses not only the function of adaptive learning but also the function of fuzzy information describing and processing, and judgment and decision making. ANFIS is different from ANN in that ANN uses the connection weights to describe a system while ANFIS uses fuzzy language rules from fuzzy inference to describe a system.

The ANFIS approach adopts Gaussian functions (or other membership functions) for fuzzy sets, linear functions for the rule outputs, and Sugeno's inference mechanism (R.E. Spekman, J.W. Kamau! Jr., N. Myhr., 1998). The parameters of the network are the mean and standard deviation of the membership functions (antecedent parameters) and the coefficients of the output linear functions as well (consequent parameters). The ANFIS learning algorithm is then used to obtain these parameters. This learning algorithm is a hybrid algorithm consisting of the gradient descent and the least-squares estimate. Using this hybrid algorithm, the rule parameters are recursively updated until an acceptable level of error is reached. Each iteration includes two passes, forward and backward. In the forward pass, the antecedent parameters are fixed and the consequent parameters are obtained using the linear least-squares estimation. In the backward pass, the consequent parameters are fixed and the error signals propagate backward as well as the antecedent parameters are updated by the gradient descent method. An ANFIS architecture is equivalent to a two-input first-order Sugeno fuzzy model with nine rules, where each input is assumed to have three associated membership functions (MFs) (Z.Zhang., D.Ding., L.Rao., and Z.Bi., 2006). Sub-attributes associated with reliability, flexibility, responsiveness, cost, and asset are used as input variables; simultaneously, construction supply chain performance is considered as output variables. These input variables were used in the measurement of the supply chain performance by (G.M.D. Ganga, L.C.R. Carpinetti., 2011). Fig 1 is an ANFIS architecture that is equivalent to a two-input first-order Sugeno fuzzy model with nine rules, where each input is assumed to have three associated membership functions (MFs) (J. Jassbi, S.M. Seyedhosseini, and N. Pilevari., 2010).

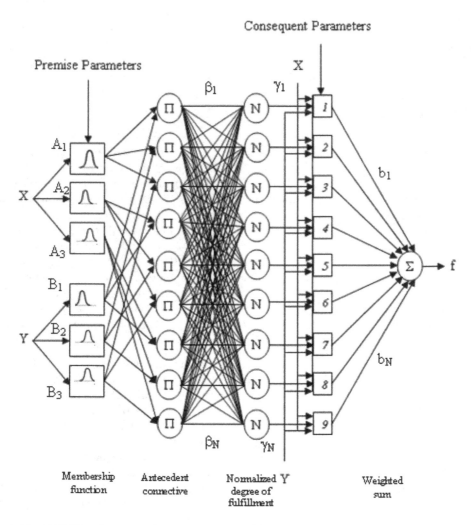

Fig. 1. The ANFIS architecture for two input variables

For proving the applicability of the model and illustration, the proposed model was applied in twenty-five of the construction companies in Thailand. The first step to apply the model was to construct the decision team. The stakeholders involved in the construction stage became the decision team including main contractor, domestic subcontractors, nominated subcontractors, project manager, material suppliers, plant/equipment suppliers, designers, financial institution, insurance agency, and regulatory bodies. For training the ANFIS, a questionnaire was designed including the identified criteria. The decision team was asked to give a score to them, based on their knowledge associated with the construction stage. A Matlab programme was generated and compiled. The pre-processed input/output matrix which contained all the necessary representative features, was used to train the fuzzy inference system. Fig 2 shows the structure of the ANFIS; a Sugeno fuzzy inference system was used in this investigation. Based on the collected data, 150 data sets were used to train the ANFIS and the rest (50) for checking and validation of the model. For rule generation, the subtractive clustering was employ where the range of influence, squash factor, acceptance ratio, and rejection ratio were set at 0.5, 1.25, 0.5 and 0.15, respectively during the process of subtractive clustering. The trained fuzzy inference system includes 20 rules (clusters) as present in Fig 3. Because by using subtractive clustering, input space was categorized into 20 clusters. Each input has 20 Gaussian curve built-in membership functions. During training in ANFIS, sets of processed data were used to conduct 260 cycles of learning.

By inserting ANFIS output to the system the flexibility level of the supply chain management can be derived. In addition, the trend of training error and checking error has been shown in Fig 4. The researcher continued the training process to 500 epochs because the trend of checking error started to increase afterward and over fitting occurred. The value of checking error by 500 epochs was 1.45 which is acceptable. Then the value of supply chain flexibility is derived by a trained ANFIS. The ANFIS output in Thai construction companies is calculated.

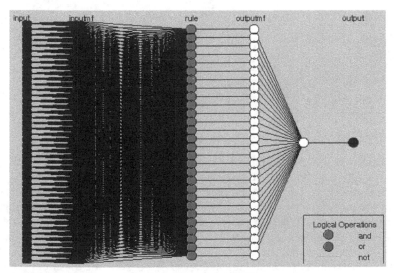

Fig. 2. Network of innovation performance by the ANFIS

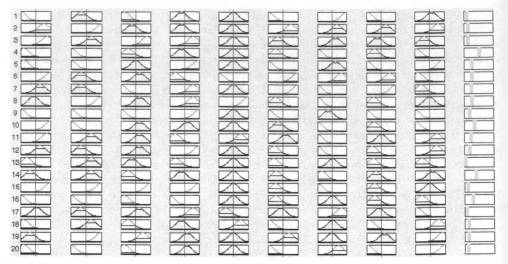

Fig. 3. Trained main ANFIS surface of supply chain performance

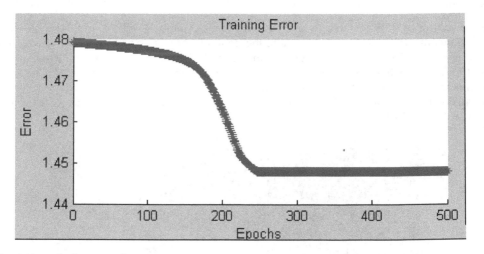

Fig. 4. Trend of errors of trained fuzzy system

Fig 5 depicts a three dimensional plot that represents the mapping from reliability (in1) and flexibility (in2) to supply chain performance (out1). As the reliability and flexibility increases, the predicted supply chain performance increases in a non-linear piecewise manner, this being largely due to non-linearity of the characteristic of the input vector matrix derived from the collected data. This assumes that the collected data are fully representative of the features of the data that the trained FIS is intended to model. However the data are inherently insufficient and training data cannot cover all the features of the data that should be presented to the trained model. The accuracy of the model, therefore, is affected under such circumstances.

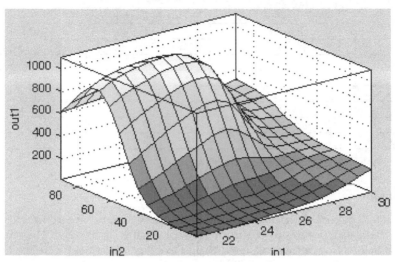

Fig. 5. Network of construction supply chain performance by the ANFIS

The rate of sub-attributes associated with flexibility, responsiveness & quickness, competency and cost and the output of ANFIS have been shown in Table 2 and 3, respectively. The twenty-five scenarios were used to test the performance the proposed method. The results indicate that the output values obtained from ANFIS are closer to the values given by experts in most scenarios being tested. The average and standard deviation of the differences between the estimated and the output values obtained from expert produced by ANFIS are calculated to be 12.6% and 8.75% respectively. As far as ANFIS is concerned, its biggest advantage is that there is no need to know the concrete functional relationship between outputs and inputs. Any relationship, linear or nonlinear, can be learned and approximated by an ANFIS such as a five-layer with sufficient large number of neurons in the hidden layer. In the case that the functional relationship between outputs and inputs is not known or cannot be determined, ANFIS definitely outperforms regression, which requires the relationship between output and inputs be known or specified. Another remarkable advantage of ANFIS is its capability of modelling the data of multiple inputs and multiple outputs. ANFIS has no restriction on the number of output. The relationships can be learned simultaneously by an ANFIS with multiple inputs and multiple outputs.

| No. | Criteria | | | | |
|---|---|---|---|---|---|
| | Reliability | Flexibility | Responsiveness | Cost | Asset |
| 1 | 23 | 54 | 31 | 31 | 20 |
| 2 | 20 | 65 | 65 | 28 | 26 |
| 3 | 19 | 75 | 75 | 30 | 23 |
| : | : | : | : | : | : |
| 98 | 20 | 65 | 65 | 28 | 31 |
| 99 | 26 | 70 | 70 | 32 | 65 |
| 100 | 23 | 70 | 25 | 31 | 75 |

Table 2. Input values for the trained ANFIS

| No | Value of output | | |
|---|---|---|---|
| | Expert's | ANFIS | Percent Difference |
| 1 | 11 | 72 | 15.4 |
| 2 | 20 | 75 | 15.08 |
| 3 | 19 | 75 | 19.67 |
| : | | | |
| 98 | 18 | 66 | 10.17 |
| 99 | 26 | 30 | 28.46 |
| 100 | 28 | 55 | 8.77 |

Table 3. Possible value obtained form ANFIS method

## 5. Conclusion

This paper has discussed the need for flexibility assessment of the construction supply chain. The particular features of construction supply chains highlighted. The need for and potential benefits of, construction supply chain flexibility assessment were then examined and the conceptual model of a flexibility assessment model for the supply chain presented. Case studies of the use of the model in assessing the construction organizations were also presented. The following conclusions can be drawn from the work presented in this paper: The way to improve the construction supply chain delivers projects is necessary to achieve client satisfaction, efficiency, effectiveness and profitability. It is important to perform the flexibility assessment of the construction supply chain in order to ensure that maximum benefit can be obtained. Since agile supply chain is considered as a dominant competitive advantage in recent years, evaluating supply chain flexibility can be useful and applicable for managers to make more informative and reliable decisions in anticipated changes of construction markets. The development of an appropriate flexibility assessment tool or model for the construction supply chain is necessary, as existing models are not appropriate in their present form. The results reveal that the ANFIS model improves flexibility assessment by using fuzzy rules to generate the adaptive neuro-fuzzy network, as well as a rotation method of training and testing data selection which is designed to enhance the reliability of the sampling process before constructing the training and testing model. The ANFIS model can explain the training procedure of outcome and how to simulate the rules for prediction. It can provide more accuracy on prediction.

Further research is necessary to compare efficiency of different models for measuring flexibility in supply chain. Although this study has been performed in the construction companies, the proposed methodology is applicable to other companies, e.g. consulting companies. Enablers in flexibility evaluation should be determined and the impact of them on capabilities must be studied in further researches. In addition, the relations between enablers should be considered in order to design a dynamic system for the supply chain management evaluation.

## 6. References

Al-Othman, W.B.E., Lababidi, H.M.S., Alatiqi, I.M., Al-Shayji, K., (2008) Supply chain optimization of petroleum organization under uncertainty in market demands and prices. *European Journal of Operational Research*, Vol. 189, No.3, pp. 822–840.

Bollapragada, R., Rao, U.S., Zhang, J. (2004) Managing inventory and supply performance in assembly systems with random supply capacity and demand. *Management Science* Vol.50, No.12, pp.1729–1743.

Bolstorff, P., Rosenbaum, R. (2007) *Supply chain excelence*. A handbook for Dramatic Improvement Using the SCOR Model. AMACOM, NY.

Coello, C.A.C. (2005) An introduction to evolutionary algorithms and their applications. Advanced Distributed Systems. Springer, Berlin, Heidelberg.

Dong, J., Zhang, D., Yan, H., Nagurney, A., (2005) Multitiered supply chain networks: Multicriteria mecision-making under uncertainty. *Annals of Operations Research*, Vol.135, No.1, pp. 155–178.

Edwards L. (2004). *Practical risk management in the construction industry*, London: Thomas Telford.

Flanagan R, Norman G.(1993) *Risk management and construction*, Cambridge: Backwell Scientific.

Ganga, G.M.D., Carpinetti, L.C.R. (2011) A fuzzy logic approach to supply chain performance management, *Int. J. Production Economics*.

Ismail, H. and Sharif. (2005) Supply chain design for supply chain: A balanced approach to building agile supply chain, *Proceeding of the International conference on Flexibility*.

Jassbi, J., Seyedhosseini, S.M. and Pilevari, N. (2010) An adaptive neuro fuzzy inference system for supply chain flexibility evaluation, *International Journal of Industrial Engineering & Production Research*, Vol. 20, pp.187–196.

Kalyanmoy, D. (2001) Multi-objective Optimization Using Evolutionary Algorithms. John Wiley and Sons, New York.

Lapide, L. (2000) What about measuring supply chain performance? *Achieving Supply Chain Excellence through Technology*, Vol. 2, pp. 287–297.

Pilcher R. (1985) *Project cost control in construction*, London: Collins.

Leung, S.C.H., Tsang, S.O.S., Ng, W.L., Wu, Y., (2007) A robust optimization model for multi-site production planning problem in an uncertain environment, *European Journal of Operational Research*, Vol.181, No.1, pp. 224–238.

Liang, T.F. (2008) Integrating production-transportation planning decision with fuzzy multiple goals in supply chains. *International Journal of Production Research*, Vol. 46, No.6, pp.1477–1494.

Mula, J., Peidro, D., Dıaz-Madroₒero, M., Vicens, E., (2010) Mathematical programming models for supply chain production and transport planning, *European Journal of Operational Research*, Vol.204, No.3, pp. 377–390.

O zer, O., Wei, W., (2004) Inventory Control with Limited Capacity and Advance Demand Information, *Operations Research*, Vol. 52, No.6, pp.988–1000.

Petrovic, D., Roy, R., Petrovic, R. (1999) Supply chain modeling using fuzzy sets. International *Journal of Production Economics*, Vol. 59, No.1–3, pp.443–453.

Popescu, I. (2007) Robust Mean-Covariance Solutions for Stochastic Optimization. *Operations Research*, Vol. 55, No.1, pp.98–112.

Ray, S., Li, S., Song, Y. ( 2005) Tailored supply chain decision making under price sensitive stochastic demand and delivery uncertainty. *Management Science*, Vol. 51, No.12, pp.1873–1891.

Santoso, T., Ahmed, S., Goetschalckx, M., Shapiro, A. (2005) A stochastic programming approach for supply chain network design under uncertainty. *European Journal of Operational Research*. Vol.167 , No.1, pp. 96–115.

Schultmann, F., Frohling, M., Rentz, O. (2006) Fuzzy approach for production planning and detailed scheduling in paints manufacturing. *International Journal of Production Research*, Vol. 44, No.8, pp. 1589–1612.

Seyedhosseini, S.M., Jassbi, J., and Pilevari, N.(2010) Application of adaptive neuro fuzzy inference system in measurement of supply chain agility: Real case study of a manufacturing company, *African Journal of Business Management*, Vol.4, No. 1, pp. 083-096.

Siemieniuch, C.E., and Sinclair, M.A. (2000) Implications of the supply chain for role definitions in concurrent engineering, *International Journal of Human Factors and Ergonomics in Manufacturing*, Vol. 10, No.3, pp. 251-272.

Spekman, R.E., Kamau Jr. J.W., Myhr, N. (1998) An empirical investigation into supply chain management*A perspective on partnerships, *International Journal of Physical Distribution and Logistics Management*, Vol. 28, No. 8, pp. 630-650.

Supply-Chain Council (SCC). (3 June 2011). Availableat: /http://www.supply-chain.org

Weng, Z.K., McClurg, T., (2003) Coordinated ordering decisions for short life cycle products with uncertainty in delivery time and demand. *European Journal of Operational Research*, No. 151, No.1, pp.12–24.

Wullink, G., Gademann, A.J.R.M., Hans, E.W., Van Harten, A. (2004) Scenario-based approach for flexible resource loading under uncertainty. *International Journal of Production Research*, Vol. 42, No.24, pp.5079–5098.

Zhang, Z., Ding, D., Rao, L., and Bi, Z. (2006) An ANFIS based approach for predicting the ultimate bearing capacity of single piles, *Foundation Analysis and Design : Innovative Methods (GSP 153) ASCE*.

# Part 2

# Techniques and Implementation

# 8

# Fuzzy Logic Approach for QoS Routing Analysis

Adrian Shehu and Arianit Maraj

*Polytechnic University of Tirana,*
*Albania*

## 1. Introduction

One of the main challenges nowadays for managing IP networks is guaranteeing quality of service. One of the proposed solutions is traffic management with MPLS protocol. However, requirement characterization and the network state are very difficult tasks, taking into account that requirements for different services are random, where as a result the network condition varies dynamically and randomly. This is reason why researches have used fuzzy logic for solving a lot of problems that can occur in very dynamic networks. In this chapter we will analyze MPLS network routing metrics using fuzzy logic. We will pay attention the most appropriate defuzzification methods for finding the path that fulfills the QoS requirements for multimedia services.

One of the key issues in providing end-to-end quality of service (QoS) guarantees in today's networks is how to determine a feasible route that satisfies a set of constraints. In general, finding a path subject to multiple constraints is an NP-complete problem that cannot be exactly solved in polynomial time. Accordingly, several heuristics and approximation algorithms have been proposed for this problem. Many of these algorithms suffer from either excessive computational cost or low performance.

Selecting feasible paths that satisfy various QoS requirements of applications in a network is known as QoS routing [1]. In general, two issues are related to QoS routing: state distribution and routing strategy. State distribution addresses the issue of exchanging the state information throughout the network. Routing strategy is used to find a feasible path that meets the QoS requirements. In this chapter we will present the fuzzy logic approach for QoS routing analysis in a network which is able to offer multimedia services, such is MPLS network [2] [3] [4] [5] [6]. Fuzzy sets offer powerful mathematical structure that has to do with non-preciosity and uncertainty of real word. Linguistic variables allow representation of numerical values with fuzzy sets. Knowing that networks nowadays are very dynamic, which means that networks have parameters that are affected from unexpected overloads, failures and other concerns, fuzzy logic offers promising approach for addressing different network problems [7] [8]. Applying of fuzzy logic in telecommunication networks is done lately and is proved to be a very economic and efficient method compared with other methods used in automatic control. Recent researches on application of fuzzy logic in telecommunication networks have to do with: packet queuing, buffer management, call acceptance, QoS routing, channel capacity sharing, traffic management etc.

Some problems can occur during multimedia service transmission, therefore it is a good idea to design some control mechanisms for solving such problems. As a result of the complex nature of control mechanisms, more and more is being done in designing intelligent controlled techniques. One of the intelligent controlled techniques that will be part of this chapter is Fuzzy Logic Controller, a technique that is based on fuzzy logic. In this chapter we will use main metrics of MPLS network as input parameters of FLC, and we will try to choose the most appropriate defuzzification method for finding better crisp values in aspect of link utilization, in the output of Fuzzy Logic controller.

In this chapter we will firs explain shortly QoS routing principle, MPLS technology in aspect of QoS routing metrics. Also, here we will give the main attention to the fuzzy logic approach, especially FLC used for QoS routing analysis in MPLS network. In this aspect we will try to find the best defuzzification method for gaining better crisp values for link optimization in MPLS network.

## 2. QoS routing

The main goal of QoS based routing is to select the most suitable path according to traffic requirements for multimedia applications. Selection of suitable transmission paths is done through routing mechanisms based on existing network resources and QoS requirements. Multimedia applications might suffer degradation in quality in traditional networks such as Internet [9]. This problem can be solved in networks that contain dynamic path creation features with bandwidth-guaranteed and constrained delays [10]. Real–time applications impose strict QoS requirements. These application requirements are expressed by parameters such as acceptable and end-to-end delays, necessary bandwidth and acceptable losses. For example, audio and video transmissions have strict requirements for delay and losses. Wide bandwidth must be guaranteed for high capacity transmission. Real time traffic, video in particular, quite often utilizes most important quantities of network resources. Efficient management of network resources will reduce network service cost and will allow more applications to be transmitted simultaneously. The task of finding suitable paths through networks is treated by routing protocols. Since common routing protocols are reaching their acceptable complexity limits, it is important that complexity proposed by QoS based routing [11] should not damage scalability of routing protocols. MPLS is a multiple solution for a lot of current problems faced by Internet [12]. By a wide support for QoS and traffic engineering, MPLS is establishing itself as a standard of the next generation's network.

## 3. MPLS network

MPLS is a data transmission technology which includes some features of circuit switched networks through packet switched network. MPLS actually works at both Layer 2 and Layer 3 in OSI model and it is often referred to as a Layer 2.5 technology. It is designed to provide transport possibilities of data for all users. MPLS techniques can be used as a more efficient tool for traffic engineering than standard routing in IP networks. Also, MPLS can be used for path control of traffic flow, in order to utilize network resources in an optimal way. Network paths can be defined for sensitive traffic, high security traffic etc, guaranteeing different CoS (Class of Service) and QoS. Main MPLS feature is virtual circuit configuration through IP network. These virtual circuits are called LSP.

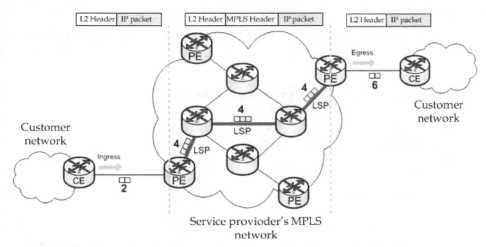

Fig. 1. MPLS network

MPLS supports traffic engineering for QoS provision and traffic prioritization, for example: provision of wider bandwidth and lower delays for gold customers who are able to pay more for better quality services. Another example a lot of paths can be defined through edge points by ensuring lower levels of interferences and backup services in case of any network failure. This is like using routing metrics in IP network to enforce traffic flowing in one or another direction, but in this case MPLS is much more powerful. An important aspect in MPLS is the priority concept of LSP [13]. LSPs can be configured with higher or lower priority. LSPs with higher priority have advantages in finding new paths compared with those of lower priority.

Figure 1 shows MPLS network and its corresponding elements. The core part represents the MPLS network. MPLS combines the advantages of packet forwarding which is based on layer 2 and routing properties of the 3'd layer. MPLS also offers traffic engineering (TE). TE is process of selecting suitable routes for data transmission on the network, that has to do with efficient use of network resources and improving network performance, thus increasing network revenue and QoS. One of the main goals of TE is efficient and reliable functionality of the network. Also, TE calculates the route from the source to the destination based on different metrics such as channel capacity (bandwidth), delays and other administrative requirements.

## 4. Routing metrics in MPLS network

Routing metrics have a significant role, not just in complexity of route calculation but also in QoS. The use of multiple metrics is able to model the network in a more precise way, but the problem for finding appropriate path can become very complex [9] [10]. In general, there are 3 types of metrics:

- Additive,
- Multiplicative and
- Concave.

They are defined as below:

If $m$ $(n_1, n_2)$ are metrics for link $(n_1, n_2)$. For one path $P = (n_1, n_2, ..., n_i, n_j)$, metric $m$ is $(n_1, n_2, ..., n_i, n_j)$:

-   Let d $(i, j)$ be a metric for link $(i, j)$.

For any path $p = (i, j, k, ..., l, m)$, we say metric d is additive if:

$$d\ (p) = d(i, j) + d\ (j,k) + ... + d(l, m) \tag{1}$$

-   We say that metric d is multiplicative if:

$$d\ (p) = d(i, j)\ x\ d\ (j,k)\ x\ ...\ x\ d(l, m) \tag{2}$$

-   We say that metric d is concave if:

$$d(p) = min[d(i, j),\ d\ (j,k),\ ...\ d(l, m)] \tag{3}$$

In MPLS network there are a lot of metrics that we can take into consideration, but in this chapter, for sake of simplicity, we will consider three main metrics: delay, losses and bandwidth. Those metrics play a direct role in quality of service in MPLS network. In order to consider multiple metrics simultaneously, we will use fuzzy logic controller. FLC is intelligent technique that can manipulate with two or more input parameters simultaneously without any problem.

## 5. Soft computing

Soft Computing is more tolerable in uncertainty and partial truth than Hard Computing. The model in which soft computing is based in human mind. The main components of soft computing are: Fuzzy Logic, Neural Networks, Probabilistic reasoning and Genetic algorithms. The most important component of soft computing is Fuzzy logic, which will be part of this chapter. Fuzzy logic will be used for a lot of applications. Applications of fuzzy logic in telecommunications networks are recent. Fuzzy Logic is organized into three main efforts: modeling and control, management and forecasting, and performance estimation.

### 5.1 Fuzzy logic

Idea for fuzzy logic has born in 1965. Lotfi Zadeh has published one seminar for fuzzy which was the beginning for fuzzy logic [14]. Fuzzy logic is tolerant in imprecise data, nonlinear functions and can be mixed with other techniques for different problems solving. The main principle of fuzzy logic is using fuzzy groups which are without crisp boundaries.

## 6. QoS routing analysis using FLC – Fuzzy Logic Controller

As we have mentioned above, for QoS routing analysis we will use FLC as intelligent controlling technique. A Fuzzy Logic Controller [15] is a rule based system in which fuzzy rule represents a control mechanism. In this case, a fuzzy controller uses fuzzy logic to simulate human thinking. In particular the FLC is useful in two special cases [15]:

- When the control processes are too complex to analyze by conventional quantitative techniques
- When the available sources of information are interpreted qualitatively or uncertainly.

Fuzzy logic controller consists of: fuzzifier, rule base, fuzzy inference and defuzzifier (see Figure 2).

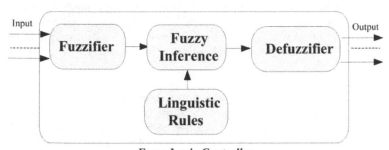

*Fuzzy Logic Controller*

Fig. 2. Fuzzy Logic Controller

**Fuzzifier:** A fuzzifier operator has the effect of transforming crisp value to fuzzy sets. Fuzzifier is presented with $x=fuzzifier(x_0)$, where $x_0$ is input crisp value; $x$ is a fuzzy set and fuzzifier represents a fuzzification operator.

**Rule-Base (Linguistic Rules):** Contains IF-THEN rules that are determined through fuzzy logic.

***Example***: if $x$ is $A_i$ and $Y$ is $B_i$ the $Z$ is $C_i$, Where $x$ and $y$ are inputs and $z$ is controlled output; $A_i$, $B_i$ and $C_i$ are linguistic terms, like: low, medium, high etc.

**Fuzzy Inference:** Is a process of converting input values into output values using fuzzy logic. Converting is essential for decision making. Fuzzy Inference process includes: membership functions and logic operations

**Defuzzifier:** can be expressed by: $y_{ou}=defuzzifier(y)$, where $y$ identifies fuzzy controller action, $y_{ou}$ identifies crisp value of control action and defuzzifier presents defuzzifier operator. Converting process of fuzzy terms in crisp values is called defuzzification. There are some defuzzification methods: COG (Centre of Gravity), COGS (Centre of Gravity for Singletons), COA (Centre of Area), LM (Left Most Maximum) and RM (Right Most Maximum).

## 7. MPLS network metrics and membership functions

For solving QoS routing problem, we will use fuzzy logic approach. Fuzzy logic is proved to be very effective in a lot of applications, such as intelligent control, decision making process etc. Fuzzy logic is based in a set of metrics which can be or not connected with each other. Calculating the best route cannot be done using complex mathematical solutions, but is based in intuitive rules.

Fuzzy logic applies to all those routes that are candidates for being chosen whereas the chosen path in this way is the path that has better quality. In this chapter we will use the Fuzzy logic controller for solving QoS routing problems and the routing algorithm refers to the fuzzy logic (fuzzy routing algorithm). This algorithm is able to choose the path with better transmission parameters. For solving such a problem using fuzzy logic, first we have to take into consideration some input parameters, acting at the entrance of FLC, which in our case must be the MPLS network metrics. These input variables can be crisp or fuzzy values. Whereas the main disadvantageous of MPLS network consist in: losses, delay and bandwidth, then these three metrics will be taken as network parameters. These metrics match with the main factors which affect for choosing the best route for transmission of multimedia services. Each network metric has the value from 0 to 1. These metrics are:

## a.   Channel capacity (B)

Channel capacity is one of the main MPLS network parameters. In this chapter, channel capacity is combined with linguistic data for selecting the optimal route from the source to destination. In this particular case we took three membership functions that indicate the potential scale of the channel capacity: LOW, MEDIUM and HIGH. Channel capacity is presented by triangular membership functions. Figure x shows the membership function for the channel capacity. Triangular number $B = (b_1, b_2, b_3)$ in limited in his left hand with value b1 and in his right hand with the value $b_3$. In this way, decision taker can calculate that channel capacity in a certain link cannot be smaller than $b_1$ or greater than $b_2$. Figure 3 shows the fuzzy set of linguistic data for channel capacity.

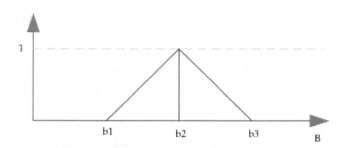

Fig. 3. Fuzzy Triangular number for channel capacity - B

It can be seen from the figure x that each value has the upper and lower limit.

## b.   Delays (D)

For most applications, especially real time applications, the delay for transmission of information between two points is one of the most important parameters for meeting QoS requirements. For delay we set 3 membership functions in triangular form to show the potential scale of the delays: ACCEPTABLE, TOLERABLE and INTOLERABLE. Figure 4 represents the membership function $\mu_s(D_s)$ for the delay. From this function it is indicated that the greatest value of membership is (=1) for $D_s = d_s$.

### c.   Losses (L)

For losses we will use 3 membership functions. For two membership functions we will use triangular form (ACCEPTABLE and TOLERABLE), while for one of membership functions we will use rectangular form (INTOLERABLE).

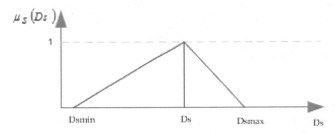

Fig. 4. Fuzzy triangular number for delay-D

In table x are given details about metrics in the input of the fuzzy system and fuzzy sets corresponding such inputs.

| Input parameters for MPLS network | Fuzzy sets |
|---|---|
| Channel capacity (bandwidth) | {LOW, MEDIUM, HIGH}-*Mbps* |
| Delays | {ACCEPTABLE, TOLERABLE, INTOLERABLE}- *ms* |
| Losses | { ACCEPTABLE, TOLERABLE, INTOLERABLE }-% |

Table 1. Input parameters and fuzzy sets

Mathematical relations of 3 input parameters can be given by the below expression:

$$f(p) = \frac{B(p)}{D(p) \times L(p)} \tag{4}$$

Where $p$ is the calculated path, $B(p)$ is channel capacity, $D(p)$ is the delay among transmission, and $L(p)$ is the probability of packet loss.

## 8. Limits of fuzzy sets for MPLS network parameters

Packet switching networks commonly are used for transmission of multimedia services. This trend continued in MPLS network also. Real time traffic is sensitive to delays, such as: voice, video etc, constitute an important part of real time traffic. Such traffic has more strict requirements for quality of service (QoS), especially in the aspect of delays between two end points and packet losses. The table below shows standard requirements for QoS for multimedia services.

| | Maximum rate | Average rate | Probability of packet loss |
|---|---|---|---|
| Voice | 32 KBits/sec | 11.2 KBits/sec | 0.05 |
| Voice | 11.6 MBits/sec | 3.85 MBits/sec | 10**(-5) |

Table 2. Bit rate for voice transmission

According to ITU recommendations for delay, packet loss and channel capacity, we have defined the boundaries of fuzzy sets.

| Delays in one direction | Characterization of quality |
|---|---|
| 0 to 150 *ms* | Acceptable for most of applications |
| 150 to 400 *ms* | May impact in some applications |
| Above 400 *ms* | Unacceptable for most of applications |

Table 3. ITU recommendation for delays

**Delays**

Delays up to 150 ms are acceptable
Delays between 150 and 400 ms are tolerable for special applications
Delays higher than 400 ms are intolerable

**Packet loss percentage**

Lower than 2% - acceptable
From 2 – 6% - tolerable
Higher than 6 % - intolerable

**Channel capacity:**

Low:  from 0 *Mbps* to 200 *Mbps*.
Medium:  from 180 *Mbps* to 500 *Mbps*.
High:  from 470 *Mbps* to 1000 *Mbps*.

## 9. Fuzzy logic toolbox in Matlab software

Fuzzy logic tool in Matlab is used for solving different problems dealing with Fuzzy Logic. Fuzzy logic is a very valuable tool for planning because it makes a very good for problems that have high importance and require high precision – something that human beings have done long time ago. Fuzzy logic tool allows users to do important jobs, but the most important thing is to allow users to create fuzzy conclusions (fuzzy inference). It is also possible to use fuzzy logic tool through command line, but in general it is easier to build a system through the GUI. There are five primary GUI tools for building, editing and reviewing systems in fuzzy logic toolbox:

1.   FIS (Fuzzy Inference System) editor
2.   Membership function editor
3.   Rules editor
4.   Rule Viewer
5.   Surface viewer

The interactions of these tools can be seen in the figure below (Figure 5).

Rule viewer and surface viewer are used for survey, compared with FIS editor, which is used for editing. So, they are read-only tools. These GUI dynamically are connected with each other and changes in FIS can be seen in other open GUIs.

Membership function for channel capacity, delays, losses and the output of the fuzzy system will be seen in the following figure (where the values are taken for real tie applications). Based on the above limits for fuzzy sets, using Matlab software we can create the membership functions main parameters of the MPLS network.

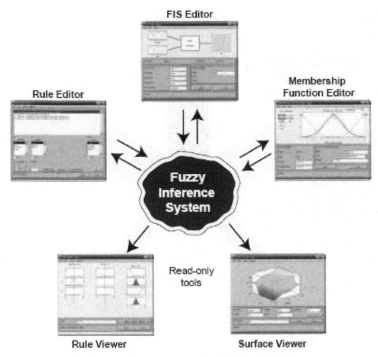

Fig. 5. Fuzzy system and its integral components in MATLAB software

[System]
Name='fuzzy_link'
Type='mamdani'
Version=2.0
NumInputs=3
NumOutputs=1
NumRules=4
AndMethod='min'
OrMethod='max'
ImpMethod='min'
AggMethod='max'
DefuzzMethod='Centre of Gravity'

[Input1]
Name='bandwidth'
Range=[0 1000]
NumMFs=3

MF1='low':'trimf',[-400 0 400]
MF2='medium':'trimf',[100 500 900]
MF3='high':'trimf',[600 1000 1400]

[Input2]
Name='delays'
Range=[0 600]
NumMFs=3
MF1='acceptable':'trimf',[-240 0 240]
MF2='tolerable':'trimf',[60 300 540]
MF3='highintolerable':'trimf',[360 600 840]

[Input3]
Name='losses'
Range=[0 10]
NumMFs=3
MF1='acceptable':'trimf',[-4 0 4]
MF2='tolerable':'trimf',[1 5 9]
MF3='intolerable':'trimf',[6 10 14]
[Output1]
Name='link optimization'
Range=[0 100]
NumMFs=3
MF1='low':'trimf',[-40 0 40]
MF2='medium':'trimf',[10 50 90]
MF3='high':'trimf',[60 100 140]

[Rules]
1 1 1, 1 (1) : 1
2 1 1, 2 (1) : 1
3 1 1, 3 (1) : 1
3 2 3, 1 (1) : 1

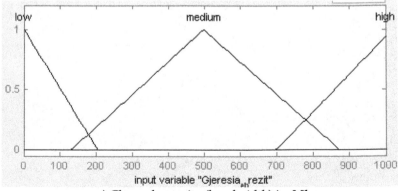

a) Channel capacity (bandwidth) in **Mbps**

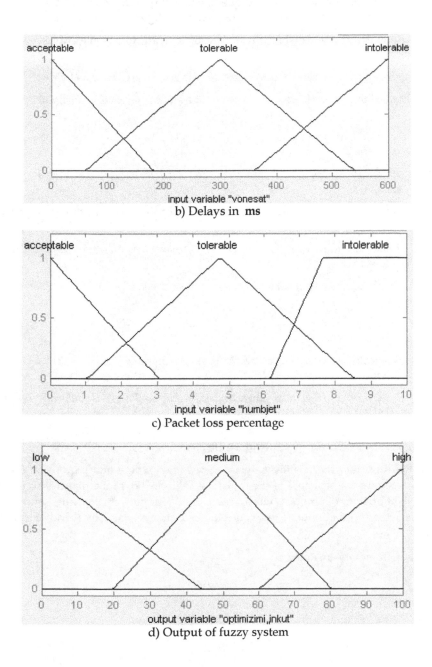

b) Delays in **ms**

c) Packet loss percentage

d) Output of fuzzy system

Fig. 6. a) Membership function of channel capacity, b) delays, c) packet loss percentage and d) output of fuzzy system

With this simple program are created the membership functions for abovementioned parameters. These membership functions are seen in the figure 6 (a, b, c and d)

Once the variable and membership functions are assigned, fuzzy rules can be written for corresponding variables.

**Some of the fuzzy rules derived from Rule editor (Matlab) are listed as below:**

*Rule 1:* If (bandwidth is low) and (delay is acceptable) and (loss is acceptable) then (link optimization is Low)

*Rule 2:* If (bandwidth is Medium) and (delay is acceptable) and (loss is acceptable) then (link optimization is Medium)

*Rule 3:* If (bandwidth is High) and (delay is Acceptable) and (loss is Acceptable) then (link optimization is High)

*Rule 4:* If (bandwidth is Low) and (delay is Tolerable) and (loss is Acceptable) then (link optimization is Low)

*Rule 5:* If (bandwidth is Medium) and (delay is Tolerable) and (loss is Tolerable) then (link optimization is Medium)

*Rule 6:* If (bandwidth is High) and (delay is Tolerable) and (loss is Intolerable) then (link optimization is Medium)

*Rule 7:* If (bandwidth is Low) and (delay is Intolerable) and (loss is Acceptable) then (link optimization is Low)

*Rule 8:* If (bandwidth is Medium) and (delay is Intolerable) and (loss is Tolerable) then (link optimization is Low)

*Rule 9:* If (bandwidth is High) and (delay is Intolerable) and (loss is Intolerable) then (link optimization is Low)

## 10. Fuzzy relations for QoS routing analysis

Here we will illustrate the relation between input fuzzy value and required output. The figure below shows the structure of the proposed solution. So, in the figure is shown fuzzy controller comprising of: inputs (which react in the input), fuzzy rules and outputs. Parameters acting on the input of this controller are: channel capacity (bandwidth), delays and losses.

Three input parameters are noted as:

$$\mu A(B) \tag{5}$$

Where $A = \{Low, Medium, High\}$

$$\mu B(D) \tag{6}$$

Where $B = \{Acceptable, Tolerable, Intolerable\}$

$$\mu C(L) \hspace{6cm} (7)$$

Where $C = \{Acceptable, Tolerable, Intolerable\}$

While, $\mu A(B)$, $\mu B(D)$ and $\mu C(L)$ are membership functions for channel capacity, delays and losses.

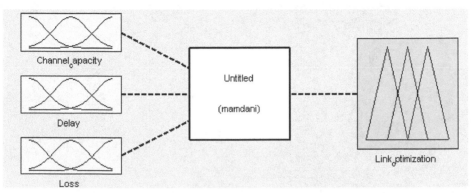

Fig. 7. The structure of the fuzzy controller system for MPLS network analysis

The role of Linguistic rules is to connect these input parameters with output of fuzzy system, which in our case is link optimization. The output comprises from three membership functions: LOW, MEDIUM and HIGH. Each rule determines one fuzzy relation. In our case, each rule represents the relation between 3 input parameters and required output that is written as:

$\mu_O(L)$ - Membership function for output of the fuzzy system.

Where $O = \{Low, Medium, High\}$

Fuzzy controller considered here is Mamdani type and consists of: Fuzzifier, fuzzy inference, linguistic rules and defuzzifier. This fuzzy controller is shown in figure x.

## 11. Defuzzification process

It is well known that in some cases the output of fuzzy process needs to be a single scalar value. Defuzzification is the process of converting the fuzzy quantity to a precise value. The output of a fuzzy process can be the union of two or more fuzzy membership functions. To see this better, we will take into consideration one example. Let suppose a fuzzy output comprises from two parts: 1) Triangular membership shape and 2) Triangular membership shape. The union of these two membership functions means that we will use the max operator, which graphically will look like in figure below.

There are a lot of methods that have been proposed recently as defuzzification methods. We will explain shortly each of these methods and we will analyze which one is the best for gaining more accurate values in the output.

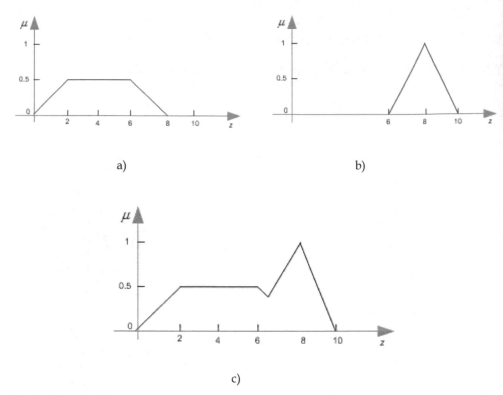

a)                                                                b)

c)

Fig. 8. a) Triangular membership shape, b) Triangular membership shape c) The union of these two membership (a and b)

## 12. Selection of defuzzification method for finding crisp value for link optimization

For finding the appropriate path for transmission of multimedia services one important role plays selection of defuzzification method. Using fuzzy logic technique, the "not accurate" data are presented by linguistic values which depend on user preferences.

There are 5 defuzzification methods: Centre of Gravity (COG), bisectorial, LOM (largest of maximum), MOM (middle of maximum) and SOM (smallest of maximum). Three most important methods are: COG, MOM and LOM. It is important to find which method gives better results in aspect of link optimization in MPLS network. To see which method is most suitable for defuzzification, first we will explain shortly each abovementioned method .

### 12.1 Centre of gravity

This method determines the centre of zone that is gained from membership functions with AND and OR logic operators. Formula with which we can calculate the defuzzified crisp output $U$ is given:

$$U = \frac{\int\limits_{Min}^{Max} u\,\mu(u)\,du}{\int\limits_{Min}^{Max} \mu(u)\,du} \qquad (8)$$

Where $U$ is defuzzification result, $u$ = *output variable*, $\mu$ = *membership function* , *Min=minimum limit for defuzzification, Max=maximum limit for defuzzification*

With formula (1) we can calculate the surface of zone that is shown in figure below and also we can find one central point in this zone. Projecting this point in the abscissa axis determines the crisp value after defuzzification.

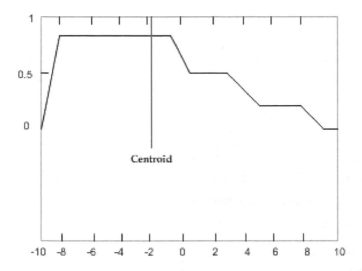

Fig. 9. COG method

## 12.2 Bisectorial method

This method divides a certain zone into two equal regions by a vertical line. This can be seen in figure below (Figure 10).

## 12.3 Middle, smallest and largest of maximum methods

In some cases MOM and LOM methods are better than COG method, but in general, for the most of cases, no matter what zone we will have, COG method shows better results. In this chapter we will analyze which method is better with MATLAB software in 3 D. LOM method determines the largest of maximum value in the zone that is obtained from membership functions with AND and OR logic operators whereas MOM method determines Middle of maximum value in that zone.

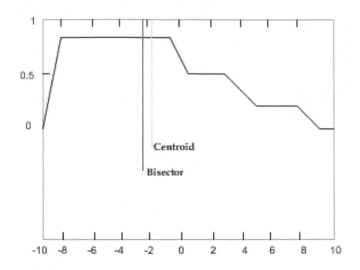

Fig. 10. Bisectorial Method

These three methods have to do with the maximum value of the sum of membership functions. In this example, since in this graph (figure x) is a flat curve at the maximum point, then these three methods have different values from each other. In case when we have a single maximum point, then three methods have the same value.

Finding defuzzification values using the above-mentioned methods can e done like below:

x3 = defuzz(x,mf1,'mom')
x4 = defuzz(x,mf1,'som')
x5 = defuzz(x,mf1,'lom')
set([h2 t2],'Color',gray)
h3 = line([x3 x3],[-0.7 1.2],'Color','k');
t3 = text(x3,-0.7,' MOM','FontWeight','bold');
h4 = line([x4 x4],[-0.8 1.2],'Color','k');
t4 = text(x4,-0.8,' SOM','FontWeight','bold');
h5 = line([x5 x5],[-0.6 1.2],'Color','k');
t5 = text(x5,-0.6,' LOM','FontWeight','bold');
x3 =    -5
x4 =    -2
x5 =    -8

These values are represented graphically like in figure 11.

Methods that are used mostly for defuzzification are: COGM MOM and LOM. Although, in some cases MOM and LOM methods give very favorable values, COG method gives better results whatever the case that we are analyzing. The performance comparison offered by three methods can be better seen through examples by surface viewer in 3D.

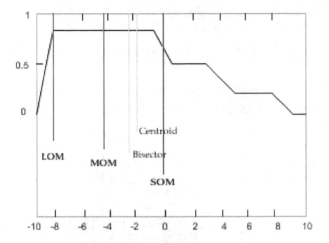

Fig. 11. LOM, MOM and SOM defuzzification methods

## 13. Analysis and examples for different defuzzification methods

Here we will use some examples taking different rules derived from rule editor of Matlba's toolbox. Also we will analyze which of the defuzzification method is better and which of the rules gives us better result in aspect of link utilization.

If we use rule number 3 (derived from rule editor):

*If (bandwidth is High) AND (delay is Acceptable) AND (loss is Acceptable) THEN (link optimization is High)*

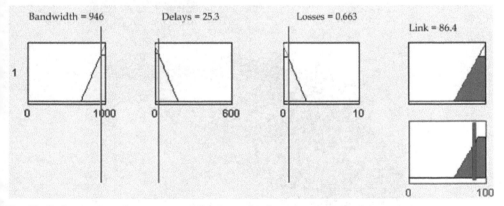

Fig. 12. Rule viewer when it is used COG method

Whereas, if we take the values for channel capacity (bandwidth) as "high" (946 Mbps), Delays 25.3 ms and losses 0.663 %, then link optimization for MPLS network will be 86.4 %. This can be shown graphically using rule viewer. So, from this figure, it is clearly seen that link optimization is high (according to determination of link optimization using membership functions). This value is obtained using COG method. Based on the results obtained here, we will conclude that this method is very effective.

The 86.4 % value represents the value after defuzzification. While, the surface viewer in 3D for three main defuzzification methods will look like in figure below.

If we use rule number 9 (derived from rule editor):

*If (bandwidth is High) AND (delay is Intolerable) AND (loss is Intolerable) THEN (link optimization is Low)*

Then, link optimization will be 20 % (see Figure 14). As we can see, in this case, link optimization is very low. So we can freely conclude that in a case when we have intolerable delays and intolerable losses, we will not have high QoS. The reason is because multimedia applications are very sensitive in delays and losses.

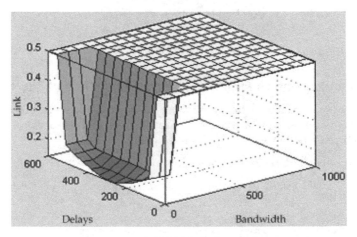

*a) COG Method*

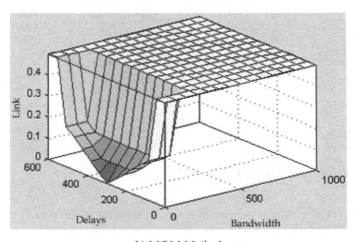

*b) MOM Method*

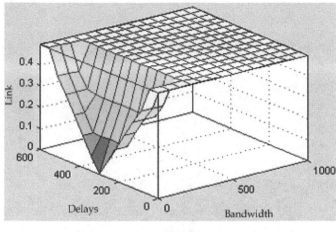

*c) LOM Method*

Fig. 13. Surface viewer for 3 defuzzification methods: a) COG, b) MOM and c) LOM

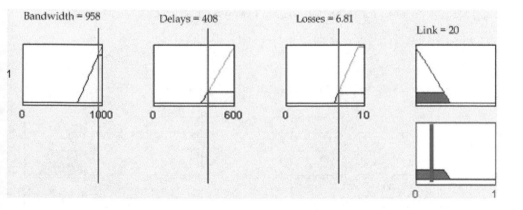

Fig. 14. Rule viewer when it is used COG method for rule 9

While, 3 D surface viewer using three main defuzzification methods is the same and is depicted in the figure below. From this graph, it is clearly seen that we have high bandwidth, but delays and percentage of packet losses are also high, resulting thus in low link optimization.

In this case we have a very low link usage, and this is the reason why surface viewer is approximately same for three defuzzification methods (low link optimization).

If we use rule number 5 (derived from rule editor):

*If (bandwidth is Medium) and (delay is Tolerable) and (loss is Tolerable) then (link optimization is Medium)*

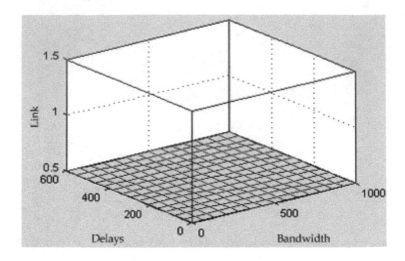

Fig. 15. Surface viewer for rule 9, for defuzzification methods: COG, MOM and LOM

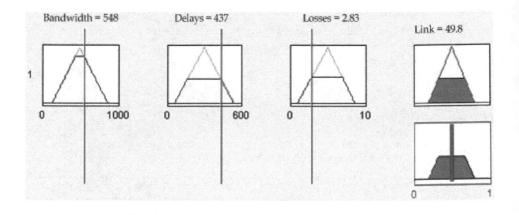

Fig. 16. Rule viewer when we use COG method for rule 5

In this case, the value for bandwidth is 548 Mbps, delays = 437 ms (tolerable) and losses are tolerable (2.83%). From the analysis we have shown that the link optimization is medium. This means that using the parameters above, we can transmit almost every multimedia service.

While, 3 D surface viewer for 3 main defuzzification methods will look like below:

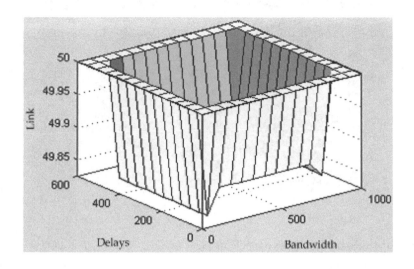

a) COG method

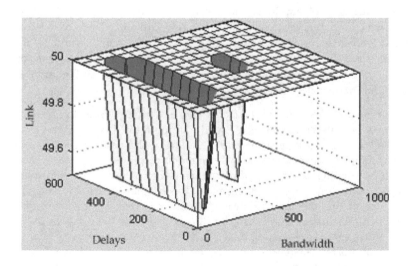

b) MOM method

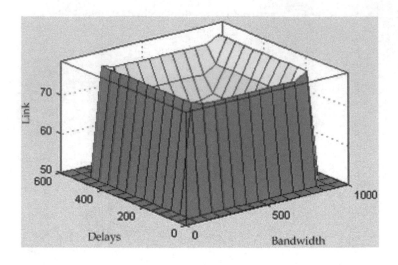

c) LOM method

Fig. 17. Surface viewer for rule 5 when it is used: a) COG, b) MOM and c) LOM

From the above examples can be clearly seen that COG defuzzification method gives better result in aspect of link utilization. This can be seen with surface viewer and rule viewer as presented in the above examples using different rules.

## 14. Conclusion

In the past, routing problem in communication networks was relatively simple. The applications have used a modest percentage of bandwidth and no one of those applications had QoS requirements. However, the existing routing protocols should be improved or replaced with algorithms that meet different QoS requirements. Thus, it is necessary to present an architecture that supports new services in Internet and guarantees QoS for multimedia applications.

In this chapter we introduced the MPLS technology as a multiple solution for a lot of current problems faced by Internet today. By a wide support for QoS and traffic engineering capability, MPLS is establishing itself as a standard of the next generation's network. In MPLS network, some problems can occur during multimedia service transmission, therefore it is a good idea to design some control mechanisms for solving such problems. As a result of the complex nature of control mechanisms, in this chapter we used intelligent controlled techniques. One of the intelligent controlled techniques that we analyzed here is Fuzzy Logic Controller, a technique that is based on fuzzy logic. We have shown that fuzzy logic approach is suitable for QoS routing analysis in MPLS network. In this chapter we used main metrics of MPLS network acting in the input of FLC and we found the most appropriate defuzzification method for finding better crisp values in the aspect of link utilization in MPLS network. Also, we have shown that the most important part of FLC is defuzzifier, which converts fuzzy values into crisp values. In this chapter we explained the methods that are used mostly for defuzzification, that are: COGM MOM and LOM. The performance comparison offered by three methods we have described through examples by surface viewer in 3D. Through these analyses using Matlab's toolbox we have shown that COG method gives better results in all analyzed cases.

## 15. References

[1] Mario Marchese, "*QoS over heterogeneous networks*", Copyright © 2007 John Wiley & Sons Ltd, The Atrium, Southern Gate, Chichester, West Sussex, PO19 8SQ, England

[2] Pragyansmita Paul and S V Raghavan–"Survey of QoS Routing"- Proceedings of the 15th international conference on Computer communication, p.50-75, August 12-14

[3] Santiago Alvarez, "*QoS for IP/MPLS Networks*", Cisco Press, Pub Date: June 02, 2006, ISBN: 1-58705-233-4

[4] Shigang Chen and Klara Nahrstedt -"Distributed QoS routing"

[5] Monique Morrow, Azhar Sayeed, "*MPLS and Next-Generation Networks: Foundations for NGN and Enterprise Virtualization*", Cisco Press, Pub Date: November 06, 2006, ISBN: 1-58720-120-8

[6] Arianit Maraj, B. Shatri, I. Limani, A. Abdullahu, S. Rugova "Analysis of QoS Routing in MPLS Network in Kosova using Fuzzy Logic"-Proceedings of the 7th WSEAS International Conference on Signal Processing, Robotics and Automation (ISPRA '08)

[7] Runtong Zhang and Jian Ma - Fuzzy QoS Management in Diff-Serv Networks- Systems, Man, and Cybernetics, 2000 IEEE International Conference on Volume 5, Issue , 2000 Page(s): 3752 - 757 vol.5

[8] A .Vasilakos, C .Ricudis, K. Anagnostakis, W .Pedrycz, A. Pitsillides-"Evolutionary-Fuzzy Prediction for Strategic QoS Routing in Broadband Networks", 0-7803-4863-W98 @10.0001998 IEEE

[9] A .Vasilakos, C .Ricudis, K. Anagnostakis, W .Pedrycz, A. Pitsillides-"Evolutionary-Fuzzy Prediction for Strategic QoS Routing in Broadband Networks", 0-7803-4863-W98 @10.0001998 IEEE

[10] Balandin, S. Heiner, A.P, SPF protocol and statistical tools for network simulations in NS-2"- Information Technology Interfaces, 2002. ITI 2002. Proceedings of the 24th International Conference on Publication Date: 2002

[11] By Eric Osborne, Ajay Simha, "*Traffic Engineering with MPLS*", Cisco Press, Pub Date: July 17, 2002, ISBN: 1-58705-031-5

[12] Baolin Sun, Layuan Li, Chao Gui - Fuzzy QoS Controllers Based Priority Scheduler for Mobile Ad Hoc Networks- This paper appears in: Mobile Technology, Applications and Systems, 2005 2nd International Conference on Publication Date: 15-17 Nov. 2005

[13] B. Shatri, A.Abdullahu, S. Rugova, Arianit Maraj, "VPN Creation in IP/MPLS Network in Kosova" icn, pp. 318-323, Seventh International Conference on Networking (icn 2008), 2008

[14] K. H. Lee, "Firs Course on fuzzy theory and applications" [book], pages: 253-279, ISBN 3-540-22988-4 Springer Berlin Heidelberg NewYork, Springer-Verlag Berlin Heidelberg 2005

[15] D. Driankov, H. Hellenndoorn and M. Reinfrank "An Introduction to fuzzy Control", Springer – Verlang, Berlin, New York, 1993

# 9

# Artificial Intelligence Techniques of Estimating of Torque for 8:6 Switched Reluctance Motor

Amin Parvizi
*University of Malaya,*
*Malaysia*

## 1. Introduction

Switched reluctance motor (SRM) is one of the best candidates for industrial and household applications. Owing to its superior abilities such as high torque to inertia ratio, easy cooling, high speed capability and ease of repair, SRM has been taken into consideration by researchers. one of the major difficulties is the nonlinear relation between current, rotor position and flux linkage. Due to the mentioned nonlinearity, it is essential to have an accurate model to deal with nonlinear characteristics of SRM. The essence of this research work is to develop the SRM model based on artificial techniques (AI) such as fuzzy logic, adaptive neuro-fuzzy. In the papers (Chancharoensook& Rahman,2002;Geldhof&Van den Bossche& Vyncke&Melkebeek,2008; Mirzaeian-Dehkordi& Moallem, 2006; Gobbi, Ramar;2008; Rajapakse& Gole& Muthumuni& Wilson& Perregaux,2004; Wai-Chuen Gan& Cheung& Li Qiu,2008) SRM models presented based on the look-up tables.

In this short communication, rule based system are considered in order to find a model to deal with nonlinear characteristics of SRM. We call it rule based due to have fixed data point. Fuzzy logic and adaptive neuro-fuzzy are employed to develop a comprehensive model for nonlinear characteristics of 8:6 SRM. Torque profile is simulated based on fuzzy logic, adaptive neuro-fuzzy techniques via MATLAB software. In the line above, error analysis is conducted for those models. Data is tabled and compared with the published data. The result of error analysis reflects the precision of the method and the capability of the approach for the further simulation.

## 2. Background theory

Switched reluctance motor (SRM) is a type of synchronous machine. Figure 1 shows the classification of the SRM. This initial classification is made by considering the method of movement.

Stator and rotor are two basic parts of SRM. One of the most important features of the SRM comes back to its simple structure. This type of electrical machine has no winding or magnet in rotor part. Both of stator and rotor have salient poles. Thus, it is named double salient machine. Figure 2 shows the typical structure of SRM.

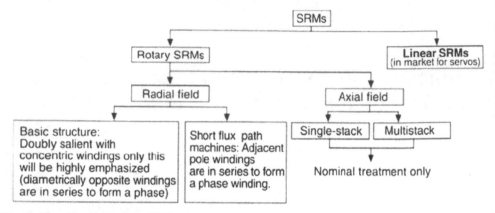

Fig. 1. Classification of the SRM

The number under the configuration (6/4 or 8/6) means SRM with 6 or 8 poles on stator and 4 or 6 poles on rotor.

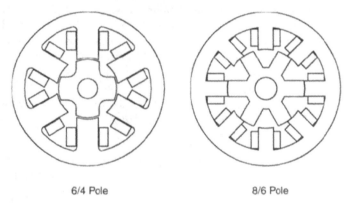

6/4 Pole                                    8/6 Pole

Fig. 2. SRM configuration

## 3. Operation of the SRMs

The key of understanding rotor movement is rising from the tendency of rotor to place in minimum reluctance position at the instance of excitation. While two rotor poles are in front of two stator poles, called align position. In align position; another set of rotor pole is out of alignment position there for another set of stator pole will be excited to move the rotor poles until the time to reach minimum reluctance. Figure 3 shows a 6:4 SRM. In the figure, at the first situation, suppose that $r_1$ and $r_1'$ are two poles of rotor and in align position with $c$ and $c'$ which are the stator poles. When $a$ is excited in the direction that is shown, stator poles tends to pull the rotor poles toward itself. Therefore, $r_2$ and $r_2'$ are in front of the a and a', respectively. After they are aligned, the stator current is turned off and the corresponding situation is shown in Figure 3(b). Now, b is excited and pulls the $r_1$ and $r_1'$ toward b and b, respectively. Hence, the rotor is rotating in a clockwise direction.

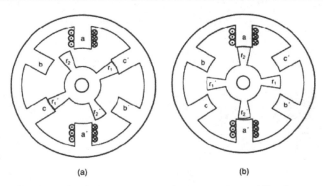

(a)                                           (b)

Fig. 3. Operation of switched reluctance motor a)Phase c aligned b) Phase a aligned

Following figure shows the lamination profile of 8:6 SRM in align position with magnetic potential contour.

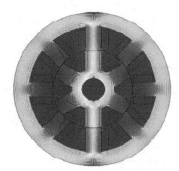

Fig. 4. Lamination profile of 8:6 SRM (Parvizi, Hassani, Mehbodnia, Makhilef, & Tamjis, 2009)

## 4. Single – Phase SRMs

During the past years, single-phase SRMs have attracted much attention due to resemblance to universal and single phase induction machines and also, single-phase SRMs are low-cost manufacture as well as induction and universal machines. Specific applications of single-phase SRMs come up in where high-speed motors are needed. When the stator and rotor poles are in front of each other which means the align position, the current that relevant to stator phase is turned off and the rotor keeps moving toward the adjacent stator pole due to kinetic energy which is stored. Adjacent stator phase is energized to attract the rotor pole toward itself. This process subsequently will be continued.

The major problem of single-phase SRMs operation come up when the rotor and stator are in align position at the instant of starting or the rotor at a position where the load torque at the starting is greater than the produced load. Permanent magnet has been used as a solution. It pulls the rotor away from the stator or at the right position in which motor can produce a torque greater than the load torque. As the figure 5 shows the rotor and stator are in unaligned position.

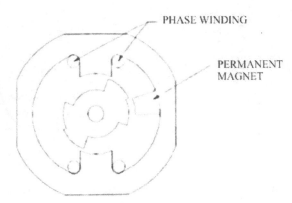

Fig. 5. Single-phase SRM with permanent magnet

Maximum duty cycle of single-phase SRM is 0.5, thus, noise and high ripple torque are deduced from a torque discontinuity which arises from duty cycle. Applications, in which torque ripple and noise are not important, are good for this machine such as home appliances and hand tool.

## 5. Magnetization characteristic of SRM

Due to saturation and varying reluctance with rotor position, there is no simple analytical solution to express the field which is produced by phase winding. Energy conversion approach that is presented in is used to analyze energy conversion.

Figure 6 shows a typical magnetization curve. Flux linkage is a function of both rotor position and excitation current and also, it is nonlinear function. One of the most important parameter which affects on flux linkage is air gap. As it can be seen clearly, in unaligned position, flux linkage is a linear function due to big air gap. In other words, the gap between stator pole and rotor pole is big. In contrast, in aligned position, due to small air gap, the magnetization curve is heavily saturated.

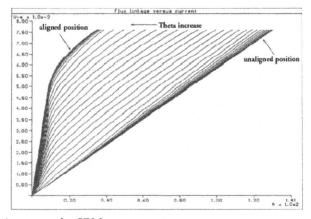

Fig. 6. Magnetization curve for SRM

Figure 7 shows a magnetization curve under specific condition. Rotor angle is locked in somewhere between aligned and unaligned position. Energy and co-energy are defined in any point of that respectively by:

$$W_f = \int_0^{\lambda_a} i \, d\lambda(i, \theta) \tag{1}$$

$$\dot{W} = \int_0^{i_a} \lambda(\theta, i) \, di \tag{2}$$

$\lambda(\theta, i)$ represents the flux linkage as a nonlinear function of rotor position and current. As figure 7 shows, the area behind the magnetization curve until $\lambda_a$ called stored field energy $(W_f)$ that this energy is stored in the iron core (rotor and stator) and in the air gap. The area under the magnetization curve until $i_a$ called co-energy $(\dot{W})$.

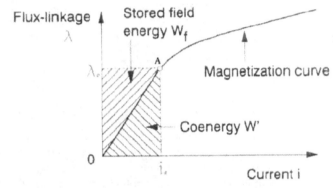

Fig. 7. Concept of stored field energy and co-energy

In the next step, suppose that rotor is released. In this situation, rotor moves toward the adjacent stator pole until place in align position. For an infinitesimal movement $\Delta\theta$ , suppose that $i_a$ is considered constant, thus the flux linkage changes from point A to point B as shown in figure 8. By considering the conservation of energy, the mechanical work $\Delta w_m$ which has been done by rotor during the $\Delta\theta$ movement is equal to the change in the stored field energy $(\Delta W_f)$.

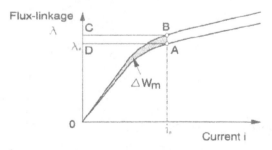

Fig. 8. Mechanical work area

The area $\Delta W_m$ equals to the change in co-energy because of the $\Delta\theta$ movement. Thus, the mechanical energy can be stated as following:

$$\Delta W_m = \Delta \dot{W} = \int_0^{i_a} \lambda(\theta_B, i)di - \int_0^{i_a} \lambda(\theta_A, i)di \tag{3}$$

And also

$$\Delta W_m = T\Delta\theta \tag{4}$$

There for, the mechanical torque can be expressed as:

$$T = \frac{\Delta W_m}{\Delta \theta} = \frac{\int_0^{i_a} \lambda(\theta_B, i)di - \int_0^{i_a} \lambda(\theta_A, i)di}{\Delta \theta} \tag{5}$$

By considering that the movement goes zero($\Delta\theta \to 0$) , for any current, the instantaneous torque can be written as following:

$$T = \frac{\partial}{\partial \theta} \int_0^i \lambda(\theta, i)di \tag{6}$$

For a linear flux model:

$$\lambda(\theta, i) = L(\theta)i \tag{7}$$

Therefore:

$$T = \int_0^i \frac{\partial \lambda(\theta, i)}{\partial \theta} di = \int_0^i \frac{dL}{d\theta} idi = \frac{dL}{d\theta} \int_0^i i\, di = \frac{1}{2} i^2 \frac{dL}{d\theta} \tag{8}$$

Therefore, the magnetization curve has been analyzed and instantaneous torque has been elaborated. Under specific condition such as being current in certain value (in linear flux region and no saturation effect), the relationship between the flux linkage and current can be assumed linear. As the current increases, the saturation effect occurs and the nonlinearity of the flux linkage will be appeared. Figure 9 shows the data of torque profile of 8:6 SRM published in (Bhiwapurkar& Jain& Mohan,2005).

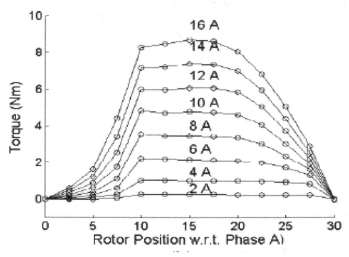

Fig. 9. Torque profile of SRM

# 6. Torque estimation model using fuzzy logic technique (FIS)

The modeling process for estimation of torque starts from analyzing data from plotted curve and will be continued by fuzzy rule base and FIS structure and ends in mapping surface. By considering 8:6 SRM's torque profile (Figure 10); Fuzzy Logic approach will be explained.

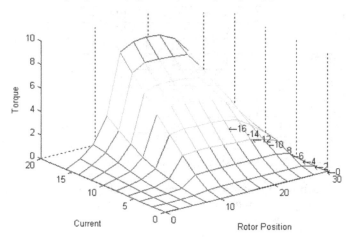

Fig. 10. Simulated Torque profile Via MATLAB

## 6.1 Establishing the fuzzy rules table

In the first step, from plotted curve, exact data should be extracted. For the torque estimation model, current and rotor angle are defined as inputs and torque is output. Based on analyzing the findings data from plotted curve minimum and maximum of each those inputs and output should be determined. Based on the division each of those inputs and output which is called fuzzy region, number of regions will determine and also, related linguistic variable will be assigned in order to settle the obstacle in establishing the fuzzy rule table. Table 1 show the input and output domain for 8:6 SRM. This table shows the inputs and output variable with their respective number of region and linguistic variable assigned for the region.

| Input/output | Range | No. of regions | Variable |
|---|---|---|---|
| Current I(A) | 2-16 | 8 | s4-m-b3 |
| Rotor position,($\theta°$) | 0-30 | 13 | s6-m-b6 |
| Torque | 0-9.54 | 21 | s10-m-b10 |

Table 1. Input and output domains for 8:6 SRM

Once domains are determined, forming fuzzy rule base table starts. To convert the torque profile characteristics to fuzzy rule base table, right interpret from the extracted data to linguistic variable is very important. Table 2 shows the fuzzy rule base table for 8:6 SRM. According to the number of the fuzzy region and the linguistic variable, this table is established.

|     | s4   | s3   | s2   | s1   | M    | b1   | b2   | b3   |
|-----|------|------|------|------|------|------|------|------|
| s6  | s10  | s10  | s10  | s10  | s10  | s10  | s10  | s10  |
| s5  | s10  | s10  | s10  | s9   | s9   | s8   | s8   | s8   |
| s4  | s10  | s9   | s9   | s8   | s8   | s7   | s7   | s6   |
| s3  | s9   | s8   | s8   | s7   | s6   | s5   | s3   | s2   |
| s2  | s8   | s7   | s5   | s2   | b1   | b3   | b6   | b9   |
| s1  | s8   | s7   | s4   | s1   | b2   | b5   | b7   | b10  |
| M   | s8   | s7   | s4   | s1   | b2   | b5   | b7   | b10  |
| b1  | s8   | s7   | s4   | s1   | b1   | b4   | b7   | b10  |
| b2  | s8   | s7   | s5   | s2   | b1   | b4   | b6   | b8   |
| b3  | s8   | s7   | s5   | s2   | M    | b2   | b4   | b6   |
| b4  | s8   | s7   | s5   | s4   | s2   | M    | b1   | b2   |
| b5  | s9   | s8   | s6   | s5   | s5   | s4   | s3   | s3   |
| b6  | s10  | s10  | s10  | s10  | s10  | s10  | s10  | s10  |

Table 2. Fuzzy rule base table for 8:6 SRM

It should be noted that wrong interpretation of each of rules will influence on overall output and as a result, wrong model will come up. Therefore, this part of work should be done carefully and without any wrong rule.

### 6.2 Formation of Fuzzy Inference System (FIS)

For the formation of the fuzzy inference system, fuzzy logic toolbox of MATLAB is used. Figure 11 shows the FIS structure that current and rotor angle are the inputs and torque is the output.

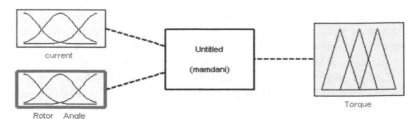

Fig. 11. Fuzzy SRM FIS structure

### 6.3 Assigning the FIS membership functions

Once the FIS structure is completed, membership functions for each of the inputs and the output will be formed. Toolbox of MATLAB has 11 built-in membership functions (MFs) which some of those are trimf, gbellmf, gaussmf, gauss2mf, sigmf, psigmf. One of these MFs that are formed by straight lines is called triangular MFs. These MFs are used here in account of simple structure and well suited for the modeling.

Current and rotor angle as the inputs have 8 MFs and 13 MFs respectively for itself and torque as the output has 21 MFs for 8:6 SRM. Figure 12 , figure 13 and figure 14 show the MF for current, rotor angle and torque, respectively.

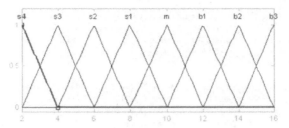

Fig. 12. Membership functions for current

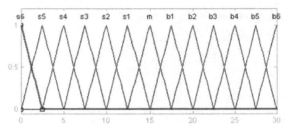

Fig. 13. Membership functions for rotor angle

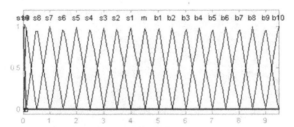

Fig. 14. Membership functions for torque

## 6.4 Constructing FIS rule

The most important part of the modeling is the constructing FIS rules because of the outcome of this part will define output fuzzy set. In other words, torque as the output is a fuzzy set that basically are formed by the results of the constructing FIS rules. Table 2 is used to constructing FIS rules. In Mamdani's type a set of if-then called rules. Thus, the conditional statements are formulated by if-then form. For instance,

Rule 1: If current is s6 and rotor angle is s4 then torque is s10

Degree of membership function is a value between 0 and 1 which is the output of the membership function. Now, degree of a rule can be defined the multiple of the degree of the inputs and output. For example, degree of the mentioned rule can be as following:

Degree (Rule 1) = $\mu$ (s6).$\mu$ (s4).$\mu$ (s10)

FIS editor is used to produce the rules which are shown in figure 15. Also, figure 15 shows a part of rules for 8:6 SRM and the number of total rules are 80.

70. If (current is b3) and (rotor__position is b4) then (torque is s14) (1)
71. If (current is b4) and (rotor__position is s5) then (torque is s14) (1)
72. If (current is b4) and (rotor__position is s4) then (torque is s8) (1)
73. If (current is b4) and (rotor__position is s3) then (torque is s3) (1)
74. If (current is b4) and (rotor__position is s2) then (torque is b14) (1)
75. If (current is b4) and (rotor__position is s1) then (torque is b14) (1)
76. If (current is b4) and (rotor__position is m) then (torque is b14) (1)
77. If (current is b4) and (rotor__position is b1) then (torque is b10) (1)
78. If (current is b4) and (rotor__position is b2) then (torque is b5) (1)
79. If (current is b4) and (rotor__position is b3) then (torque is b1) (1)
80. If (current is b4) and (rotor__position is b4) then (torque is s14) (1)

Fig. 15. Constructing rules using rule editor

The surface viewer is used to show the dependency of the output to both of inputs. There for, it generates torque surface map. Figure 16 shows the torque for 8:6.

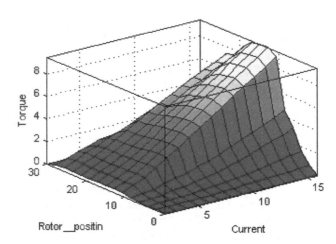

Fig. 16. Surface viewer of the FIS for 8:6 SRM

## 7. Torque estimation model using Adaptive Neuro-Fuzzy Inference System (ANFIS)

ANFIS is an acronym of Adaptive Neuro-Fuzzy Inference System. Adaptive Neuro-Fuzzy is a technique which provides a learning method from the desired input and output to adjust the MFs parameters. During this process, back propagation and hybrid are two algorithms that are used so that the best parameters for the MFs will be achieved.

## 7.1 Forming ANFIS

By considering the graphical representative of torque (figure 9), rotor angle and current are defined as inputs and torque as output. Figure 17 shows the FIS editor for ANFIS that two inputs and one output has been shown clearly.

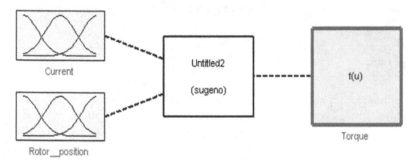

Fig. 17. Neuro-Fuzzy SRM FIS structure

## 7.2 Training scheme of FIS

Once the data set are obtained from the torque curve, loading data starts. The loaded data set should be in three columns matrix format. First and second belong to the inputs and the third one present the torque data.

The training data appears in the plot in center of the ANFIS editor as a set of circle as shown in figure 18 for 8:6 SRM.

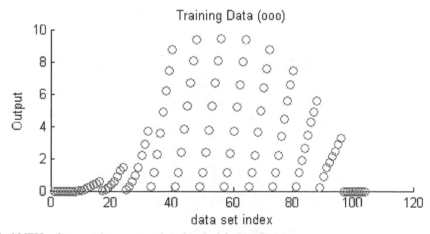

Fig. 18. ANFIS editor with training data loaded for 8:6 SRM

## 7.3 Initializing and generating FIS

Once data set is loaded, next step is initializing the MFs. There are two partitioning method for initializing the MFs:

1.   Grid partition
2.   Subtractive clustering

Second method is employed in account of having one-pass algorithm which estimates the number of clusters.

Figure 19 shows the cluster parameters which are:

1.   Range of influence
2.   Squash factor
3.   Accept ratio
4.   Reject ratio

For varying both of inputs "range of influence" is set to 0.15. Other parameters remain in their previous value because those values are acceptable for training scheme. Once the parameters are set, the outcome FIS generates 104 numbers of MFs for both of the inputs, and output.

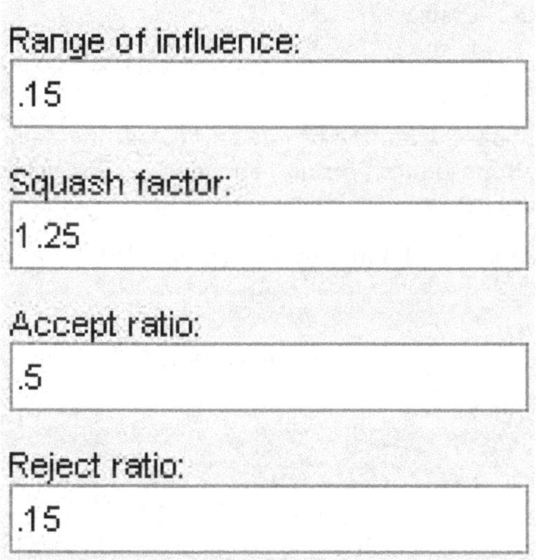

Range of influence:

.15

Squash factor:

1.25

Accept ratio:

.5

Reject ratio:

.15

Fig. 19. Parameters set for subtractive clustering

## 7.4 ANFIS training

In order to optimize the obtained parameters, two methods are available:

1.   Hybrid method: this method is a combination of least squares and back propagation method.
2.   Back propagation: this method consists of steepest descend method for MFs.

The first method is considered for data training. Error tolerance is established to create halt criterion. The error training will stop after certain epoch which is set. The number of epochs for both of 8:6 is 150.

The final error training is 3.014e -7 which is shown in figure 18 after 150 epochs.

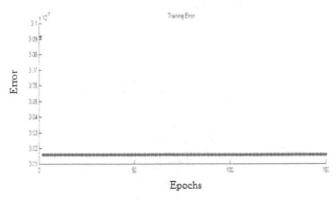

Fig. 20. ANFIS training with hybrid method

## 7.5 Viewing ANFIS structure

Figure 21 shows the ANFIS model structure for 8:6 SRM. There are two inputs (rotor angle and current) and one output (torque). There are total 104 MFs for each of inputs.

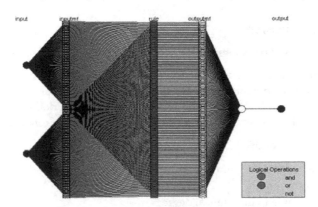

Fig. 21. ANFIS model structure for 8:6 SRM

The summarized modeling description is shown in table 3 for 8:6 SRM.

| Modeling Description | Setting |
|---|---|
| Number of Inputs | 2 |
| Number of Output | 1 |
| Method | Subtractive Clustering |
| Number of MFs | 104 |
| Optimized Method | Hybrid |
| Epochs | 150 |

Table 3. Fuzzy rule base table for 8:6 SRM

The mapping surface of 8:6 SRM using neuro-fuzzy technique is shown in figure 19.

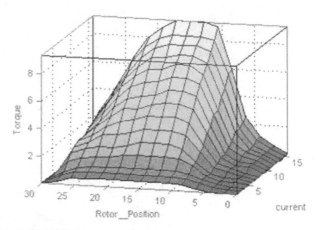

Fig. 22. Surface view of 8:6 SRM

## 8. Result and discussion

### 8.1 Error analysis for torque estimation model using fuzzy logic technique

Torque estimation based on fuzzy logic technique has been presented. Thus, 8 and 13 membership functions were formed for the inputs and 21 for the torque as the output for 8:6 RM. Error analysis is conducted to obtain the accuracy of the model. Appendix D shows the computed torque values in term of comparison with the desired measured values.

**From the results in appendix A:**

- N = Number of data points= 104
- I = phase current(A)
- $\theta$ = Rotor angle in mechanical degree
- $T_m$ = Measured torque in Newton-meter
- $T_f$ = Computed torque in Newton-meter
- $\sum(T_m)$ = Sum of the measured torque $T_m$=270.95
- $\sum(T_f)$ = Sum of the computed torque $T_f$=282.4614
- $\sum(|\varepsilon|)$ = Calculated total absolute error=16.2222

Thus,

Mean $T_f = \dfrac{282.4614}{104} = 2.716$

Average% error $= \left[\dfrac{\sum|\varepsilon|}{Mean\,T_f * N}\right] * 100\%$

$$= \dfrac{16.2222}{2.716 * 104} * 100\% = 5.7431$$

## 8.2 Error analysis for torque estimation model using adaptive neuro-fuzzy inference system technique

ANFIS is one the best approaches due to the capability of learning without dependency to human knowledge. In other worlds, in fuzzy logic approach, membership functions have been formed by the human knowledge but ANFIS because of having training algorithm and independency to human knowledge is more capable to produce accurate data. In this section, error analysis shows the preciseness of the mode:

**From the results in appendix B:**

- N = Number of data points= 104
- I = phase current(A)
- $\theta$ = Rotor angle in mechanical degree
- $T_m$ = Measured torque in Newton-meter
- $T_f$ = Computed torque in Newton-meter
- $\Sigma(T_f)$ = Sum of the computed torque =2.71E+02
- $\Sigma(T_m)$ = Sum of the measured torque =270.95
- $\Sigma(|\varepsilon|)$ = Calculated total absolute error= 4.61 e-011

Thus,

Mean $T_f = \frac{2.71E+02}{104} = 2.6058$

Average% error= $\left[\frac{\Sigma|\varepsilon|}{Mean\ T_f * N}\right] * 100\%$

$$= \frac{4.61e - 011}{2.6058 * 104} * 100 = 1.7011e - 011$$

## 9. Conclusion

Error analysis is conducted for the two approaches. Table 4 reflects the average percentage error of each models.

|                             | FIS      | ANFIS           |
|-----------------------------|----------|-----------------|
| Average Percentage Error    | 5.7431%  | 1.701e − 011%   |

Table 4. Error analysis result

As it can been seen clearly, table above shows the ANFIS model is the best among those. ANFIS technique is used in order to develop predictive model for obtaining precision outcome. This approach can be used for any nonlinear function with arbitrary accuracy.

Torque profile of switched reluctance motor is a nonlinear function and the inherent nonlinear characteristics lead us toward artificial intelligence approaches. Due to the mentioned nonlinearity a predictive model is needed. ANFIS model owing to its abilities to predict is opted. The reason being is due to the ANFIS modeling approach possessing learning characteristic capability that allows it to learn from the data values through the training scheme, thus avoids on the dependency of human knowledge with regard to the systems(Parvizi.A&Hassani&Mehbodnia&Makhilef&Tamjis,2009) . Besides, ANFIS method dose not have the complexity of FIS method which makes it much easier to understand and utilize. Average percentage error shows that the outcome is in good agreement with the published data. Torque profile is simulated and results reveals that ANFIS modeling method is a trustable model for further research. In addition, this approch can be used in order to control the turn-off angle of the SRM which leades to a SRM with low torque ripples.

## 10. Acknowledgment

This work is dedicated to my parents, Mohammad and Fatemeh for their kindness and support.The author like to thank Dr.Aris Ramlan, Mr.Peter Nicoll and Dr.M. Beikzadeh for reviewing and his right-on-target comments.

## 11. Appendix A

Error analysis for torque Using Fuzzy logic Technique

| Current | Rotor Angle | Measured torque | Computed torque | $\lvert \varepsilon \rvert$ |
|---------|-------------|-----------------|-----------------|-----|
| 2 | 0 | 0 | 0.1723 | 0.1723 |
| 4 | 0 | 0 | 0.1723 | 0.1723 |
| 6 | 0 | 0 | 0.1723 | 0.1723 |
| 8 | 0 | 0 | 0.1723 | 0.1723 |
| 10 | 0 | 0 | 0.1723 | 0.1723 |
| 12 | 0 | 0 | 0.1723 | 0.1723 |
| 14 | 0 | 0 | 0.1723 | 0.1723 |
| 16 | 0 | 0 | 0.1723 | 0.1723 |
| . | . | . | . | . |
| . | . | . | . | . |
| 2 | 30 | 0 | 0.1723 | 0.1723 |
| 4 | 30 | 0 | 0.1723 | 0.1723 |
| 6 | 30 | 0 | 0.1723 | 0.1723 |
| 8 | 30 | 0 | 0.1723 | 0.1723 |
| 10 | 30 | 0 | 0.1723 | 0.1723 |
| 12 | 30 | 0 | 0.1723 | 0.1723 |
| 14 | 30 | 0 | 0.1723 | 0.1723 |
| 16 | 30 | 0 | 0.1723 | 0.1723 |
| 936 | 1560 | 270.95 | 282.4614 | 16.2222 |

## 12. Appendix B

*Error analysis for the ANFIS model of 8:6 SRM*

| Current | Rotor Angle | Measured Torque | Computed Torque | $|\varepsilon|$ |
|---------|-------------|-----------------|-----------------|-----------------|
| 2 | 0 | 0 | 7.99e-014 | 7.99E-14 |
| 4 | 0 | 0 | 6.49e-014 | 6.49E-14 |
| 6 | 0 | 0 | 6.61e-014 | 6.61E-14 |
| 8 | 0 | 0 | 3.72e-14 | 3.72E-14 |
| 10 | 0 | 0 | 2.14e-13 | 2.14E-13 |
| 12 | 0 | 0 | 2.36e-13 | 2.36E-13 |
| 14 | 0 | 0 | 3.11e-13 | 3.11E-13 |
| 16 | 0 | 0 | 3.08e-014 | 3.08E-14 |
| . | . | . | . | . |
| . | . | . | . | . |
| 2 | 30 | 0 | -1.18e-013 | 1.18E-13 |
| 4 | 30 | 0 | -4.62e-012 | 4.62E-12 |
| 6 | 30 | 0 | -6.92e-012 | 6.92E-12 |
| 8 | 30 | 0 | 3.25e-012 | 3.25E-12 |
| 10 | 30 | 0 | 1.15e-012 | 1.15E-12 |
| 12 | 30 | 0 | 3.34e-012 | 3.34E-12 |
| 14 | 30 | 0 | 1.36e-012 | 1.36E-12 |
| 16 | 30 | 0 | 2.43e-011 | 2.43E-11 |
| 936 | 1560 | 270.95 | 2.71E+02 | 4.61E-11 |

## 13. References

Chancharoensook, P.& Rahman, M.F. , "Dynamic modeling of a four-phase 8/6 switched reluctance motor using current and torque look-up tables," *IECON 02 [Industrial Electronics Society, IEEE 2002 28th Annual Conference of the]* , vol.1, no., pp. 491- 496 vol.1, 5-8 Nov. 2002

Geldhof, K.R. & Van den Bossche, A. & Vyncke, T.J. & Melkebeek, J.A.A. , "Influence of flux penetration on inductance and rotor position estimation accuracy of switched reluctance machines," *Industrial Electronics, 2008. IECON 2008. 34th Annual Conference of IEEE* , vol., no., pp.1246-1251, 10-13 Nov. 2008

Mirzaeian-Dehkordi, B. & Moallem, P. , "Genetic Algorithm Based Optimal Design of Switching Circuit Parameters for a Switched Reluctance Motor Drive," *Power Electronics, Drives and Energy Systems, 2006. PEDES '06. International Conference on* , vol., no., pp.1-6, 12-15 Dec. 2006

Gobbi, R. & Ramar, K. , "Practical current control techniques for torque ripple minimization in SR motors," *Power and Energy Conference, 2008. PECon 2008. IEEE 2nd International*, vol., no., pp.743-748, 1-3 Dec. 2008

Rajapakse, A.D. & Gole, A.M.; Muthumuni, D. & Wilson, P.L.; Perregaux, A. , "Simulation of switched reluctance motors embedded in large networks," *Power System Technology,*

*2004. PowerCon 2004. 2004 International Conference on* , vol.1, no., pp. 695- 700 Vol.1, 21-24 Nov. 2004

Wai-Chuen Gan& Cheung, N.C. & Li Qiu , "Short distance position control for linear switched reluctance motors: a plug-in robust compensator approach," *Industry Applications Conference, 2001. Thirty-Sixth IAS Annual Meeting. Conference Record of the 2001 IEEE* , vol.4, no., pp.2329-2336 vol.4, 30 Sep-4 Oct. 2001

Bhiwapurkar, N.; Jain, A.K.; Mohan, N.; , "Study of new stator pole geometry for improvement of SRM torque profile," *Electric Machines and Drives, 2005 IEEE International Conference on* , vol., no., pp.516-520, 15-15 May 2005

Parvizi.A&Hassani.M&Mehbodnia.A&Makhilef.S&Tamjis.M.R    *"Adaptive Neuro-Fuzzy Approach of Estimating of torque for 8:6 Switched Reluctance Motor"* International Conference for Technical Postgraduates TECHPOS conference, Malaysia. IEEE conference proceeding , page(s): 1-4,2009

# 10

# Term Weighting for Information Retrieval Using Fuzzy Logic

Jorge Ropero, Ariel Gómez, Alejandro Carrasco,
Carlos León and Joaquín Luque
*Department of Electronic Technology, University of Seville,*
*Spain*

## 1. Introduction

The rising quantity of available information has constituted an enormous advance in our daily life. However, at the same time, some problems emerge as a result from the existing difficulty to distinguish the necessary information among the high quantity of unnecessary data. Information Retrieval has become a capital task for retrieving the useful information. Firstly, it was mainly used for document retrieval, but lately, its use has been generalized for the retrieval of any kind of information, such as the information contained in a database, a web page, or any set of accumulated knowledge. In particular, the so-called Vector Space Model is widely used. Vector Space Model is based on the use of index terms, which represent some pieces of knowledge or Objects. Index terms have associated weights, which represent the importance of them in the considered set of knowledge.

It is important that the assignment of weights to every index term - called Term Weighting - is automatic. The so-called TF-IDF method is mainly used for determining the weight of a term (Lee et al., 1997). Term Frequency (TF) is the frequency of occurrence of a term in a document; and Inverse Document Frequency (IDF) varies inversely with the number of documents to which the term is assigned (Salton, 1988). Although TF-IDF method for Term Weighting has worked reasonably well for Information Retrieval and has been a starting point for more recent algorithms, it was never taken into account that some other aspects of index terms may be important for determining term weights apart from TF and IDF: first of all, we should consider the degree of identification of an object if only the considered index term is used. This parameter has a strong influence on the final value of a term weight if the degree of identification is high. The more an index term identifies an object, the higher value for the corresponding term weight; secondly, we should also consider the existance of join terms.

These aspects are especially important when the information is abundant, imprecise, vague and heterogeneous. In this chapter, we define a new Term Weighting model based on Fuzzy Logic. This model tries to replace the traditional Term Weighting method, called TF-IDF. In order to show the efficiency of the new method, the Fuzzy Logic-based method has been tested on the website of the University of Seville. Web pages are usually a perfect example of heterogeneous and disordered information. We demonstrate the improvement introduced by the new method extracting the required information. Besides, it is also possible to extract related information, which may be of interest to the users.

## 2. Vector Space Model and Term Weighting

In the Vector Space Model, the contents of a document are represented by a multidimensional space vector. Later, the proper classes of the given vector are determined by comparing the distances between vectors. The procedure of the Vector Space Model can be divided into three stages, as seen in Figure 1 (Raghavan & Wong, 1986):

- The first step is document indexing, when most relevant terms are extracted.
- The second stage is based on the introduction of weights associated to index terms in order to improve the retrieval relevant to the user.
- The last stage classifies the document with a certain measure of similarity.

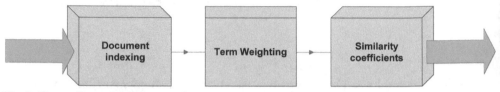

Fig. 1. Vector Space Model procedure

In this chapter, we are focusing in the second stage. It was in the late 50's when the idea of text retrieval came up - a concept that was later extended to general information retrieval -. Text retrieval was founded on an automatic search based on textual content through a series of identifiers. It was Gerard Salton who laid the foundations for linking these identifiers and the texts that they represent during the 70's and the 80's. Salton suggested that every document could be represented by a term vector in the way D = ($t_i$, $t_j$,..., $t_p$), where every $t_k$ identifies a term assigned to a document D. A formal representation of the vector D leads us not to consider only the terms in the vector, but to add a set of weights representing the term weight, it is to say, its importance in the document.

A Term Weighting system should improve efficiency in two main factors, recall and precision. Recall takes into account the fact that the objects relevant to the user should be retrieved. Precision considers the fact that the objects that are not wanted by the user should be rejected. In principle, it is desirable to build a system that rewards both high recall, - retrieving all that is relevant - and high precision - discarding all unwanted objects (Ruiz & Srinisavan, 1998). Recall improves using high-frequency index terms, i.e. terms which occur in many documents of the collection. This way, it is expected to retrieve many documents including such terms, and thus, many of the relevant documents. The precision factor, however, improves when using more specific index terms that are capable of isolating the few relevant articles of the mass of irrelevant. In practice, compromises are utilized; using frequent enough terms to achieve a reasonable level of recall without causing a too low value of precision. The exact definitions of recall and precision are shown in Equations 1 and 2.

$$\text{Recall} = \frac{retrieved \ relevant \ objects}{total \ number \ of \ relevant \ objects}$$

Equation 1. Definition of recall

$$\text{Precision} = \frac{retrieved\ relevant\ objects}{total\ number\ of\ retrieved\ objects}$$

Equation 2. Definition of precision

So firstly, terms that are mentioned frequently in individual documents or extracts from a document, appear to be useful for improving recall. This suggests the use of a factor known as Term Frequency (TF) as part of a Term Weighting system, measuring the frequency of occurance of a term in a document. The TF factor has been used for Term Weighting for years in automatic indexing environments. Secondly, the TF factor solely does not ensure an acceptable retrieval. In particular, when the high frequency terms are not concentrated in specific documents, but instead are frequent in the entire set, all documents tend to be recovered, and this affects the precision factor. Thus, there is the need to introduce a new factor that favours the terms that are concentrated in only a few documents in the collection. The Inverse Document Frequency (IDF) is the factor that considers this aspect. The IDF factor is inversely proportional to the number of documents (n) to which a term is assigned in a set of documents N. A typical IDF factor is log (N / n) (Salton & Buckley, 1996). So the best index terms to identify the contents of a document are those able to distinguish certain individual documents from the rest of the set. This implies that the best terms should have high term frequencies, but low overall collection frequencies. A reasonable measure of the importance of a term can be obtained, therefore, by the product of term frequency and inverse document frequency (TF x IDF). It is usual to describe the weight of a term $i$ in a document $j$ as shown in Equation 3.

$$w_{ij} = tf_{ij} \times idf_j$$

Equation 3. Obtention of term weights; general formula

This formula was originally designed for the retrieval and extraction of documents. Eventually, it has also been used for the retrieval of any object in any set of accumulated knowledge, and has been revised and improved by other authors in order to obtain better results in Information Retrieval (Lee et al., 1997), (Zhao & Karypis, 2002), (Lertnattee & Theeramunkong, 2003), (Liu & Ke, 2007).

In short, term weights must be related somehow to the importance of an index term in the corresponding set of knowledge. There are two options for defining these weights:

- The evaluation of the weights by an expert in the field. This is based on his own perception of the importance of index terms. This method is simple, but it has the disadvantage of relying solely on the criterion of the engineer of knowledge, it is very subjective and is not able of being automated.
- Automated generation of weights using a set of rules. The most widely used method for Term Weighting, as said above, is the TF-IDF method. In this chapter, we propose a novel Fuzzy Logic-based Term Weighting method, which obtains better results for Information Retrieval.

To calculate the weight of a term, the TF-IDF approach considers two factors:

- TF: Frequency of occurrence of the term in the document. So $tf_{ik}$ is the frequency of occurrence of the term $T_k$ in document i.

-   IDF: varies inversely with the number of documents $n_k$ where the term $T_k$ has been assigned in a set of N documents. The typical IDF factor is represented by the expression $\log(N / n_k + 0.01)$.

Introducing standardization to simplify the calculations, the formula finally obtained for the calculation of the weights is defined in Equation 4 (Liu et al., 2001)

$$W_{ik} = \frac{tf_{ik} \times \log(N / n_k + 0.01)}{\sqrt{\sum_{k=1}^{m} tf_{ik} \times \log(N / n_k + 0.01))^2}}$$

Equation 4. Obtention of term weights. Used formula.

A third factor that is commonly used is the document length normalization factor. Long documents usually have a much larger set of extracted terms than short documents. This fact makes it more likely that long documents are retrieved (Van Rijsbergen, 1979), (Salton & Buckley, 1996). The term weight obtained using a length normalization factor is given by Equation 5.

$$W_{ik} = \frac{w_{ik}}{\sqrt{\sum_{i=1}^{m} (w_i)^2}}$$

Equation 5. Obtention of term weights using a length normalization factor

In Equation 5, $w_i$ correspond to the weights of the other components of the vector.

All Term Weighting tasks are shown in Figure 2.

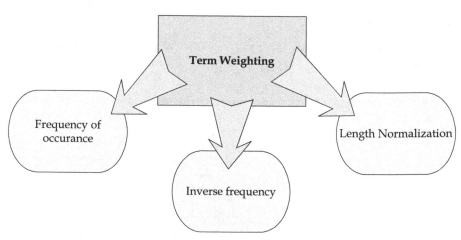

Fig. 2. Term Weighting tasks

## 3. Term Weighting method comparison

### 3.1 Term Weighting methods

The TF-IDF method works reasonably well, but has the disadvantage of not considering two aspects that we believe key:

- The first aspect is the degree of identification of the object if a determined index term is solely used in a query. This parameter has a strong influence on the final value of a weight of term if the degree of identification is high. The more a term identifies an object, a higher value has its correspondent weight. However, this parameter creates two disadvantages in terms of practical aspects when a systematic, automated Term Weighting scheme is neccessary. On the one hand, the degree of identification is not deductible from any feature of the index term, so it must be specified by the Knowlegde Engineer. The assigned values may therefore be subjective, not systematic and not univocal. On the other hand, the same index term may have a different relationship with different objects.
- The second aspect is related to the join index terms, i.e. terms that are linked to others. Join terms have lower weights as the fact that these keywords are linked is what really determines the principal object. The appearance of one of these words could refer to another object.

This chapter describes, firstly, the operation of TF-IDF method. Then, the new Term Weighting Fuzzy Logic-based method is introduced. Finally, both methods are implemented for the particular case of Information Retrieval for the University of Seville web portal, obtaining specific results of the operation of both of them. A web portal is a typical example of a disordered, vague and heterogenous set of knowledge. With this aim, an intelligent agent was designed to allow an efficient retrieval of the relevant information. This system should be valid for any set of knowledge. The system was designed to enable users to find possible answers to their queries in a set of knowledge of a great size. The whole set of knowledge was classified into different objects. These objects represent the possible answers to user queries and were organized into hierarchical groups (called Topic, Section and Object). One or more standard questions are assigned to every object and some index terms are extracted from them.

The last step is Term Weigthing; the assigned weight depends on the importance of an index term for the identification of the object. The way in which these weights are assigned is the main issue of this chapter. All the process is shown in Figure 3.

As an example of the classical TF-IDF Term Weighting method functioning, we are using the term 'library', used in the example shown in Table 1.

At Topic hierarchic level:

- 'Library' appears 6 times in Topic 6 ($tf_{ik}$ = 6, K=6).
- 'Library' appears 10 times in other Topics ($n_k$ = 3)
- There are 12 Topics in total (N=12) - for normalizing, it is only necessary to know the other $tf_{ik}$ and $n_k$ for the Topic-.
- Substituting, $W_{ik}$ = 1.00.

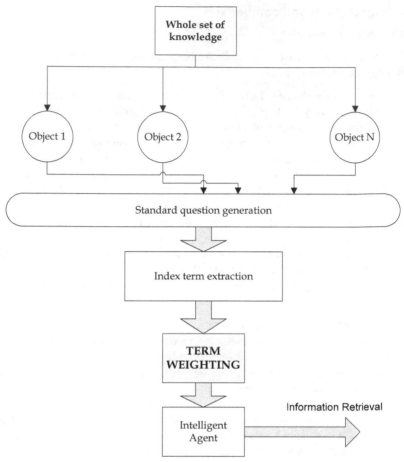

Fig. 3. Information Retrieval process.

As well, an example of the followed methodology is shown in Table 1.

| STEP | EXAMPLE |
|---|---|
| Step 1: Web page identified by standard/s question/s | - Web page: http://bib.us.es/index-ides-idweb.html<br>- Standard question: What online services are offered by the Library of the University of Seville? |
| Step 2: Locate standard/s question/s in the hierarchical structure. | Topic 6: Library<br>Section 3: Online services<br>Object 1. |
| Step 3: Extract index terms | Index terms: 'Library', 'services', 'online' |
| Step 4: Term weighting | Explained below |

Table 1. Example of the followed methodology.

At Section hierarchic level:

- 'Library' appears 6 times in Section 6.3 ($tf_{ik} = 6$, K= 3)
- 'Library' appears 4 times in other Sections in Topic 6 ($n_k = 6$)
- There are 6 Sections in Topic 6 (N=6).
- Substituting, $W_{ik} = 0.01$. In fact, 'Library' appears in most of the Sections in Topic 6, so it is not very relevant to distinguish the desired Section inside the Topic.

At Object hierarchic level:

- 'Library' appears once in Object 6.3.1 ($tf_{ik} = 1$, K = 1). – Logically a term can only appear once in an Object -.
- 'Library' appears 3 times in other Topics ($n_k = 3$).
- There are 4 Objects in Section 6.3 (N=3).
- Substituting, $W_{ik} = 0.01$.

Consequently, 'Library' is relevant to find out that the Object is in Topic 6, but not very relevant to find out the definite Object, which should be found according to other terms in a user consultation.

As said above, TF-IDF has the disadvantage of not considering the degree of identification of the object if only the considered index term is used and the existance of join terms. The FL-based method provides a solution for these problems: the solution is to create a table of all the index terms and their corresponding weights for each object. This table will be created in the process of extracting the index words from the standard questions. Imprecision practically does not affect the method due to the fact that Term Weighting is based on fuzzy logic. This fact minimizes the effect of possible variations of the assigned weights.

Furthermore, the Fuzzy Logic-based method provides two important advantages:

- Term Weighting is automatic.
- The level of expertise required is much lower. Moreover, there is no need for an operator of any kind of knowledge about Fuzzy Logic, but only has to know how many times an index term appears in a certain subset and the answer to two simple questions:
- How does an index term define an object by itself?
- Are there any join terms tied to the considered index term?

For example, in the case of a website, the own web page developer may define standard questions. These questions are associated with the object - the web page -. He also should define the index for each object and answer the two questions proposed above. This greatly simplifies the process and leaves the possibility of using collaborative intelligence.

Fuzzy Logic based Term Weighting method is defined below. Four questions must be answered to determine the weight of an Index Term:

- Question 1 (Q1): How often does an index term appear in other subsets?  - Related to IDF factor -.
- Question 2 (Q2): How often does an index term appear in its own subset?  - Related to TF factor -.
- Question 3 (Q3): Does an index term undoubtedly define an object by itself?
- Question 4 (Q4): Is an index term joined to another one?

With the answers to these questions, a set of values is obtained. These values are the inputs to a fuzzy logic system, a Term Weight Generator. The Fuzzy Logic system output sets the weight of an index term for each hierarchical level (Figure 4).

Fig. 4. Term Weighting using Fuzzy Logic.

Next it is described how to define the system input values associated with each of the four questions (Qi). Qi are the inputs to the Fuzzy Logic system

*Question 1*

Term weight is partly associated to the question 'How often does an index term appear in other subsets?'. It is given by a value between 0 – if it appears many times – and 1 - if it does not appear in any other subset -. To define weights, we are considering the times that the most used terms in the whole set of knowledge appear. The list of the most used index terms is shown in Table 2.

| Number of order | Index term | Number of appearances in the accumulated set of knowledge |
|---|---|---|
| 1 | Service | 31 |
| 2 | Services | 18 |
| 3 | Library | 16 |
| 4 | Research | 15 |
| 5 | Address | 14 |
|  | Student | 14 |
| 7 | Mail | 13 |
|  | Access | 13 |
| 9 | Electronic | 12 |
|  | Computer | 12 |
|  | Resources | 12 |
| 12 | Center | 10 |
|  | Education | 10 |
|  | Registration | 10 |
|  | Program | 10 |

Table 2. List of the most used words.

Provided that there are 1114 index terms defined in our case, we think that 1 % of these words must mark the border for the value 0 (11 words). Therefore, whenever an index term appears more than 12 times in other subsets, we will give it the value of 0. Associated values for every Topic are defined in Table 3.

| Number of appearances | 0 | 1 | 2 | 3 | 4 | 5 | 6 |
|---|---|---|---|---|---|---|---|
| Associated value | 1 | 0.9 | 0.8 | 0.7 | 0.64 | 0.59 | 0.53 |
| Number of appearances | 7 | 8 | 9 | 10 | 11 | 12 | ≥13 |
| Associated value | 0.47 | 0.41 | 0.36 | 0.3 | 0.2 | 0.1 | 0 |

Table 3. Input values associated to Q1 for topic hierarchic level.

Between 0 and 3 times appearing - approximately a third of the possible values - , we consider that an index term belongs to the so called HIGH set. Therefore, it is defined in its correspondant fuzzy set with uniformly distributed values between 0.7 and 1, as may be seen in Figure 5. Analogously, we distribute all values uniformly according to different fuzzy sets. Fuzzy sets are defined by linguistic variables LOW, MEDIUM and HIGH. Fuzzy sets are triangular, on one hand for simplicity and on the other hand because we tested other more complex types of sets (Gauss, Pi type, etc), but the results did not improve at all.

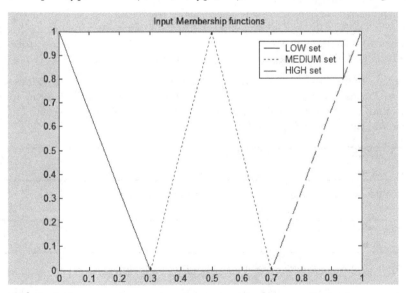

Fig. 5. Input fuzzy sets.

On the other hand, given that at each hierarchical level, a different term weight is defined, it is necessary to consider other scales to calculate the fuzzy system input values for the other hierarchical levels. As for the level of topic was considered the top level - the whole set of knowledge - , for the level of Section we consider the number occurrences of an index term on a given topic. Keeping in mind that all topics are considered, we take as reference the value of the topic in which the index term appears more often. The process is analogous to the above described, obtaining the values shown in Table 4.

| Number of appearances | 0 | 1 | 2 | 3 | 4 | 5 | ≥ 6 |
|---|---|---|---|---|---|---|---|
| Associated value | 1 | 0.7 | 0.6 | 0.5 | 0.4 | 0.3 | 0 |

Table 4. Input values associated to Q1 for section hierarchic level.

To find the term weight associated with the object level, the method is slightly different. It is also based on the definition of fuzzy sets, but we do not take into account the maximum number of words per secion, but the value associated to Q1 directly passes the border between fuzzy sets when the number of objects in which it appears increases in one unit, as seen in Table 5.

| Number of appearances | 0 | 1 | 2 | ≥ 3 |
|---|---|---|---|---|
| Associated value | 1 | 0.7 | 0.3 | 0 |

Table 5. Input values associated to Q1 for object hierarchic level.

*Question 2*

To find the imput value to the FL system of FL with question 2, the reasoning is analogous to the one for Q1, Though, we only have to consider the frequency of occurance of an index term within a single subset of knowledge, and not the frequency of occurrence in other subsets. Logically, the more times a term appears in a subset, the greater the probability that the query is related to it. Question Q2 corresponds to the TF factor.

Looking again at the list of index terms used in a topic, we obtain the values shown in Tables 6 and 7. It has been taken into account that the more times an index term appears in a topic or section, the greater should be the input value. These tables correspond to the values for the hierarchical levels of Topic and Section, respectively.

| Number of appearances | 1 | 2 | 3 | 4 | 5 | ≥ 6 |
|---|---|---|---|---|---|---|
| Associated value | 0 | 0.3 | 0.45 | 0.6 | 0.7 | 1 |

Table 6. Input values associated to Q2 for topic hierarchic level.

| Number of appearances | 1 | 2 | 3 | 4 | 5 | ≥ 6 |
|---|---|---|---|---|---|---|
| Associated value | 0 | 0.3 | 0.45 | 0.6 | 0.7 | 1 |

Table 7. Input values associated to Q2 for section hierarchic level.

Q2 is meaningless to determine the input value for the last hierarchical level. At this level, an index term appears only once on every object.

*Question 3*

For Question 3, the answer is completely subjective. In this chapter, we propose the values "Yes", "Rather" and "No". Table 8, shows the input values associated with Q3. This value is independent of hierarchical level.

| Answer (Does the term itself define the Object?) | Yes | Rather | No |
|---|---|---|---|
| Associated value | 1 | 0.5 | 0 |

Table 8. Input values associated to Q3.

For example, the developer of a web page would only have to answer "Yes", "Rather" or "No" to Question 3, without complicated mathematical formulas to describe it.

*Question 4*

Finally, question 4 deals with the number of index terms joined to another one. If an index term is joined to another one, its weight is lower. This is due to the fact that the term must be a join term to refer to the object in question. We propose term weight values for this question in Table 9. Again, the values 0.7 and 0.3 are a consequence of considering the border between fuzzy sets.

| Joined terms to an index term | 0 | 1 | 2 | ≥ 3 |
|---|---|---|---|---|
| Associated value | 1 | 0.7 | 0.3 | 0 |

Table 9. Input values associated to Q3.

After considering all these factors, fuzzy rules must be defined. In the case of Topic and Section hierarchical levels, we must consider the four input values that are associated with questions Q1, Q2, Q3 and Q4. Four output fuzzy sets have been also defined: HIGH, MEDIUM-HIGH, MEDIUM-LOW AND LOW. For the definition of the fuzzy rules for the Term Weighting system, we have used basically the following criteria:

- A high value of Q1 (IDF-related factor) implies that the term is not very present in other sets of knowledge. In this case, the output will be high, unless the term itself has very little importance (low Q3) or it is joined to many terms (low Q4).
- A high value of Q2 (TF-related factor), usually implies a high output value, since the index term is very present in a set of knowledge. However, if Q1 has a low value means that the term is present throughout the whole set of knowledge, so it is not very useful for extracting information.
- Q3 is a very important parameter, since if one term defines itself very well to a particular object, it is much easier to find the object.
- A low value of Q4 makes an index term less important, since it is associated with other terms. This fact causes a lower output value.

The combination of the four inputs and the three input fuzzy sets provides 81 possible combinations, which are summarized in Table 10.

In the object level (the last hierarchic level), Question 2 is discarded. Therefore, there is a change in the rules, although the criteria for the definition of fuzzy rules are similar to the previous case. An input less reduces the number of rules to twenty seven.

## 3.2 Example of the followed methodology

An example of the followed methodology is shown below. A comparision with the classical TF-IDF is done, starting from the definition of an object in the database of the Web portal of the University of Seville. The following example shows the difference between applying the TF-IDF method and applying the Fuzzy Logic-based one.

| Rule number | Rule definition | Output |
|---|---|---|
| R1 | IF Q1 = HIGH and Q2 ≠ LOW | At least MEDIUM-HIGH |
| R2 | IF Q1 = MEDIUM and Q2 = HIGH | At least MEDIUM-HIGH |
| R3 | IF Q1 = HIGH and Q2 = LOW | Depends on other Questions |
| R4 | IF Q1 = HIGH and Q2 = LOW | Depends on other Questions |
| R5 | IF Q3 = HIGH | At least MEDIUM-HIGH |
| R6 | IF Q4 = LOW | Descends a level |
| R7 | IF Q4 = MEDIUM | If the Output is MEDIUM-LOW, it descends to LOW |
| R8 | IF (R1 and R2) or (R1 and R5) or (R2 and R5) | HIGH |
| R9 | In any other case | MEDIUM-LOW |

Table 10. Fuzzy rules.

In the Web portal database, Object 6.3.1 (http://bib.us.es/index-ides-idweb.html) is defined by the following standard question:

*What online services are offered by the Library of the University of Seville?*

If we consider the term 'library':

At Topic hierarchic level:

- 'Library' appears 6 times in other Topics in the whole set of knowledge, so that the value associated to Q1 is 0.53.
- 'Library' appears 10 times in Topic 6, so that the value associated to Q2 is 1.
- The response to Q3 is 'Rather' in 7 of the 10 times and 'No' in the other three, so that the value associated to Q3 is a weighted average: $(7*0.5 + 3*0)/10 = 0.35$.
- Term 'Library' is tied to one term 7 times and it is tied to two terms once. Therefore, the average is 1.1 terms. A linear extrapolation leads to a value associated to Q4 of 0.66.
- With all the values as inputs for the fuzzy logic engine, we obtain a term weight of 0.56.

At Section hierarchic level:

- 'Library' appears 6 times in other Sections corresponding to Topic 6, so that the value associated to Q1 is 0.
- 'Library' appears 4 times in Topic 6, so that the value associated to Q2 is 0.6.
- The response to Q3 is 'Rather' in three of the four cases, so that the value associated to Q3 is $(3*0.5 + 1*0)/4 = 0.375$.
- Term 'Library' is tied to one term 5 times and it is tied to two terms once so that the value associated to Q4 is 0.63.

- With all the values as inputs for the fuzzy logic engine, we obtain a term weight of 0.13.

At Object hierarchich level:

- 'Library' appears 3 times in other Objects corresponding to Section 6.3, so that the value associated to Q1 is 0.
- The response to Q3 is 'Rather', so that the value associated to Q3 is 0.5.
- Term 'Library' is tied to one term twice and it is tied to two terms once so that the value associated to Q4 is 0.57.
- With all the values as inputs for the fuzzy logic engine, we obtain a term weight of 0.33.

A summary of the values for the index term 'library' is shown in Table 11.

| Hierarchic levels | | Q1 value | Q2 value | Q3 value | Q4 value | Term Weight |
|---|---|---|---|---|---|---|
| Topic level (Topic 6) | TF-IDF Method | - | - | - | - | 1 |
| | Fuzzy Logic-based method | 0.53 | 1 | 0.35 | 0.66 | 0.56 |
| Section level (Section 3) | TF-IDF Method | - | - | - | - | 0.01 |
| | Fuzzy Logic-based method | 0 | 0.6 | 0.375 | 0.63 | 0.13 |
| Object level (Object 1) | TF-IDF Method | - | - | - | - | 0.01 |
| | Fuzzy Logic-based method | 0 | - | 0.5 | 0.57 | 0.33 |

Table 11. Comparison of Term Weight values.

We may see the difference with the corresponding weight for the TF-IDF method - a value $W_{ik} = 0.01$ had been obtained), but this is just what we were looking for: not only the desired object is found, but also the ones that are more closely related to it. The word 'library' has a small weight for the TF-IDF method because it can not distinguish between the objects of Section 6.3. However, in this case all the objects will be retrieved, as they are interrelated. The weights of other terms determine the object which has a higher level of certainty.

# 4. Tests and results

## 4.1 General tests

Tests were held on the website of the University of Seville. 253 objects were defined, and grouped in a hierarchical structure, with 12 topics. Every topic has a variable number of sections and objects. From these 253 objects, 2107 standard questions were extracted. More than half of them were not used for these tests, as they were similar to others and did not contribute much to the results. Finally, the number of standard questions used for the tests was 914. Also, several types of standard questions were defined.

Depending on the nature of the considered object, we defined different types of standard questions, such as:

- A single primary standard question, which is the one that best defines an object. This question must always be associated to every object, the others types of standard questions are optional.
- Standard questions that take into account synonyms of some of the index terms used in the main standard question (e.g., "report" as a synonym for "document").We have called them synonim standard questions.
- Standard questions that take into account that a user may search for an object, but his question may be inaccurate or may be he does not know the proper jargon (e.g., "broken table" for "repairing service"). We have called them imprecise standard questions.
- Standard questions that are related to the main question associated with the object, but are more specific (e.g., "I'd like to find some information about the curriculum of Computer Science" to "I'd like to find some information about the curriculum for the courses offered by the University of Seville "). We have called them specific standard questions.
- Standard questions created by a feedback system. Most frequent user queries may be used.

For our tests, we considered the types of standard questions shown in Table 12.

| Type of standard question | Number of questions |
|---|---|
| Main standard questions | 252 |
| Synonim standard questions | 308 |
| Imprecise standard questions | 125 |
| Specific standard questions | 229 |
| Feedback standard questions | 0 |
| Total standard questions | 914 |

Table 12. Types of standard questions.

The standard questions were used as inputs in a Fuzzy Logic-based system. The outputs of the system are the objects with a degree a certainty greater than a certain threshold. To compare results, we considered the position in which the correct answer appears among the total number of answers identified as probable.

First of all, we shall define the thresholds to overcome in the Fuzzy Logic system. Thus, topics and sections that are not related to the object to be identified are removed. This is one of the advantages of using a hierarchical structure. Processing time is better as many subsets of knowledge are discarded. Anyway, it is desirable not to discard too many objects, in order to also obtain the related ones. The ideal is to retrieve between one and five answers for the user. The results of the consultation were sorted in 5 categories:

- Category Cat1: the correct answer is retrieved as the only answer or it is the one that has a higher degree of certainty between the answers retrieved by the system.
- Category Cat2: The correct answer is retrieved between the three answers with higher degree of certainty -excluding the previous case -.
- Category Cat3: The correct answer is retrieved between the five answers with higher degree of certainty - excluding the previous cases -.
- Category Cat4: The correct answer is retrieved, but not between the five answers with higher degree of certainty.
- Category Cat5: The correct answer is not retrieved by system.

Results are shown in Table 13

| Method | Cat1 | Cat2 | Cat3 | Cat4 | Cat5 | Total |
|--------|------|------|------|------|------|-------|
| TF-IDF method | 466 (50.98%) | 223 (24.40%) | 53 (5.80%) | 79 (8.64%) | 93 (10.18%) | 914 |
| FL-based method | 710 (77.68%) | 108 (11.82%) | 27 (2.95%) | 28 (3.06%) | 41 (4.49%) | 914 |

Table 13. Information Retrieval results of using both Term Weighting methods.

The results obtained with the TF-IDF method are quite reasonable. 81.18% of the objects are retrieved among the top 5 choices and more than half of the objects are retrieved in the first place, Fuzzy Logic-based method is clearly better. 92.45% of the objects are retrieved and more than three-quarters are retrieved in the first place.

## 4.2 Tests according to the type of standard questions

In order to refine the conclusions about both Term Weighting methods, it is important to make a more thorough analysis of the results. We submitted to both Term Weighting methods to a comprehensive analysis according to the type of standard question. Results are shown in the Table 14.

According to the results, the TF-IDF method works relatively well considering the number of objects retrieved. Though, the Fuzzy Logic-based method is more precise, retrieving 91.67% of the objects in the first place. On the other hand, good results for this type of questions are logical, since questions correspond to supposedly well-made user queries.

For synonymous standard questions, the conclusions are similar: the results obtained using the Fuzzy Logic-based method are better than those achieved with TF-IDF method, especially in regard to precision. Though, the TF-IDF method also ensures good results. However, queries are not precise, so the performance is worse for the TF-IDF method than it is for the Fuzzy Logic-based method. This fact gives an idea of fuzzy logic as an ideal tool for adding more flexibility to the system. Anyway, the results are quite similar to those obtained for the main standard questions. They are only slightly worse, since synonim standard questions are similar to the main standard questions.

The difference is even more noticeable in regard to imprecise standard questions and specific standard questions. Imprecise standard questions are detected nearly as well as the main standard questions in the case of Fuzzy Logic-based method. This is another reason to confirm the appropriateness of using Fuzzy Logic. As for the specific standard questions, we

| Type of standard question | | Cat1 | Cat2 | Cat3 | Cat4 | Cat5 | Total |
|---|---|---|---|---|---|---|---|
| Main standard questions | TF-IDF Method | 171 (67.86%) | 58 (23.02%) | 6 (2.38%) | 6 (2.38%) | 11 (4.37%) | 252 |
| | Fuzzy Logic-based method | 231 (91.67%) | 13 (5.16%) | 2 (0.79%) | 0 (0.00 %) | 6 (2.38%) | 252 |
| Synonim standard questions | TF-IDF Method | 177 (57.46%) | 86 (27.92%) | 13 (4.22%) | 15 (4.87%) | 17 (5.52%) | 308 |
| | Fuzzy Logic-based method | 252 (81.82%) | 41 (13.31%) | 3 (0.97%) | 5 (1.62%) | 47 (2.27%) | 308 |
| Imprecise standard questions | TF-IDF Method | 74 (59.20%) | 32 (25.60%) | 6 (4.80%) | 1 (0.80%) | 12 (9.60%) | 125 |
| | Fuzzy Logic-based method | 111 (88.80%) | 5 (4.00%) | 0 (0.00 %) | 0 (0.00 %) | 9 (7.20%) | 125 |
| Specific standard questions | TF-IDF Method | 46 (20.08%) | 49 (21.40%) | 26(11.35%) | 55(24.01%) | 52 (22.71%) | 229 |
| | Fuzzy Logic-based method | 107 (46.72%) | 53 (23.14%) | 24 (10.48%) | 23(10.04%) | 22 (9.61%) | 229 |

Table 14. Information Retrieval results of using both Term Weighting methods, according to the type of standard question.

get the worst result by far among all classes of standard questions. This is a logical fact, considering that these questions are associated with the main standard question, but it is more concrete. In fact, it is usual for such specific questions to belong to a list within a whole. This way, there may be objects that are more related to the query than the requiered object itself. This is hardly a drawback, since both objects are retrieved to the user - the more specific one and the more general one -. The own user must choose which one is the most accurate. This case shows more clearly that the fact of using Fuzzy Logic allows the user to extract a larger number of objects.

### 4.3 Tests according to the number of standard questions

Another aspect to consider in the analysis of the results is the number of standard questions assigned to every object. Obviously, an object that is well defined by a single standard question is very specific. Thus, it is easy to extract the object from the complete set of knowledge. However, there are objects that contain very vague or imprecise information, making it necessary to define several standard questions for every object. For this study, the objects are grouped into the following:

- Group 1: the object is defined by a single standard question.
- Group 2: the object is defined by two to five standard questions.
- Group 3: the object is defined by six to ten standard questions.
- Group 4: the object is defined by more than ten standard questions.

Obviously, groups 1 and 2 are more numerous, since it is less common that many questions have the same response. However, the objects from the groups 3 and 4 correspond to a wide range of standard questions, so they are equally important. In Table 15 the number of objects for each of these groups is defined.

| Group number | Number of standard questions per object | Number of objects |
|---|---|---|
| Group 1 | 1 | 95 |
| Group 2 | 2-5 | 108 |
| Group 3 | 6-10 | 22 |
| Group 4 | > 10 | 28 |

Table 15. Groups according to the number of standard questions per object.

To analyze the results, the position in which the required object is retrieved must be considered. We consider the retrieval of most of the standard questions that define that object. For example, if an object is defined by 15 standard questions and, for 10 of them, the object is retrieved in second place, it is considered that the object has actually been retrieved in second place.

In short, this study does not focus on the answers to standard questions, but on the correctly retrieved objects. This provides a new element for the system analysis. Results are shown in Table 16.

For group 1, the results are almost perfect for the Fuzzy Logic-based method, as nearly all the objects are retrieved in the first place (about 94%). However, the TF-IDF method, though not as accurate, resists the comparison. This behaviour is repeated in group 2. The objects are often retrieved by both methods among the top three items. Though, the Fuzzy Logic-based method is better for its accuracy, retrieving over 92% of the objects in the first place. In view of the tests, we conclude that the results are very good for both methods when up to five standard questions are defined. Although the results are better for the novel Fuzzy Logic-based Term Weighting method, they are also quite reasonable for the classical TF-IDF Term Weighting method.

However, the largest advantage of using Fuzzy Logic for Term Weighting occurs when many standard questions per object are defined, i.e. when the information is confusing, disordered or imprecise. For the case of group 3, where objects are defined by among six and ten standard questions per object type, we observe that there is a significant difference between the TF-IDF classical method and the proposed Fuzzy Logic-based method. Although both methods retrieve all the objects, there is a big difference in the way they are retrieved, especially on the accuracy of the information extraction. 86% of the objects are retrieved in first place using the Fuzzy Logic-based method, while only 45% using the TF-IDF classical method.

| Type of standard question | | Cat1 | Cat2 | Cat3 | Cat4 | Cat5 | Total |
|---|---|---|---|---|---|---|---|
| Group 1 | TF-IDF Method | 74 (77.89%) | 16 (16.84%) | 1 (1.05%) | 1 (1.05%) | 3 (3.16%) | 95 |
| | Fuzzy Logic-based method | 89 (93.68%) | 3 (3.16%) | 2 (2.10%) | 0 (0.00 %) | 1 (1.05%) | 95 |
| Group 2 | TF-IDF Method | 86 (79.63%) | 21 (19.44%) | 1 (0.93%) | 0 (0.00 %) | 0 (0.00 %) | 108 |
| | Fuzzy Logic-based method | 100 (92.59%) | 7 (6.48%) | 0 (0.00 %) | 0 (0.00 %) | 1 (0.93%) | 108 |
| Group 3 | TF-IDF Method | 10 (45.45%) | 9 (40.91%) | 3 (13.63%) | 0 (0.00 %) | 0 (0.00 %) | 22 |
| | Fuzzy Logic-based method | 19 (86.36%) | 3 (13.63%) | 0 (0.00 %) | 0 (0.00 %) | 0 (0.00 %) | 22 |
| Group 4 | TF-IDF Method | 10 (35.71%) | 10 (35.71%) | 3 (10.71%) | 2 (7.14%) | 3 (10.71%) | 28 |
| | Fuzzy Logic-based method | 21 (75.00%) | 4 (14.29%) | 1 (3.57%) | 1 (3.57%) | 1 (3.57%) | 28 |

Table 16. Information Retrieval results of using both Term Weighting methods, according to the number of standard questions per object.

The difference is even more marked when more than ten standard questions per object are defined. In this case, it is obvious that none of the questions clearly define the object, so that information is clearly vague. While using the Fuzzy Logic-based method, more than 96% of the objects are retrieved - with 75% of them in the first place -, with the TF-IDF method correctly, only 82% of the objects are retrieved. Furthermore, only 35.7% of these objects are extracted in the first place.

In view of the table, we observe that the more standard questions per object, the better the results of the Fuzzy Logic-based method, compared with those obtained with the classical TF-IDF method. Therefore, the obvious conclusion is that the more convoluted, messy and confusing is the information, the better the Fuzzy Logic-based Term Weighting method is compared to the classical one. This makes Fuzzy Logic-based Term Weighting an ideal tool for the case of information extraction in a web portal.

## 5. Future research directions

We suggest the application of other Computational Intelligence techniques apart from Fuzzy Logic for Term Weighting. Among these techniques, we believe that the so-called neuro-fuzzy techniques represent a very interesting field, as they combine human reasoning provided by Fuzzy Logic and the connection-based structure of Artificial Neural Networks, taking advantage of both techniques. One possible application is the creation of fuzzy rules by means of an Artificial Neural Network system.

Another possible future direction is to check the validity of this method in other environments containing inaccurate, vague and heterogeneous data.

## 6. Conclusion

The difficulty to distinguish the necessary information from the huge quantity of unnecessary data has enhanced the use of Information Retrieval recently. Especially, the so-called Vector Space Model is much extended. Vector Space Model is based on the use of index terms. These index terms are associated with certain weights, which represent the importance of these terms in the considered set of knowledge. In this chapter, we propose the development of a novel automatic Fuzzy Logic-based Term Weighting method for Vector Space Model. This method improves the TF-IDF Term Weighting classic method for its flexibility. The use of Fuzzy Logic is very appropiate in heterogeneous, vague, imprecise, or not in order information environments.

Fuzzy Logic-based method is similar to TF-IDF, but also considers two aspects that the TF-IDF does not: the degree of identification of the object if a determined index term is solely used in a query; and the existance of join index terms. Term Weighting is automatic. The level of expertise required is low, so there is no need for an operator of any kind of knowledge about Fuzzy Logic. Therefore, an operator only has to know how many times an index term appears in a certain subset and the answer to two simple questions.

Although the results obtained with the TF-IDF method are quite reasonable, Fuzzy Logic-based method is clearly superior. Especially when user queries are not equal to the standard query or they are imprecise, we observe that the performance declines more for the TF-IDF method than for the Fuzzy Logic-based method. This fact gives us an idea of how suitable is the use of Fuzzy Logic to add more flexibility to an Information Retrieval system.

## 7. References

Lertnattee, V. & Theeramunkong, T. (2003). Combining homogenous classifiers for centroid-based text classification. *Proceedings of the 7th International Symposium on Computers and Communications*, pp. 1034-1039.

Lee, D.L., Chuang, H., Seamons, K., 1997. *Document ranking and the vector-space model*. IEEE Software, Vol. 14, Issue 2, pp. 67 – 75.

Liu, S., Dong, M., Zhang, H., Li, R. & Shi, Z. (2001). An approach of multi-hierarchy text classification. *Proceedings of the International Conferences on Info-tech and Info-net*. Beijing. Vol 3, pp. 95 – 100.

Raghavan, V.V. & Wong, S.K. (1986). A critical analysis of vector space model for information retrieval. *Journal of the American Society for Information Science*, Vol.37 (5), p. 279-87.

Ruiz, M. & Srinivasan, P. (1998). Automatic Text Categorization Using Neural Networks. *Advances in Classification Research vol. 8: Proceedings of the 8th ASIS SIG/CR*

*Classification Research Workshop*. Ed. Efthimis Efthimiadis. Information Today, Medford:New Jersey, pp 59-72.

Salton, G. (1988). *Automatic Text Processing*. Addison-Wesley Publishing Company.

Salton, G. & Buckley, C. (1996). Term Weighting Approaches in Automatic Text Retrieval. *Technical Report TR87-881, Department of Computer Science, Cornell University, 1987. Information Processing and Management* Vol.32 (4), pp. 431-443.

Van Rijsbergen, C.J. (1979). *Information retrieval*. Butterworths.

Zhao, Y. & Karypis, G. (2002). Improving precategorized collection retrieval by using supervised term weighting schemes. *Proceedings of the International Conference on Information Technology: Coding and Computing*, pp 16 – 21.

# 11

# Fault Diagnostic of Rotating Machines Based on Artificial Intelligence: Case Studies of the Centrais Elétricas do Norte do Brazil S/A – Eletrobras-Eletronorte

Marcelo Nascimento Moutinho

*Centrais Elétricas do Norte do Brasil S/A – ELETROBRAS-ELETRONORTE,*
*Brasil*

## 1. Introduction

The efficiency of the maintenance techniques applied in energy generation power plants is improved when expert diagnosis systems are used to analysis information provided by the continuous monitoring systems used in these installations. There are a large number of equipments available in the power plants of the Centrais Elétricas do Norte do Brazil S/A - ELETROBRAS-ELETRONORTE (known as ELETRONORTE). These equipments operate continuously because are indispensable for the correct functioning of the generation and transmission systems of the company. Anomalies in the operation of these devices can be detected with the use of intelligent diagnosis tools which analysis the information of the continuous monitoring systems and, based in a set of qualitative rules, indicate the best procedures to avoid the fail of the equipments.

The best maintenance strategy used in each equipment operated by ELETRONORTE should consider factors as: equipments importance for the production process, acquisition cost and failure rate. To accomplish this task, one of the three maintenance techniques more used nowadays is chosen: corrective, preventive or predictive [1]. In the predictive maintenance, an operational report of the equipment's condition is emitted using the information collected by the continuous monitoring system. The formulation of such report is a task divided in the following stages: 1) Anomaly identification that can be occurring in the equipment; 2) Detection of the anomalous component; 3) Evaluation of the severity of the fault; and 4) Estimation of the remaining life time of the equipment. The predictive maintenance policies is an efficient practice to identify problems in hydrogenerators that will increase reliability, decrease maintenance costs, limit service failures and increase the life of the machines.

There is a vast literature on techniques for detection and identification of faults known to the FDI (Fault Detection and Isolation). A possible classification of these techniques that consider the aspects related to the type of information available about the process analysis defines three categories: methods based on quantitative models, methods based on qualitative models or semi-qualitative, and methods based on historical data [2]. The first two categories are commonly named Model Based Fault Detection and Isolation (MBFDI) [3].

A MBFDI algorithm consists of two components: the residues generator and the process of decision making: the residues generator compares the current values of inputs, outputs or states of the process with the estimated model that describes the normal behavior; the process decision is the logic that converts the residue signal (quantitative knowledge) on a qualitative information (normal operating condition or abnormal). The bases of MBFDI algorithms are described in [3], [4] and [5]. The main difficulty in implementing a MBFDI algorithm lies in the fact that the fidelity of the model affects the sensitivity of the fault detection mechanism and the diagnosis precision. Many real systems are not susceptible to conventional modeling techniques due to: the lack of precise knowledge about the system, the strongly nonlinear behavior, the high degree of uncertainty, or the time-varying characteristics.

Recently, well successfully applications of predictive techniques have been reported. In [6 to 9] are presented intelligent systems for predictive maintenance addressed to the diagnosis in real-time of industrial processes. In [10] a fault detection and isolation scheme of sensor and actuator is presented. The project considers multivariate dynamic systems with uncertainties in the mathematical model of the process. Detailed studies on the robustness of anomalous systems of identification in presence of modeling errors is also reported in the survival paper [2].

Nowadays, the expert diagnosis technologies available in the market are in maturation process. The tools commercially available have restrictions in the information exchange with the company's legacy systems. The users normally can't change the software structure and don't know the conceptual data base model. Due to these limitations, the company who uses this kind of paradigm is in a difficult situation when software modifications, not considered in the initial project, are necessary to adjust it to a specific application.

In this chapter is described the procedures for designing and test MBFDI system. Two types of models will be used: autoregressive models and fuzzy models. The proposed system is evaluated experimentally using real monitoring data from a synchronous compensator and a synchronous generator. The synchronous compensator analyzed is in operation at Vila do Conde substation, located at Pará state, Brazil. The synchronous generator studied is in operation at Tucuruí Hydroelectric, located at Pará state too. Both equipments are operated by ELETRONORTE.

## 2. Fuzzy system and regression models for use in diagnosis systems

To design the fault detection system proposed in this work mathematical models are used to describe the relationships between the variables monitored in the equipment analyzed. Two types of models will be used: autoregressive models and fuzzy models. The purpose of this section is describe the two structures used.

### 2.1 System identification with regression models

The following structure, known in literature as Autoregressive model with exogenous inputs (ARX), will be used [14]:

$$y(t) + a_1 y(k-1) + ... + a_{n_a} y(k-n_a) =$$
$$b_0 u(k-d) + b_1 u(k-1-d) + ... + b_{n_b} u(k-d-n_b)$$

(1)

where $y(k)$ and $u(k)$ are, respectively, the values of the output and input signals at the discrete time $k$, an integer multiple of the sampling interval $T_s$, $n_a$ and $n_b$ are the number of regressors is the output and input signals, respectively, and $d \geq 1$ is the output transport system delay as an integer multiple of the sampling interval. Using the discrete delay operator, $(q^{-1})^1$, the following polynomial representation of Eq. (1) can be obtained:

$$A(q^{-1})y(t) = q^{-d}B(q^{-1})u(t) \tag{2}$$

where $A(q^{-1})$ and $B(q^{-1})$ are as follow:

$$A(q^{-1}) = 1 + a_1 q^{-1} + a_2 q^{-2} + ... + a_{n_a} q^{-n_a} \tag{3}$$

$$B(q^{-1}) = b_0 + b_1 q^{-1} + b_2 q^{-2} + ... + b_{n_b} q^{-n_b} \tag{4}$$

It is interesting to add stochastic characteristics in the model representing as realistically as possible the nature of the process. This can be done considering that the output signal is affected by uncorrelated noise. Thus, the following representation can be obtained:

$$y(k) = \phi^T(k)\theta(k) + e(k) \tag{5}$$

where $e(k)$ is a Gaussian white noise; $\phi(k)$ is the vector of regressors and $\theta(k)$ is the vector of model parameters. The vectors $\phi(k)$ and $\theta(k)$ are represented as follows:

$$\phi(k) = \left[ -y(k-1) \, ... - y(k - n_a) \, u(k-d) \, ... \, u(t - d - n_b) \, \right]^T \tag{6}$$

$$\theta(t) = \left[ a_1 \, a_2 ... \, a_{n_a} \, b_0 \, b_1 ... \, b_{n_b} \right]^T \tag{7}$$

The non-recursive least squares method [14] will be used in order to estimate the vector $\hat{\theta}(k)$, which represents approximately the parameter vector $\theta(k)$ of Eq. (5). The objective of the method is to minimize the sum of the squares of the prediction error between the estimated model output and the real output of the plant. Substituting in equation (5) $k = 1,2, .., N$, we obtain, in matrix notation:

$$\mathbf{y} = \begin{bmatrix} y(1) \\ y(2) \\ \vdots \\ y(N) \end{bmatrix}, \mathbf{\Phi} = \begin{bmatrix} \phi(1)^T \\ \phi(2)^T \\ \vdots \\ \phi(N)^T \end{bmatrix}, \varepsilon = \begin{bmatrix} \xi(1) \\ \xi(2) \\ \vdots \\ \xi(N) \end{bmatrix} \tag{8}$$

$$\mathbf{y} = \mathbf{\Phi}\hat{\theta} + \varepsilon \tag{9}$$

where. $\xi(k) = y(k) - \phi^T(k)\hat{\theta}$. The following quadratic performance index must be minimized:

---

[1] Represented as follows $q^{-1}y(k) = y(k-1)$

$$J(\hat{\theta}) = \frac{1}{2}\sum_{k=1}^{N}\xi(t)^2 \tag{10}$$

The value of $\hat{\theta}$ that minimizes the Eq. (10) is [15]:

$$\theta_{MQ} = (\Phi^T\Phi)^{-1}\Phi^T y \tag{11}$$

## 2.2 Identification of predictive models based on fuzzy logic

In this subsection the structure of the fuzzy model used in this work will be described. The following discrete nonlinear system representation is used:

$$y(k) = f\left[\Psi(k-1)\right] \tag{12}$$

where $f(.)$ is a nonlinear function of the *Information Vector* $\Psi$, defined as:

$$\Psi(k-1) = \left[y(k-1)\cdots y(k-n_a)\ldots u(k-d)\ldots u(k-d-n_b)\right]^T \tag{13}$$

where: $n_a$ and $n_b$ represent the number of regressors of discrete output signals, $y(k)$ and input $u(k)$, respectively, $d$ is the output transport delay as an integer multiple of the sampling interval $T_s$; $e(k)$ is a random signal that supposedly corrupts the signals of the model is designed in a stochastic environment. This model is known as Non-linear Auto-regressive with exogenous inputs (NARX).

We consider the existence of a measurable set of variables that characterize the operating conditions of the system (12) at every moment. Using these variables, you can define a set of rules that describe, approximately, the behavior of the function $y(k)$:

$$R^{(l)}: \text{IF} < V_1 \text{ is } V_{1,i}^l > \text{AND} < V_2 \text{ is } V_{2,j}^l > \text{AND} \ldots \text{AND} < V_k \text{ is } V_{k,p}^l > \text{THEN } y_l(k) = f_l(k) \tag{14}$$

where: $l=1,2, \ldots, M$; $i = 1,2, \ldots, n_1$; $j = 1,2, \ldots, n_2$; and $p = 1,2,\ldots, n_k$. The terms, $V_1, V_2, \ldots, V_k$ are fuzzy linguistic variables that are part of the vector $\Psi$ and were chosen to describe the system (12). The domain of these variables is uniformly partitioned into $n_i = n_1, n_2, \ldots, n_k$ fuzzy sets (for example, the partitions of $V_i$ are: $V_{i,1}, V_{i,2}, \ldots, V_{i,ni}$. In this work the function $f_i(.)$ is represented by the following linear combination:

$$f_l(k) = c_l^0 + c_l^1 V_1 + c_l^2 V_2 + \cdots + c_l^k V_k \tag{15}$$

onde $c_l^i$ $i=1,2,\ldots,k$ are coefficients to be estimated.

At a given instant of discrete time $k$ each linguistic variable, $V_i$, will have a membership value $\mu_{V_{i,j}}[V_i(t)]$ associated with the fuzzy set $j$ ($j = 1,2, \ldots, n_i$). For mathematical simplicity, the membership functions used to represent these sets are triangular and trapezoidal, with the trapezoidal used only in two extreme sets, as shown in Figure 2. It is easy to see that, for each fuzzy variable, at most two and at least one fuzzy set has a membership value different from zero and the sum of these values always is equal one.

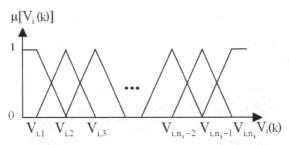

Fig. 2. Membership functions of the $n_i$ fuzzy sets associated with the Linguistic variable $V_i(k)$.

The set of M rules defined by (14) describe a fuzzy system of Sugeno [16], a mathematical tool that can represent globally and approximately the system described in Eq (12). It is a universal nonlinear approximator, a mathematical function that represents with an arbitrary degree of precision, dynamic systems governed by nonlinear relationships.

According to the theory of fuzzy systems [16], the output signal $\hat{y}(k)$ of the fuzzy system defined by the set of rules (14) is obtained by weighted average of the individual outputs of each of the M rules:

$$\hat{y}(k) = \frac{\sum_{l=1}^{M} \omega_l y_l(k)}{\sum_{l=1}^{M} \omega_l} \tag{16}$$

The weights, $\omega_l$, are called Functions Validation. They are calculated in terms of the vector $\Psi$ as follows:

$$\omega_l = \mu_{V_{1,i}^l}(V_1(t)) \times \mu_{V_{2,j}^l}(V_2(t)) \times \cdots \times \mu_{V_{k,p}^l}(V_k(t)) \tag{17}$$

According to Eq.(16), the value of the signal output of the model is a function of the $\omega_l$ weights and functions $f_l(.)$. Therefore, for a given set of values of signal $y(k)$ can be found an optimal setting of the parameters of fuzzy membership functions defined on each input and the parameters of the functions $f_l(.)$ that minimizes the difference $y(k) - \hat{y}(k)$ for the entire set. The details of the procedure for identification of these parameters will be the subject matter of section IV which will be described a procedure for identifying models based on real data from a continuous monitoring system described in the next section.

## 2.3 Prediction techniques based on Adaptive-Network-based Fuzzy Inference Systems (ANFIS)

### 2.3.1 Synchronous compensator monitoring system – VIBROCOMP

This monitoring system was designed as predictive maintenance tool for Synchronous Compensators (SC). These equipments are large rotary machines of 150 MVAr where the constant evaluation of its physical parameters is critical. In the State of Pará, Eletronorte operates three SC that are part of its transmission system: two are installed in Vila do Conde substation, located in Para State, and one is installed in the Marabá substation. These three equipments are monitored by VibroComp. Figure 3 shows a photograph of CPAV-01, one of SC monitored in the substation of Vila do Conde. This equipment, a member of the National Interconnected System (SIN), is used for voltage regulation. The main features of CPAV-01 are presented in Table 1.

Fig. 3. Synchronous Compensator 01 of the substation Vila do Conde.

| Characteristics | Value |
|:---:|:---:|
| Power | 150 MVAR |
| Speed | 900 RPM |
| Voltage | 13.8 KV |
| Current | 6.275 A |
| Frequency | 60Hz |

Table 1. Nominal Characteristics of CPAV-01.

The VibroComp system consists of the following parts:

1. *Hardware:*
   - Sources, sensors, transmitters and signal conditioners;
   - Aquisition Computers, Database Computers, data acquisition cards, serial cards, cables, etc..;
2. *Software:*
   - Data Acquisition Module;
   - Database Module;
   - Expert Diagnosis System;
   - Client Module

The signal conditioning hardware and monitoring software were developed at the Centro de Tecnologia da ELETRONORTE, known as the Laboratório Central (LACEN). Further details on the development of VibroComp can be obtained in [17].

To evaluate the operational condition of a SC, mechanical, electrical and thermal properties are monitored. Table 2 shows some of the signs monitored by VibroComp that are used in this work.

| Tag | Description | Unit | Type |
|---|---|---|---|
| $M_{lah}$ | Vibr. Bearing Ring - Horizontal | µm | Vibration |
| $M_{laa}$ | Vibr. Bearing Ring - Axial | µm | Vibration |
| $M_{lav}$ | Vibr. Bearing Ring - Vertical | µm | Vibration |
| $M_{lbh}$ | Vibr. Pump Bearing - Horizontal | µm | Vibration |
| $M_{lba}$ | Vibr. Pump Bearing - Axial | µm | Vibration |
| $M_{lbv}$ | Vibr. Pump Bearing - Vertical. | µm | Vibration |
| $L_{dh1}$ | Vibr. Left - Horizontal 1 | µm | Vibration |
| $L_{eh2}$ | Vibr. Left - Horizontal 2 | µm | Vibration |
| $P_{h2}$ | Pressure of Cooling Hydrogen | bar | Pressure |
| $R_{ot}$ | Compensator Speed | RPM | Speed |
| $P$ | Active Power | MW | Power |
| $Q$ | Reactive Power | MVAR | Power |
| $T_{bea87}$ | Temp. stator bars - slot 87 | C° | Temperature |
| $T_{bea96}$ | Temp. stator bars - slot 96 | C° | Temperature |
| $T_{bea105}$ | Temp. stator bars - slot 105 | C° | Temperature |
| $T_{aer}$ | Temp. Cooling Water - Input | C° | Temperature |
| $T_{hsr}$ | Temp. Cooling Hydrogen - Output | C° | Temperature |
| $T_{her}$ | Temp. Cooling Hydrogen - Input | C° | Temperature |

Table 2. Some signals monitored by VibroComp.

The Data Acquisition Module is a client/server application that uses the TCP/IP protocol to send information to the Client Module and Database Module. The Client Module was developed in order to be the interface between the user and the Acquisition and Database modules. The client can get the waveforms of the measured signals from the acquisition module and also make the trend analysis and event analysis. The Expert Diagnosis System is used to analyze the information stored in the Database Module. The application runs on the client module and provides to the analyst the possibility of each fails of the equipment. To do this is used a Fuzzy Inference Engine. In Figures 4 and 5 some of the interfaces of VibroComp are presented.

In the next section will present the procedure for the identification of predictive models used in this work. The modeling techniques presented in section II will be used.

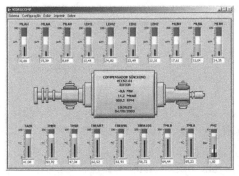

Fig. 4. Main Interface of Client Module of VibroComp

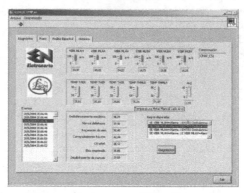

Fig. 5. Interface of the Expert Diagnosis System of VibroComp

## 3. Case studies 1: System modeling of a synchronous compensator

### 3.1 Synchronous compensator predictive models

In this section we present a case study where we identified the parameters of mathematical models that describe, approximately, the behavior of a SC operating in a normal condition.

The equipment CPAV-01, located in the Vila do Conde substation was examined. The models proposed in this work were estimated and validated with real data from the VibroComp monitoring system. The analyzed period was 03/01/2008 to 25/03/2008. The SC was under normal conditions without showing any anomaly.

The identification of mathematical models to describe the behavior of CPAV-01 in this period is a practical procedure that can be divided into the following steps:

1. Statistic analysis of the monitored signals to identify dynamic relationships;
2. Choose the structure of the models;
3. Models Estimation and validation;

The objective of the first step is to identify the correlations that exist in the monitored signals. In this work two mathematical functions are used: Autocorrelation Function (ACF) and Cross-Correlation Function (CCF):

The ACF was used to identify correlations in time of a discrete signal $y(k)$. The formulation used is as follows:

$$r_\tau = \frac{\sum_{k=\tau+1}^{N}[y(k)-\bar{y}][y(k-\tau)-\bar{y}]}{\sum_{k=1}^{N}[y(k)-\bar{y}]^2} \tag{18}$$

where: $\bar{y}$ is the average value of the signal $y(k)$ and $k$ is the discrete time, an integer multiple of the sampling interval, $T_s$.

The ACF analysis revealed that some of the monitored signals ($P(k)$ and $R_{ot}(k)$) behaves approximately like random and uncorrelated white noise. Other signs ($T_{aer}(k)$, $P_{h2}(k)$, $M_{lah}(k)$, $P(k)$, $T_{bea87}(k)$ and $L_{dh1}(k)$) are auto-correlated and can be characterized by models with Autoregressive Moving Average (ARMA) [18]. The profile of the ACF shows signs of a fixed pattern for the first time delays followed by a pattern composed of combinations of exponential and damped sinusoidal functions. In Figure 6, for example, is shown the profile of the auto-correlation signal $T_{bea87}(k)$.

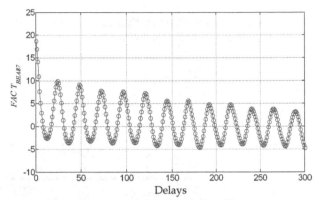

Fig. 6. Profile Auto-correlation function of the signal $T_{bea87}(k)$.

The CCF is used to assess correlations between two discrete signals $u(k)$ and $y(k)$. The following formulation was used:

$$r_{yu} = \frac{\sum_{k=\tau+1}^{N}[y(k)-\bar{y}][u(k-\tau)-\bar{u}]}{\sum_{k=1}^{N}[y(t)-\bar{y}]^2} \tag{19}$$

where $\bar{u}$ is the average value of the signal $u(k)$.

In the Figure 7 is presented the profile of the CCF between the signal $T_{aer}(k)$ and the signal $T_{bea87}(k)$. The analysis of the CCF of the $T_{aer}(k)$ indicates that this signal is more correlated to the signs $T_{bea87}(k)$, $P_{h2}(k)$ and $Q(k)$.

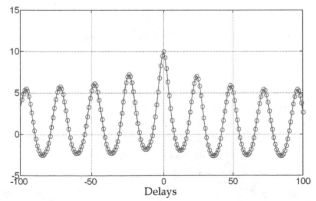

Fig. 7. Profile of the cross-correlation function between the signal $T_{aer}(k)$ and the signal $T_{bea87}(k)$.

A similar analysis realized for the signal $T_{aer}(k)$ was performed for all other signs in Table 2. The final result of the statistic analysis is presented in Table 3. The interpretation of this table is as follows: the signals in the left column are related to the central column signals at delays intervals specified in the right column. For example, the signal $T_{aer}(k)$, is self-correlated and is also related with the signs $T_{bea87}(k)$, $T_{bea87}(k-1)$, $P_{h2}(k-1)$, $P_{h2}(k-2)$, $P_{h2}(k-3)$ and so on. The order of presentation of the signs in the center column is proportional to the intensity of the relationship with the signals in the left column.

| Tag | Correlations | Delays |
|---|---|---|
| $L_{dh1}$ | $M_{lah}$, $T_{bea87}$ e $L_{eh2}$ | [1 7], [1 7] e [1 7] |
| $P_{h2}$ | $Q$, $T_{bea87}$ e $T_{aer}$ | [1 3], [1 3] e [1 3] |
| $Q$ | $P_{h2}$, $T_{bea87}$ e $T_{hsr}$ | [1 3], [1 2] e [1 3] |
| $T_{bea87}$ | $T_{bea105}$, $Q$, e $T_{her}$ | [1 2], [1 2] e [1 2] |
| $T_{aer}$ | $T_{aer}$, $T_{bea87}$, $P_{h2}$, $Q$ | [1 4], [0 2], [0 2] e [0 2] |

Table 3. Correlations of Signals Monitored by VibroComp.

The choice of the model structure, the goal of the second step of the identification procedure was based on information in Table 3. The statistical characteristics of the signals indicate that Auto-regressive Moving Average with Exogenous Input (ARMAX) models are good alternatives to explain the dynamic relationships of the monitored signals. However, it is suspected that there are nonlinear relationships between the monitored signals. These relationships are better described by a universal nonlinear approximate operator. For comparison purposes in this paper will be use three types of mathematical models: Single-input single-output (SISO) ARMAX, multi-inpult single-output (MISO) ARX and a MISO Sugeno fuzzy system. For exemplification purposes, details of the procedure for identification of the $T_{aer}(k)$ model will be presented. The other signs presented in Table 3. can be estimated by a similar procedure.

The first model analyzed for the sign $T_{aer}(k)$ is the SISO ARMAX with the following structure:

$$T_{aer}(k) = \sum_{i=1}^{4} a_i T_{aer}(k-i) + \sum_{i=0}^{1} b_i T_{bea87}(k-i) + \varepsilon(k) + c_1 \varepsilon(k-1) \tag{20}$$

where $\varepsilon$ is an uncorrelated noise that supposedly corrupts the data, since the model is designed in a stochastic environment. For the sake of structural simplicity, only the signal $T_{bea87}(k)$ was chosen as the input for this model. As shown in Table 3, this signal has higher values for the CCF with the $T_{aer}(k)$. Under an intuitive point of view, it is coherent to suppose that the temperature of cooling water is dependent on the temperature values of the stator bars of SC.

A second more complex MISO ARX model was proposed to explain the behavior of the signal $T_{aer}(k)$. In this case, the other relationships identified in Table 3 were used. The following structure was chosen:

$$A(q^{-1})y(k) = B(q^{-1})U(k) + \varepsilon(k)$$
$$y(k) = T_{aer}(k)$$
$$U(k) = \left[ P_{h2}(k) \; T_{bea87}(k) \; Q(k) \right]^{T}$$
$$A(q^{-1}) = 1 + a_1 q^{-1} + a_2 q^{-2} + a_3 q^{-3} + a_4 q^{-4}$$
$$B(q^{-1}) = \left[ B_0(q^{-1}) + B_1(q^{-1}) + B_2(q^{-1}) \right]$$
$$B_0(q^{-1}) = b_{00} + b_{01} q^{-1} + b_{02} q^{-2}$$
$$B_1(q^{-1}) = b_{10} + b_{11} q^{-1} + b_{12} q^{-2}$$
$$B_2(q^{-1}) = b_{20} + b_{21} q^{-1} + b_{22} q^{-2}$$

(21)

The third model proposed model uses a fuzzy inference system to represent the signal $T_{aer}(k)$. Table 4 presents details of the two topologies used. All models are Sugeno fuzzy systems with weighted average defuzzifier and number of outputs equal to the number of rules.

| Inputs | Sets | Function | Parameters |
|--------|------|----------|------------|
| Fuzzy Model Topology 1: MFT1 | | | |
| $T_{aer}$, $T_{bea87}$ | 2-3 | Bell | 50 ou 135 |
| Fuzzy Model Topology 2: MFT2 | | | |
| $T_{aer}$, $T_{bea87}$, $P_{h2}$ | 2-3 | Gaussiana | 44 ou 96 |
| Fuzzy Model Topology 3: MFT3 | | | |
| $T_{aer}$, $T_{bea87}$ | 2 | Gaussian | 212 |

Table 4. Structure of Fuzzy Models for Signal $T_{aer}(k)$

The nomenclature used to identify the models is as follows: MFT1 represents the Fuzzy Model Topology 1. The interpretation of other fields in the Table 4 is as follows: in each model are specified the inputs, the number of sets on each input and the type of membership function. The model MFT1, for example, uses two inputs with two or three Bell fuzzy sets in each input. The number of parameters in the model is 50 or 135, depending on the chosen combination. The Bell and Gaussian function used are as follows.

$$f_{Bell}(x,a,b,c) = \frac{1}{1 + \left| \dfrac{x-c}{a} \right|^{2b}}$$

(22)

$$f_{Gauss}(x,\sigma,c) = e^{\left( \frac{-x+c}{\sqrt{2}\sigma} \right)^{2}}$$

(23)

The parameter estimation was performed in the MATLAB environment. To estimate the models of the linear equations (20) and (21) we used the System Identification Toolbox [19]. The estimation method used was the non-recursive least squares. The mass of data was divided into two parts: the first was used for the estimation of the model and the second part was used for validation. Figure 8 shows the time domain validation of the model of

Equation (20). The sampling interval used in the model is $T_s = 1$ hour. The model can explain the dynamics of the signal in most of the time interval analyzed. The identified parameters are presented in the Table 5.

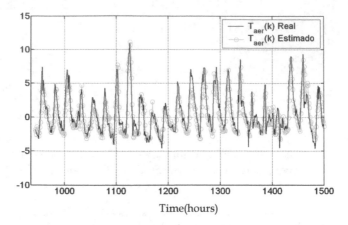

Fig. 8. Comparison between the output signal of the SISO Model and the real signal $T_{aer}(k)$.

| Parameters | Values | Parameters | Values |
|:---:|:---:|:---:|:---:|
| $a_1$ | -1.054051 | $b_0$ | 0.624452 |
| $a_2$ | 0.130458 | $b_1$ | -0.531587 |
| $a_3$ | 0.036976 | $c_1$ | -0.296779 |
| $a_4$ | 0.016368 | - | - |

Table 5. Coefficients of the Linear SISO Model for Signal $T_{aer}(k)$.

Figure 9 shows the time domain validation of the MISO model of equation (21). Table 5 shows the values of the estimated coefficients.

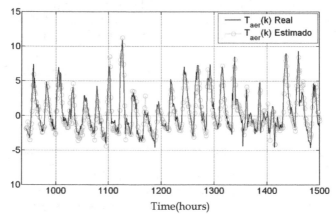

Fig. 9. Comparison between the output signal of the MISO Model and the real signal $T_{aer}(k)$.

Fuzzy models presented in Table 6 were estimated with the algorithm ANFIS (Adaptive-Network-based Fuzzy Inference System) proposed by Jyh-Shing [20] and available on Fuzzy Systems Toolbox of MATLAB, MathWorks (2002). ANFIS is an algorithm for parameter adjustment of Sugeno fuzzy systems based on training data. In Figure 10 presents the results of the comparison between the output of the model $MFT2$ and the real signal $T_{aer}(k)$.

| Parameters | Values | Parameters | Values |
|:---:|:---:|:---:|:---:|
| $a_1$ | -0.546560 | $b_{10}$ | 0.624452 |
| $a_2$ | -0.194398 | $b_{11}$ | -0.531587 |
| $a_3$ | -0.031782 | $b_{12}$ | -0.296779 |
| $a_4$ | 0.035349 | $b_{20}$ | -0.024828 |
| $b_{00}$ | 0.829278 | $b_{21}$ | 0.002835 |
| $b_{01}$ | -0.450037 | $b_{22}$ | 0.013416 |
| $b_{02}$ | -0.145693 | - | - |

Table 6. Coefficients of the Linear MISO Model for Signal $T_{aer}(k)$.

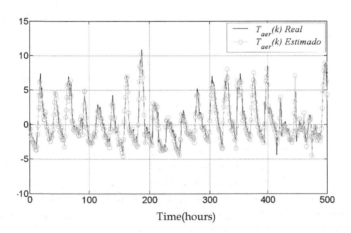

Fig. 10. Comparison between the output signal of the $MFT2$ model and the real signal $T_{aer}(k)$.

A similar procedure to that described for the signal $T_{aer}(k)$ was performed for all other signals in Table 3. Annex A shows the identified models. The set of models obtained represents the normal behavior of CPAV-01. Comparing the behavior estimated by the standard model with the actual behavior of the equipment is possible to identify the occurrence of malfunctions. The performance of predictive models of the signal $T_{aer}(k)$ will be presented in the next section.

### 3.2 Performance evaluation of predictive models

In this section we present the results of performance evaluation of predictive models estimated in Section IV-A. The criteria used are as follows:

- Structural Complexity (SCO);
- Computational Effort for Estimation (CEE);
- Mean Square Error (EMQ);

The Structural Complexity (SCO) can be evaluated by the total number of adjustable parameters. For the fuzzy models the number of rules and membership sets are also considered.

The Computational Effort for Estimation (CEE) can be measured by the number of training epochs until a good model is estimated. In this work the efficiency of the estimation method is not considered. Therefore, a simplifying assumption will be used to assume that the cost estimation is associated only to the number of training epochs until a certain level of accuracy of the model is achieved.

The quality of a model depends on the value of the Mean Square Error Training ($EMQ_T$) and the Mean Squared Validation ($EMQ_V$). In this work the following index will be used:

$$EMQ_x = \frac{1}{N}\sum_{k=0}^{N}\left[\hat{T}_{aerx}(k) - T_{aerx}(k)\right]^2 \tag{24}$$

where $\hat{T}_{aerx}(k)$ is the signal is estimated; $T_{aerx}(k)$ is the real measured signal, and $x \in [T\ V]$ indicates the error is calculated with training or validation data.

In the Table 7 are presented the results of the training of the fuzzy models. In some situations the increase in the number of membership functions results in improved performance during the training but decreased performance in the validation. This observation can be proved for the model *MFT1* comparing lines 1 and 2 with lines 3 and 4 and for the model *MFT2* comparing lines 5 and 6 with rows 7 and 8.

The increase in the number of training epochs can also exert a deleterious effect on the $EMQ_V$. For the model *MFT1*, this effect is observed comparing lines 1 with 2 and 3 with 4. For the model *MFT2* this increase in $EMQ_V$ is observed comparing the line 7 to line 8. The cause of this behavior is to decrease the generalize ability of the model during the training, phenomenon known as overfitting. The best performance in the training was obtained with the model *MFT3* on line 10 and the best performance in the validation phase was observed in line 6 with the model *MFT2*.

Comparing the model MFT3 with the models MFT1 and MFT2 it's observed that increasing the number of inputs improves performance in training data. However, this relationship was not observed when the validation data are analyzed.

The comparison between the models of Equations (20) and (21) shows that the MISO is beter. In this case the increase in the SCO resulted in better performance.

In all simulations the performance of the Fuzzy model was superior to linear models in the training data. However, when the validation data are considered this relationship is not always true. An example is the comparison between lines 12 and 4 where we observe an increase in the SCO and a degradation of performance in the validation data.

Fault Diagnostic of Rotating Machines Based on Artificial Intelligence: Case Studies of the Centrais Elétricas do
Norte do Brazil S/A – Eletrobras-Eletronorte

225

| ID | Training | $EMQ_T$ | $EMQ_V$ |
|----|----------|---------|---------|
| | | MFT1 | |
| | 2 sets, 50 parameters, 8 rules | | |
| 1 | 20 | 0.7071 | 1.029 |
| 2 | 150 | 0.6009 | 1.231 |
| | 3 sets, 135 parameters, 27 rules | | |
| 3 | 10 | 0.4936 | 3.4069 |
| 4 | 50 | 0.4762 | 6.1030 |
| | | MFT2 | |
| | 2 sets, 44 parameters, 8 rules | | |
| 5 | 10 | 0.6597 | 1.0083 |
| 6 | 250 | 0.6064 | 0.9085 |
| | 3 sets, 96 parameters, 27 regras | | |
| 7 | 10 | 0.4692 | 3.8152 |
| 8 | 20 | 0.4663 | 4.1179 |
| | | MFT3 | |
| | 2 sets, 212 parameters, 32 rules | | |
| 9 | 10 | 0.3434 | 4.4351 |
| 10 | 20 | 0.3405 | 4.3070 |
| | | ML1 | |
| | 0 sets, 7 parameters, 0 rules | | |
| 11 | 1 | 1.7053 | 4.4881 |
| | | ML2 | |
| | 0 sets, 13 parameters, 0 rules | | |
| 12 | 1 | 1.2130 | 3.9079 |

Table 7. Results of Fuzzy Models Training for the Signal $T_{aer}(k)$.

# 4. Case studies 2: Development of a Fuzzy expert system for a synchronous compensator

## 4.1 Project of the fuzzy expert system

This section describes the project of a Fuzzy Expert System used to faults diagnosis of a SC based on a Mandan fuzzy system [16]. The design methodology is formed by the following steps:

1. Selection of input variables - the choice depends on the quantity and quality of information provided by the monitoring system. The cause and effect relationships involved in the operation of the equipment helps in this selection. A detailed study of the correlation between variables can help eliminate redundancy of information simplifying the inference unit;
2. Selection of Output Variables - At this stage the following question must be answered: What are the faults to be detected?
3. Selection of Membership Functions – For each input and output, acceptable and not acceptable levels should be determined. In addition, the number of sets and the overlap must be specified for each variable;

4. Formulation of Rules – Standard fuzzy IF-THEN rules that considers the normality conditions;
5. Selection of Operators – Plausibility and continuity should be used for this selection;
6. Adjust of Rule Base – Simulation using trial and error procedure used to detect inconsistencies in the rule base. Mathematical models of the monitored system also can be used;

In the first stage two approaches have been proposed: the first strategy considers only the global values of the signals monitored by VibroComp as inputs and the second approach uses the spectral information of the vibration signals as inputs. In this paper, only the conventional approach will be used because the data base structure of the Expert System of VibroComp has not using spectrum information. The input signals to be used are: $M_{lah}$, $M_{lav}$, $M_{laa}$, $M_{lba}$, $M_{lbh}$ and $M_{lbv}$. A description of these abbreviations can be found in Table 2.

The output variables are the faults to be detected. For each fault the expert maintenance engineers of the company defined default probability values of the fault. Table 8 shows the outputs of the fuzzy expert system and the probabilities values defined.

| ID | Fail | Values |
|----|------|--------|
| F1 | Mechanical Unbalance | 10%, 20%, 70%, 90% |
| F2 | Faulty bearing | 10%, 20%, 70%, 90% |
| F3 | Rubbing Axis | 20%, 30%, 50%, 70% |
| F4 | Housing/Support Loose | 10%, 20%, 70%, 90% |
| F5 | Oil Whirl | 10%, 20%, 70%, 90% |
| F6 | A bent shaft | 10%, 30%, 40%, 60% |
| F7 | Misalignment of Bearings | 10%, 20%, 30%, 70% |

Table 8. Outputs of Synchronous Compensator Fuzzy Expert System

The structure defined in the expert system outputs is so peculiar: for each fault are defined the expected possibilities. The table 8 was determined from the experience of the company's maintenance experts. The validation tests of the fuzzy expert system proposed show that this feature can be better used if each fault is described by a finite number of fuzzy sets equal to the number of possibilities provided by the experts. From a practical point of view, this project choice is based on the following argument: defining a finite number of fault possibilities ensures that the diagnostic system will present expected results.

This project choice, however, does not guarantee the accuracy of the diagnosis. The distribution of fuzzy membership sets in the output variables is a very important aspect of the fuzzy expert system. There are significant inconsistencies between the output values of the fuzzy expert system and the expected values when the membership functions uniformly distributed throughout the universe of discourse of the output variables. So uniformly in the distribution the membership functions, which is a common practice in most applications described in the literature [16], did not show satisfactory results for any kind of defuzzifier used. The solution was to specify non-overlapping fuzzy sets, located in a rather narrow

around the values of precision defined by the expert engineers. Triangular functions with no
more than 10% of base showed satisfactory results. Figure 11 is shown an example of
distribution of membership functions of the output variable F7. It was observed that this
distribution has great influence on the behavior of the diagnostic system.

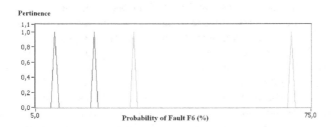

Fig. 11. Membership functions for variable F7, misalignment of bearings.

Fifteen rules were defined by the expert engineers, so that the diagnostic system can detect
the faults described in Table 8. These rules use only vibration and temperature variables.
Below is one of the specified rules:

**Regra 1:** IF $M_{lah}$ IS Alarme 1 AND $M_{lbh}$ IS Alarme 1 THEN
F1 IS 70% AND F2 IS 30% AND F3 IS 20% AND F4 IS 10% AND F5 IS 10% AND F6 IS 10%
AND F7 IS 20%.

In this and all other rules provided by the experts can be observed another unique feature:
the antecedents are short combinations of the monitored signals and the consequents are
long combinations of faults. Table 9 shows the characteristics of the membership functions
of input variables.

| Universe [0 100] | Function | |
|---|---|---|
| Fuzzy Sets | Type | Interval |
| Normal | Trapezoidal | [0 0 30 40] |
| Alarm - 1 | Triangular | [40 45 50] |
| Alarm - 2 | Trapezoidal | [50 60 100 100] |

Table 9. Membership Functions of Vibration Inputs: $M_{lah}$, $M_{lav}$, $M_{laa}$, $M_{lbh}$, $M_{lbv}$ and $M_{lba}$.

Changes made in the distribution of the membership functions in the output variables and
the choice of the precision of the faults resulted in satisfactory performance. In the
validation tests were observed differences of performance related to the defuzzifier used.
This is a project choice and the most appropriate defuzzifier depends on the application.

The other operators of the inference unit have not great influence on the performance. The
Fuzzy Expert System, in its current state of development, allows the use of the following
methods: T-Norm, Min operator; Mandani implication and Maximum aggregation method.

## 4.2 Experimental evaluation of the fuzzy expert system

To evaluate the fault detection methodology proposed in this work will be presented a case study where it was possible to detect an anomalous behavior based on the residual analysis of the reference models of the SC.

In the figure 12 is presented the analyzed event which was monitored by VibroComp on 11/03/2008 11:47:56 AM in CPAV-01 at $t$ = 1560 hours of operation. In this situation was detected a considerable increase in the stator bars temperatures $T_{bea87}(k)$, $T_{bea96}(k)$ and $T_{bea105}(k)$. We also observed an increase in the value of reactive power that reached the value of $Q(k)$ = 148,5 MVAR, close to the nominal limit of apparent power of the equipment (150MVA). In Table 10 are presented the recorded values and the normal limits of each monitored signal. Is note the scope of this work explain the causes of the dynamic behavior observed in CPAV-01 based on laws of physics and mechanical models. To establish clearly these cause and effect relationships, mechanical engineering and dynamic vibration knowhow are required, The author of this article does not have this knowhow. The main objective of this work is not to explain. The intention is to describe the mechanical behavior of the studied system and classify this dynamic in patterns or signatures using mathematical models estimated and validated based on real monitoring data. Using these models a fault detection system is projected based on MBFDI techniques.

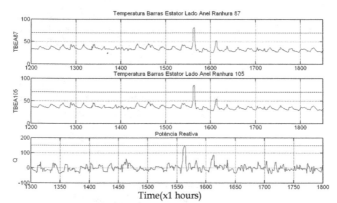

Fig. 12. Experimental evaluation of fuzzy expert system with case study in CPAV-01. Signals monitored during the event and normal limits.

| Tag | Value | Limit of Normality |
|-----|-------|--------------------|
| $T_{bea87}(k)$ | 82°C | 70° C |
| $T_{bea96}(k)$ | 82,23°C | 70° C |
| $T_{bea105}(k)$ | 82,53°C | 70° C |
| $Q(k)$ | 148,5 MVAR | 150 MVAR |

Table 10. Values monitored by VibroComp during the stator temperature event.

Figures 13 to 15 are presented the results of the analysis of the event using the MBFDI technique presented in this work. *MFT2*, the SISO linear model of Equation (20) and the MIMO linear model of Equation (21) are used as reference models, respectively. In the condition of normality, the residual signal has a mean near zero and a low standard

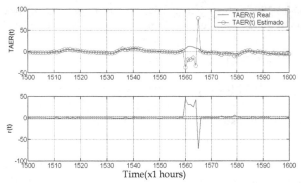

Fig. 13. Increase in the stator bars temperatures - Results of the event analysis using the
MBFDI technique with Fuzzy *MFT2*.

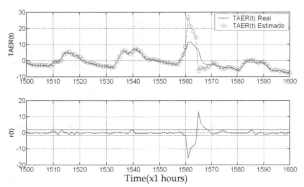

Fig. 14. Increase in the stator bars temperatures - Results of the event analysis using MBFDI
technique with the SISO linear model.

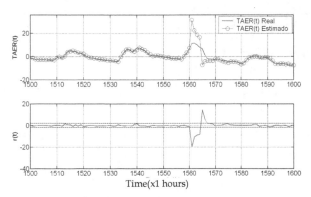

Fig. 15. Increase in the stator bars temperatures - Results of the event analysis using MBFDI
with MISO Linear Model.

deviation. At the beginning of the anomalous behavior, the residues signal increases in the
three models, which allows a rapid and reliable detection of the failure. In the model the

increase is greater $MFT2$ indicating that this model has a higher sensitivity for the detection of such failures. The two linear models have approximately the same level of residue during the event.

One of the rules used for the residues evaluation is shown:

$$\text{IF } (\,|r(k)| > r_{Taer}\,) \text{ AND } (\,T_{bea87}(k)\; Real > LT)$$
$$\text{THEN}$$
$$\text{FAILURE} = \text{Stator Temperature out of Range} \qquad (25)$$
$$r(k) = T_{aer}(k)\; Real\; -\; T_{aer}(k)\; Estimated$$

where: $r(k)$ represents the residual of signal $T_{aer}(k)$; $r_{Taer}$ is the maximum allowed residue in the normal condition, and $LT$ represents the thermal limit of the stator winding.

## 5. Conclusions

In this paper we presented the design and experimental evaluation of a MBFDI system used for SC. The predictive models used in the proposed system were estimated based on real data obtained from the monitoring of the studied equipment during normal conditions. With these models is still possible to detect failures in a fledgling state from the comparison between model output and real signs monitored, as was presented in a case study where it was possible to detect the moment of occurrence of a failure.

## 6. Appendix A: Structure of the models of the signs *Mlah, Ldh1, Ph2, Q, Tbea87*

The structure of the SISO linear model for the signal $T_{bea87}$ is as follows:

$$T_{bea87}(k) = \sum_{i=1}^{4} a_i T_{bea87}(k-i) + \sum_{i=0}^{3} b_i T_{bea105}(k-i) + \varepsilon(k) + c_1 \varepsilon(k-1) \qquad (26)$$

In the figure 16 is presented the results of the estimation of the SISO model of Eq. (26).

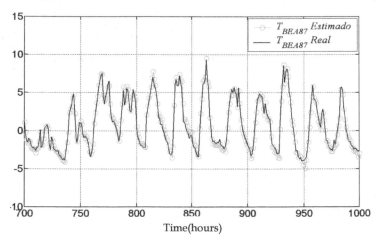

Fig. 16. Comparison between the signal estimated by the linear SISO model and the real signal $T_{bea87}(k)$.

The structure of the MISO linear model for the signal $T_{bea87}$ is as follows:

$$A(q^{-1})y(k) = B(q^{-1})U(k) + \varepsilon(k)$$
$$y(k) = T_{bea87}(k)$$
$$U(k) = \begin{bmatrix} T_{bea105}(k) & T_{her}(k) & Q(k) \end{bmatrix}^T$$
$$A(q^{-1}) = 1 + a_1 q^{-1} + a_2 q^{-2} + a_3 q^{-3} + a_4 q^{-4}$$
$$B(q^{-1}) = \begin{bmatrix} B_0(q^{-1}) + B_1(q^{-1}) + B_2(q^{-1}) \end{bmatrix} \tag{27}$$
$$B_0(q^{-1}) = b_{00} + b_{01}q^{-1} + b_{02}q^{-2}$$
$$B_1(q^{-1}) = b_{10} + b_{11}q^{-1} + b_{12}q^{-2}$$
$$B_2(q^{-1}) = b_{20} + b_{21}q^{-1} + b_{22}q^{-2}$$

In the figure 17 is presented the results of the estimation of the MISO model of Eq. (27).

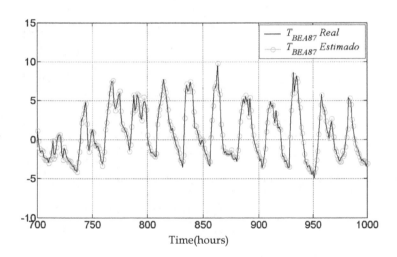

Fig. 17. Comparison between the signal estimated by the linear MISO model and the real
signal $T_{bea87}(k)$.

The structure of the SISO linear model for the signal $Q(k)$ is as follows:

$$Q(k) = \sum_{i=1}^{7} a_i Q(k-i) + \sum_{i=0}^{1} b_i T_{bea87}(k-i) + \varepsilon(k) + c_1 \varepsilon(k-1) \tag{28}$$

In the figure 18 is presented the results of the estimation of the SISO model of Eq. (28).

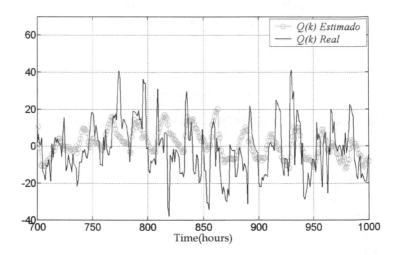

Fig. 18. Comparison between the signal estimated by the linear SISO model and the real signal $Q(k)$.

The structure of the MISO linear model for the signal $Q(k)$ is as follows:

$$A(q^{-1})y(k) = B(q^{-1})U(k) + C(q^{-1})\varepsilon(k)$$
$$y(k) = Q(k)$$
$$U(k) = \left[ T_{bea87}(k)\ T_{aer}(k)\ T_{hsr}(k) \right]^T$$
$$A(q^{-1}) = 1 + a_1 q^{-1}$$
$$B(q^{-1}) = \left[ B_0(q^{-1}) + B_1(q^{-1}) + B_2(q^{-1}) \right] \qquad (29)$$
$$B_0(q^{-1}) = b_{00} + b_{01} q^{-1} + b_{02} q^{-2}$$
$$B_1(q^{-1}) = b_{10} + b_{11} q^{-1} + b_{12} q^{-2}$$
$$B_2(q^{-1}) = b_{20} + b_{21} q^{-1} + b_{22} q^{-2}$$
$$C(q^{-1}) = 1 + c_1 q^{-1} + c_2 q^{-2}$$

In the figure 19 is presented the results of the estimation of the MISO model of Eq. (29).

Fault Diagnostic of Rotating Machines Based on Artificial Intelligence: Case Studies of the Centrais Elétricas do
Norte do Brazil S/A – Eletrobras-Eletronorte

233

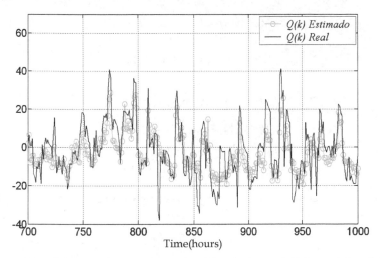

Fig. 19. Comparison between the signal estimated by the linear MISO model and the real signal $Q(k)$.

The structure of the SISO linear model for the signal $P_{h2}(k)$ is as follows:

$$P_{h2}(k)=\sum_{i=1}^{5} a_i P_{h2}(k-i)+\sum_{i=0}^{8} b_i T_{aer}(k-i)+\varepsilon(k)+c_1\varepsilon(k-1) \qquad (30)$$

In the figure 20 is presented the results of the estimation of the SISO model of Eq. (30).

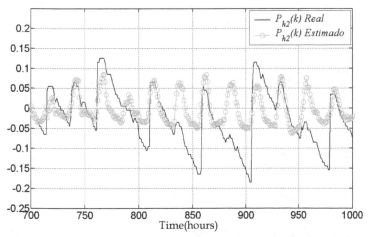

Fig. 20. Comparison between the signal estimated by the linear SISO model and the real signal $P_{h2}(k)$.

The structure of the MISO linear model for the signal $P_{h2}(k)$ is as follows:

$$A(q^{-1})y(k) = B(q^{-1})U(k) + \varepsilon(k)$$
$$y(k) = P_{h2}(k)$$
$$U(k) = \left[ Q(k)\ T_{bea87}(k)\ T_{aer}(k) \right]^T$$
$$A(q^{-1}) = 1 + a_1 q^{-1}$$
$$B(q^{-1}) = \left[ B_0(q^{-1}) + B_1(q^{-1}) + B_2(q^{-1}) \right] \tag{31}$$
$$B_0(q^{-1}) = b_{00} + b_{01}q^{-1} + b_{02}q^{-2} + b_{03}q^{-3}$$
$$B_1(q^{-1}) = b_{10} + b_{11}q^{-1} + b_{12}q^{-2} + b_{13}q^{-3}$$
$$B_2(q^{-1}) = b_{20} + b_{21}q^{-1} + b_{22}q^{-2} + b_{23}q^{-3}$$

In the figure 21 is presented the results of the time comparison of the estimated MISO model of Eq. (31).

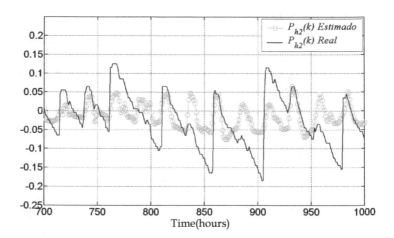

Fig. 21. Comparison between the signal estimated by the linear MISO model and the real signal $P_{h2}(k)$.

The structure of the SISO linear model for the signal $L_{dh1}(k)$ is as follows:

$$L_{dh1}(k) = \sum_{i=1}^{2} a_i L_{dh1}(k-i) + \sum_{i=0}^{2} b_i T_{bea87}(k-i) + \\ + \varepsilon(k) + \sum_{i=1}^{2} c_i \varepsilon(k-1) \tag{32}$$

The structure of the MISO linear model for the signal $L_{dh1}(k)$ is as follows:

$$A(q^{-1})y(k) = B(q^{-1})U(k) + \varepsilon(k)$$
$$y(k) = L_{dh1}(k)$$
$$U(k) = \begin{bmatrix} T_{bea87}(k) & M_{lah}(k) & L_{eh2}(k) \end{bmatrix}^T$$
$$A(q^{-1}) = 1 + a_1 q^{-1}$$
$$B(q^{-1}) = \begin{bmatrix} B_0(q^{-1}) + B_1(q^{-1}) + B_2(q^{-1}) \end{bmatrix} \qquad (33)$$
$$B_0(q^{-1}) = \sum_{i=0}^{7} b_{0i} q^{-i}$$
$$B_1(q^{-1}) = \sum_{i=0}^{7} b_{1i} q^{-i}$$
$$B_2(q^{-1}) = \sum_{i=0}^{7} b_{2i} q^{-i}$$

In the figures 22 and 23 are presented the results of the time comparison of the estimated
SISO and MISO models Eq. (32) and Eq. (33).

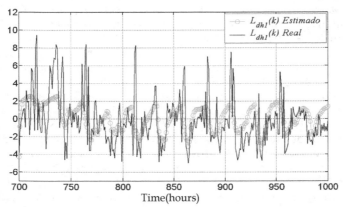

Fig. 22. Comparison between the signal estimated by the linear SISO model and the real
signal $L_{dh1}(k)$.

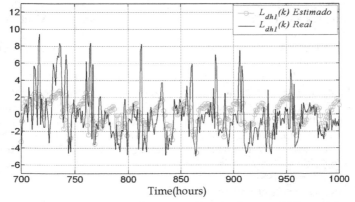

Fig. 23. Comparison between the signal estimated by the linear MISO model and the real
signal $L_{dh1}(k)$.

# 7. References

[1] Nepomuceno, L. X.; *Técnicas de Manutenção Preditiva*; Editora Edgard Blücher Ltda; Volume 2; 1989

[2] Venkat Venkatasubramanian, Raghunathan Rengaswamy, Kewen Yin, Surya N. Kavuri; *A review of process fault detection and diagnosis Part I: Quantitative model-based methods*. Computers and Chemical Engineering, 27, 2003, 293-311.

[3] Patton, R. J., Frank, P. M., and Clark, R. N.; *Fault Diagnosis in Dynamic Systems, Theory and Application*. Control Engineering Series. Prentice Hall, London 1989.

[4] Chen, J. and Patton, R. J. *Robust Model Based Fault Diagnosis for Dynamic Systems*. Kluwer Academic, 1999.

[5] Basseville, M. and Nikiforov, I. V. *Detection of Abrupt Changes: Theory and Application*. Prentice Hall, 1993.

[6] Mari Cruz Garcia, Miguel A. Sanz Bobi and Javier del Pico *SIMAP - Intelligent System for Predictive Maintenance Application to the health condition monitoring of a windturbine gearbox*, Elsevier, Computers in Industry, vol 57, 2006, 552568;

[7] Moutinho, Marcelo N. *Sistema de Análise e Diagnóstico de Equipamentos Elétricos de Potência - SADE*. II Semana Eletronorte do Conhecimento e Inovação (II SECI). 21 a 23 de outubro de 2009, São Luís - MA.

[8] Moutinho, Marcelo N. *Fuzzy Diagnostic Systems of Rotating Machineries, some ELETRONORTE's applications*. The 15th International Conference on Intelligent System Application to Power Systems, Curitiba - Brazil, 2009.

[9] Moutinho, Marcelo N. *Classificação de Padrões Operacionais do Atuador Hidráulico do Distribuidor de um Hidrogerador Utilizando Técnicas de Estimação Paramétrica e Lógica Fuzzy - Resultados Experimentais*. XIX SNPTEE - Seminário Nacional de Produção e Transmissão de Energia Elétrica. Florianópolis, SC. 23 a 26 Outubro de 2011.

[10] ]Zhengang Han, Weihua Li and Sirish L. Shah; *Fault detection and isolation in the presence of process uncertainties*; Elsevier, Control Engineering Practice 13, 2005, pag 587-599;

[11] Paul M. Frank, *Fault Diagnosis in Dynamic Systems Using Analytical and Knowledge-based Redundancy A Survey and Some New Results*, Automatica, Vol. 26, No. 3, pp. 459-474, 1990;

[12] Alexandre Carlos Eduardo; *Diagnóstico de Defeitos em Sistemas Mecânicos Rotativos através da Análise de Correlações e Redes Neurais Artificiais*, Tese de doutorado apresentada à Comissão de Pós-Graduação da Faculdade de Engenharia Mecânica, como requisito para a obtenção do título de Doutor em Engenharia Mecânica. Campinas, 2003, S.P. - Brasil.

[13] VibroSystM. *Zoom 5 Software Guia do Usuário*. P/N: 9476-26M1A-100. VibroSystM Inc. 2005.

[14] Aguirre, L. A., *Introdução à Identificação de Sistemas*, 2ª edição, UFMG, 2004.

[15] Karl J. Aström and Björn Wittenmark, Computer *Controlled Systems*, Prentice-Hall, 1984.

[16] L. X. Wang, *A course in Fuzzy Systems and Control*, Prentice-Hall International, Inc.,1997,

[17] Norberto Bramatti. *Desenvolvimento e Implantação de um Sistema de Monitoração on-line de Compensadores Síncronos*. Dissertação de Mestrado. Universidade Federal do Pará, Centro Tecnológico, Programa de Pós-graduação em Engenharia Elétrica. 2002.

[18] Lennart Ljung, *System Identification - Theory for the User*, PTR Prentice Hall, Englewood Cliffs, New Jersey, 1987;

[19] Lennart Ljung; *System Identification Tolbox 7 User's Guide*.

[20] Jang, J.-S. R., *ANFIS: Adaptive-Network-based Fuzzy Inference Systems, IEEE Transactions on Systems, Man, and Cybernetics*, Vol. 23, No. 3, pp. 665-685, May 1993.

# 12

# Engine Knock Detection Based on Computational Intelligence Methods

Adriana Florescu[1], Claudiu Oros[1] and Anamaria Radoi[2]
*[1]University Politehnica of Bucharest,*
*[2]Ecole Politechnique Federale de Laussane,*
*[1]Romania*
*[2]Switzerland*

## 1. Introduction

*Artificial intelligence* emerged from human thinking that has both logical and intuitive or subjective sides. The logical side has been developed and utilized, resulting advanced von Neumann type computers and expert systems, both constituting the *hard computing* domain. However, it is found that hard computing can't give the solution of very complicated problems by itself. In order to cope with this difficulty, the intuitive and subjective thinking of human mind was explored, resulting the *soft computing* domain (also called *computational intelligence*). It includes *neural networks*, *fuzzy logic* and *probabilistic reasoning*, the last gathering *evolutionary computation* (including *genetic algorithms* with related efforts in *genetic programming* and *classifier systems*, *evolution strategies* and *evolutionary programming*), *immune networks*, *chaos computing* and parts of *learning theory*. In different kind of applications, all pure artificial intelligence methods mentioned above proved to be rather complementary than competitive, so that combined methods appeared in order to gather the advantages and to cope with the disadvantages of each pure method. The scope of this chapter is to study and finaly compare some representative classes of pure and combined computational intelligence methods applied in engine knock detection.

The internal-combustion engine is one of the most used vehicle power generators in the world today. When looking at the characteristics of a vehicle - and therefore the ones of the engine that drives it - , some of the most important are the emissions, fuel economy and efficiency. All three of these variables are affected by a phenomenon that occurs in the engine called knock. *Engine knock* (also known as *knocking, self-combustion, detonation, spark knock* or *pinging*) in spark-ignition internal combustion engines occurs when combustion of the mixture of fuel and air in the cylinder starts off correctly because of the ignition by the spark plug, but one or more pockets of the mixture explode outside the normal combustion front. The importance of knock detection comes from the effects it generates; these can range from increased fuel consumption and pollution, the decrease of engine power and up to partial or complete destruction of the cylinders, pistons, rods, bearings and many other damages around the engine bay.

Internal combustion engines present an optimum working cycle that is right on the edge of self-combustion or knock. If engine knock occurs and is detected in a cycle then the ignition timing (spark angle) needs to be modified so that the next cycle does not suffer from the same phenomenon. This is why the detection needs to be done in under a cycle (Bourbai, 2000; Li&Karim, 2004; Hamilton&Cowart, 2008; Erjavec, 2009).

Engine knock can be detected using a series of devices placed in and around the engine bay like: pressure sensors mounted inside each cylinder, devices that measure the ionization current in the spark plug or accelerometers mounted on the engine to measure vibrations etc. The best and most accurate information on knock is given by the *pressure sensors* but the easiest and less expensive way to detect it is by using *vibration sensors* mounted on the engine (Erjavec, 2009; Gupta, 2006; Bosch, 2004; Thomas et al., 1997; Ettefag, 2008, Fleming, 2001). The knock detection methods used so far for extracting information from the engine sensors include *time, frequency (spectrum)* or a diversity *time-frequency analysis (Wavelet)* based solutions (Adeli&Karim, 2005; Park&Jang, 2004; Radoi et al., 2009; Midori et al., 1999; Lazarescu et al., 2004; Jonathan et al., 2006). The restriction of average detection rates and the complexity of information needed for the Wavelet analysis support further developments and hybridization with mixed techniques that proved useful in other fields of application than the one explored in this chapter: *wavelet-fuzzy* (Borg et al., 2005), *wavelet-neural* (Zhang&Benveniste, 1992; Billings&Wei, 2005; Wu&Liu, 2009; Banakar&Azeem, 2008) and *wavelet-neuro-fuzzy* (Ylmaz&Oysal, 2010).

Among the pure computational intelligence methods described in (Wang&Liu, 2006; Prokhorov, 2008; Mitchell, 2010;Wehenkel, 1997), different types of neural network applications have been employed with better detection rates than the previous non-neural methods but no clear comparative analysis results have been presented so far for engine knock detection. The methods taken into account and finally compared in this chapter start with the *Fuzzy Kwan-Cai Neural Network* (Kwan&Cai, 1994) - for the application of which other neuro-fuzzy or fuzzy logic models were studied (Zhang&Liu, 2006; Ibrahim,2004; Liu&Li, 2004; Hui, 2011; Chen, 2005) -, expand to the *Kohonen Self-Organizing Map (SOM)* (Kohonen, 2000, 2002; Hsu, 2006; Lopez-Rubio, 2010) and end with *Bayes Classifier* (Larose, 2006) to which results of this chapter conforming with other work (Auld et al., 2007) published so far have proved needing hybridization.

Work started using two sizes of training and testing sample groups, both belonging to the Bosch Group database in order to see how data size can affect the results. The applications were built to handle both pressure and vibration samples in order to see which of them can supply the most valuable information. In addition, due to the lack of chapters available on this subject, through the analysis of the results, we can get a better impression of the nature of these types of signals, the coherence of samples and evolution of detection rates with every new sample added. Also, to complete the analysis, a comparison of the responses from pressure and vibration families of samples is made for the three methods.

## 2. Mathematical background of used computational intelligence methods

### 2.1 Fuzzy Kwan-Cai neural network

The Fuzzy Kwan-Cai neural network shown in Fig.1 has four layers, each of them being a fuzzy block represented by a different type of fuzzy neurons with their own specific purpose and functions (Kwan&Cai, 1994).

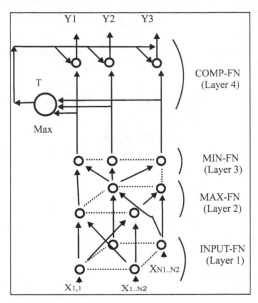

Fig. 1. The Fuzzy Kwan-Cai Neural Network structure

The first layer represents the input and is built with fuzzy input neurons, each one selecting a characteristic of the original sample vector. In the case of a two dimensional sample containing N1xN2 vector elements we will have a first layer that has N1xN2 neurons. For the neuron on the (i, j) position the equations are:

$$s_{ij}^{[1]} = z_{ij}^{[1]} = x_{ij} \,, \tag{1}$$

$$y_{ij}^{[1]} = s_{ij}^{[1]} / P_{v\max} \,, \tag{2}$$

for i=1, 2, ..., N1; j=1, 2, ..., N2, where $s_{ij}^{[1]}$ represents the state of the neuron on the (i, j) position for the first layer, $z_{ij}^{[1]}$ is it's input value, $x_{ij}$ is the value of the element (i, j) in the input sample pattern, ($x_{ij} \geq 0$), $y_{ij}^{[1]}$ is its output value and $P_{v\max}$ is the maximum value of all the input elements. The notation will be kept for neurons belonging to all the following layers.

The second layer is built of N1xN2 neurons and its purpose is to perform the fuzzification of the input patterns by means of the weight function $w(m,n)$ - also called the fuzzification function - , defined as:

$$w(m,n) = e^{-\beta^2 (m^2 + n^2)} \,, \tag{3}$$

where parameters m=-(N1-1), ..., +(N1-1), n=-(N2-1), ..., +(N2-1) and β determines how much of the sample vector each fuzzy neuron sees. Each neuron from the second layer has M outputs, one for each neuron in the third layer. The output for the second layer neuron on position (p, q) is:

$$y^{[2]}_{pqm} = q^{[2]}_{pqm} , \tag{4}$$

for p=1, ..., N1; q=1, ..., N2; m=1,...,M, where $y^{[2]}_{pqm}$ is the $m^{th}$ output of the second layer neuron on position (p,q) to the $m^{th}$ third level neuron. The output function $q_{pqm}$ is determined within the training algorithm. For a more simplified approach, we can choose isosceles triangles with the base α and the height 1, mathematically defined as:

$$y^{[2]}_{pqm} = q_{pqm}\left(s^{[2]}_{pq}\right) = \begin{cases} 1 - \dfrac{2\left|s^{[2]}_{pq} - \theta_{pqm}\right| \le \frac{q}{2}}{\alpha}, & \text{for } \left|s^{[2]}_{pq} - \theta_{pqm}\right| \le \dfrac{\alpha}{2}, \\ 0, & \text{other} \end{cases} \tag{5}$$

where $\alpha \ge 0$, p=1, ..., N1; q=1, ..., N2; m=1, ..., M. Parameter $\theta_{pqm}$ is the center of the isosceles triangle base. By means of the training algorithm, p, q and m values corresponding to α and $\theta_{pqm}$ are determined.

The third layer is made-up of M neurons each of them representing a learned pattern and so the value for M can only be determined at the end of the learning process. It can be seen as a fuzzy deduction (inference) layer. The output for the third layer neuron is:

$$y^{[3]}_m = s^{[3]}_m = \min_{p=1...N1}(\min_{q=1...N2}(y^{[2]}_{pqm})), \tag{6}$$

for m=1,..., M.

The fourth and final layer is the network's output layer and is made up of competitive neurons one for each pattern that is learned; it is the defuzzification layer. If an input pattern is more similar to the mth pattern that was learned, then the output of the mth comparative neuron will be attributed value 1 and the others value 0:

$$y^{[4]}_m = s^{[4]}_m = z^{[4]}_m , \tag{7}$$

$$y^{[4]}_{pqm} = q[s^{[4]}_m - T] = \begin{cases} 0, & \text{if } s^{[4]}_m < T \\ 1, & \text{if } s^{[4]}_m = T \end{cases} \tag{8}$$

$$T = \max_{m=1...M}(\max_{j=1...N2}(y^{[3]}_m)), \tag{9}$$

for m=1,..., M, where T is defined as the activation threshold for all the neurons in the forth layer.

The flowchart in Fig.2 summarizes the procedure of adapting and implementing the Fuzzy Kwan-Cai algorithm to the application proposed in the chapter. The differences from the standard theoretical algorithm are that the sample databases are first imported and validated for integrity and then separated into pressure and vibration, respectively training and testing classes. The standard classification steps follow and the algorithm ends with the calculation of the detection rate.

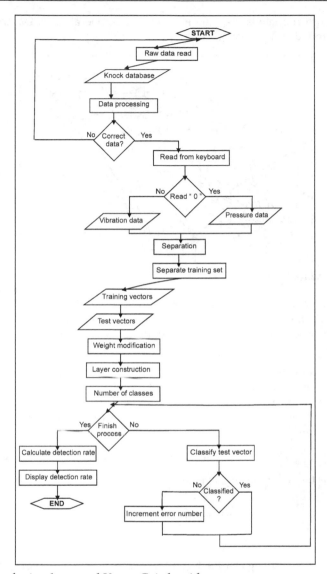

Fig. 2. Flowchart for implemented Kwan-Cai algorithm

## 2.2 Kohonen Self-Organizing Map (SOM)

The Kohonen Self-Organizing Map (SOM) with the structure presented in Fig.3 is a neural network characterized by the fact that neighboring neurons (cells) communicate among themselves by mutual-lateral interactions transforming into detectors of specific classes when given input patterns. The learning can be unsupervised or supervised (Kohonen, 2000, 2002; Hsu, 2006; Lopez-Rubio, 2010) In this chapter the supervised learning algorithm was used.

The network transforms similarities among vectors into neural vicinities (the similar input patterns will be found as neighbors).

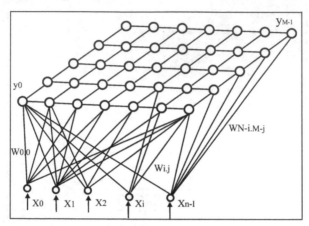

Fig. 3. The SOM neural network

From a structural point of view, the Kohonen neural network is composed of two layers out of which the first one is an input layer made of transparent neurons with no processing functions. Its purpose is to receive the input pattern and send it to the second layer. This first layer has the same size as the input pattern.

The second layer contains M output neurons, a number equal or higher than the number of classes desired in order to classify the entry patterns. They can be arranged planar, linear, circular, as a torus or sphere, the training and performances being dependent on the network shape. The planar network can also be rectangular or hexagonal depending on the placement of neurons.

An input vector $X_p \in R^n$ is applied in parallel to all the neurons of the network, each of them being characterized by a weight vector:

$$W_{j=}(w_{0j}, w_{1j}, ..., w_{n-11j})^T \in R^n,$$  (10)

for j=0, 1, …, M-1.

In order to choose the winning neuron j* with its associated weight vector $W_j$* for an input pattern we must calculate the Gaussian distance $d_j$ between that pattern and each of the neuron's weight vectors. The winner will be chosen by the lowest distance $d_j^*$ of all:

$$d_j = \left\| X_p - W_j \right\|,$$  (11)

$$d_j^* = \min\{d_j\},$$  (12)

for j=0, 1, …, M-1.

After the winner determination process has finished the weights refining one is started and this must not have an effect on all the neurons but only in a certain vicinity $V_j^*$ around the winner j*. Outside this perimeter the influence of this process is considered null. The radius of this vicinity starts out big and keeps on getting smaller and smaller with the refining process.

The learning rate can have many expressions. In this application, the chosen expression was:

$$\eta(t) = \eta_0 \exp[-\|r_k - r_j^*\| / \sigma^2], \tag{13}$$

where $r_j^*$ and $r_k$ are position vectors in the network representing the characteristic of the neural center of the vicinity and the neuron with the index k for which the refining process is taking place. Function $\eta_0 = \eta_0(t)$ decrease in time, representing the value of the learning rate in the center of the vicinity:

$$\eta_0(t) = a / t^p, \tag{14}$$

The parameter $\sigma$ controls the speed of decreasing the learning rate, depending on the radius of the vicinity.

After the refining process for the current input vector is finished the next one is selected and so on until all the input vectors are used and the stop training condition is inspected. A useful stopping condition is the moment when the weights of the network cease being refined (are no longer being modified):

$$\|w_{ij}(t+1) - w_{ij}(t)\| < \varepsilon, \tag{15}$$

where i=0, 1, ..., n-1 and j=0, 1, ..., M-1.

The flowchart in Fig.4 summarizes the procedure of adapting and implementing the Kohonen Self-Organizing Map algorithm to the application proposed in the chapter. The differences from the standard theoretical algorithm are the same as those described for the Fuzzy Kwan-Cai algorithm in Fig. 2.

## 2.3 Bayes classifier

For the Bayes Classifier working with Gaussian classes (Larose, 2006) considering first the case of two (R=2) 1-dimensional classes (n=1), the density of probability being of Gaussian nature can be defined:

$$g_r(x) = p(x \mid \omega_r) \cdot P(\omega_r) = \frac{1}{\sqrt{2\pi} \cdot \sigma_r} \cdot e^{-\frac{(x-m_r)^2}{2\sigma_r^2}} \cdot P(\omega_r), \tag{16}$$

where parameter $r \in \{1; 2\}$ .

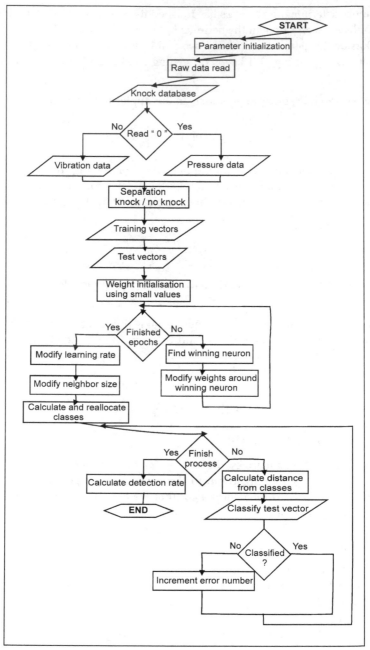

Fig. 4. Flowchart for implemented Kohonen Self- Organizing Map algorithm

Making an expansion to the n-dimensional case, the formula (16) for the Gaussian dispersion becomes:

$$p(x \mid \omega_r) = \frac{1}{(2\pi)^{n/2} \left| C_r \right|^{1/2}} e^{-\frac{1}{2}(x-m_r)^T C_j^{-1}(x-m_r)} , \tag{17}$$

where $m_r = E_r\{x\}$ represents the means of vectors in class r, $C_r = E_r\{(x - m_r)(x - m_r)^T\}$ is the matrix of covariance for the vectors in class r and $E_r\{\bullet\}$ is an operator that determines the mean value and that is used to make estimations concerning $m_r$ and $C_r$ based on a finite number $N_r$ of patterns from $\omega_r$. Their formulae are:

$$m_r = \frac{1}{N_r} \sum_{x \in \omega_r} x , \tag{18}$$

$$C_r = \frac{1}{N_r} \sum_{x \in \omega_r} xx^T - m_r m_r^T , \tag{19}$$

$C_r$ being a positive semi-defined symmetrical matrix. The discriminant function based on the Gaussian density of probability will be:

$$g_r(x) = \ln P(\omega_r) - \frac{1}{2}\ln\left|C_j\right| - \frac{1}{2}[(x - m_r)^T C_r^{-1}(x - m_r)], \tag{20}$$

The flowchart in Fig.5 summarizes the procedure of adapting and implementing the Bayes Classifier algorithm to the application proposed in the chapter. The differences from the standard theoretical algorithm are the same as those described for the Fuzzy Kwan-Cai algorithm in Fig.2 and the Kohonen Self-Organizing Map in Fig.4.

## 3. Experimental results for each method

### 3.1 Methodology description, results and analysis

The algorithms treated in this chapter were tested on a Bosch Group database using two sizes of vector sample groups: one of 100 vectors and one of 1000, both of them containing pressure and vibration samples. In each case two thirds of the group was used for training and one third for testing.

The vectors that make up the database represent samples taken from petrol engines, some corresponding to knock situations and some not. The signals related to these samples were taken from pressure and vibration sensors mounted in and around the engine bay. The change in pressure caused by knock activity is seen as an immediate rise in pressure due to causes outside the normal engine piston cycle. On the other hand, the vibration sensors will detect vibrations – knocking noises – representing abnormal combustion fields being generated inside the pistons.

The applications have to declare knock or no knock for every sample vector received and, after testing the database, reach a verdict on the error of the process or in this case the identification rate. When knock is encountered actions can be taken to return the engine to a non-knock state.

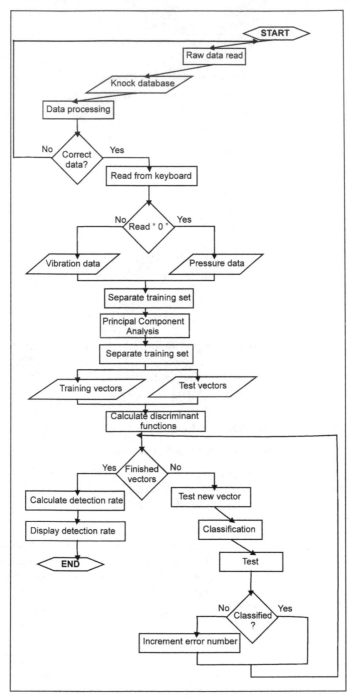

Fig. 5. Flowchart for implemented Bayes Classifier

The testing method for both algorithms (Fuzzy Kwan-Cai and Kohonen Self-Organizing Map) is the following: one parameter varies between its theoretical limits whereas the others remain constant. It is obvious that the difference between the bigger training group and the smaller one should be the higher detection rate.

The following tables contain only the significant part of the experimental results in order to outline the highest detection rates obtained.

## 3.2 Fuzzy Kwan-Cai neural network results

This type of neural network does not need training cycles because it learns as it studies the vectors it receives and builds its own classes in the testing process. In order not to get the wrong idea from the start we have to mention that the high number of classes observed in Table I and Table II for this neural network is due to the second nature of the application which acts like a "focusing lens", examining the internal structure of the two main classes. Therefore it must be stated that the number of classes we are interested in, for this experiment, is two. The significance and proper function limits of this application for parameters given in Table I and Table II are: $\alpha$ which is the base of isosceles triangles ($\alpha \in [1.5; 3.5]$), $\beta$ that determines how much of the sample vector each fuzzy neuron sees ($\beta \in [0.1; 1.6]$) and Tf that represents the neural network's sensitivity to errors (Tf $\in [0.1; 0.35]$).

The first vector generates a class of its own, the next ones either are found relatives of one of the vectors that have come before and therefore are put in the same class or start a new class. The maximum detection results in the tables mentioned above are outlined by being bolded. Unsatisfactory results with high detection rates are presented in italic.

Tables Ia and Ib present the pressure sample detection rate results for the Fuzzy Kwan-Cai neural network using the small sample database and the large sample database. According to Table Ia, the highest detection rate value of 68% was obtained for combination (3.5; 0.15; 1) where parameters Tf and $\beta$ are kept constant whereas $\alpha$ varies.

The same method has been used for Table Ib showing the combinations used by changing the parameter Tf while keeping constant the other two. Combinations are from (3.5; 0.35; 1) down to (3.5; 0.15; 1). A maximum correct detection rate of 93.40% was obtained for the (3.5; 0.22; 1) group.

The detection rate results in Tables Ia and Ib show that from this point of view the Fuzzy Kwan-Cai neural network is very stabile, small variations of its parameters not affecting the experimental outcome. It is clear from the results presented that an increase in the sample database leads to an increase in the detection rates, the network not being affected by sample vectors that are not cohesive in nature with the rest of their class.

Tables IIa and IIb contain the vibration sample detection results. Table IIa represents the small sample database and Table IIb the large one. Table IIa uses the same method of parameter variation as Tables Ia and Ib but valid variations are not achieved because for a result to be considered satisfactory it should at least be higher than 50%.

The first part of Table IIb contains results obtained by using combinations in the same way as Tables Ia, Ib and IIa, the parameter that varies being Tf whereas the others are kept constant. Used combinations start at (3.5; 0.35; 1) and end at (3.5; 0.15; 1). In this first set the

| α | Tf | β | Rate [%] | No. classes |
|---|----|---|----------|-------------|
| 3.5 | 0.15 | 1 | 68% | 2 |
| 3.4 | 0.15 | 1 | 64% | 4 |
| 3.3 | 0.15 | 1 | 64% | 4 |
| 3.2 | 0.15 | 1 | 64% | 4 |
| 3.1 | 0.15 | 1 | 64% | 4 |
| 3 | 0.15 | 1 | 48% | 5 |
| 2.9 | 0.15 | 1 | 48% | 5 |
| 2.8 | 0.15 | 1 | 48% | 7 |
| 2.7 | 0.15 | 1 | 48% | 7 |
| 2.6 | 0.15 | 1 | 48% | 7 |
| 2.5 | 0.15 | 1 | 72% | 9 |
| 2.4 | 0.15 | 1 | 60% | 9 |
| 2.3 | 0.15 | 1 | 58% | 11 |
| 2.2 | 0.15 | 1 | 58% | 11 |
| 2.1 | 0.15 | 1 | 58% | 11 |
| 2 | 0.15 | 1 | 68% | 12 |

Table Ia. Pressure detection rates- small database

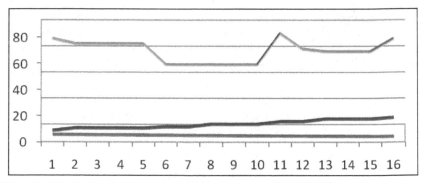

Fig. 6. Plot of α (blue) ,Rate[%](green) and No. classes (red) (Table Ia)

| α | Tf | β | Rate [%] | No. classes |
|---|----|---|----------|-------------|
| 3.5 | 0.35÷0.23 | 1 | 93.40% | 1 |
| 3.5 | 0.22 | 1 | 93.40% | 2 |
| 3.5 | 0.21 | 1 | 93.40% | 3 |
| 3.5 | 0.2 | 1 | 93.40% | 3 |
| 3.5 | 0.19 | 1 | 93.40% | 4 |
| 3.5 | 0.18 | 1 | 93.40% | 5 |
| 3.5 | 0.17 | 1 | 93.40% | 5 |
| 3.5 | 0.16 | 1 | 93.40% | 8 |
| 3.5 | 0.15 | 1 | 93.40% | 10 |
| 3.5 | 0.35÷0.23 | 1 | 93.40% | 1 |

Table Ib. Pressure detection rates- large database

| α | Tf | β | Rate [%] | No.classes |
|-----|-----------|----------|----------|------------|
| 3.5 | 0.35÷0.29 | 1 | 48% | 2 |
| 3.5 | 0.28 | 1 | 48% | 3 |
| 3.5 | 0.27 | 1 | 62% | 6 |
| 3.5 | 0.26 | 1 | 62% | 6 |
| 3.5 | 0.25 | 1 | 68% | 9 |
| 3.5 | 0.24 | 1 | 68% | 9 |
| 3.5 | 0.23 | 1 | 62% | 9 |
| 3.3 | 0.3 | 1 | 48% | 3 |
| 3.3 | 0.3 | 0.9 | 48% | 3 |
| 3.3 | 0.3 | 0.8 | 48% | 3 |
| 3.3 | 0.3 | 0.7÷0.3 | 48% | 2 |
| 3.3 | 0.3 | 0.2 | 48% | 1 |

Table IIa. Vibration detection rates- small database

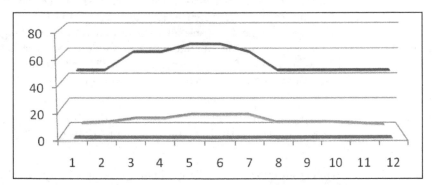

Fig. 7. Plot of Tf (blue),Rate[%] (red) and No.classes (green) (Table IIa)

| α | Tf | β | Rate [%] | No. classes |
|-----|-----------|----------|----------|-------------|
| 3.5 | 0.35÷0.24 | 1 | 93.40% | 1 |
| **3.5** | **0.24** | **1** | **93.40%** | **2** |
| 3.5 | 0.23 | 1 | 93.40% | 3 |
| 3.5 | 0.22 | 1 | 93.40% | 5 |
| 3.5 | 0.21 | 1 | 93.40% | 9 |
| 3.5 | 0.2 | 1 | 82.05% | 10 |
| 3.5 | 0.19 | 1 | 93.13% | 32 |
| 3.5 | 0.18 | 1 | 92.34% | 57 |
| 3.5 | 0.17 | 1 | 90.23% | 107 |
| 3.5 | 0.16 | 1 | 85.75% | 143 |
| 3.5 | 0.15 | 1 | 85.75% | 200 |
| 3.3 | 0.3 | 1 | 85.10% | 3 |
| 3.3 | 0.3 | 0.9 | 85.10% | 3 |
| 3.3 | 0.3 | 0.8 | 85.10% | 3 |
| **3.3** | **0.3** | **0.7÷0.3** | **85.10%** | **2** |
| 3.3 | 0.3 | 0.2 | 85.10% | 1 |

Table IIb. Vibration detection rates- large database

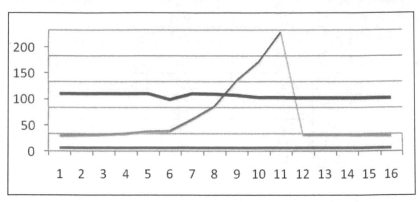

Fig. 8. Plot of Tf (blue) ,Rate[%](red) and No.classes (green) (Table IIb)

maximum correct detection rate of 93.40% is achieved for (3.5; 0.24; 1) – values bolded. Set two contains combinations from (3.3; 0.3; 1) down to (3.3; 0.3; 0.2), parameter β varying between 1 and 0.2 and the other two staying constant. A detection value not as high but equally as important as the maximum one obtained in the previous set is showed in combinations from (3.3; 0.3; 0.7) to (3.3; 0.3; 0.3). The value is 85.10% and presents interest because it is a much higher value than the ones constantly obtained and also represents a correct class detection of two classes.

The vibration situation presented in Tables IIa and IIb leads us to the same results revealed by Tables Ia and Ib, that an increase in the database size will lead to a substantial increase in the detection rate.

In the case of the large sample group shown in Tables Ia and Ib, respectively in Tables IIa and IIb, the neural network does not show any difference in maximum detection rates, differences being observed only for the small sample group. Both tables also present the same maximum detection rate, showing that the network can learn to identify both types of samples with the same accuracy.

Table III presents the time situation. It contains the average detection time situation for both pressure and vibration samples and also from a small and large database point of view. It is clear that the large database obtains better results with almost equally small detection times – 0.0022s for pressure and 0.0046s for vibration – and that pressure vectors have the tendency of being faster detected than vibration ones because the pressure group is more coherent and homogenous than vibration group.

| Average detection time [s] | Pressure | Vibration |
|---|---|---|
| Large database | **0.0022** | **0.0046** |
| Small database | 0.0052 | 0.0056 |

Table III. Average detection times representing pressure and vibration for both small and large databases

What can be observed from the start is that the bigger sample group has almost equal detection times in both pressure and vibration cases to the smaller group, a significant increase being shown in the detection rates. The average detection times in Table III show that via optimization the network can be used in real–time knock applications with very good detection rates and with no prior in-factory learning processes.

One can observe for the Fuzzy Kwan-Cai algorithm that different combinations of parameters can produce the same detection rates, so that a linear variation in any of the parameters will not always lead to a linear variation in the detection rate.

### 3.3 Kohonen Self–Organizing Map neural network results

The Kohonen–Self Organizing Map has a separate learning stage taking place before the detection process begins and being composed of epochs. After the learning stage has ended it does not need to be repeated and the processing of the test batch begins.

For this neural network three sizes of neural maps were used – nine, one-hundred and four-hundred neurons –, as shown in Tables IV, V, VI. They were tested on both pressure and vibration samples.

Table IVa contains only the pressure sample detection rate results for the small vector database using the one hundred–neuron configuration. By keeping the number of epochs constant at 100 and the learning rate at 0.2 and by means of a variation of the neighborhood size from 90 down to 10, we obtained the following spike values: a detection rate of 80% marked bold-italic for the (100; 0.2; 83) group and the maximum value of the detection rate for the small database 82.85% marked bold for the (100; 0.2; 82) combination.

Table IVb contains the pressure sample detection rates using the large database. From the start, using the nine-neuron map, an important fact appears: the nine-neuron map can not cope with the large database due to the small number of neurons that have to remember a large amount of samples, leading to confusion and very low detection rates. The variation methods are the same ones as in the complete version of Table IVa but, even by varying each of the parameters and keeping the other two constant, we can not obtain a spike value higher than 29.78% marked italic, value resulting from the combination (100; 0.4; 5). Performing the same variation techniques as in Table IVa, the maximum value for the detection rate in Table IVb results of 90.57% from the (400; 0.2; 400) and (500; 0.2; 400) combinations – both marked bold - , with lower but not less important spikes of 89.66% for (100; 0.2; 400) and (100; 0.3; 400) – marked bold-italic.

Table Va contains the vibration sample detection rates for the small database. The same variation methods as those in Tables IVa and IVb were used for the exact same values. The one-hundred-neuron network encounters its top value of 80% for the (100; 0.2; 95) combination and also a smaller spike of 74.28% for (100; 0.2; 60). The four-hundred-neuron network tops out at the 82.85% detection rate for the (300; 0.2; 400) combination of parameters. The same marking methods as in the previous tables were also used here and in the following ones.

The large database results for the vibration sample vectors are found in Table Vb. These values have come from the same methods of testing and values used in Tables IVa, IVb and Va. As in the case of the complete Table IVa (from which only the one-hundred neuron

| No. neurons | Epochs | Learning rate | Neighborhood | Rate [%] |
|---|---|---|---|---|
| 100 | 100 | 0.2 | 90 | 68.57 |
| *100* | *100* | *0.2* | *83* | *80* |
| **100** | **100** | **0.2** | **82** | **82.85** |
| 100 | 100 | 0.2 | 80 | 77.14 |
| 100 | 100 | 0.2 | 70 | 74.28 |
| 100 | 100 | 0.2 | 60 | 68.57 |
| 100 | 100 | 0.2 | 50 | 71.42 |
| 100 | 100 | 0.2 | 40 | 71.42 |
| 100 | 100 | 0.2 | 30 | 71.42 |
| 100 | 100 | 0.2 | 20 | 77.14 |
| 100 | 100 | 0.2 | 10 | 65.71 |

Table IVa. Pressure detection rates- small database

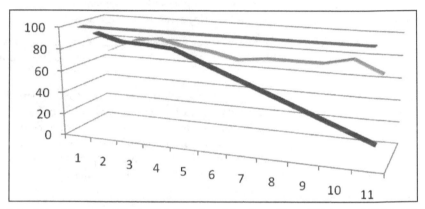

Fig. 9. Plot of No. Neurons (blue), Neighborhood (red) and Rate[%] (green)(Table IVa)

| No. neurons | Epochs | Learning rate | Neighborhood | Rate [%] |
|---|---|---|---|---|
| 9 | 100 | 0.2 | 5 | 23.03 |
| 9 | 100 | 0.3 | 5 | 27.35 |
| *9* | *100* | *0.4* | *5* | *29.78* |
| *9* | *100* | *0.5* | *5* | *28.57* |
| 9 | 100 | 0.6 | 5 | 19.75 |
| 9 | 100 | 0.7 | 5 | 20.06 |
| **400** | **100** | **0.2** | **400** | **89.66** |
| **400** | **100** | **0.3** | **400** | **89.96** |
| 400 | 100 | 0.4 | 400 | 87.84 |
| 400 | 100 | 0.5 | 400 | 88.75 |
| 400 | 100 | 0.6 | 400 | 89.96 |
| 400 | 100 | 0.7 | 400 | 88.75 |
| **400** | **100** | **0.2** | **400** | **89.66** |
| 400 | 200 | 0.2 | 400 | 89.36 |
| 400 | 300 | 0.2 | 400 | 88.75 |
| **400** | **400** | **0.2** | **400** | **90.57** |
| **400** | **500** | **0.2** | **400** | **90.57** |

Table IVb. Pressure detection rates- large database

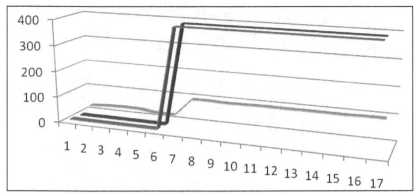

Fig. 10. Plot of No. Neurons (blue), Neighborhood (red) and Rate[%] (green)(Table IVb)

| No. neurons | Epochs | Learning rate | Neighborhood | Rate [%] |
|---|---|---|---|---|
| **100** | **100** | **0.2** | **95** | **80** |
| 100 | 100 | 0.2 | 90 | 65.71 |
| 100 | 100 | 0.2 | 80 | 65.71 |
| 100 | 100 | 0.2 | 70 | 57.14 |
| **100** | **100** | **0.2** | **60** | **74.28** |
| 100 | 100 | 0.2 | 50 | 65.71 |
| 100 | 100 | 0.2 | 40 | 65.71 |
| 100 | 100 | 0.2 | 30 | 68.57 |
| 100 | 100 | 0.2 | 20 | 60 |
| 400 | 100 | 0.2 | 400 | 65.71 |
| 400 | 200 | 0.2 | 400 | 71.42 |
| **400** | **300** | **0.2** | **400** | **82.85** |
| 400 | 400 | 0.2 | 400 | 65.71 |
| 400 | 500 | 0.2 | 400 | 62.85 |
| 400 | 600 | 0.2 | 400 | 71.42 |

Table Va. Vibration detection rates- small database

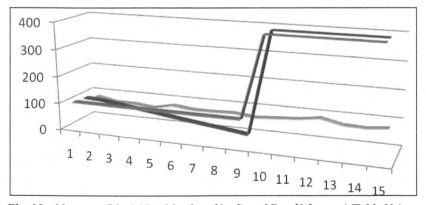

Fig. 11. Plot No. Neurons (blue) Neighborhood(red) and Rate[%] green)(Table Va)

| No. neurons | Epochs | Learning rate | Neighborhood | Rate [%] |
|---|---|---|---|---|
| 100 | 100 | 0.2 | 95 | 79.63 |
| 100 | 100 | 0.2 | 90 | 79.93 |
| 100 | 100 | 0.2 | 80 | 79.02 |
| *100* | *100* | *0.2* | *70* | *81.15* |
| 100 | 100 | 0.2 | 60 | 78.11 |
| **100** | **100** | **0.2** | **50** | **81.76** |
| 100 | 100 | 0.2 | 40 | 75.98 |
| 100 | 100 | 0.2 | 30 | 79.93 |
| 100 | 100 | 0.2 | 20 | 76.59 |
| 400 | 100 | 0.2 | 400 | 87.53 |
| *400* | *100* | *0.2* | *375* | *89.05* |
| 400 | 100 | 0.2 | 350 | 88.75 |
| *400* | *100* | *0.2* | *325* | *89.36* |
| 400 | 100 | 0.2 | 300 | 86.83 |
| 400 | 100 | 0.2 | 275 | 86.62 |
| **400** | **100** | **0.2** | **250** | **89.66** |
| 400 | 100 | 0.2 | 225 | 88.75 |
| 400 | 100 | 0.2 | 200 | 88.44 |
| 400 | 100 | 0.2 | 175 | 88.44 |

Table Vb. Vibration detection rates- large database

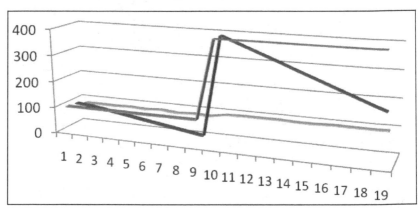

Fig. 12. Plot of No. Neurons (blue), Neighborhood (red) and Rate[%] (green) (Table Vb)

section has been presented in this chapter), the nine-neuron network in the complete Table Vb is not suited for working with such a large database, the network becoming confused. This shows in constant results under 50% which can not be taken into account as valid experimental results. These values can only be used as examples of exceptional cases. The one-hundred-neuron network section presented in Table Vb obtains a maximum detection rate of 81.76% for combinations (100; 0.2; 50), another important value over 80% being of 81.15 % for (100; 0.2; 70) . The four-hundred-neuron network tops out at 89.66% for combinations (100; 0.2; 250) and present other important values of 89.36% for (100; 0.2, 325) and of 89,05% for (100; 0.2; 375).

Table VI represent the average detection times using both pressure and vibration vectors for both small and large databases. With values of 0.0023s (small database) and 0.0024s (large database) the pressure samples obtain smaller detection times than the vibration samples with 0.0027s (small database) and 0.0028s (large database). This situation is representative for the four-hundred-neuron network, this also being the slowest solution but with the highest detection rates. The nine-neuron network, even though it has the best detection times, can not be taken into account as a real application because it is not able to cope with large database. The one-hundred-neuron network is the best compromise between detection speed and detection rates as shown in this table.

As with the previous described algorithms, the SOM results shown in Tables IV and V that an increase in the sample group size (training set case) will lead to an increase in detection rates. In this case, the two separate groups are not separated by big detection rate gaps.

| Average detection time [s] | Small database | | Large database | |
|---|---|---|---|---|
| | Pressure samples | Vibration samples | Pressure samples | Vibration samples |
| SOM - 400 neurons | 0.0023 | 0.0027 | 0.0024 | 0.0028 |
| SOM - 100 neurons | 0.000193 | 0.000478 | 0.000538 | 0.000498 |
| SOM - 9 neurons | 0.0000576 | 0.0000579 | 0.0000535 | 0.0000872 |

Table VI. Pressure and vibration average detection times for both small and large sample databases

As in theory, the experimental results in Tables IV, V and VI show that with the increase in neurons there is an increase in detection rates but a decrease in detection times because more neurons translate to more detail that can be remembered, so the distinction between knock and non-knock situations can be more precisely done - therefore a compromise must be made. Being interested not only in obtaining high detection rates but also detection times that would be coherent to the task at hand (samples must be processed in under an engine cycle so the modifications can be brought to the next one), the one-hundred-neuron map seems to be the best option from the three methods tested. The nine-neuron map, even if it produces very high detection times, has a very poor detection rate in both pressure and vibration groups making it useless for any further applications.

The four-hundred-neuron map presented the highest detection rates for this neural network, values that are a little bit smaller than the Fuzzy Kwan-Cai but with detection times very similar to it, the only difference being that the SOM needs separate training. In this case, looking at the detection times in Table VI, the SOM does not seem to make any difference between pressure and vibration signals, the medium detection times showing very small variations. There is a small difference in detection rates between pressure and vibration samples; the SOM seems to handle both models very well.

A very important factor in the good working of the Kohonen Self-Organizing Map is getting the number of epochs and the learning rate well calibrated. A greater than necessary number of epochs would lead to the situation where the network learns in the necessary time period but it is left with more epochs that are not used for learning. This situation, in combination with a high learning rate, would lead to the network learning everything very fast in the first epochs and then forgetting or distorting the knowledge in the following ones.

## 3.4 Bayes classifier results

The Bayes Classifier, as described by its name, is not a neural network but has been included in this chapter as a basic reference point for the evaluation of the two neural networks. It uses a method of calculating the minimum distance from a sample to one of the knock or non-knock class centers - classes that are considered Gaussian by nature. That is why it presents the worst detection times, as shown in Table VIII.

Table VIIa represents the combined pressure and vibration detection rates status for the small database. The way the testing has been done for this algorithm is by progressively growing from a small comparison group (the batch of samples chosen to represent the known classes for testing) versus large test group situation, to a large comparison group versus small test group situation.

The process starts out with a balance of 11 training vectors and 90 testing ones, which leads to a detection rate starting from 65.50% for pressure and 55.55% for vibration and grows (for training vectors) versus shrinks (for testing vectors) in a progressive way to 85 training vectors and 16 testing vectors, leading to a detection rate ending at 43.75% for pressure and 81.25% for vibration. An interesting detail can be observed in this table: the pressure vectors seem to present a constant state even though more and more are added to the learning group every time the detection rates stay approximately between 50% and 72.50%, the last value being the highest pressure detection rate.

The change of state occurs at the end of the table where we can observe a decrease in the learning rate for the combinations of (80 training vectors; 21 testing vectors) with a detection rate of 42.85% and (85 training vectors; 16 testing vectors) with a detection rate of 43.75%.

This decrease is due to the inclusion in the learning group of vectors that are radically different from their stated class; therefore, the knock or non-knock distinction can not be made. In the case of the vibration sample vectors the progression is of almost uniform growth from 55.55% to 81.25%, the last being also the maximum detection rate for the small database experiment.

Table VIIb follows the same type of progression, only that the large database is used for both pressure and vibration samples. The progression goes from a combination of (371 training vectors; 629 testing vectors) with a detection rate of 93.64% for pressure and 90.30% for vibration samples to a combination of (671 training vectors; 329 testing vectors) with the maximum detection rate achieved in this table of 95.44% for pressure samples and 92.40% for vibration samples. Within this progression it can be seen more clearly that the pressure samples are very cohesive in nature and that, given enough samples, the algorithm goes past the problems it has with radically different sample vectors, maintaining a detection rate over 90% in every case.

Table VIII represents the average detection times for both the small and large databases using both pressure and vibration samples.

Being a simple comparative algorithm, we can see in Table VIII that an increase in the database size leads to a slowing down of the process because the comparison must be made with more vectors. In the case of the small database, pressure vectors are detected faster

| Training vectors | Test vectors | Press. rate [%] | Vib. rate [%] |
|---|---|---|---|
| 11 | 90 | 65.50 | 55.55 |
| 12 | 89 | 56.17 | 58.42 |
| **13** | **88** | **72.50** | **60.22** |
| 15 | 86 | 51.16 | 53.48 |
| 21 | 80 | 63.75 | 66.25 |
| 28 | 73 | 54.79 | 64.38 |
| 35 | 66 | 59.09 | 60.60 |
| 41 | 60 | 68.33 | 70 |
| 47 | 54 | 59.25 | 68.51 |
| 55 | 46 | 56.52 | 73.91 |
| 61 | 40 | 67.50 | 70 |
| 65 | 36 | 52.77 | 77.77 |
| 67 | 34 | 68.57 | 74.28 |
| 75 | 26 | 50 | 76.92 |
| 80 | 21 | 42.85 | 76.19 |

Table VIIa. Pressure - vibration detection rates- small database

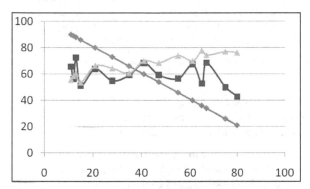

Fig. 13. Test vectors (blue), pressure (red) and vibration rates(green) (Table VIIa)

| Training vectors | Test vectors | Press. rate [%] | Vib. rate [%] |
|---|---|---|---|
| **371** | **629** | **93.64** | **90.30** |
| 391 | 609 | 93.43 | 90.14 |
| 411 | 589 | 93.20 | 90.32 |
| 431 | 569 | 92.97 | 89.98 |
| 451 | 549 | 92.71 | 89.79 |
| 471 | 529 | 92.43 | 89.60 |
| 491 | 509 | 92.14 | 89.58 |
| 511 | 489 | 91.82 | 89.77 |
| 531 | 469 | 91.42 | 89.55 |
| **551** | **449** | **91.09** | **89.08** |
| **571** | **429** | **90.67** | **89.04** |
| **591** | **409** | **91.44** | **89.48** |
| 611 | 389 | 92.28 | 90.23 |
| 631 | 369 | 93.22 | 91.32 |
| 651 | 349 | 94.26 | 92.26 |

Table VIIb. Pressure - vibration detection rates- large database

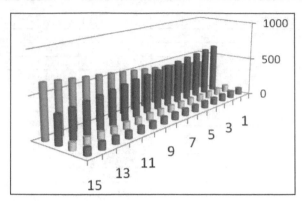

Fig. 14. Test vectors (red), training vectors (blue), pressure rates (green) and vibration rates (violet)

| Average detection time [s] | Pressure | Vibration |
|---|---|---|
| Small sample database | **0.0287** | 0.0297 |
| Large sample database | 0.0948 | **0.094** |

Table VIII. Pressure and vibration average detection times for both small and large sample databases

(0.0287s) than vibration samples (0.0297s). The large database experiments lead to almost equal average detection times between pressure (0.0948s) and vibration (0.094s) samples, with a tendency to better recognize vibration samples.

There is little relevance in the detection rates for the small sample group, even though a small variation between pressure and vibration can be seen. The increase in detection rates due to a bigger knowledge database can also be seen from Tables VIIa and VIIb.

The greatest importance of the Bayes Classifier in this chapter comes from its great sensitivity to change. When the knowledge group includes vectors that are incoherent with the others or that are more different, the detection rate goes down immediately. In this case, the algorithm can not classify properly because one or both classes contain vectors that are very far away from their centers and vectors from one class may get tangled up with the other one. By doing this the Bayes Classifier acts as a monitor for change in the constitution of the sample classes or a "magnifying glass" reacting to the internal composition of the data groups.

Given a big enough knowledge database that is also very coherent in the nature of its classes, the detection rates go up and can be comparable to the neural networks but at a great cost in speed.

## 4. Comparison among the three tested methods

The first discussion will be based on the database size point of view. As we can see from Fig.15 and Fig.16 that summarize results in Tables I, II, IV, V and VII, the size of the learning, training or comparison database is very important in the good functioning of all three tested algorithms.

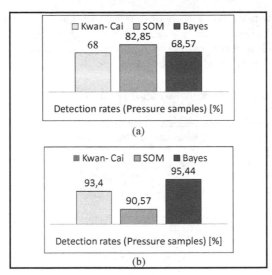

Fig. 15. Pressure sample detection rates using the small database (a) and the large database (b) for the Kwan- Cai, SOM neural networks and the Bayes Classifier

An increase in the database size from one hundred to one thousand sample vectors will lead to a minimum increase of ten percent in the detection rates. For the small database, the Fuzzy Kwan-Cai neural network obtains maximum detection rates for the pressure samples at 68% that are higher than the ones for vibration samples at 48%, but after using the large data set the maximum pressure and vibration detection rates become equal at 93.40%. The difference in detection rates for the pressure and vibration samples using the small database shows that the pressure samples are more coherent and therefore easier to classify. The same evolution as shown by the Fuzzy Kwan- Cai is also true for the Kohonen Self-Organizing Map (SOM). Even more so, the increase in learning database size will lead to a theoretical increase in the detection rate of the Bayes Classifier.

The second discussion will be based on the detection rate point of view. As shown in Fig.15 and Fig.16, the Bayes Classifier seems to show the best detection rates. Its fault is that it needs large amounts of comparison data in order to create classes that are comprehensive enough. Out of the three algorithms tested in this chapter, it is also the less stabile due to the fact that it calculates distances to the center of the comparison classes. If these classes are not well defined and separated, the detection rates fall dramatically. This can be seen in Table VIIb. The Fuzzy Kwan-Cai obtains the highest detection rates of all three algorithms - these being valid detection rates that are not influenced by the nature of learned vectors leading to the great stability of this method. The learning method used employs the automatic generation of learning classes as it goes through the sample set. The fuzzy logic creates a more organic representation of the knowledge classes than the boolean one. The Kohonen Self-Organizing Map (SOM) presents the second highest detection rates and a more controlled and stabile learning and training environment then the other two algorithms. Because the learning is done prior to the start of the testing process and in repetitive epochs, the neural network has the chance to go through the data set again and again until a complete image is formed. The two neural networks show no considerable preference between pressure and vibration samples and present high stability to drastic variations in training samples which in a non-neural method could cause a decrease in detection rates. The nature of these types of signals and their differences are outlined by the Bayes Classifiers sensitivity to unclear classes and the way in which the Fuzzy Kwan-Cai neural network works by showing the internal structure of the classes.

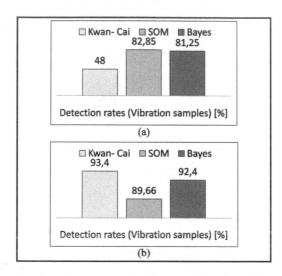

Fig. 16. Vibration sample detection rates using the small database (a) and the large database (b) for the Kwan-Cai, SOM neural networks and the Bayes Classifier

The third discussion will be based on the detection time point of view. As present in Fig.17 and Fig.18 that summarize results in Tables III, VI and VIII, it is clear at first glance that the neural networks are far superior to the normal non-neural classification algorithm. The Bayes Classifier obtains the longest detection times due to the process of comparing each new vector to the knowledge classes. The best, valid, detection times are shown by the Kohonen Self-Organizing Map with the one-hundred-neurons configuration. This configuration, given optimization of the code, can lead to detection times coherent to the engine combustion cycles in which the knock detection needs to take place. Any number of neurons under one hundred will make it hard for the network to give satisfactory detection rates even though the detection times will decrease dramatically. In this chapter we are interested in maximizing the balance between high detection rates and low detection times and not achieving the two extremes and having to compromise one outcome. The second best detection times that are also very close to one another belong to the Fuzzy Kwan-Cai and SOM with the configuration of four-hundred-neurons.

These two algorithms also show the highest detection rates from the methods tested in this chapter. In a real-time application there should not be any problem with the SOMs separate training stage because it would be performed only once inside the factory. The Fuzzy Kwan-Cai neural network presents a different advantage in that it can learn as it goes along, not needing a separate training stage and continuously receiving information and gaining knowledge.

It is clear from the information presented in this chapter that the best detection rates correlated to very good detection times belong to the Kohonen Self-Organizing Map with a configuration of one-hundred-neurons.

The SOM with a configuration of four-hundred-neurons obtains results almost similar to the Fuzzy Kwan-Cai. The difference between these two networks is that the SOM requires a separate training stage where the separated and well defined learning classes are given to it and the Fuzzy Kwan-Cai learns as it receives sample vectors and builds its own classes.

The Bayes Classifier is very useful for showing the nature of the knock and non-knock classes how well they are defined and separated due to its sensitivity to drastic variations in sample vectors. Its detection rate depends on the size of the knowledge database and its coherence making it useless in real-world applications.

From a real-world application point of view, in order to further maximize detection rates, it is clear that a parallel process composed of a pressure-vibration analysis and detection becomes necessary, based on the experimental results. Due to the developments in digital signal processing (DSP) technology, the parallel process would not lead to an increasing detection times.

## 5. Concluding remarks

In order to avoid overcrowding, this final chapter contains general concluding remarks due to the fact that details and accurate conclusions have already been widely presented in chapters III and IV above.

Three methods of knock detection were studied and compared in this chapter. Testing was performed on a Bosch Group database. Two of the three algorithms used are of neural nature: Fuzzy Kwan-Cai neural network – presenting the unsupervised learning approach and fuzzy inference core - and Kohonen Self-Organizing Map (SOM) – with a separate supervised learning stage - and the third is non-neural: Bayes Classifier.

The three algorithms were either trained or had comparison classes and were tested on two different database sizes, one small of one hundred samples vectors and one large representing one thousand samples in order to show how the database size would affect the detection outcome.

Experiments were made on both pressure and vibration sample vectors in order to see which of these are more coherent in nature, leading to results that show an overall greater coherence with slightly more increased detection rates and how this coherence might affect the algorithms being tested. The experiments performed have led to results that prove the superiority of the neural methods in contrast to the normal classification – the situation being looked at from a rate-time point of view as seen in Fig.15, Fig.16, Fig.17, Fig.18.The difference between the neural and non neural methods is represented by an average scale factor of 0,001s in favour of the neural. This superiority should be seen also from a stability to errors point of view as seen in Table VIIb where a stray vector can distort the judgement of the non neural Bayes Classifier so that detection rates fall.

Comparisons were made between the algorithms leading to experimental results enabling us to draw conclusions on which methods are superior to others, in what way and also on the properties and nature of the database used in the experiments.

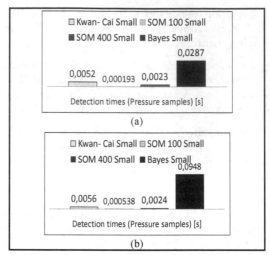

Fig. 17. Pressure sample detection times using the small database (a) and the large database (b) for the Kwan- Cai, SOM neural networks and the Bayes Classifier

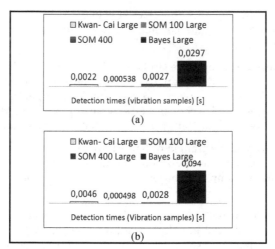

Fig. 18. Vibration sample detection times using the small database (a) and the large database (b) for the Kwan- Cai, SOM neural networks and the Bayes Classifier

Suggestions for real-world applications were made in the prior chapter leading to further optimizations around the strengths and weaknesses of each algorithm.

The three algorithms and most of all the two neural networks have long been used for varied applications showing great robustness and stability. The versions of these applications used in this paper are presented and have been used and tested in their standard form as presented in (Kohonen, 2000, 2002) and (Kwan&Cai, 1994) using as method of verification direct comparison of the outcome of detection and the optimal known value for each vector at a time and incremented into an error counter. The databases were verified to be consistent of their description.

## 6. Acknowledgement

This work was supported by CNCSIS – UEFISCSU, project number PNII – IDEI code 1693/2008.

## 7. References

Adeli, H. & Karim , A. (2005). Wavelets in Intelligent Transportation Systems (1st edition) , Ed. Wiley, ISBN-13: 978-0470867426, England

Auld, T.; Moore, A.W. & Gull, S.F. (2007). Bayesian Neural Networks for Internet Traffic Classification, vol. 18, issue. 1, pp. 223–239, ISSN: 1045-9227

Banakar A. & Azeem M. F. (2008). Artificial wavelet neural network and its application in neuro-fuzzy models, Appl. Soft Comput., vol. 8, no. 4, pp. 1463–1485, ISSN: 1568-4946

Billings, S.A. & Wei H.L. (2005). A new class of wavelet networks for nonlinear system identification, vol. 16, issue. 4, pp. 862 – 874, ISSN: 1045-9227

Borg, J.M., Cheok K.C, Saikalis G. & Oho, S (2005). Wavelet-based knock detection with fuzzy logic, in IEEE International Conference on Computational Intelligence for Measurement Systems and Applications – CIMSA 2005, , pp.26-31, ISBN: 978-1-4244-2306-4, Sicily Italy 14-16 July 2005

Bosch, R. (2004). Bosch-Gasoline-Engine Management, Ed. Robert Bosch GmbH, ISBN-13: 978-0837611006

Boubai, O. (2000). Knock detection in automobile engines, vol.3, issue 3, pp. 24-28, ISSN: 1094-6969

Chen, P.C. (2005). Neuro-fuzzy-based fault detection of the air flow sensor of an idling gasoline engine, vol.219, no. 4, pp.511-524, ISSN 0954-4070

Erjavec, J. (2009). Automotive Technology: A System Approach (5th edition), Ed. Delmar Cengage Learning, ISBN-13: 978-1428311497, Clifton Park NY USA

Ettefagh, M M., Sadeghi, H., Pirouzpanah, V. H. & Arjmandi T. (2008). Knock detection in spark ignition engines by vibration analysis of cylinder block: A parametric modeling approach, vol. 22, Issue 6, pp. 1495-1514, august 2008, ISSN: 0888-3270

Fleming, W.J. (2001). Overview of Automotive Sensors, vol.1, issue 4, pp.296-308, ISSN: 1530-437X

Gupta, H.N. (2006). Fundamentals of Internal Combustion Engines, Ed. Prentice-Hall of India Private Limited, ISBN-13: 978-8120328549, New Delhi India

Hamilton, L J. & Cowart, J S. (2008). The first wide-open throttle engine cycle: transition into knock experiments with fast in-cylinder sampling, vol. 9, no. 2, pp. 97-109, ISSN 1468-0874

Hsu, C.C. (2006). Generalizing self-organizing map for categorical data, vol. 17, issue.2, pp. 294 - 304, ISSN: 1045-9227

Hui, C.L. P. (2011). Artificial Neural Networks - Application, Publisher: InTech, ISBN 978-953-307-188-6, Croatia

Ibrahim, A. M. (2004). Fuzzy logic for embedded systems applications, Ed. Elsevier Science, ISBN-13: 978-0750676052, MA USA

Jonathan, M.B., Saikalis, G., Oho, S.T. & Cheok, K.C. (2006). Knock Signal Analysis Using the Discrete Wavelet Transform, No. 2006-01-0226, DOI: 10.4271/2006-01-0226

Kohonen, T. (2000).Self-organizing Maps (3rd edition), Ed. Springer, ISBN-13: 978-3540679219, Berlin

Kohonen, T. (2002). The self-organizing map, vol. 78, no. 9., pp. 1464-1480, ISSN: 0018-9219

Kwan, H.K. & Cai, T (1994). A fuzzy neural network and its applications pattern recognition, IEEE Transactions on Fuzzy Systems, vol.2, issue.3, pp. 185-193, ISSN: 1063-6706

Larose, D.T. (2006).Data Mining Methods and Models, Wiley-IEEE Press, ISBN-13: 978-0471666561, USA

Lazarescu, D., Radoi, C. & Lazarescu, V. (2004). A Real-Time Knock Detection Algorithm Based on Fast Wavelet Transform, in International Conference Communications 2004, Bucharest, pp. 65-68., ISBN: 0-7803-8533-0, Bucharest 20-24 June 2004

Li, H. & Karim , G. A. (July 2004). Knock in spark ignition hydrogen engines, vol. 29, issue 8, pp. 859-865, ISSN: 0360-3199

Liu, P. & Li, H.X. (2004). Fuzzy neural network theory and application, Publisher: World Scientific Publishing Company, ISBN-13: 978-9812387868, Singapore

Lopez-Rubio E. (2010). Probabilistic Self-Organizing Maps for Continuous Data, vol.21, issue.10, pp. 1543 - 1554, ISSN: 1045-9227

Midori, Y., Nobuo, K. & Atsunori K. (1999). Engine Knock Detection Using Wavelet Transform, Dynamics & Design Conference, Issue B, , pp. 299-302, Tokio, 1999

Mitchell, T.M. (2010). Machine Learning (3rd edition), Ed. New York: McGraw Hill Higher Education, ISBN 0070428077, Oregon USA

Park, S.T. & Jang J. (2004). Engine knock detection based on Wavelet transform, Proceeding of the 8th Russian-Korean International Symposiom on Science and Technology – KORUS 2004, vol.3, pp. 80-83, ISBN: 0-7803-8383-4, 26 June-3 July 2004

Prokhorov, D.(2008). Computational Intelligence in Automotive Applications (1st Edition), Ed.Springer, ISBN 978-3-540-79256-7

Radoi, A., Lazarescu V., & Florescu A. (2009). Wavelet Analysis To Detect The Knock On Internal Combustion Engines, tome 54, no.3, pp. 301-310, ISSN: 0035-4066

Thomas, J.H., Dubuisson, B. & M.A. Dillies-Peltier (1997). Engine Knock Detection from Vibration Signals Using Pattern Recognition, Mecanica, vol.32, no 5, pp. 431-439

Wang, F.Y.& Liu, D. (2006). Advances in Computational Intelligence: Theory And Applications (1st edition), Ed. World Scientific Publishing Company,. ISBN-13: 978-9812567345, Singapore

Wehenkel, L.A. (1997) Automatic Learning Technique in Power Systems, Kluwer Academic Publishers, ISBN-13: 978-0792380689 , USA

Wu J.D. & Liu, C.H. (2009). An expert system for fault diagnosis in internal combustion engines using wavelet packet transform and neural network, vol. 36, issue 3, pp. 4278-4286, ISSN: 0957-4174

Yilmaz, S. & Oysal, Y. (2010). Fuzzy Wavelet Neural Network Models for Prediction and Identification of Dynamical Systems, vol. 21 , issue 10, pp. 1599 – 1609, ISSN: 1045-9227

Zhang, Q. & Benveniste A. (1992). Wavelet networks, vol. 3, issue. 6, pp. 889–898, ISSN: 1045-9227

Zhang, H. & Liu, D. (2006). Fuzzy Modeling and Fuzzy Control (Control Engineering) (1st edition) , Ed. Birkhauser Boston, ISBN-13: 978-0817644918, MD USA

# 13

# Understanding Driver Car-Following Behavior Using a Fuzzy Logic Car-Following Model

Toshihisa Sato and Motoyuki Akamatsu
*Human Technology Research Institute,*
*National Institute of Advanced Industrial Science*
*and Technology (AIST),*
*Japan*

## 1. Introduction

Recently, automatic systems that control driving speeds and headway distances while following a vehicle have been developed worldwide. Some products, such as adaptive cruise control systems, have already been installed in upper segments of passenger vehicles. Car following is an important operation in safe and comfortable driving on straight and/or curved roads. The number of traffic accidents involving rear-end collisions is the highest over the last decade in Japan (Iwashita et al., 2011). A rear-end collision occurs when the distance between two vehicles decreases due to deceleration of the lead vehicle and/or higher speed of the following vehicle. The automatic vehicle control system maintains a safe headway distance while following a vehicle and controls velocity according to the relative speed of the leading vehicle, in order to avoid a rear-end collision.

If the system's automatic controls do not match the driver's manual controls, driver acceptance of the automatic vehicle control systems decreases, and the driver is not likely to use them. For example, when a lead vehicle speeds up and the inter-vehicle distance increases, one driver may accelerate strongly, whereas another driver may accelerate slightly; and other drivers may not accelerate. The system's automatic hard acceleration does not suit drivers whose acceleration is slight and those who do not accelerate, and they may regard such automatic systems as dangerous. Therefore, it is expected that drivers will accept longitudinal control systems that operate in a manner similar to their own usual car-following behavior. Drivers' car-following behavior must be investigated in a real road-traffic environment to develop vehicle control and driver support systems that are compatible with drivers' typical car-following behavior.

Car-following behavior consists of two aspects: how much distance drivers allow for a leading vehicle as an acceptable headway distance, and how they control acceleration according to the movements of the leading vehicle. Figure 1 presents an example of a typical following process. This car-following behavior data was recorded using an instrumented vehicle on a real motorway in Southampton (Sato et al., 2009a). The relative distance and speed were detected by microwave radar. The data length was 5min. Car-following behavior is a goal-seeking process depicted by several spirals as drivers attempt to maintain the desired following headway behind a vehicle in a car-following situation.

In this chapter, the range of headway distances that drivers leave for leading vehicles is the "static" aspect of car-following behavior. A driver's acceleration controls based on the relationship between the driver's own vehicle and the leading vehicle is termed the "dynamic" aspect. Following distances, Time Headway (THW) (defined by the relative distance to a leading vehicle divided by the driving speed of driver's own vehicle), and Time to Collision (TTC) (defined by the relative distance to a leading vehicle divided by the relative speed between the leading and drivers' own vehicles) are indicators for evaluating the static aspect. A number of car-following models deal with the dynamic aspect.

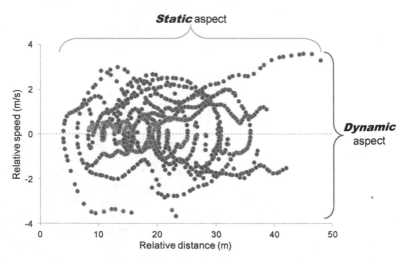

Fig. 1. Example of car-following behavior data collected using an instrumented vehicle on an actual road. (For details of the data collection method, please see section 3.2.)

## 1.1 Brief review of car-following models

Car-following models have been developed since the 1950s (e.g., Pipes, 1953). Many models describe the accelerative behavior of a driver as a function of inter-vehicle separation and relative speed. The following are representative car-following models (for details, please see Brackstone & McDonald, 1999).

General Motors Model:

The fundamental concept behind the General Motors Model is the stimulus-response theory (Chandler et al., 1958). Equation (1) presents a representative formulation.

$$_F(t + T) = \alpha \left[ \frac{[v_F(t)]^m}{[X_L(t) - X_F(t)]^l} \right] [V_L(t) - V_F(t)] \tag{1}$$

where $a_F(t+T)$ is the acceleration or deceleration rate of the following vehicle at time $t+T$; $V_L(t)$ is the speed of the lead vehicle at time $t$; $V_F(t)$ is the speed of the following vehicle at time $t$; $X_L(t)$ is the spacing of the lead vehicle at time $t$; $X_F(t)$ is the spacing of the following vehicle at time $t$; $T$ is the perception-reaction time of the driver; and $m$, $l$, and $\alpha$ are constants to be determined.

Basically, the response is the acceleration (deceleration) rate of the following vehicle. This is a function of driver sensitivity and the stimulus. The stimulus is assumed to be the difference between the speed of the lead vehicle and that of the following vehicle. Driver sensitivity is a function of the spacing between the lead and following vehicles and the speed of the following vehicle. Several derived equations have been proposed in the last 20 years (see Mehmood et al., 2001).

However, one weakness of the General Motors Model is that the response of the following vehicle is determined by one stimulus, speed relative to the leading vehicle. When the relative speed between the two vehicles is zero, the acceleration or deceleration response is zero. This is not a realistic phenomenon, because a driver decelerates to increase inter-vehicle separation when the relative speed is zero but the spacing is too short. To overcome this problem, Helly developed a linear model that includes the additional stimulus term of the desired headway distance (Helly, 1959):

$$a_F(t + T) = C_1[V_L(t) - V_F(t)] + C_2\{[X_L(t) - X_F(t)] - Dn(t + T)\}$$

$$Dn(t + T) = \alpha + \beta V_F(t) + \gamma a_F(t) \tag{2}$$

where $D_n(t+T)$ is the desired following distance at time $t+T$; and $\alpha$, $\beta$, $\gamma$, $C_1$, and $C_2$ are calibration constants.

Another limitation is the assumption of symmetrical behavior under car-following conditions. For example, a lead vehicle has a positive relative speed with a certain magnitude, and another lead vehicle has a negative relative speed with the same magnitude. In these situations, the General Motors Model gives the same deceleration rate in the first case as the acceleration rate in second case. In a real road-traffic environment, deceleration in the second case is greater than acceleration to avoid risk.

Stopping-Distance Model:

The Stopping-Distance Model assumes that a following vehicle always maintains a safe following distance in order to bring the vehicle to a safe stop if the leading vehicle suddenly stops. This model is based on a function of the speeds of the following and leading vehicles and the follower's reaction time. The original formulation (Kometani & Sasaki, 1959) is:

$$\Delta x(t-T) = \alpha v^2_L(t-T) + \beta_1 v^2_F(t) + \beta v_F(t) + b_0 \tag{3}$$

where $\Delta x$ is the relative distance between the lead and following vehicles; $v_L$ is the speed of the lead vehicle; $v_F$ is the speed of the following vehicle; $T$ is the driver's reaction time; and $\alpha$, $\beta$, $\beta_1$, and $b_0$ are calibration constants.

The Stopping-Distance Model is widely used in microscopic traffic simulations (Gipps, 1981), because of its easy calibration based on a realistic driving behavior, requiring only the maximal deceleration of the following vehicle. However, the "safe headway" concept is not a totally valid starting point, and this assumption is not consistent with empirical observations.

Action-Point Model:

The Action-Point Model is the first car-following model to incorporate human perception of motion. The model developed by Michaels suggests that the dominant perceptual factor is changes in the apparent size of the vehicle (i.e., the changing rate of visual angle) (Michaels, 1963):

$$\frac{d\theta}{dt} = \frac{4*W_L}{4*[X_L(t)-X_F(t)]^2+W_L^2}\,[V_L(t) - V_F(t)] \tag{4}$$

where $W_L$ is the width of the lead vehicle.

This model assumes that a driver appropriately accelerates or -decelerates if the angular velocity exceeds a certain threshold. Once the threshold is exceeded, the driver chooses to decelerate until he/she can no longer perceive any relative velocity. Thresholds include a spacing-based threshold that is particularly relevant in close headway situations, a relative speed threshold for the perception of closing, and thresholds for the perception of opening and closing for low relative speeds (a recent work suggests that the perception of opening and that of closing have different thresholds (Reiter, 1994)). Car-following conditions are further categorized into subgroups: free driving, overtaking, following, and emergency situation. A driver engages in different acceleration behaviors in different situations when the perceived physical perception exceeds the thresholds.

The Action-Point Model takes into account the human threshold of perception, establishing a realistic rationale. However, various efforts have focused on identifying threshold values during the calibration phase, while the adjustment of acceleration above the threshold has not been considered, and the acceleration rate is normally assumed to be a constant. Additionally, the model dynamic (switching between the subgroups) has not been investigated. Finally, the ability to perceive speed differences and estimate distances varies widely among drivers. Therefore, it is difficult to estimate and calibrate the individual thresholds associated with the Action-Point Model.

## 2. Fuzzy logic car-following model

Drivers perform a car-following task with real-time information processing of several kinds of information sources. The car-following models discussed above have established a unique interpretation of drivers' car-following behaviors. A driver in a car-following situation is described as a stimuli-responder in the General Motors Model, a safe distance-keeper in the Stopping-Distance Model, and a state monitor who wants to keep perceptions below the threshold in the Action-Point Model. However, these models include non-realistic constraints to describe car-following behavior in real road-traffic environments: symmetry between acceleration and deceleration, the "safe headway" concept, and constant acceleration or deceleration above the threshold.

The fuzzy logic car-following model describes driving operations under car-following conditions using linguistic terms and associated rules, instead of deterministic mathematical functions. Car-following behavior can be described in a natural manner that reflects the imprecise and incomplete sensory data presented by human sensory modalities. The fuzzy logic car-following model treats a driver as a decision-maker who decides the controls based on sensory inputs using a fuzzy reasoning. There are two types of fuzzy inference system that uses fuzzy reasoning to map an input space to an output space, Mandani-type and

Sugeno-type. The main difference between the Mamdani and Sugeno types is that the output membership functions are only linear or constant for Sugeno-type fuzzy inference. A typical rule in the Sugeno-type fuzzy inference (Sugeno, 1985) is:

If input $x$ is $A$ and input $y$ is $B$ then output $z$ is $x*p+y*q+r$;

where $A$ and $B$ are fuzzy sets and $p$, $q$, and $r$ are constants.

The constant output membership function is obtained from a singleton spike ($p=q=0$).

## 2.1 Overview

The fuzzy logic car-following model was developed by the Transportation Research Group (TRG) at the University of Southampton (Wu et al., 2000). McDonald et al. collected car-following behavior data on real roads and developed and validated the proposed fuzzy logic car-following model based on the real-world data (briefly mentioned in 2.2 and 2.3; please see Wu, 2003; Zheng, 2003 for further explanation).

The fuzzy logic model uses relative velocity and distance divergence (DSSD) (the ratio of headway distance to a desired headway) as input variables. The output variable is the acceleration-deceleration rate. The DSSD is the average of the headway distance that is observed when the relative speeds between vehicles are close to zero. This model adopts fuzzy functions (fuzzy sets described by membership functions) as the formula for the input-output relationship. Figure 2 depicts the structure of the fuzzy logic car-following model.

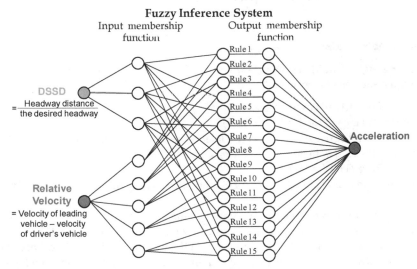

Fig. 2. Structure of the fuzzy inference system in the fuzzy logic car-following model

Specifications of the fuzzy inference system are as follows.

- Type of inference system: Sugeno
- Type of input membership function: Gaussian
- Type of output membership function: Constant

- Number of partitions for input (Relative Velocity): 5 (closing+, closing, about zero, opening, and opening+)
- Number of partitions for input (DSSD): 3 (close, ok, and far)
- Initialization of fuzzy inference system: grid partition method
- Learning algorithm: combination of back-propagation and least square methods
- Defuzzification method: weighted average

The parameter of the fuzzy inference system is estimated using the following combination of back-propagation and least square methods. The initial fuzzy inference system adopts the grid partition method in which the membership functions of each input are evenly assigned in the range of the training data. Next, the membership function parameters are adjusted using the hybrid learning algorithm. The parameters of output membership functions are updated in a forward pass using the least square method. The inputs are first propagated forward. The overall output is then a linear combination of the parameters of output membership functions. The parameters of input membership functions are estimated using back propagation in each iteration, where the differences between model output and training data are propagated backward and the parameters are updated by gradient descent. The parameter optimization routines are applied until a given number of iterations or an error reduction threshold is reached.

The input-output mapping specified by the fuzzy inference system has a three-dimensional structure. We focus on relative velocity-acceleration mapping in order to analyze the dynamic aspect of car-following behavior (i.e., drivers' acceleration controls based on the variation in relative speeds).

## 2.2 Input variable validation

The following eight candidates were applied to the fuzzy inference system estimation in order to obtain satisfactory performance of the fuzzy logic model.

- Velocity of the driver's own vehicle ($V_d$)
- Headway distance to the lead vehicle (HD)
- Relative velocity between the lead vehicle and the driver's vehicle (RV = d(HD)/dt)
- Velocity of the lead vehicle ($V_l = V_d + RV$)
- Time headway (THW = HD /$V_d$)
- Inverse of time to collision (1/TTC, TTC = HD/RV, where the value is infinite when RV = 0.)
- Angular velocity (This value is calculated using the following approximate formula: (width*RV)/HD$^2$, where the width of the lead vehicle is assumed to be 2.5m.)
- Distance divergence (DSSD, calculated from HD divided by the desired headway. The desired headway was chosen to be the average of the headway observed when the relative speeds between vehicles were close to zero.)

The performance of the fuzzy logic model was evaluated by the Root Mean Square Error (RMSE) of the model prediction:

$$RMSE = \sqrt{\frac{\sum_{i=1}^{N}(\hat{Y}_i - Y_i)^2}{N}} \tag{5}$$

where $\hat{Y}_i$ is a predicted value using the fuzzy logic model at time increment i, $Y_i$ is raw data at time increment i, and N is the number of data.

All possible model formulations (a single variable, combination of two variables, and combination of three variables) were tested. The data were collected on real motorways using a TRG instrumented vehicle. Although a three-input model suggested better RMSE performance than a one-input model or a two-input model, the two-input model using relative speed and distance divergence was adopted because of the complexity of the model structure and its applicability to a wide range of car-following situations. For details of the input variable validation, refer to Zheng, 2003.

## 2.3 Model validation

The developed fuzzy logic car-following model was validated in terms of reproducing a single vehicle's car-following behavior, as well as reproducing traffic flow under car-following conditions (a platoon of vehicles).

The single vehicle's car-following behavior was evaluated from empirical data, and the average RMSE of acceleration was $0.20 \text{m}/\text{s}^2$. The platoon behavior was evaluated using simulation. The response of a platoon of 20 vehicles to step changes of acceleration or deceleration of a lead vehicle was assessed in order to investigate the influence of the movement of the lead vehicle on a line of vehicles. The results validated that the fuzzy logic car-following model could reproduce both stable and unstable traffic behavior. For details of the model validation, refer to Wu et al., 2003 and Zheng, 2003.

## 3. Case study 1: Car-following behavior comparison between the UK and Japan

### 3.1 Motivation

This section introduces a case study focusing on a comparison of drivers' car-following behavior in the UK and in Japan (Sato et al., 2009b). The fuzzy logic car-following model was developed using naturalistic data collected in Southampton. We applied this model to behavioral data collected in Japan. One objective is to confirm whether Japanese car-following behavior can be described by the fuzzy logic model with the same structure as the UK model. Another objective is to investigate cross-cultural variations of the car-following behaviors of drivers in the two countries.

With increasing globalization of automotive markets, it is important to understand the differences between driving behavior in different countries. Car-following behavior may differ due to differences in nationality and the road traffic environments of different countries. The findings may contribute to designing human-centered automatic vehicle control systems based on international differences in driving behavior.

### 3.2 Methods

### 3.2.1 Instrumented vehicles

An AIST instrumented vehicle and a TRG instrumented vehicle are used for behavioral data collection (Brackstone et al., 1999; Sato & Akamatsu, 2007). Both vehicles are equipped with various sensors and driving recorder systems in order to detect the vehicle driving status and to measure the driver's operations. Velocity is measured using a speed pulse signal, and acceleration is detected by a G-sensor. The relative distance and relative speed to the leading and following vehicles are recorded with laser radar units (AIST instrumented vehicle) or microwave radar (TRG instrumented vehicle) that are fixed within the front and rear bumpers. Figure 3 presents an overview of the AIST instrumented vehicle. This vehicle collects the following data:

- Driving speed by speed pulse signal,
- Relative distance and speed to the leading and following vehicles by laser radar units,
- Vehicle acceleration by G-sensor,
- Angular velocity by gyro sensor,
- Geographical position by D-GPS sensor,
- Application of gas and brake pedals by potentiometers,
- Position of driver's right foot by laser sensors,
- Steering wheel angle by encoder,
- Turn signal activation by encoder, and
- Visual images (forward and rear scenes, lane positions, and driver's face) by five CCD cameras.

Fig. 3. AIST instrumented vehicle with sensors and a recorder system for detecting nearby vehicles

The velocity of the following vehicle was calculated based on the velocity of the instrumented vehicles and the relative speed. The visual image of the rear scenes was used for better understanding of the traffic conditions while driving and for clarifying uncertainties identified in the radars.

### 3.2.2 Road-traffic environment

Figure 4 depicts the road environment in the Southampton (UK) and Tsukuba (Japan) routes. The driving route in Tsukuba was 15km long (travel time 30min). This route included urban roads with several left and right turns at intersections, with a traffic lane that was mostly one lane, and a bypass that had one and two traffic lanes. The driving route in Southampton included trunk roads and motorways with two and three lanes and roundabout junctions. The driving behavior data in Southampton was collected as part of an EC STARDUST project (Zheng et al., 2006). The field experiments at the two sites were conducted during the morning from 9:00 to 10:45.

### 3.2.3 Variables

The passive mode was used for the data collected (Fig. 5), reflecting random drivers who followed the instrumented vehicle. The passive mode can collect and evaluate a large population of drivers, rather than just the participating driver in the instrumented vehicle, in a short period and at a lower level of detail (Brackstone et al., 2002). The measured data in the passive mode enable evaluation of car-following behavior trends in each country.

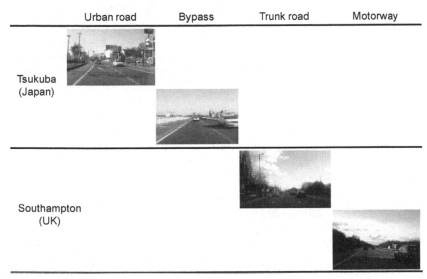

Fig. 4. Road environments used for car-following behavior analyses

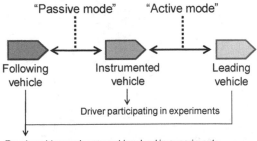

Fig. 5. Active and passive modes in car-following conditions

In the analysis, the car-following condition was defined as a situation in which a driver followed a leading vehicle with relative speeds between 15km/h and -15km/h. The relative distance to a following vehicle under car-following conditions was obtained from the measured data. The rear distances collected were divided into two sets in terms of the associated driving speeds: 30 to 49km/h and 50 to 69km/h. The speed range of 30 to 49km/h corresponds to driving on an urban road (Tsukuba) and on a trunk road (Southampton), while the speed of 50 of 69km/h corresponds to driving on a bypass (Tsukuba) and on a motorway (Southampton).

The THW of the passive mode (defined by the relative distance between the following vehicle and the instrumented vehicle divided by the driving speed of the following vehicle) was calculated, and the distributions of the THW at each set were compared for analysis of the static aspect of car-following behavior.

In addition to the rear distances, the relative speeds and acceleration of the following vehicle were used for the fuzzy logic car-following model. Although this model can be used to describe individual drivers' acceleration-deceleration behavior, we applied the model to the passive mode data in order to compare general features of the dynamic aspect of car-following behavior between Tsukuba and Southampton. The continuous data for more than 20sec was input to the model specification within the measured car- following data.

### 3.3 Results

### 3.3.1 Static aspect

Figure 6 presents the distributions of the THW for each speed range and proportions of the time when drivers take the relevant THW to the total time while driving at the corresponding velocity.

In the lower speed range (30 to 49km/h), the proportion of Southampton drivers taking very short THW (0.5 to 1s) exceeds that of Tsukuba drivers. The proportion of Tsukuba drivers taking THW longer than 3s exceeds that of Southampton drivers. In the higher speed range (50 to 69km/h), no difference in THW between the two regions is observed. Both Tsukuba drivers and Southampton drivers spend more time with the short THW (0.5s to 1.5s). As mentioned in previous research (Brackstone et al., 2009), THW tends to decrease as velocity increases.

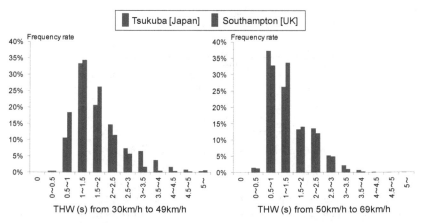

Fig. 6. Comparison of THW between two countries for each speed range

### 3.3.2 Dynamic aspect

Figure 7 presents the relative velocity–acceleration mapping obtained from the fuzzy inference specification in Tsukuba and Southampton. The two sites have similar traces (Southampton, 15; Tsukuba, 14) and data length (Southampton, 511.5sec; Tsukuba, 522.9sec). The RMSEs of the predicted acceleration and the measured data in the estimated fuzzy logic model were 0.15m/sec² in Tsukuba and 0.17m/sec² in Southampton. These findings indicate a satisfactory model-to-data fit compared to other published works (Wu et al., 2003).

The deceleration of Tsukuba drivers is greater than that of Southampton drivers when their vehicle approaches the leading vehicle. When the distance between vehicles is opening, the acceleration of Southampton drivers is greater than that of Tsukuba drivers. Thus, the acceleration-deceleration rate of Tsukuba drivers indicates a tendency opposite that of Southampton drivers.

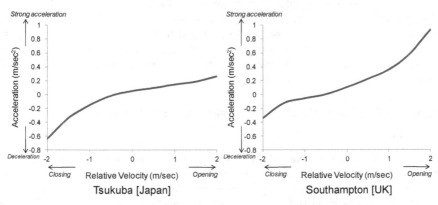

Fig. 7. Results of fuzzy logic model specification: Relative velocity–acceleration mapping between Tsukuba and Southampton

### 3.4 Discussion

The low RMSE of the Tsukuba acceleration rate suggests that the proposed fuzzy logic model is well-suited to Japanese car-following behavior. The findings imply that Japanese drivers use relative velocity and distance divergence for adjusting acceleration and deceleration while following a vehicle.

The THW of Tsukuba drivers was longer at slow velocity. When Tsukuba drivers approached a preceding vehicle in the same traffic lane, they decelerated more strongly. In addition, Tsukuba drivers accelerated less as the distance to the leading vehicle increased. Strong deceleration while moving toward the leading vehicle and weak acceleration when following a preceding vehicle led to long headway distances.

Southampton drivers tended to adopt shorter THW when in car-following in the low driving speed range. The acceleration rate of Southampton drivers was higher than that of Tsukuba drivers when overtaking a vehicle. It is assumed that such strong acceleration contributes to maintaining a short headway distances in car-following situations.

Tsukuba car-following behavior data were collected on urban roads and a bypass. When driving on urban roads, a leading vehicle often has to decelerate suddenly due to other vehicles at crossroads, a change of traffic signals, and the emergence of pedestrians or bicycles. The leading vehicle might also slow down suddenly on the bypass because a merging car may cut in front of it. Drivers adopted longer headway distances and decelerated more strongly in closing inter-vehicle separations when driving on roads where they should pay more attention to the movements of the leading vehicle.

Southampton car-following behavior data were collected on major roads with two or three lanes. In the speed range of 30 to 69km/h, traffic was quite congested in the morning peak when the field experiments were conducted. The drivers kept short headway distances in order to avoid lane changes of vehicles in front of them, leading to strong acceleration with opening inter-vehicle distances.

The road traffic environment in which the behavior data are collected is an important factor in the differences between car-following behavior in Southampton and that in Tsukuba, indicating that the road-traffic environment influences car-following behavior, regardless of the country of data collection. These findings imply that a single operational algorithm would suffice even when using vehicle control and driver support systems in different counties, although different algorithms would be necessary for different road types (e.g., roads in a city and roads connecting cities).

## 4. Case study 2: Longitudinal study of elderly drivers' car-following behavior

### 4.1 Motivation

This section introduces another case study focusing on the assessment of elderly drivers' car-following behavior, using the proposed fuzzy logic car-following model. The number of elderly drivers who drive their own passenger vehicles in their daily lives has increased annually. Driving a vehicle expands everyday activities and enriches the quality of life for the elderly. However, cognitive and physical functional changes of elderly drivers may lead to their increased involvement in traffic accidents. Thus, it is important to develop advanced driver assistance and support systems that promote safe driving for elderly drivers. Automatic vehicle control systems are expected to enhance comfort as well as safety when elderly drivers follow a vehicle. Understanding elderly drivers' car-following behavior is essential for developing automatic control systems that adapt to their usual car-following behavior.

Various studies comparing physical and cognitive functions between young and elderly drivers have been conducted in order to investigate the influence of age-related functional decline on driving (e.g., Owsley, 2004). Driving behavior is influenced by several driver characteristics (e.g., driving skill and driving style); and individual drivers' characteristics differ, especially between young and elderly drivers. Thus, a comparison of the driving behaviors of young and elderly drivers includes the influence of drivers' characteristics as well as the impact of the age-related decline of cognitive functions.

We have been involved in a cohort study on the driving behaviors of elderly drivers on an actual road (Sato & Akamatsu, 2011). A cohort study conducted in real road-traffic environments is expected to focus on changes in elderly drivers' cognitive functions because their cognitive functional changes may be greater than changes in their driving skills or driving styles within a few years. One aim of this study is to clarify how elderly drivers follow a lead vehicle, based on analysis of how car-following behavior changes with aging. We collected car-following behavior data of elderly drivers determined in one year and compared it with that determined five years later. The distributions of THW in the two field experiments were compared in order to investigate the static aspect of car-following behavior. For analysis of the dynamic aspect, the fuzzy logic car-following model was applied to compare elderly drivers' accelerative behavior while following a vehicle.

## 4.2 Methods

### 4.2.1 Procedures

Field experiments were conducted in 2003 (first experiment) and in 2008 (second experiment). The two experiments were conducted using the same instrumented vehicle, the same driving route, and the same participants. The AIST instrumented vehicle was used for the data collection (Fig. 3). Almost all the sensors and the driving recorder system were fixed inside the trunk, so that the participating drivers could not see them, in order to encourage natural driving behaviors during the experiment trials.

The experiments were conducted on rural roads around Tsukuba. The route included several left and right turns, and the travel time was 25min (total distance 14km). The participant rode alone in the instrumented vehicle during the experiment trials. Before the recorded drives, the participants performed practice drives from the starting point to the destination without using a map or an in-vehicle navigation system.

Four elderly drivers (three males and one female) with informed consent participated in the two experiments. Their ages ranged from 65 to 70 years (average 67.3 years) in the first experiment and from 70 to 74 years (average 72.0 years) in the second experiment. Their annual distance driven ranged from 5,000 to 8,000km in the first experiment and from 2,000 to 10,000km in the second experiment (average 6,500km in both experiments).

The participants were instructed to drive in their typical manner. In the first experiment, the recorded trip for each elderly participant was made once a day on weekdays, for a total of 10 trips. In the second experiment, the trial was conducted twice a day on weekdays, for a total of 30 trips. The participants took a break between the experiment trials in the second experiment.

### 4.2.2 Data analysis

Figure 8 depicts a target section for the analysis of elderly drivers' car-following behavior. We focused on a two-lane bypass, the same road environment as that in section 3.2.2. We included only drives with a leading vehicle, excluding drives without a leading vehicle on the target section.

The active mode (distance between the instrumented vehicle and the leading vehicle) was used in the analysis of the elderly drivers' car-following behavior. We also used the passive mode (distance between the instrumented vehicle and the following vehicle) to investigate traffic characteristics on the analyzed road. The latter is expected to indicate whether changes in elderly drivers' car-following behaviors are influenced by their functional declines or by changes in traffic characteristics on the target road.

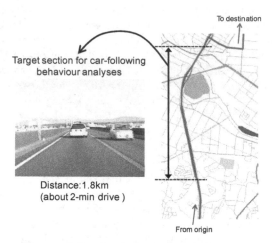

Fig. 8. Road section used for car-following behavior analysis

## 4.3 Results

### 4.3.1 Static aspect

Figure 9 presents the distributions of THW for leading and following vehicles. The THW distributions suggest the proportion of time experienced in each category to the total time of the car-following conditions. There were no differences in the distribution of THW to following vehicles between the first and second experiments.

The peak of the distribution of THW to leading vehicles is found in the category from 1 to 1.5s in the first experiment. However, the peak is found in the category from 1.5 to 2s in the second experiment, indicating that the THW in the second experiment exceeds that in the first experiment.

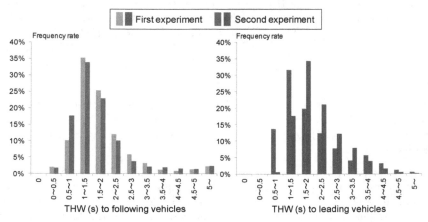

Fig. 9. Comparison of THW to leading and following vehicles between the first and second experiments

### 4.3.2 Dynamic aspect

Figure 10 compares the relative velocity–acceleration mapping of the first and second experiments. In the fuzzy logic model specification, there is a total of 27 traces (data length 770.5sec) in the first experiment and 29 traces (data length 1481.0sec) in the second experiment.

The RMSEs between the predicted and measured accelerations in the estimated fuzzy logic model were $0.25m/sec^2$ in the first experiment and $0.14m/sec^2$ in the second experiment, which are within adequate errors compared to those estimated based on other real-world data (Wu et al., 2003).

The deceleration when the elderly participants approach the lead vehicle was the same in the two experiments. However, the elderly drivers accelerate more strongly in the second experiment than in the first experiment, when the leading vehicle goes faster and the headway distance is opening.

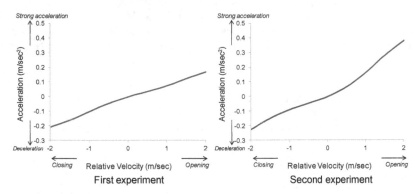

Fig. 10. Results of fuzzy logic model specification of elderly drivers: Relative velocity–acceleration mapping between the first and second experiments

### 4.4 Discussion

Comparison of THW to following vehicles between the first and second experiments indicates no change in traffic flow on the target section in five years. In contrast, THW to leading vehicles is longer in the second experiment than in the first experiment, suggesting that elderly drivers take longer THW and the static aspect of their car-following behaviors changes over five years.

The task-capability interface model (Fuller, 2005) helps clarify why elderly drivers' car-following behavior changes with aging. In this model, drivers adjust task difficulty while driving in order to avoid road accidents. Task difficulty can be described as an interaction between the driver's capability and task demands. When the driver's capability exceeds the task demands, the task is easy and the driver completes the task successfully. When the task demands exceed the driver's capability, the task is difficult and a collision or loss of control occurs because the driver fails to accomplish the task. Here, the driver's capability is determined by the individual's physical and cognitive characteristics (e.g., vision, reaction time, and information processing capacity), personality, competence, skill, and driving style.

Task demands are determined by the operational features of the vehicle (e.g., its control characteristics), environmental factors (e.g., road surface and curve radii), interactions with other road users (e.g., slowing down of a lead vehicle and crossing of pedestrians or bicycles), and human factors (e.g., choice of driving speeds, headway distances, and acceleration control). The longitudinal assessment in this study is conducted using the same participant, the same instrumented vehicle, and the same route. These experiment settings lead to no differences in driver personality affecting capability or in vehicle operational features and road traffic environments influencing task demands. The decline in physical and cognitive functions may lead to a decrease in the elderly driver's capability. Therefore, elderly drivers reduce task demands by adopting longer THW to a leading vehicle, and they seek to maintain capability higher than the reduced task demands.

The results of the fuzzy logic car-following model estimation suggest that the acceleration rate when the inter-vehicle distance is opening becomes higher after five years, although the deceleration rate while approaching the vehicle in front does not change. The stronger acceleration may be a compensating behavior for maintaining the driver's capability by increasing the task demand temporarily, because the driver's capability interacts with the task demands, and drivers can control the task demands by changing their driving behavior in order to improve their capability (e.g., increasing speed, to wake up when feeling sleepy while driving).

Our findings imply that when a leading vehicle drives faster and the headway distances are opening while driving on multi-traffic lanes or while approaching a merging point, information or warning about the movements of the surrounding vehicles is helpful to elderly drivers because they accelerate more strongly and the temporal task demand is higher in this situation.

## 5. Limitations

The fuzzy logic car-following model deals mainly with two vehicles: a vehicle in front and the driver's own vehicle. When drivers approach an intersection with a traffic light under car-following conditions, they may pay more attention to the signal in front of the leading vehicle and manage their acceleration based on the traffic light. Drivers allocate their attention to the forward road structure instead of the leading vehicle when they approach a tight curve; thus, they may reduce their driving speed before entering the curve even if the headway distance is opening. The car-following behavior before intersections or tight curves can be influenced by environmental factors other than a lead vehicle. Further car-following models should be developed to reproduce the car-following behavior in these situations.

## 6. Conclusion

This chapter describes the fuzzy logic car-following model, including a comparison with other car-following models. We introduce two case studies that investigate drivers' car-following behavior using the fuzzy logic car-following model. This model can determine the degree to which a driver controls longitudinal acceleration according to the relationship between the preceding vehicle and his/her vehicle. The fuzzy logic model evaluates the driver's acceleration and deceleration rates using a rule base in natural language. This model contributes to interpretation of the difference in headway distances between Tsukuba and Southampton and changes in elderly drivers' headway distances with aging.

In the cross-cultural study, we compared the car-following behavior gathered on roads where driving is on the left side of the road. Further research will be addressed to compare the car-following behavior between left-hand driving and right-hand driving (e.g., in the United States).

In the longitudinal study, we investigated the car-following behavior of small samples. The next step is to collect and analyze more elderly driver car-following behaviors to validate the findings of this study. Additionally, further study should be conducted to examine individual differences in car-following behaviors to clarify which cognitive function influences changes in car-following behavior with aging. We will assess the relationship between car-following behavior on a real road and elderly drivers' cognitive functions (e.g., attention, working memory, and planning (Kitajima & Toyota, 2012)) measured in a laboratory experiment. Analysis of the relationship between driving behavior and a driver's cognitive functions will help determine how driver support systems may assist driving behavior and detect the driver's cognitive functions based on natural driving behavior.

## 7. Acknowledgments

The authors are grateful to Prof. M. McDonald of the University of Southampton and Prof. P. Zheng of Ningbo University for useful discussions on estimation methodologies and results of the fuzzy logic car-following model.

## 8. References

Brackstone, M., McDonald, M., & Sultan, B.; (1999). Dynamic behavioural data collection using an instrumented vehicle. *Transportation Research Record,* No.1689, (1999), pp. 9-17, ISSN 0361-1981

Brackstone, M. & McDonald, M.; (1999). Car-following: a historical review. *Transportation Research Part F,* Vol.2, No.4, (December 1999), pp. 181-196, ISSN 1369-8478

Brackstone, M., Sultan, B., & McDonald, M.; (2002). Motorway driver behaviour: studies on car following. *Transportation Research Part F,* Vol.5, No.1, (March 2002), pp. 31-46, ISSN 1369-8478

Brackstone, M., Waterson, B, & McDonald, M.; (2009). Determinants of following headway in congested traffic. *Transportation Research Part F,* Vol.12, No.2, (March 2009), pp. 131-142, ISSN 1369-8478

Chandler, R.E., Herman, R. & Montroll, E.W.; (1958). Traffic dynamics: Studies in car following. *Operations Research,* Vol.6, No.2, (March 1958), pp. 165-184, ISSN 0030-364X

Fuller, R.; (2005). Towards a general theory of driver behaviour. *Accident Analysis and Prevention,* Vol.37, No.3, (May 2005), pp. 461-472, ISSN 0001-4575

Gipps, P.G.; (1981). A behavioural car following model for computer simulation. *Transportation Research Part B,* Vol.15, No.2, (April 1981), pp. 105-111, ISSN 0191-2615

Helly, W.; (1959). Simulation of Bottlenecks in Single Lane Traffic Flow. *Proceedings of the Symposium of Theory of Traffic Flow,* pp. 207-238, New York, USA, 1959

Iwashita, Y., Ishibashi, M., Miura, Y., & Yamamoto, M.; (2011). Changes of Driver Behavior by Rear-end Collision Prevention Support System in Poor Visibility. *Proceedings of First International Symposium on Future Active Safety Technology toward zero-traffic-accident,* Tokyo, Japan, September 5-9, 2011

Kitagima, M. & Toyota, M.; (2012). Simulating navigation behaviour based on the architecture model Model Human Processor with Real-Time Constraints (MHP/RT). *Behaviour & Information Technology*, Vol.31, No.1, (November 2011), pp. 41-58, ISSN 1362-3001

Kometani, E. & Sasaki, T.; (1959). Dynamic behaviour of traffic with a nonlinear spacing-speed relationhip. *Proceedings of the Symposium of Theory of Traffic Flow*, pp. 105-119, New York, USA, 1959

Mehmood, A., Saccomanno, F., & Hellinga, B.; (2001). Evaluation of a car-following model using systems dynamics. *Proceedings of the 19th International Conference of the System Dynamics Society*, Atlanta, Georgia, USA, July 23-27, 2001

Michaels, R.M.; (1963). Perceptual factors in car following. *Proceedings of the Second International Symposium on the Theory of Road Traffic Flow*, pp. 44-59, Paris, France, 1963

Owsley, C.; (2004). Driver capabilities. *Transportation in an Aging Society A Decade of Experience (Transportation Research Board Conference Proceedings 27)*, pp. 44-55, ISSN 1027-1652, Washington, D.C., USA, 2004

Pipes, L.A.; (1953). An operational analysis of traffic dynamics. *Journal of Applied Physics*, Vol.24, No.3, (March 1953), pp. 274-281, ISSN 0021-8979

Reiter, U.; (1994). Empirical studies as basis for traffic flow models. *Proceedings of the Second International Symposium on Highway Capacity*, pp. 493-502, Sydney, Australia, 1994

Sato, T., & Akamatsu, M.; (2007). Influence of traffic conditions on driver behavior before making a right turn at an intersection: analysis of driver behavior based on measured data on an actual road. *Transportation Research Part F*, Vol.10, No.5, (September 2003), pp. 397-413, ISSN 1369-8478

Sato, T., Akamatsu, M., Zheng, P., & McDonald, M.; (2009a). Comparison of Car-Following Behavior between Four Countries from the Viewpoint of Static and Dynamic Aspects. *Proceedings of 17th World Congress on Ergonomics (IEA 2009)*, Beijing, China, August 9-14, 2009

Sato, T., Akamatsu, M., Zheng, P., & McDonald, M.; (2009b). Comparison of Car Following Behavior between UK and Japan. *Proceedings of ICROS-SICE International Joint Conference 2009*, pp. 4155-4160, Fukuoka, Japan, August 18-21, 2009

Sato, T, & Akamatsu, M.; (2011). Longitudinal Study of Elderly Driver's Car-Following Behavior in Actual Road Environments. *Proceedings of First International Symposium on Future Active Safety Technology toward zero-traffic-accident*, Tokyo, Japan, September 5-9, 2011

Sugeno, M.; (1985). *Industrial Applications of Fuzzy Control*, Elsevier Science Inc., ISBN 0444878297, New Yorkm USA

Wu. J., Brackstone, M., & McDonald, M.; (2000). Fuzzy sets and systems for a motorway microscopic simulation model. *Fuzzy Sets and Systems*, Vol.116, No.1, (November 2000), pp. 65-76, ISSN 0165-0114

Wu, J., Brackstone, M., & McDonald, M.; (2003). The validation of a microscopic simulation model : a methodological case study. *Transportation Research Part C*, Vol.11, No.6, (December 2003), pp. 463-479, ISSN 0968-090X

Zheng, P.; (2003). *A microscopic simulation model of merging operation at motorway on-ramps*, PhD Thesis, University of Southampton, Southampton, UK

Zheng, P., McDonald, M., & Wu, J.; (2006). Evaluation of collision warning-collision avoidance systems using empirical driving data. *Transportation Research Record*, No.1944, (2006), pp. 1-7, ISSN 0361-1981

# Permissions

The contributors of this book come from diverse backgrounds, making this book a truly international effort. This book will bring forth new frontiers with its revolutionizing research information and detailed analysis of the nascent developments around the world.

We would like to thank Elmer P. Dadios, for lending his expertise to make the book truly unique. He has played a crucial role in the development of this book. Without his invaluable contribution this book wouldn't have been possible. He has made vital efforts to compile up to date information on the varied aspects of this subject to make this book a valuable addition to the collection of many professionals and students.

This book was conceptualized with the vision of imparting up-to-date information and advanced data in this field. To ensure the same, a matchless editorial board was set up. Every individual on the board went through rigorous rounds of assessment to prove their worth. After which they invested a large part of their time researching and compiling the most relevant data for our readers. Conferences and sessions were held from time to time between the editorial board and the contributing authors to present the data in the most comprehensible form. The editorial team has worked tirelessly to provide valuable and valid information to help people across the globe.

Every chapter published in this book has been scrutinized by our experts. Their significance has been extensively debated. The topics covered herein carry significant findings which will fuel the growth of the discipline. They may even be implemented as practical applications or may be referred to as a beginning point for another development. Chapters in this book were first published by InTech; hereby published with permission under the Creative Commons Attribution License or equivalent.

The editorial board has been involved in producing this book since its inception. They have spent rigorous hours researching and exploring the diverse topics which have resulted in the successful publishing of this book. They have passed on their knowledge of decades through this book. To expedite this challenging task, the publisher supported the team at every step. A small team of assistant editors was also appointed to further simplify the editing procedure and attain best results for the readers.

Our editorial team has been hand-picked from every corner of the world. Their multi-ethnicity adds dynamic inputs to the discussions which result in innovative outcomes. These outcomes are then further discussed with the researchers and contributors who give their valuable feedback and opinion regarding the same. The feedback is then collaborated with the researches and they are edited in a comprehensive manner to aid the understanding of the subject.

Apart from the editorial board, the designing team has also invested a significant amount of their time in understanding the subject and creating the most relevant covers. They scrutinized every image to scout for the most suitable representation of the subject and create an appropriate cover for the book.

The publishing team has been involved in this book since its early stages. They were actively engaged in every process, be it collecting the data, connecting with the contributors or procuring relevant information. The team has been an ardent support to the editorial, designing and production team. Their endless efforts to recruit the best for this project, has resulted in the accomplishment of this book. They are a veteran in the field of academics and their pool of knowledge is as vast as their experience in printing. Their expertise and guidance has proved useful at every step. Their uncompromising quality standards have made this book an exceptional effort. Their encouragement from time to time has been an inspiration for everyone.

The publisher and the editorial board hope that this book will prove to be a valuable piece of knowledge for researchers, students, practitioners and scholars across the globe.

# List of Contributors

**Kazuhisa Takemura**
Waseda University, Japan

**Hashim Habiballa**
University of Ostrava, Czech Republic

**Jorma K. Mattila**
Lappeenranta University of Technology, Finland

**Arturo Tellez, Heron Molina, Luis Villa, Elsa Rubio and Ildar Batyrshin**
IPN, CIC, Mexico City, Mexico

**Agnes Achs**
University of Pecs Faculty of Engineering, Hungary

**Heydy Castillejos and Volodymyr Ponomaryov**
National Polytechnic Institute of Mexico, Mexico

**Thoedtida Thipparat**
Faculty of Management Sciences, Prince of Songkla Universit, Kohong Hatyai, Songkhla, Thailand

**Adrian Shehu and Arianit Maraj**
Polytechnic University of Tirana, Albania

**Amin Parvizi**
University of Malaya, Malaysia

**Jorge Ropero, Ariel Gómez, Alejandro Carrasco, Carlos León and Joaquín Luque**
Department of Electronic Technology, University of Seville, Spain

**Marcelo Nascimento Moutinho**
Centrais Elétricas do Norte do Brazil S/A – ELETROBRAS-ELETRONORTE, Brazil

**Adriana Florescu and Claudiu Oros**
University Politehnica of Bucharest, Romania

**Anamaria Radoi**
Ecole Politechnique Federale de Laussane, Switzerland

**Toshihisa Sato and Motoyuki Akamatsu**
Human Technology Research Institute, National Institute of Advanced Industrial Science and Technology (AIST), Japan

Printed in the USA
CPSIA information can be obtained
at www.ICGtesting.com
JSHW011457221024
72173JS00005B/1112

9 781632 382115